LEGAL UNHOUSING
Power, Rights, and Housing Precarity

Edited by Anna Jane Samis Lund
and Sarah Buhler

UBCPress · Vancouver

Originally printed in Canada
Printed and bound by CPI Group (UK) Ltd, Croydon, CR0 4YY

UBC Press is an eBOUND Digital Certified publisher. The epub version of this book meets stringent accessibility standards, ensuring it is available to people with diverse needs.

Library and Archives Canada Cataloguing in Publication

Title: Legal unhousing : power, rights, and housing precarity / edited by Anna Jane Samis Lund and Sarah Buhler.
Names: Lund, Anna Jane Samis, editor | Buhler, Sarah, editor.
Series: Law and society series (Vancouver, B.C.)
Description: Series statement: Law and society series | Includes bibliographical references and index.
Identifiers: Canadiana (print) 2026017615X | Canadiana (ebook) 20260176184 | ISBN 9780774873291 (softcover) | ISBN 9780774873314 (EPUB) | ISBN 9780774873307 (PDF)
Subjects: LCSH: Housing—Law and legislation—Canada. | LCSH: Right to housing—Canada. | LCSH: Housing policy—Canada.
Classification: LCC KE5295 .L44 2026 | LCC KF5730 .L44 2026 kfmod | DDC 344.71/063635—dc23

Canada Council for the Arts | Conseil des arts du Canada
Canada
British Columbia Arts Council
British Columbia

UBC Press gratefully acknowledges the financial support for our publishing program of the Government of Canada, the Canada Council for the Arts, and the British Columbia Arts Council.

This book has been published with the help of a grant from the Canadian Federation for the Humanities and Social Sciences, through the Scholarly Book Awards, using funds provided by the Social Sciences and Humanities Research Council of Canada.

This book was supported by funds from the Estey Chair in Business Law. It was established in 2012 by John and Bill Estey in honour of their father, the late Willard "Bud" Estey, a former Justice of the Supreme Court of Canada.

UBC Press is situated on the traditional, ancestral, and unceded territory of the xʷməθkʷəy̓əm (Musqueam) people. This land has always been a place of learning for the xʷməθkʷəy̓əm, who have passed on their culture, history, and traditions for millennia, from one generation to the next.

UBC Press
The University of British Columbia
www.ubcpress.ca

Contents

Part 2: Legal Unhousing of Homeowners

LEGAL UNHOUSING

Introduction

ANNA JANE SAMIS LUND AND SARAH BUHLER

The Importance of Housing and Home

The importance of housing and home for human beings cannot be overstated. Housing provides shelter from the elements and from outside threats. But we need more than four walls and a roof. We also need our dwelling places to provide opportunities for us to meet emotional, psychological, relational, and cultural needs. In short, we need a place to call *home.* Home is "vested with emotion."[1] The concept and experience of home are connected to our need for belonging and tied up with our identities as human beings. As Alison Blunt and Robyn Dowling write, one's sense of self is "related to and produced through lived and metaphorical experiences of home."[2] In her article "Homeplace: A Site of Resistance," bell hooks describes homes as places where "Black people could affirm one another and by so doing heal many of the wounds inflicted by racist domination."[3] Similarly, Evelyn Peters and Carol Lafond note that Indigenous participants in their research discussed their homes as places to pass on cultural identities and practise cultural traditions.[4] Echoing and expanding on these insights, Jesse Thistle notes that Indigenous concepts of home encompass a "web of relationships and responsibilities involving connections to human kinship networks; relationships with animals, plants, spirits, and elements; relationships with the Earth, lands and waters, and territories; and connections to traditional stories, songs, teachings, names and ancestors."[5]

The concept of "home" is intangible and laden with layers of feeling, meaning, and culture, but the materiality of four walls and a roof still matters. As Lindsey McCarthy writes, "home is relational, intangible, portable, psychosocial and emotional *but so is the roof over one's head, and all the things underneath it, of critical importance*."[6] It is unsurprising that safe and secure physical housing is a key determinant of health, well-being, and quality of life.[7] In this collection, we acknowledge that "housing" and "home" have distinct meanings and associations, but we also insist on the close connection between the two concepts. Thus, home is more than housing: it is a multi-scalar concept, with "housing" as one of its scales. As we discuss further below, the loss of housing is not simply the loss of a roof and four walls; it is a loss of home or an aspect of home. Any process or force that leads to an involuntary loss of housing therefore affects one of the deepest needs of human beings.

Yet we are living in an age of ever-increasing displacement, dispossession, and home disruption. Globally, the world is seeing its highest-ever number of refugees and displaced persons because of war, geopolitical instability, extractive and accumulative economic practices, and climate change. Sociologist Saskia Sassen uses the term "expulsion" to describe the forces that have led to rising numbers of global socio-economic and environmental dislocations of people.[8] In Canada, fires exacerbated by rising temperatures have razed towns and destroyed homes, displacing families and dislocating communities.[9] People everywhere in the country are finding that their dwelling places and homemaking practices have become increasingly unstable because of escalating costs, threats of redevelopment,[10] discrimination,[11] or other factors. Growing numbers of people reside in places that are unsafe and inadequate. For too many (especially women and members of vulnerable groups), their housing is not a place of rest and safety but a site of violence and inequality.[12] Indeed, attention to the reality that not all could "stay home and stay safe" was heightened during the COVID-19 pandemic.[13] Growing numbers of people, especially youth, find themselves couch-surfing or staying temporarily with relatives, and they might experience this as a form of hidden homelessness.[14] And increasing numbers of people find themselves literally with no roof over their heads, forced to try to find security and shelter in encampments, on the street, or in other precarious places.

Just as home is a deeply important human need, so too the loss of home can have profound impacts on those who experience it. The loss of home not only entails the loss of physical shelter but also can encompass a huge range of deprivations, including the "loss of bodily comfort, love, privacy, rootedness, and hope."[15] Research has shown that eviction from rental housing, for example, is associated with negative outcomes, including loss of employment, disruptions to education, child apprehension, and poor mental and physical health. Respondents in a recent Canadian study used the language of trauma to describe the impacts of eviction on their lives.[16] And extensive research discusses the physical and mental health tolls of homelessness.[17] Loss of home can also be connected to deep spiritual, emotional, and community losses. Thistle has written that "Indigenous homelessness is not [only] defined as lacking a structure of habitation; rather, it is more fully described and understood through a composite lens of Indigenous worldviews. These include individuals, families and communities isolated from their relationships to land, water, place, family, kin, each other, animals, cultures, languages and identities."[18] It is important to emphasize that the harms of displacement and loss of home are never distributed evenly among communities: the most vulnerable and marginalized members of society are always those most deeply affected.

Housing and Homelessness in Canada: Power and Precarity

Growing numbers of people in Canada are facing problems with obtaining and retaining adequate and affordable housing. Although the language of "crisis" is widely applied to describe the housing situation in this country, critical scholars have pointed out that the term "crisis" can distract attention from the fact that for some the status quo is highly profitable and therefore desirable. For example, Ricardo Tranjan writes that Canada's "housing crisis" is in fact "a permanent state of affairs that harms people in, or in need of, rental housing ... [while] ... landlords, real estate investment firms, and developers operate in a stable and lucrative business environment."[19] Yet, from the point of view of low-income, marginalized, and, increasingly, middle-class families, housing does appear to be in a state of crisis. In the words of Gregor Craigie,

> there's a huge and growing segment of society whose lives are dominated by the difficult question – where will I live? Some simply give up on their dreams of buying a home. Others spend their free time looking for a better place to rent. Some have been evicted by landlords cashing in on those high prices. Others are plagued by panic attacks every time a rental application is rejected and are terrified of ending up homeless. And for those experiencing homelessness, of course, every day is a crisis.[20]

In Canada, the number of people experiencing homelessness has continued to grow since the early 2000s and has increased dramatically across the country in recent years. For example, Vancouver saw a 32 percent increase in street-based homelessness in the three years between 2020 and 2023.[21] In Saskatoon, a survey in 2024 identified at least 1,499 people experiencing homelessness there – nearly triple the number recorded just two years earlier.[22] At least 235,000 people in Canada experience homelessness every year.[23] In addition, as of 2021, at least 1.5 million people in Canada (or 10 percent of all households) experienced what is known as "core housing need," meaning that they would need to spend more than a third of their income to secure adequate housing.[24] Many people must resort to unsafe or overcrowded housing and are unable to meet other essential needs such as food and clothing.[25] Furthermore, as the National Housing Council has recently reported, core housing need "is deepest and most prevalent among people who have historically been marginalized and disadvantaged, including women, lone-parent households, people with disabilities, seniors, immigrants, 2SLGBTQI+, racialized communities and Indigenous People."[26] In short, it is increasingly difficult for a significant number of people in Canada to meet their basic housing needs.[27]

Current levels of widespread housing instability and homelessness have not always been the norm in Canada. The federal government invested heavily in housing following the Second World War by building social housing, providing rental subsidies, and offering mortgage protection measures.[28] However, around 1980, inspired by neoliberal economic policies that touted small governments and privatization of public and social goods, the federal government started down a path of "dehousing."[29] This move was characterized by deep disinvestment and retrenchment. By 1993, the federal government had completely withdrawn from the provision of financial support for new social and public housing (except for inadequate contributions to some housing on First Nations reserves).[30] What ensued was an era when an increasingly deregulated private market was expected to fill the gaps: this approach failed to protect vulnerable people and is "widely considered to mark the beginning of the homelessness crisis in Canada."[31]

It was not until 2017 that the federal government re-entered the housing policy landscape with the launch of the National Housing Strategy. The strategy and the subsequent *National Housing Strategy Act* (*NHSA*) of 2019,[32] have been criticized for not meeting housing needs across the country. A recent report by the National Housing Council, for example, noted that Canada is "losing affordable housing faster and in greater quantities than the National Housing Strategy is producing it ... [T]he production of affordable housing planned by the National Housing Strategy is dramatically insufficient."[33] In other words, the net overall number of affordable rental homes is diminishing in Canada.[34] The Canadian Centre for Housing Rights explains that this is the result of rapid rental increases as well as the systematic redevelopment or demolition of affordable rental housing.[35]

In addition to public disinvestment, a myriad of powerful interests and structural and systemic factors work together to produce homelessness and housing instability. In Canada, the phenomenon known as the "financialization of housing" has gained recent attention.[36] Although most housing in Canada is in the realm of private markets (and Canada has the lowest rate of subsidized housing in the OECD),[37] the financialization of housing heralds a new stage in the commodification of housing. Spring and Rosol write that financialization denotes the transformation of housing into a "product for investors – creating a new asset class that enriches them via business strategies based on tenant dispossession."[38] In practice, financialization refers to financial firms' acquisitions of multi-family rental housing whose investors then access an income stream derived from tenants' monthly rental payments.[39] Financialized real estate firms, including Real Estate Investment Trusts (or REITs), are buying up large numbers of rental housing units across the country. By 2017, all but three of the top sixteen apartment landlords owning over 7,500 units were financialized landlords.[40] Researchers show that they squeeze maximum profits from renters by raising rents, cutting their own costs (e.g., for maintenance), and adding new fees for tenants. They also "reposition" buildings by converting lower-rent units into higher-rent units.[41] Andrew Crosby observes that "enabled by state policies and legislation, REITs and financialized property management firms have thrived as apartment investors, bringing with them evolving sets of accumulation strategies that have accelerated the gentrification of lower-income buildings and neighbourhoods, as well as eroded affordable housing stock, in Canadian cities."[42] Kaitlin Schwan concludes that in a financialized housing market, "housing is no longer understood as a social good or the basis of human life and community. It is – first and foremost – a way to make money."[43] Two chapters in this book deal directly with financialization. Jason Leslie's chapter examines how the federal government has promoted the financialization of housing through its mortgage-backed securities and mortgage bond programs and argues that the primary beneficiaries of these programs have been lenders and not home buyers. David Wiseman's chapter examines how residents in a rental community targeted by financialized landlords used strategies of legal and social organization to advocate for their right to housing.

In Canada, another key structural factor underlying homelessness and unstable housing is colonialism. Theorists of settler colonialism have described it as a structure and relation of power predicated on the occupation of Indigenous lands: it "aims to force Indigenous people out of place, temporally and spatially."[44] Indigenous people's experiences of housing, home, and homelessness are uniquely shaped by the dynamics of colonialism. Discussing homelessness experienced by Indigenous people in urban centres in Alberta, Gabrielle Weasel Head and Yale Belanger have described the profound irony for Indigenous people of being homeless in one's homeland.[45] Thistle has written that

> colonialism has ... disrupted Indigenous homemaking practices by displacing Indigenous people from their ancestral lands, separating children from their families, and implementing exclusionary socio-spatial structures, all of which have undermined social determinants of Indigenous health, ranging from proximal determinants like housing and poverty to the distal determinants of cultural continuity, self-determination, and an Indigenous sense of home.[46]

The legacies of colonialism have created particular and troubling housing problems for Indigenous people, including high rates of unsheltered homelessness in urban centres and the disproportionate incarceration of Indigenous women. Two chapters in this collection examine the overrepresentation of Indigenous people in homeless encampments. Belanger traces the connections between this contemporary phenomenon and the long history of racist law, policies, and ideas. Alexandra Flynn and Estair Van Wagner draw from the *United Nations Declaration on the Rights of Indigenous Peoples* (*UNDRIP*)[47] and section 35 of the *Constitution Act, 1982,*[48] to chart a potential path forward. Meanwhile, Caydence Marley focuses on the housing conditions facing incarcerated Indigenous women and highlights the myriad ways in which prison-as-housing is deeply inadequate and contrary to human rights requirements.

Law's Contradictory and Complex Relationships with Housing and Home

Although home has often been conceptualized as a private space, separate from the "outside" world of politics and power, this conception is misguided. Social, economic, political, and – as this book explores – legal conditions powerfully shape and produce people's experiences of housing and home. Feminist scholars have led the analysis of how so-called private spaces of home can be sites where patriarchal power relations play out (and are resisted). As Dowling and Blunt put it, "the embodied, intimate, and personal spaces of home are closely bound up with, rather than separate from, wider power relations."[49] This book shows how law is ever present in these dynamics: law actively shapes people's lived experiences of housing precarity and loss of housing. This book also shows that law can be a source of powerful rights-based claims to home and housing.

So where is law when it comes to housing precarity, displacement, and homelessness? What does law have to say to the human need for home? Does law protect people who are threatened with the loss of home or who need a home? How and why does it play a role in unhousing people – expelling and dispossessing them from their homes? As Lorna Fox O'Mahony and James Sweeney have written, the "idea of home is both present and absent in law."[50] On the one hand, issues to do with housing, claims to housing, and loss of housing are foundational to many legal issues – from division of family property to mortgage law and practice, to residential tenancies, to regulation of the activities of homeless people. Refugee law encounters people who have lost a homeland and are seeking a new one. Criminal law allows state agents to contain people within prisons – those most un-home-like places. And, of course, many legal claims by Indigenous Nations are fundamentally about rights to their homelands. On the other hand, law often fails to account for the deeply human elements underlying claims to housing and home. Fox writes that "the idea of home in law has not carried much weight, particularly when balanced against easily measurable, legally definable, proprietary and contractual interests in property."[51]

The right to housing has been recognized as a human right in international human rights law, and Canada recognized the right in its 2019 *NHSA*. Yet Canadian law has a persistently complex and contradictory relationship with housing and home, and different and uneven approaches have evolved across different legal fields.

Although lawyers and legal insiders might make claims about law's neutrality, critical scholars have shown that when it comes to housing and displacement of people from their homes, law is far from neutral and instead tends to reproduce existing power relations. A large body of scholarship documents law's relationship with capitalist power relations and the protection and accumulation of private property. For example, Katherina Pistor documents how law provides the basic building blocks of capitalism in her book *The Code of Capital: How the Law Creates Wealth and Inequality.*[52] Scholars have also shown how law is mobilized to oppress members of marginalized groups and evict vulnerable people from public spaces in a stark reminder of "who is considered a rightful citizen."[53] Similarly, researchers have explained how civil courts reproduce "racial capitalism" – that is, producing profit for those with capital and reinforcing and perpetuating systems of social and economic injustice against racialized communities.[54] In her detailed discussion of American eviction courts, for example, Kathryn Sabbeth concludes that these courts actively sustain and entrench power imbalances between landlords and tenants by legitimizing the objectives of extracting wealth and imposing control.[55]

Other researchers argue that dispossession and eviction of vulnerable groups are at the foundation of the capitalist and colonial relations that lie at the heart of property law. For example, Alexander Baker points out that capitalism is constantly seeking new practices of "accumulation by dispossession."[56] And Brenna Bhandar argues that the very development of modern property law relied on the "attribution of value to the lives of those defined as having the capacity, will, and technology to appropriate."[57] She writes that there "cannot be a history of private property law ... that is not at the same time a history of land appropriation ... [M]odern property laws emerged along with and through colonial modes of appropriation."[58] In short, colonial law has always been actively implicated in processes by which people lose their homes and homelands.

Although the focus of this volume is squarely on dominant Canadian law and legal systems, we know that Indigenous laws that speak to home, and the relations and obligations of people relating to home, continue to exist. Indigenous laws invoke what Bhandar calls a "radically different political imaginary of property" that embraces an "embodied and conceptual relationship to the land, animals, and plants that reflect ways of being quite alien to capitalist, commoditized visions of land."[59] Indigenous legal scholars and communities are doing deeply important work animating and revitalizing Indigenous laws relating to property and relations to home and land.[60]

Legal Unhousing

This book introduces the concept of "legal unhousing" to describe how law and legal processes work across varied fields – including foreclosure law, residential tenancy law, judgment enforcement law, and prison law – to remove people from their housing and homes. By asking questions – including How does law "unhouse" people across a variety of legal terrains and circumstances? How does law internally justify displacing people from their dwelling places? How does law adjudicate competing claims for a place that is someone's home? – we witness something about law's power as a force of expulsion and dispossession. We also witness a variety of normative and doctrinal approaches to housing and loss of housing across legal fields depending on traditions and norms developed in the particular field. As this book shows, the legal unhousing landscape in Canada is made even more uneven by varied approaches to the same area of law across provincial and territorial jurisdictions.[61] Conversely, we are also able to observe how law and legal claims can be brought forward to highlight the importance of housing and home to people's well-being, dignity, and humanity. This book explores how law can become a force that promotes the human right to housing, and how it can be transformed or developed to incorporate a sense of the deep value and importance of home.

Although legal unhousing is a concept that we have coined and introduced in this book, scholars in disciplines outside law have produced research that helps us to think about the meaning and significance of the loss of housing. For example, Richard Baxter and Katherine Brickell discuss the phenomenon of what they call "home-unmaking." They define it as "the precarious process by which material and/or imaginary components of home are unintentionally or deliberately, temporarily or permanently, divested, damaged or even destroyed."[62]

Other authors refer to the concept of "unhoming." For example, Daniel Manson and Danya Fast describe various processes that lead to unhoming of youth, including being evicted, getting "kicked out" of childhood homes, fleeing violence, or "aging out" of child welfare systems.[63] For Adam Elliott-Cooper and his coauthors, unhoming is the severing of links between people and their communities that happens as an outcome of gentrification. It therefore entails a sense of "rupture" and destruction of one's attachments to place and home.[64] Gentrification-induced displacement as a type of unhoming, they write, is a "form of violence that removes the sense of belonging to a particular community or home-space."[65]

Finally, some authors have adopted the term "domicide," which denotes the "deliberate destruction of home by human agency in pursuit of specified goals, which causes suffering to the victims."[66] In a recent Canadian study, Andrew Crosby uses that term to discuss evictions related to gentrification and redevelopment of the Heron Gate community in Ottawa (discussed further in Wiseman's chapter in this collection). Crosby writes that "domicidal forces are remaking tattered townhomes into twinkling towers and replacing Black and Brown communities with a white, more affluent demographic."[67]

The scholars developing theories and understandings of home-unmaking, unhoming, and domicide do not centre or explicitly draw out the legal infrastructures underlying the processes that they describe. The specific contribution of this collection is to expose and investigate the often unseen role of law in reifying, but also potentially addressing, the complex and urgent problems of precarious housing and displacement in this country. We introduce the concept of legal unhousing to describe this endeavour. Our use of the term incorporates elements and ideas related to home-unmaking, unhoming, and domicide. We use the term "legal unhousing" to illuminate the specific legal processes and practices that cause people to lose their housing and homes and to highlight the idea that law works to entrench and naturalize many of the processes that lead to displacement and home dispossession. As discussed above, law operates in multiple, often contradictory ways to establish, react to, and sometimes disrupt conditions of housing precarity and loss of home.

Although law can function as an oppressive and dislocating force, and though legal unhousing processes reproduce highly unequal power relations, it is also important to emphasize the agency of those affected by legal unhousing. People continue homemaking practices despite hostile and even violent conditions, and there are long histories of activism and resistance to housing injustice in Canada.[68] This book includes rich discussions of resistance to legal unhousing as well as creative legal practices that seek to claim housing as a human right in this country. We turn now to a discussion of the origins, contexts, and meanings of the human right to housing.

The Human Right to Housing

The right to housing is recognized across a number of international instruments, but the most "comprehensive" articulation is found in section 11(1) of the *International Covenant on Economic, Social and Cultural Rights* (*ICESCR*).[69] Under that section, countries that are parties to the covenant "recognize the right of everyone to an adequate standard of living for himself and his family including adequate food, clothing and housing, and to the continuous improvement of living conditions." The Committee on Economic, Social and Cultural Rights (UNCESCR) is an eighteen-member committee of human rights experts that oversees implementation of the *ICESCR*.[70] The UNCESCR has elaborated what the right to housing entails. It is not merely a right to shelter or even a right to housing but a right to *adequate* housing.[71] The committee identified seven aspects of housing on which its adequacy can be evaluated: (1) legal security of tenure, (2) availability of services, materials, facilities, and infrastructure, (3) affordability, (4) habitability, (5) accessibility, (6) location, and (7) cultural adequacy.[72]

Security of tenure is a key theme throughout this book. It means "a set of relationships with respect to housing and land, established through statutory or customary law or informal or hybrid arrangements, that enables one to live in one's home in security, peace and dignity."[73] Forced evictions threaten security of tenure. A forced eviction is "the permanent or temporary removal against their will of individuals, families and/or communities from the homes and/or lands which they occupy, without the provision of, and access to, appropriate forms of legal or other protection."[74] Safeguarding the right to housing means that governments must refrain from taking part in forced evictions themselves and "ensure that legislative and other measures are adequate to prevent, and if appropriate, punish forced evictions carried out, without appropriate safeguards, by private persons or bodies."[75] Many of the chapters in this book consider how Canadian law protects, or too often fails to protect, security of tenure. However, the chapters also illustrate how legal unhousing is a broader concept than protection against forced evictions. Shelter falls short of being adequate housing if it is lacking in necessary services, unaffordable, uninhabitable, inaccessible, located away from key social facilities, or culturally inadequate.[76] In their chapters, Laverne Jacobs and Caydence Marley examine these other dimensions of adequate housing in the context of people with disabilities and women prisoners, respectively.

Despite a robust articulation in international human rights law of a right to housing,[77] the situation in Canada is less promising.[78] Dignity is central to the right to housing, as conceived by the UNCESCR,[79] and it is a guiding principle in the *Canadian Charter of Rights and Freedoms.*[80] The Charter protects the rights to life and security of the person,[81] yet Canadian courts have interpreted these rights narrowly.

In *Tanudjaja v Canada (Attorney General),*[82] a seminal Charter case on housing rights, four precariously housed and unhoused individual litigants joined with a housing organization to challenge the federal and Ontario governments for adopting policies that created housing insecurity. The plaintiffs argued that the governments' actions and inactions in adopting these policies violated the rights to life and security of the person of the precariously housed. They also advanced an argument that the policies violated the Charter protection against discrimination against unhoused people, who disproportionately comprise "single mothers, persons with mental and physical disabilities, Aboriginal persons, seniors, youth, racialized persons, newcomers and persons in receipt of social assistance."[83] The judge initially dismissed the claim, reasoning that section 7 of the Charter does not protect positive rights *to housing*, rather just the negative right not to have the government interfere with one's existing housing arrangements, and that section 15 was not engaged because the impugned policies did not deny a benefit to or impose a burden on the unhoused.[84] The Ontario Court of Appeal did not endorse this reasoning, but a majority held that the plaintiffs' claims were non-justiciable, meaning that the court should refrain from deciding the claims because they raised questions about government policy choices, not law.[85]

Section 7 of the Charter has provided some limited protection in terms of a right to shelter. A series of cases across Canada has taken up the question of whether unhoused people have a right to erect shelters outside when there are inadequate indoor shelter spaces. These cases often come before a court because a municipality wants to clear an encampment and is applying for a court order to allow it to proceed, or less commonly, because the encampment residents apply for an order to stop the clearance.[86] In the 2009 case of *Adams v Victoria,* the British Columbia Court of Appeal held that unhoused people have a right to erect temporary overnight shelters on public lands if there are insufficient indoor shelter spaces for them.[87] Subsequent cases have expanded this holding slightly, allowing that in some instances unhoused people might be entitled to erect shelters on a continuing basis[88] and that the availability of shelter spaces must be assessed in light of barriers to their use.[89] However, this right still only protects people who are "sleeping rough" from being displaced if there are inadequate shelter spaces.

As discussed above, the federal government launched a National Housing Strategy in 2017, which included significant funding commitments to maintain existing affordable housing, to build new units, and to provide direct support to families and individuals in housing need, through a Canada Housing Benefit.[90] The strategy also indicated that legislation including accountability measures would be passed imminently. In 2019, the federal government enacted the *NHSA.* The *NHSA* recognizes that housing is "a fundamental human right affirmed in international law" and commits the government to "the progressive realization of the right to adequate housing" as recognized in the *ICESCR.*[91]

The *NHSA* directs the minister to develop and maintain a national housing strategy. A newly created official, the federal housing advocate, is tasked with monitoring implementation of the strategy.[92] The advocate must prepare an annual report on their activities and recommendations for how Parliament can address systemic housing issues.[93] The minister must prepare a response to the annual report.[94] Both the advocate's report and the minister's response must be tabled in Parliament.[95]

The *NHSA* also provides two tools for identifying and studying systemic housing issues. The advocate might opt to study an issue and prepare a report on it, including recommendations for measures that the federal government has jurisdiction to adopt.[96] The advocate might identify a systemic issue or receive submissions from the public about issues that warrant study. The advocate can also request that the National Housing Council establish a review panel to study an issue.[97] The council is another newly created entity, tasked with "furthering housing policy,"[98] which it does by "promot[ing] participatory and evidence-based analysis."[99] When a review panel is struck, it must hold at least one public hearing on the systemic issue and do so in a manner that allows participation by "the public, particularly members of communities that are affected by the issue and groups that have expertise in human rights and housing."[100] The minister must respond to any report prepared by the advocate or a review panel on systemic issues, and these responses must be tabled in Parliament.[101]

Marie-Josée Houle was appointed as the first federal housing advocate in February 2022. In her first year, she identified three systemic issues: financialization, homeless encampments, and evictions.[102] The advocate's office has commissioned research on all three topics and issued a final report to the minister on encampments. In June 2022, the National Indigenous Feminist Housing Working Group and the Women's National Housing and Homelessness Network asked the advocate to examine what is required to meaningfully realize the right to housing for Indigenous women, girls, and gender-diverse people.[103] The advocate requested that the council establish a review panel to study this issue,[104] and the council complied with this request.[105] By 2024, the advocate had identified at least seven new systemic issues and was undertaking work to address several of them, including the homelessness of veterans and accessibility of housing for people with disabilities.[106]

As of this writing, the council has struck three review panels. The first was to study the financialization of purpose-built rental housing. It received written submissions from April to August 2023, held eight oral hearings from September to December 2023, and submitted its report to the minister of housing, infrastructure, and communities on May 27, 2024.[107] The second review panel, mentioned above, was named in 2024 to study the homelessness of women, girls, and gender-diverse people.[108] It submitted its final report on November 24, 2025.[109] In June 2025, the advocate requested that the council strike a review panel on the lack of accessible housing in Canada, and the panel started its work in the spring of 2026.[110]

Canada is a federal state, and many of the heads of power relevant to housing fall under the jurisdiction of provincial and territorial governments. Only Prince Edward Island has recognized the right to housing in the preamble of its residential tenancy legislation.[111] No other province or territory has enshrined a right to housing. Yet the federal government can and must provide leadership on the issue.[112] For example, it has coordinated with provincial and territorial governments to implement a Canada Housing Benefit that helps with housing costs for low-income renters. More recently, the federal government introduced its "Blueprint for a Renters' Bill of Rights," urging provinces and territories to incorporate various measures to strengthen tenants' rights and tying adoption of such measures to federal funding.[113] It remains to be seen whether and how provinces and territories will respond and what the impact of this blueprint will be.

Overview of the Book

The book starts with a chapter by Michèle Biss exploring the question of how the right to housing might continue to evolve in the coming years. Biss revisits the disappointing outcome in *Tanudjaja.* She reminds us that *Tanudjaja* is often cited for two propositions: governments do not have a positive obligation to provide housing under section 7 of the Charter, and houselessness is not an analogous ground under section 15.[114] However, she notes that these propositions, adopted by the Ontario Superior Court, were explicitly not affirmed on appeal. Biss then examines international and domestic legal developments suggesting that the terrain might be ripe for courts to recognize a more robust right to housing in Canada. A comprehensive right to housing is set out in international law, as an interdependent and indivisible aspect of the right to life, and Canadian courts are slowly coming to recognize that these international articulations must shape the interpretation of the right to housing of people in Canada under domestic law. Biss argues persuasively that a more robust right to housing might become legally cognizable in Canada, and the balance of the book explores the extent to which the right to housing is already protected or undermined by Canadian law.

The remaining chapters are divided into four sections, organized broadly around categories of housing: rented housing, home ownership, encampments, and institutions. Because housing is commonly litigated through the lens of contract and property, one might expect that those with a greater claim to property or contractual entitlements might fare better under our existing legal protections, and to some extent this is true. Homeowners undergoing foreclosure get more time to address financial defaults under a mortgage than renters who have missed lease payments. Renters have more protections against unhousing than people in encampments. People housed in institutions, whether carceral or therapeutic, often experience unhousing in ways that extend beyond loss of tenure to questions of availability of services, habitability, accessibility, location, and cultural adequacy. Yet, despite the disparate experiences of unhousing across these four settings, similarities emerge regarding how law can both reify power imbalances and challenge them.

Legal Unhousing of Renters

One-third of Canadians live in rented properties.[115] These tenants have some degree of security of tenure because residential tenancy law limits the reasons for which they can be evicted. Human rights legislation prohibits private landlords from discriminating against tenants on the basis of disability, race, gender, family status, and other protected grounds. Municipal bylaws can indirectly protect security of tenure by placing limits on how landlords repurpose existing rental properties. The chapters in this section explore the promises and limits of these intersecting legal regimes.

Sarah Buhler's chapter, "The Banality of Eviction: Strategic Ignorance in Eviction Decision Making," examines how residential tenancy hearing officers obscure the human element and harms of unhousing in eviction proceedings through practices of "strategic ignorance." This chapter foregrounds the rift between the lived experience of eviction as a deeply impactful process entangled with larger social and economic forces and the often mechanistic, acontextual outputs of tribunals that adjudicate landlord eviction applications. Drawing from literature that critically analyzes eviction processes, Buhler posits that eviction law and decision making are characterized by a form of strategic ignorance that encourages the avoidance of certain knowledge while actively reproducing meanings that uphold existing property and power relations. This strategic ignorance allows eviction to be seen as routine and unremarkable rather than disruptive and harmful. Buhler urges lawmakers and eviction tribunals to reject this approach and instead embrace a commitment to the human right to housing, which requires seeing eviction as a grim outcome and a last resort.

Jonnette Watson Hamilton approaches legal unhousing of renters from a different but related angle. Her chapter, "Legal Unhousing and Landlords' Unenforced Duty to Accommodate Tenants with Disabilities," examines residential tenancy evictions through the lens of human rights law, and she finds that decision makers typically ignore or downplay legal protections against disability discrimination in eviction cases. Watson Hamilton shows that people with disabilities are more likely to face eviction than many other groups. She describes how eviction decision makers fail to engage substantively with human rights laws when disability – usually mental or cognitive disability – appears to be a factor underlying the eviction application. When there is no human rights analysis in eviction proceedings, there is little to counter the stigma, stereotypes, and prejudices that people with disabilities face in Canada. Watson Hamilton's careful comparative analysis demonstrates that approaches to human rights analysis vary across jurisdictions in Canada, revealing a somewhat uneven human rights and eviction landscape facing renters with disabilities.

In his chapter, "Enabling and Resisting Financialized Legal Unhousing in Ottawa: Toward a 'Righting' of Legal Frameworks," David Wiseman examines how renters can use legal and social movement strategies to resist their displacement by financialized landlords and how legal frameworks can provide such renters with greater protections. His chapter focuses on the multiple resistance strategies used by renters in the Heron Gate Village community in Ottawa: negotiating with their landlords, advocating to politicians, staging rallies, communicating about their situation to journalists and the public, participating in city planning decisions and then challenging them at the Ontario Land Tribunal, and launching a potentially precedent-setting human rights claim. These efforts achieved a degree of success, including higher relocation payments for renters evicted early in the process and later a nondisplacement guarantee, by which the landlord undertook not to displace any renters from their housing unless and until they were provided with equivalent units with equal rent payments elsewhere in the community. The Heron Gate case study highlights the weak protections available to renters, and Wiseman draws from examples of demolition-based eviction bylaws in other municipalities and guidance from international law on forced evictions to suggest how these protections could be made more robust.

Legal Unhousing of Homeowners

The federal government has historically emphasized home ownership in its housing strategy, and Canada has become a nation of homeowners. As of 2021, two-thirds of Canadians own their homes.[116] Owners have greater security of tenure than tenants, but that security can be imperilled by a resident's financial liabilities, both voluntary and involuntary. People might voluntarily borrow money to purchase a home or borrow money against the value of a home that they already own. This manner of voluntary borrowing is ubiquitous: 60 percent of Canadian homeowners owe money on a residential mortgage.[117] Any default under the mortgage could result in the lender taking steps to seize or sell the home. Homeowners might also voluntarily borrow money not tied directly to their homes, for example, when a borrower amasses debt by using a credit card. And homeowners can become debtors involuntarily, such as when they are ordered to pay someone else money at the end of a lawsuit. In these cases, creditors can use judgment enforcement law to sell the debtor's home to satisfy the debt. The chapters in this section examine how mortgage and judgment enforcement laws run up against the right to housing.

Anna Lund's chapter considers how Canadian mortgage law could be reimagined through a right-to-housing perspective. Mortgage law is often conceived of as a matter of property and contract law, but in South Africa courts and legislators have grappled with what that country's constitutionalized right to housing means for mortgage practice. The result has been meaningful changes to the legal process facing homeowners who have defaulted on their mortgages, including mandatory judicial oversight of the process, expanded rights of redemption, greater court oversight of costs, and more scope to adjust mortgage debt using insolvency tools. Lund argues that principles driving South African courts resonate in Canadian mortgage enforcement practice: residences should be subject to greater protections than other properties, the justifiability of any sale is fact specific, and there is a significant power imbalance between lenders and borrowers. Canada can learn important lessons from the South African experience about how to ensure that mortgage enforcement proceedings comply with the right to housing.

In his chapter, Jason Leslie examines the mortgage securitization system in Canada, which he characterizes as an understudied aspect of housing financialization. He argues that mortgage securitization has entrenched home ownership as the "primary and perhaps the only legitimate way of providing Canadians with housing" while sidelining those with acute housing needs. His research draws from access to information requests that he submitted to the federal government and its housing agency, the Canada Mortgage and Housing Corporation (CMHC), to describe and critique how the system functions. Leslie finds that the federal government has both paid out significant funds and taken on sizable liabilities to support mortgage securitization. The stated aim of the system is to promote home ownership by reducing the cost of residential mortgage borrowing; however, the impact on mortgage rates has been modest, the lower interest rates can actually drive up both housing prices and rental rates, and any benefits accrue only to homeowners, not to renters. Instead, the primary beneficiaries of securitization have been financial institutions, which have used the government's securitization program to "bolster their capitalization and support other lending."[118]

Ronald CC Cuming explores the protections available to homeowners who have not paid their debts or are otherwise subject to judgment enforcement proceedings. His chapter engages with the practicalities of how the law can balance the right of creditors to recover the amounts owed to them with the need of debtors to remain housed and be protected from unjustified evictions. In many provinces, the protection of a debtor's home in judgment enforcement proceedings is partial, meaning that the home can be sold and that the debtor receives a set amount if there is any equity remaining in the home. In Saskatchewan, the protection is comprehensive, preventing the debtor's home from being sold by a judgment creditor as long as it is being used by the homeowner as an active residence. Cuming argues that Saskatchewan's comprehensive protection is justifiable because it prevents debtors and their families from the harms of forced evictions and because it is tailored: the protection is lost if the home is sold, destroyed, or expropriated, and it does not apply if the debtor has engaged in serious misconduct. Cuming concludes his chapter by examining the complexities that arise when the provincial full-home exemption is incorporated into federal bankruptcy proceedings. He provides guidance on how a creditor can recover value from a home if a bankrupt homeowner ceases to use it as an active residence following a bankruptcy and whether the bankrupt homeowner's discharge can be made conditional on the payment of some of the value of the exempt home to the creditor.

Legal Unhousing of Encampment Residents

Accurately counting the number of unhoused people across Canada at any given time is incredibly difficult. One estimate put the number at 32,000, with 25 percent of those individuals being unsheltered.[119] Many unsheltered people opt to live with others in encampments. Encampment residents have few protections against forced evictions, and some municipalities have opted to displace them, aggressively and repeatedly, even though they have nowhere else to go.[120] Indigenous people are overrepresented in encampments, and the chapters in this section explore how settler laws, policies, and ideas have led to Indigenous homelessness and how legal tools can be used to respond to this dire situation.

Yale Belanger situates homeless encampments within their broader historical context, which includes the dispossession of Indigenous Peoples from their lands and government policy choices that contribute to high rates of Indigenous people living in overcrowded, uninhabitable housing on reserves and in homeless encampments in urban areas. He illustrates this historical context by retelling the story of how the Papaschase Indian Band was annulled in 1888 and dispossessed of its reserve land in Edmonton. He then traces the echoes of that dispossession into contemporary responses of the City of Edmonton and Edmonton Police Service to Camp Pekiwewin, an encampment of unhoused people established in June 2020 near the territory of the band. Belanger uses a media scan to illuminate how the city and police used settler ideas to justify the removal of Camp Pekiwewin.

In their chapter, Alexandra Flynn and Estair Van Wagner set out the legal obligations of governments with respect to Indigenous Peoples under Canadian constitution law and the *UNDRIP*[121] and then argue that these obligations must inform all decisions about encampments and engagements with encampment residents. This means, they argue, that governments have a robust duty to consult encampment residents and ensure their meaningful participation. Their chapter outlines the magnitude of Canada's housing crisis and the degree to which Indigenous people are disproportionately affected. They summarize jurisprudence in which courts have recognized the rights of encampment residents under the Charter and refer to court decisions in which judges have engaged with the connections between Indigeneity and homelessness. Flynn and Van Wagner argue that the right to housing in Canada must be informed by constitutionally protected Indigenous rights, the *UNDRIP*, and human rights–informed case law, offering steps forward in recognizing these connections.

Legal Unhousing in Institutions

The final two chapters consider legal unhousing of incarcerated Indigenous women and people with disabilities, looking at how law and legal processes create precarity and housing instability for these constituencies. In her chapter, Laverne Jacobs examines the multiple ways in which persons with disabilities are unhoused, including through a lack of adequately designed spaces, insufficient supports in the community, and financialization. Jacobs illustrates how accessibility standards and international human rights frameworks can be used to help fulfill the right to housing for people with disabilities.

In her chapter, Caydence Marley argues that Canada's women's prisons fall well short of the standard of adequate housing as it is conceptualized in international law, especially for Indigenous women prisoners. She demonstrates that Indigenous women will continue to be overincarcerated in Canada as long as the country continues to fail in its human rights obligations related to housing and justice system involvement. Marley shows that living conditions in prisons are inadequate and that the UN standards of adequate housing can be used as a benchmark for remedying the inadequacies. Protecting and upholding the right to housing therefore require transformed approaches to prisons and criminal justice processes.

Toward the Human Right to Housing in Canada

This book takes up questions about how the law facilitates unhousing and how it can be used as a tool to promote a meaningful right to housing for Canadians. The authors examine legal unhousing across a range of contexts: residential tenancy law, municipal planning processes, judgment enforcement, mortgage securitization and enforcement, encampments of unhoused people, prisons, and housing for people with disabilities. More contexts could easily have been added to this list since legal unhousing can occur in condominiums and housing cooperatives, in postsecondary student housing, in expropriation decisions, and in family law proceedings. This book focuses on the laws promulgated or adopted by Canadian settler-state institutions of government and not Indigenous laws.

Despite these limitations, the breadth of the chapters allows us to observe trends and complexities in how law unhouses people. Across a variety of contexts, law reifies the positions of powerful actors: those who own property or otherwise benefit from treating it as a profit centre. Sometimes the law reifies the positions of powerful actors by occluding the positions of less powerful actors, namely residents. Buhler's chapter highlights how this process of occlusion occurs in residential tenancy hearings in which a tenant's claim to home is diminished by the strategic ignorance of decision makers. Wiseman's chapter reveals that Ottawa's demolition bylaws fail to account for the interests of residents and thus allow landlords to evict tenants legally en masse. The chapters by Watson Hamilton and Jacobs examine the subordination of people with disabilities by dominant legal frameworks and processes related to housing. And Marley's chapter shows how law's failure to attend to prisons as dwelling places completely obscures the housing rights of those forced to dwell in prisons.

The law also reifies the positions of powerful actors through its complexity. Sophisticated actors are better able to navigate this complexity. Cuming highlights how creditors have used the conditional discharge process in bankruptcy to deny homeowners the protections that they are entitled to under Saskatchewan's judgment enforcement legislation. The complexity created by the interplay of bankruptcy law and judgment enforcement law disadvantages homeowners. Leslie's critique of the mortgage securitization regime reveals that financial institutions have been the primary beneficiaries of a government program justified as a tool for promoting home ownership. The benefits flowing to homeowners are meagre, and the securitization program likely harms renters by driving up rental rates. Yet this inequitable state of affairs is largely hidden from view because of the legal complexity of how mortgage securitization works.

Jeannie Suk has written that "the law makes the home. The home makes us. And, of course, we make the law."[122] This book asks: Can those who make and practise law take seriously the impacts of unhousing? Can law take seriously the human rights claims of vulnerable people who have lost, or are at risk of losing, their homes? As the authors show in this book, advocates and rights holders are actively claiming the human right to housing in Canada and are using legal processes, often in conjunction with extralegal community advocacy, to assert that law is not just a tool for unhousing people. It can also be a tool for resisting unhousing and making claims about the profound importance of home. In *Tanudjaja,* the plaintiffs had their matter struck as non-justiciable, meaning that the court ruled that the matter was not capable of being resolved by a court. One way to understand the decision of the court is that it rejected the breadth of the plaintiff's claim. Legal innovations might have more purchase when they are tailored to speak to specific aspects of the right to adequate housing. They might be particularly impactful when they make visible the intangible values of home. Wiseman highlights the value of demoviction bylaws, which make it harder for financialized landlords to buy up affordable properties and evict all of the residents with the intention of demolishing the building and redeveloping the property. Such bylaws recognize the value of keeping existing communities intact. Jacobs highlights the role that accessibility legislation and standards can play in ensuring that the built form of housing enables people with disabilities to live in community, close to friends and opportunities to fulfill themselves through work and education. And Flynn and Van Wagner show how powerful legal instruments such as the *UNDRIP* and the Charter can be invoked to promote the dignity and housing rights of marginalized Indigenous Peoples by recognizing their long-standing relationships with their homelands.

Any legal innovation must grapple with the reality that law often reifies unequal power relations through how it gets implemented. There is often a gap between how law appears on the books and how it works in practice. Residential tenancy and mortgage enforcement legislation provide protection to tenants and homeowners, but people often struggle to claim those protections in legal proceedings. Lund highlights how South African courts have stepped into this gap to play an oversight role when lenders enforce against mortgaged residences. Jacobs notes that the incredible potential for accessibility standards to promote the housing rights of people with disabilities will be realized only if there is an effective method for enforcing them. Law is one tool for protecting and promoting the right of every person in Canada to adequate housing but only if we move beyond law as a theoretical abstraction and confront how it operates in our everyday lives. This collection takes up the challenge of reimagining how law can be transformed from a tool of unhousing to a safeguard for human beings, their housing, and their homes.

Addendum: Just as this book was going to print, the Ontario Superior Court of Justice released its decision in *The Regional Municipality of Waterloo v Named Respondents and Persons Unknown*, 2026 ONSC 2971. This decision has been hailed by housing advocates as a landmark decision that marks an important step for the human right to housing in Canada. Significantly, the court recognized that homelessness is an "analogous ground" under section 15 of the Charter of Rights and Freedoms. The decision also engages extensively with Canada's international human rights obligations. The impacts of this decision remain to be seen in the days and years ahead.

Acknowledgments

The introduction and this edited collection have benefited immeasurably from the research and editorial assistance of Jessica Csandl, Anjali Choudhary, and Dominique Panko as well as the generous feedback of the anonymous reviewers.

Notes

1 Lindsey McCarthy, "Homeless Women, Material Objects and Home (Un)making" (2019) 35:7 *Housing Studies* 1309–31 at 1310.

2 Alison Blunt and Robyn Dowling, *Home,* 2nd ed. (Abingdon, UK: Routledge, 2022) at 311.

3 bell hooks, *Yearning: Race, Gender, and Cultural Politics* (Toronto: Between the Lines, 1990) at 42.

4 Evelyn Peters and Carol Lafond, "'I Basically Stick with My Own Kind': First Nations Appropriation of Urban Space in Saskatoon, Saskatchewan," in *Indigenous in the City: Contemporary Identities and Cultural Innovation,* ed. Evelyn Peters and Chris Anderson (Vancouver: UBC Press, 2013), 88–109 at 105.

5 Jesse Thistle, *Definition of Indigenous Homelessness in Canada* (Toronto: Canadian Observatory on Homelessness Press, 2017) at 14.

6 McCarthy, "Homeless Women," at 1310 (emphasis added).

7 Leilani Farha, *Report of the Special Rapporteur on Adequate Housing as a Component of the Right to an Adequate Standard of Living, and on the Right to Non-Discrimination in This Context,* UNGA, 31st Sess, UN Doc A/HRC/31/54 (2015).

8 See Saskia Sassen, *Expulsions: Brutality and Complexity in the Global Economy* (Cambridge, MA: Harvard University Press, 2014).

9 John Vaillant, *Fire Weather: The Making of a Beast* (Toronto: Knopf Canada, 2023); Peter Edwards and Kevin Loring, *Lytton: Climate Change, Colonialism and Life Before the Fire* (Toronto: Random House Canada, 2024).

10 See Chapter 4 of this collection.

11 See Chapter 3 of this collection; Priya Gupta, "Racial Disparity and Discrimination in Housing in Canada" (2024) 102:3 *Canadian Bar Review* 705–36.

12 National Indigenous Feminist Housing Working Group (NIFHWG), *Homeless on Homelands: Upholding Housing as a Human Right for Indigenous Women, Girls, Two Spirit and Gender Diverse People* (Kirkland Lake, ON: Keepers of the Circle, 2022) at 19; Anna Lund, "Intersections Between Precarious Housing and Residential Tenancy Law: A Review of a Complex Exile and Recent Legal Scholarship on Residential Tenancies" (2023) 36:4 *Journal of Law and Social Policy* 44–62 at 49–50.

13 Leilani Farha and Kaitlin Schwan, "The Front Line of Defence: Housing and Human Rights in the Time of COVID-19," in *Vulnerable: The Law, Policy and Ethics of COVID-19,* ed. Colleen M. Flood, Vanessa MacDonnell, Jane Philpott, Sophie Theriault, and Srinda Venkatpuram (Ottawa: University of Ottawa Press, 2020), 355–66.

14 Sarah Buhler, *Keeping Youth Housed: Law and Legal System Reform for Youth Eviction Prevention* (Ottawa: National Right to Housing Network, 2024), https://housingrights.ca/wp-content/uploads/Sarah-Buhler-2024-Keeping-Youth-Housed.pdf [perma.cc/MGV6-GKDD].

15 Daniel Manson and Danya Fast, "Making Homes in Un-Homelike Places Among Young People in Vancouver: Implications for Homelessness Prevention" (2024) 4 *Youth* 885–904 at 888.

16 Sarah Zell and Scott McCullough, *Evictions and Eviction Prevention in Canada* (Winnipeg: Institute of Urban Studies, University of Winnipeg, 2020) at 78.

17 See the overview of this research in Chapter 2 of this collection.

18 Thistle, *Definition of Indigenous Homelessness,* at 6.

19 Ricardo Tranjan, *The Tenant Class* (Toronto: Between the Lines, 2023) at 1–3. See also Martine August, *The Financialization of Multi-Family Rental Housing in Canada: A Report for the Office of the Federal Housing Advocate,* Catalogue No. HR34-4/2022E-PDF (Ottawa: Canadian Human Rights Commission, 2022), https://homelesshub.ca/sites/default/files/attachments/august-financialization-rental-housing-ofha-en.pdf [perma.cc/9KXT-25N3] (noting how the REIT identified that withdrawal of the federal government from nonprofit residential home construction "would ensure an advantageous supply-demand imbalance" [at 6]).

20 Gregor Craigie, *Our Crumbling Foundation: How We Solve Canada's Housing Crisis* (Toronto: Penguin Random House Canada, 2024) at 1.

21 Homelessness Services Association of BC, *2023 Homeless Count in Greater Vancouver Final DATA Report* (Vancouver: Homelessness Services Association of BC, 2023).

22 City of Saskatoon, "Point in Time Community Homelessness Count Identifies Indigenous Over-Representation and More Children and Adults" (July 2, 2025), https://www.saskatoon.ca/news-releases/point-time-homelessness-count-community-report-highlights-indigenous-over-representation-and-more [perma.cc/UVB2-2GFL].

23 National Housing Council (NHC), *Renewing Canada's National Housing Strategy* (Ottawa: NHC, 2023) at 7.

24 Statistics Canada, "To Buy or to Rent: The Housing Market Continues to Be Reshaped by Several Factors as Canadians Search for an Affordable Place to Call Home," news release (September 21, 2022), https://www150.statcan.gc.ca/n1/en/daily-quotidien/220921/dq220921b-eng.pdf?st=NtMP7qDp [perma.cc/SZ58-NXSD].

25 See Charlotte Spring and Marit Rosol, "'Pay the Rent or Feed the Kids': A Scoping Review of the 'Housing-Food Insecurity Nexus' in Canada" (2022), https://osf.io/preprints/socarxiv/wd87b [perma.cc/F6GF-PCJN].

26 NHC, *Reviewing Canada's National Housing Strategy,* at 7.

27 See Spring and Rosol, "'Pay the Rent or Feed the Kids,'"at 3.

28 Ibid at 5.

29 Ibid.

30 Andy Crosby and Jacqueline Kennelly, "Hate the High Cost of Rent? Blame the 1990s" (September 12, 2022), monitormag.ca/articles/hate-the-high-cost-of-rent-blame-the-1990s-2/ [perma.cc/9DVJ-2SH8].

31 Ibid.

32 *National Housing Strategy Act,* SC 2019, c 2019, s 313 [*NHSA*].

33 NHC, *Reviewing Canada's National Housing Strategy,* at 2.

34 Canadian Centre for Housing Rights, *Preserving Affordable Homes in the Private Rental Market* (Toronto: Canadian Centre for Housing Rights, 2024) at 4, https://housingrightscanada.com/wp-content/uploads/2024/02/CCHR-PolicyBrief-PreservingAffordableHomesInThePrivateRentalMarket-HousingPolicyToolsSeries-January2024-Final.pdf [perma.cc/79NQ-2NNR].

35 Ibid.

36 NHC, *Review Panel: The Financialization of Purpose-Built Rental Housing* (Ottawa: NHC, 2024) at 19, https://cms.nhc-cnl.ca/media/PDFs/REVIEW%20PANEL%20

REPORT%20-%20The%20Financialization%20of%20Purpose-Built%20Rental%20Housing%20-%20MAY%202024.pdf [perma.cc/5L74-YMMM]; Martine August, "The Financialization of Canadian Multi-Family Rental Housing: From Trailer to Tower" (2020) 42:7 *Journal of Urban Affairs* 975–97.

37 Canadian Centre for Housing Rights, "Housing Policy News: Top Stories of 2023" (January 11, 2024), https://housingrightscanada.com/housing-policy-news-top-stories-of-2023 [perma.cc/N8MU-7BYS].

38 Spring and Rosol, "'Pay the Rent or Feed the Kids,'" at 6.

39 August, *Financialization of Rental Housing.*

40 Andrew Crosby, *Resisting Eviction: Domicide and the Financialization of Rental Housing* (Halifax: Fernwood, 2023) at 71; August, "The Financialization of Canadian Multi-Family Rental Housing," at 981, reporting that in 2017 eighteen of the twenty-five largest landlords in Canada were financialized.

41 Crosby, *Resisting Eviction,* at 71–72.

42 Ibid at 72.

43 Kaitlin Schwan, "Confronting Financialization to Prevent Homelessness," in *Ending Homelessness in Canada: The Case for Homelessness Prevention,* ed. James Hughes (Toronto: Lorimer, 2024), 34–46 at 35.

44 Lisa Slater, *Anxieties of Belonging in Settler Colonialism: Australia, Race and Place* (New York: Routledge, 2019), 43; Sarah Buhler and Patricia Barkaskas, "The Colonialism of Eviction" (2023) 36 *Journal of Law and Social Policy* 23–43.

45 See Yale D. Belanger and Gabrielle Weasel Head, "'All We Need Is Our Land': Exploring Southern Alberta Aboriginal Homelessness," in *Indigenous Homelessness: Perspectives from Canada, Australia, and New Zealand,* ed. Julia Christensen and Evelyn J. Peters (Winnipeg: University of Manitoba Press, 2016), 161–84.

46 Thistle, *Definition of Indigenous Homelessness,* at 34.

47 United Nations General Assembly (UNGA), *United Nations Declaration on the Rights of Indigenous Peoples,* UNGA, 61st Sess, UN Doc A/RES/61/295 (2007), UNGAOR Res 61/295, Supp No 49, UN Doc A/RES/61/295 [*UNDRIP*].

48 *Constitution Act, 1982,* being Schedule B to the *Canada Act 1982* (UK), 1982, c 11.

49 Blunt and Dowling, *Home,* at 27.

50 Lorna Fox O'Mahony and James A. Sweeney, *The Idea of Home in Law: Displacement and Dispossession* (Surrey, UK: Ashgate, 2011) at 1.

51 Lorna Fox, *Conceptualising Home: Theories, Law and Policies* (Oxford: Hart, 2006) at 119–20.

52 Katherina Pistor, *The Code of Capital: How the Law Creates Wealth and Inequality* (Princeton, NJ: Princeton University Press, 2019).

53 Farida Rady and Luisa Sotomayor, "Barred and Banished: Encampment Evictions, Public Space, and Permanent Displaceability in Toronto" (2024) 56:5 *Antipode* 1830–56 at 1835; see also Alexandra Potamianos, "Precarity, Property, and Homelessness in Toronto" (2025) 37:2 *Journal of Law and Social Policy* 1–21; Terry Skolnik, *Homelessness, Liberty and Property* (Cambridge, UK: Cambridge University Press, 2025); Marie-Eve Sylvestre, Nicholas Blomley, and Céline Bellot, *Red Zones: Criminal Law and the Territorial Governance of Marginalized People* (Cambridge, UK: Cambridge University Press, 2020); Joe Hermer and Janet Mosher, eds., *Disorderly People: Law and the Politics of Exclusion in Ontario* (Halifax: Fernwood, 2002).

54 Tonya L. Brito, Kathryn A. Sabbeth, Jessica K. Steinberg, and Lauren Sudeall, "Racial Capitalism and the Civil Courts" (2022) 122:5 *Columbia Law Review* 1243–86 at 1249–50.

55 Kathryn A. Sabbeth, "Eviction Courts" (2022) 18:2 *University of St. Thomas Law Journal* 359–404 at 402.

56 Alexander Baker, "From Eviction to Evicting: Rethinking the Technologies, Lives and Power Sustaining Displacement" (2021) 45:4 *Progress in Human Geography* 796–813 at 798.

57 Brenna Bhandar, *Colonial Lives of Property: Law, Land, and Racial Regimes of Ownership* (Durham, NC: Duke University Press, 2018) at 4.

58 Ibid at 3.

59 Ibid at 193–94.

60 See, generally, Angela Cameron, Sari Graben, and Val Napoleon, eds., *Creating Indigenous Property: Power, Rights and Relationships* (Toronto: University of Toronto Press, 2020).

61 See, for example, Jonnette Watson Hamilton's chapter in this volume, which shows that consideration of human rights is taken up differently in eviction decision making depending on the province or territory.

62 Richard Baxter and Katherine Brickell, "For Home *Un*Making" (2014) 11:2 *Home Cultures* 133–43 at 134.

63 Manson and Fast, "Making Homes in Un-Homelike Places," at 888.

64 Adam Elliott-Cooper, Phil Hubbard, and Loretta Lees, "Moving Beyond Marcuse: Gentrification, Displacement and the Violence of Un-Homing" (2019) 44:3 *Progress in Human Geography* 492–509 at 494, 498.

65 Ibid at 503.

66 J. Douglas Porteous and Sandra E. Smith, *Domicide: The Global Destruction of Home* (Montreal and Kingston: McGill-Queen's University Press, 2001) at 12.

67 Crosby, *Resisting Eviction,* at 29.

68 For example, Lillian Piché Shirt demonstrated against housing discrimination in Edmonton by living in a teepee in front of City Hall for twelve days in the summer of 1969; see Corinne George, "'If I Didn't Do Something, My Spirit Would Die': Grassroots Activism of Aboriginal Women in Calgary and Edmonton, 1951–1985" (MA thesis, University of Calgary, 2007) at 73–79 (says the protest lasted twelve days); "Protest Teepee Taken Down" (June 12, 1969) *Vancouver Sun* at 22 (says the protest lasted eleven days).

69 *International Covenant on Economic, Social and Cultural Rights,* December 16, 1966, 993 UNTS 3 (entered into force January 3, 1976) [*ICESCR*]; Canada, Office of the Federal Housing Advocate, *Security of Tenure in Canada: Summary Report,* by C.L. Michel, Catalogue No. HR34-21/2023E-PDF (Ottawa: Canadian Human Rights Commission, 2023) at 7. For a summary of other relevant provisions, see Office of the United Nations High Commissioner for Human Rights (OHCHR), *The Right to Adequate Housing: Fact Sheet No. 21,* 2014, UN Doc GE.14-80125 (Rev 1) at 11–12; Canada, Library of Parliament, *A Primer on Housing Rights in Canada,* background paper, by Ryan van den Berg, Publication No. 2019-16-E (Ottawa: Library of Parliament, 2019) at 2–3.

70 UNCESCR, *Fact Sheet No. 16 (Rev. 1),* OHCHR (1991) at 14.

71 UNCESCR, *General Comment No. 4: The Right to Adequate Housing (Art. 11 (1) of the Covenant),* OHCHR, 6th Sess, UN Doc E/1992/23 (1991) at para 7; on the gender blindness of the UNCESCR's general comments, see Dianne Otto, "Gender Comment: Why Does the UN Committee on Economic, Social and Cultural Rights Need a General Comment on Women?" (2002) 14:1 *Canadian Journal of Women and the Law* 1–52.

72 UNCESCR, *General Comment No. 4,* at para 8.

73 Raquel Rolnik, *Report of the Special Rapporteur on Adequate Housing as a Component of the Right to an Adequate Standard of Living, and on the Right to Non-Discrimination in This Context,* UNGA, 25th Sess, UN Doc A/HRC/25/54 (2013) at para 5, https://documents.un.org/doc/undoc/gen/g13/191/86/pdf/g1319186.pdf [perma.cc/3UKU-M57P].

74 UNCESCR, *General Comment 7: The Right to Adequate Housing (Art. 11.1 of the Covenant): Forced Evictions,* OHCHR, 16th Sess, UN Doc E/1998/22 (1997) at para 3.

75 Ibid at paras 8–9.

76 OHCHR, *Fact Sheet 21,* at 4.

77 But see Emily Paradis, "Do Us Proud: Poor Women Claiming Adjudicative Space at CESR" (2015) 24 *Journal of Law and Social Policy* 109–34, reflecting on the benefits and drawbacks of the *ICESCR* for addressing women's homelessness; critiquing the international articulation of the right as being inadequately attentive to women's experiences of housing insecurity, see Leilani Farha, "Is There a Woman in the House? Re/Conceiving the Human Right to Housing" (2002) 14:1 *Canadian Journal of Women and the Law* 118–41.

78 David DesBaillets and Sarah E. Hamill, "Coming in from the Cold: Canada's National Housing Strategy, Homelessness, and the Right to Housing in a Transnational Perspective" (2022) 37:2 *Canadian Journal of Law and Society* 273–93; Bruce Porter, *Implementing the Right to Adequate Housing Under the National Housing Strategy Act: The International Human Rights Framework* (Ottawa: Office of the Federal Housing Advocate, 2021); Bruce Porter, "Homelessness, Human Rights, Litigation and Law Reform: A View from Canada" (2004) 10:2 *Australian Journal of Human Rights* 133–64; Martha Jackman, "From National Standards to Justiciable Rights: Enforcing International Social and Economic Guarantees Through Charter of Rights Review" (1999) 14 *Journal of Law and Social Policy* 69–90.

79 UNCESCR, *General Comment No. 4,* at para 7.

80 *Canadian Charter of Rights and Freedoms,* Part I of the *Constitution Act, 1982,* being Schedule B to the *Canada Act 1982* (UK), 1982, c 11 [Charter].

81 Martha Jackman and Bruce Porter, "Rights Based Strategies to Address Poverty and Homelessness in Canada," in *Advancing Social Rights in Canada,* ed. Martha Jackman and Bruce Porter (Toronto: Irwin Law, 2014), 65–106.

82 *Tanudjaja v Canada (Attorney General),* 2014 ONCA 852 [*Tanudjaja* ONCA], affirmingg in part 2013 ONSC 5410 [*Tanudjaja* ONSC], leave to appeal dismissed 2015 CanLII 36780 (SCC). For the case, see David DesBaillets, "The International Human Right to Housing and the Canadian Charter: A Case Comment on

Tanudjaja v. Canada (Attorney General)" (2015) 32:1 *Windsor Yearbook of Access to Justice* 121–38; Tracy Heffernan, Fay Faraday, and Peter Rosenthal, "Fighting for the Right to Housing in Canada" (2015) 24:2 *Journal of Law and Social Policy* 10–45; Vasuda Sinha, Lorne Sossin, and Jenna Meguid, "Charter Litigation, Social and Economic Rights and Civil Procedure" (2017) 26:3 *Journal of Law and Social Policy* 43–67; David Wiseman, "The Past and Future of Constitutional Law and Social Justice: Majestic or Substantive Equality?" (2015) 71:22 *Supreme Court Law Review* 563–605; Margot Young, "Temerity and Timidity: Lessons from *Tanudjaja v. Attorney General (Canada)*" (2020) 61:2 *Les cahiers de droit* 469–93.

83 *Tanudjaja* ONSC at para 111.

84 Ibid at para 128.

85 *Tanudjaja* ONCA at para 19; on the court's approach to justiciability, see Margot Young, "Charter Eviction: Litigating out of House and Home" (2015) 24:3 *Journal of Law and Social Policy* 46–67; on justiciability generally, see David Wiseman, "The Charter and Poverty: Beyond Injusticiability" (2001) 51:4 *University of Toronto Law Journal* 425–58.

86 Stepan Wood, "Reconsidering the Test for Interlocutory Injunctions Affecting Homeless Encampments: A Critical Assessment of BC Case Law" (2024) 61:1 *Osgoode Hall Law Journal* 161–222 (describing the context in British Columbia in which applications are overwhelmingly brought against residents of encampments). For examples of cases in which encampment residents or litigants acting on their behalf applied for remedies related to their eviction, see *Poff v City of Hamilton*, 2021 ONSC 7224; Anna Lund, "The Edmonton Encampment Litigation and the Charter Claims We Didn't (Get to) Argue" (2024) 40 *Windsor Yearbook of Access to Justice* 229–61; *Heegsma v Hamilton (City)*, 2024 ONSC 7154.

87 *Victoria (City) v Adams*, 2009 BCCA 563; Margot Young, "Sleeping Rough and Shooting Up: Taking British Columbia's Urban Justice Issues to Court," in *Realizing Social Rights*, ed. Martha Jackman and Bruce Porter (Toronto: Irwin, 2013), 413–41; Jennifer Koshan, "Redressing the Harms of Government (In)Action: A Section 7 Versus Section 15 Charter Showdown" (2013) 22:1 *Constitutional Forum* 31–46; Jamie Chai Yun Liew, "Finding Common Ground: Charter Remedies and Challenges for Marginalized Persons in Public Spaces" (2012) 1:1 *Canadian Journal of Poverty Law* 1–31; Martha Jackman, "Charter Remedies for Socio-Economic Rights Violations: Sleeping Under a Box?," in *Taking Remedies Seriously*, ed. Robert J. Sharpe and Kent Roach (Montreal: Canadian Institute for the Administration of Justice, 2010), 279–301; Sarah Buhler, "Cardboard Boxes and Invisible Fences: Homelessness and Public Space in *City of Victoria v Adam*" (2009) 27:1 *Windsor Yearbook of Access to Justice* 209–25.

88 *Bamberger v Vancouver (Board of Parks and Recreation)*, 2022 BCSC 49 at paras 17–20; *The Regional Municipality of Waterloo v Persons Unknown and to Be Ascertained*, 2023 ONSC 670 at para 105 [*Waterloo*]; *Prince George (City) v Johnny*, 2025 BCSC 1556 at paras 103–4.

89 *Waterloo* at paras 67–72; on the evolving case law in this area, see Alexandra Flynn, Heidi Kiiwetinepinesiik Stark, and Estair Van Wagner, *Encampments and Legal Obligation: Evolving Rights and Relationships: Report for Advocates and Legal Practitioners* (Ottawa: Office of the Federal Housing Advocate, 2024); Office of the

Federal Housing Advocate, *Upholding Dignity and Human Rights: The Federal Housing Advocate's Review of Homeless Encampments – Final Report* (Ottawa: Canadian Human Rights Commission, 2024).

90 Minister of Families, Children and Social Development, *Canada's National Housing Strategy: A Place to Call Home* (Ottawa: Government of Canada, 2017), https://assets.cmhc-schl.gc.ca/sites/place-to-call-home/pdfs/canada-national-housing-strategy.pdf?rev=5f39d264-0d43-4da4-a86a-725176ebc7af [perma.cc/KR9H-R62Z].

91 *NHSA* at s 4.

92 Ibid at s 13.

93 Ibid at s 16.

94 Ibid at s 17(1).

95 Ibid at ss 16(2), 17(2).

96 Ibid at s 13.1(4).

97 Ibid at ss 13.1(2), 13.2(1).

98 Ibid at s 6(1).

99 Minister of Families, Children and Social Development, *Canada's National Housing Strategy*, at 9.

100 *NHSA* at s 16.3(b).

101 Ibid at ss 17.1, 17.2.

102 Office of the Federal Housing Advocate, *Housing Is a Human Right: The Office of the Federal Housing Advocate's 2021–2022 Annual Report to the Minister* (Ottawa: Canadian Human Rights Commission, 2022) at 5, https://2021.housing.chrcreport.ca/pdfs/office_of_the_federal_housing_advocate-annual_report_2021.pdf [perma.cc/N47E-4RCV]. See the discussion of the advocate's work on encampments in Chapter 9 of this collection.

103 NIFHWG, *Homeless on Homelands*, at 12; Women's National Housing and Homelessness Network (WNHHN) Human Rights Task Force, *The Crisis Ends with Us: Request for a Review into the Systemic Denial of the Equal Right to Housing of Women and Gender-Diverse People in Canada* (WNHHN, 2022), https://womenshomelessness.ca/wp-content/uploads/WNHHN-Claim-15-June-2022.pdf [perma.cc/9EBP-R862].

104 Office of the Federal Housing Advocate (OFHA), *Putting People First: The Federal Housing Advocate's 2023–2024 Annual Report to the Minister*, Catalogue No. CH1-44E-PDF (Ottawa: Canadian Human Rights Commission, 2024) at 18.

105 NHC, "Statement from Neha Members and Terms of Reference" (2024), https://cms.nhc-cnl.ca/media/PDFs/Terms%20of%20reference%20_%20Neha.pdf [perma.cc/WC8Q-6NPT].

106 OFHA, *Putting People First*, at 33–35.

107 NHC, *Review Panel;* NHC, "The Review Panel on the Financialization of Purpose-Built Rental Housing Submits Report to the Minister," news release (May 29, 2024), https://nhc-cnl.ca/news/post/the-review-panel-on-the-financialization-of-purpose-built-rental-housing-submits-report-to-the-minister- [perma.cc/EK7L-VUVD].

108 NHC, "Statement from Neha Members."

109 NHC, *We Are Human. We Deserve a Place to Live. It's That Simple. Final Report and Recommendations of the Neha Review Panel* (Ottawa: NHC, 2025); NHC, "Neha Review Panel Reports on the Right to Safe, Adequate and Affordable Housing for Women, Two Spirit, Trans, and Gender-Diverse People," news release (November

24, 2025), https://nhc-cnl.ca/publications/post/neha-review-panel-s-reports-on-the-right-to-safe-adequate-and-affordable-housing-for-women-two-spirit-trans-and-gender-diverse-people.

110 OFHA, "Federal Housing Advocate Calls for Hearing into Lack of Accessible Housing in Canada" (June 12, 2025), https://www.chrc-ccdp.gc.ca/resources/news room/federal-housing-advocate-calls-hearing-lack-accessible-housing-canada [perma.cc/23TT-GPAL].

111 *Residential Tenancy Act*, SPEI 2022, c 88, preamble.

112 Michel, *Security of Tenure,* at 9, citing UNCESCR, *List of Issues Prior to Submission of the Seventh Periodic Report of Canada,* 66th Sess, UN Doc E/C.12/CAN/QPR/7 (2020); Human Rights Council, *Guidelines for the Implementation of the Right to Adequate Housing,* UNGA, 43rd Sess, UN Doc A/HRC/43/43 (2019).

113 See Housing, Infrastructure and Communities Canada, "Blueprint for a Renters' Bill of Rights" (last modified September 16, 2024), https://housing-infrastructure.canada.ca/housing-logement/bill-rights-charte-droits/renters-locataires-eng.html [perma.cc/Z43U-JBGB].

114 On homelessness as an analogous ground under s 15 of the Charter, see Terry Skolnik, "Homelessness and Unconstitutional Discrimination" (2019) 15:1 *Journal of Law and Equality* 69–94.

115 Statistics Canada, *Housing Indicators by Tenure Including Presence of Mortgage Payments and Subsidized Housing, Household Type Including Census Family Structure and Period of Construction: Canada, Provinces and Territories, Census Metropolitan Areas and Census Agglomerations,* Table No. 98-10-0241-01 (Ottawa: Statistics Canada, 2023), https://www150.statcan.gc.ca/t1/tbl1/en/tv.action?pid=9810024101 [perma.cc/N8PN-68AL] (as of 2021, 4,899,925 households rent out of 14,687,350 total households).

116 Ibid (as of 2021, 9,787,420 households are homeowners out of 14,687,350 total households nationally).

117 Ibid (as of 2021, 9,787,420 households are homeowners, and 5,870,875 households have mortgages).

118 See Chapter 6 in this collection at 190.

119 Homeless Hub, "How Many People Are Homeless in Canada?" (2024), https://homelesshub.ca/collection/homelessness-101/how-many-people-homeless-canada/ [perma.cc/MSL9-97N2]. See also OFHA, *Upholding Dignity and Human Rights: The Federal Housing Advocate's Review of Homeless Encampments* (Ottawa: Canadian Human Rights Commission, 2024) at 6.

120 OFHA, *Overview of Encampments Across Canada: A Right to Housing Approach* (Ottawa: Canadian Human Rights Commission, 2022) (contains case studies of different municipal responses to encampments).

121 *UNDRIP.*

122 Jeannie Suk, *At Home in the Law: How the Domestic Violence Revolution Is Transforming Privacy* (New Haven, CT: Yale University Press, 2009) at 8.

1

Homelessness, the Right to Life, and the *National Housing Strategy Act*
The Path Forward for Canadian Jurisprudence

MICHÈLE BISS

Introduction

I start this chapter by acknowledging a harsh reality: people experiencing homelessness are needlessly losing their lives across Canada.[1] Federal and subnational governments have failed to fulfill their obligation to protect the fundamental right to life of those experiencing homelessness. Yet government lawyers continually pursue aggressive litigation strategies to shut the door further to any protection under sections 7 and 15 of the *Canadian Charter of Rights and Freedoms* (these sections protect the rights to life, liberty, and security of the person, and equality, respectively).[2] This discreditable aim is often advanced by mischaracterizing the outcome of a court decision known as *Tanudjaja v Canada (Attorney General)*[3] and ignoring the "living tree" principle established by the Judicial Committee of the Privy Council in *Edwards v Canada,* which states that our constitutional framework in Canada evolves and is not static.[4] As such, many rights holders and advocates alike have turned to international law to help raise issues concerning the right to life of those experiencing homelessness.

In this chapter, I discuss the persistent exclusion and denial of the right to life of those experiencing homelessness in Canada by what I argue is the neglect of international law and a misinterpretation of the relevance of the *Tanudjaja* case. First I review what actually happened in *Tanudjaja:* it was a loss for economic and social rights advocates but not in the ways now invoked by those opposing housing rights claims. Then, I examine how the legal context has changed, overtaking the court's reasoning in *Tanudjaja.* These changes include (1) developments in international law, which recognize the indivisibility and interdependence of the right to life and other socio-economic rights, (2) the passing of the federal *National Housing Strategy Act,*[5] and (3) the recent court decisions in *Toussaint v Canada (Attorney General)*[6] and *Disability Rights Coalition v Nova Scotia (Attorney General),*[7] which demonstrate an evolving climate for the legal interpretation of how the Charter can impose positive obligations to protect the right to life for vulnerable groups experiencing homelessness.

Unsettled Law: Homelessness, the Charter, and the *Tanudjaja* Decision

In May 2010, four persons experiencing homelessness and one institutional applicant (the Centre for Equality Rights in Accommodation – now named the Canadian Centre for Housing Rights) filed an application in court challenging the failures of Canada and Ontario to implement effective national and provincial strategies to address homelessness.[8] The applicants posited that the government failure to implement effective national and provincial housing strategies to reduce and eliminate homelessness and inadequate housing violated their rights under sections 7 and 15 of the Charter. The supporting record included 9,000 pages of evidence from experts along with affidavits of the applicants.

Two years after the application was filed, the governments of Ontario and Canada filed a "motion to strike" based on the position that the claim did not disclose a cause of action, because these governments were not subject to positive obligations to address homelessness through the Charter.[9] In other words, the government defendants argued that the court should refuse to allow the case to proceed because there was no legitimate legal issue that a court was capable of resolving.

Justice Lederer of the Ontario Superior Court of Justice granted the motion to strike. This decision was appealed, and the majority of the Court of Appeal upheld Lederer's decision. This means that the substantive legal arguments were never actually considered by a court because the proceeding was terminated before that could happen. In her dissenting opinion, Justice Feldman of the Ontario Court of Appeal noted that she would have allowed the appeal and that "the application raises significant issues of public importance."[10] As the lawyers for the applicants (Tracy Heffernan, Fay Faraday, and Peter Rosenthal) wrote, "Feldman JA ruled that the application raised justiciable legal claims, sought justiciable remedies, and that there was support in the jurisprudence for both the section 7 and section 15 claims."[11] In fact, "Feldman JA concluded that it was an error of law to strike the claim at the pleadings stage and that the evidentiary record supporting the claim should be put before the court."[12] However, certainly in the context of section 15 (equality rights) claims, court decisions about encampments have held that the *Tanudjaja* case is a precedent for a rejection of "homelessness" as an analogous ground.[13] This means that courts have taken the position that people who are homeless should not have protection under the Charter. As noted by Alexandra Flynn, Heidi Kiiwetinepinesiik Stark, and Estair Van Wagner, "as a result of [*Tanudjaja*], very few Canadian courts have fully examined the right to housing under the *Charter* to date, and certainly not since the *NHSA* was enacted."[14]

Motions to strike are decided on the pleadings (arguments and materials filed by the applicant to support the case), and thus Justice Lederer reached the decision to strike in the *Tanudjaja* case without reviewing any of the 9,000 pages of evidence. Additionally, in the appeal before the Ontario Court of Appeal, several organizations made interventions. They included Amnesty International, the ARCH Disability Law Centre, the Charter Committee on Poverty Issues, the Colour of Poverty/Colour of Change Network, the David Asper Centre for Constitutional Rights, the Ontario Human Rights Commission, and the Women's Legal Education and Action Fund. Those civil society organizations collectively hold thousands of members. An appeal was later filed with the Supreme Court of Canada, but it decided not to hear the case.[15] The apex court missed a tremendous opportunity to consider a matter of public importance.[16]

But there is something fundamentally incorrect about positioning the decision in *Tanudjaja* as settled law on whether government policy decisions involving socio-economic matters such as housing are exempt from Charter scrutiny. Indeed, as Bruce Porter and Martha Jackman have written, "with the denial of a hearing on the evidence, and the Supreme Court of Canada's refusal to grant leave to appeal the motion to dismiss in *Tanudjaja*, socio-economic rights remain in the unsettled state ... caught between two contrasting constitutional rights paradigms."[17] On the one hand, government lawyers argue that the absence of explicit reference to economic and social rights in Canada's Constitution reflects a political choice that social and economic policies be immune from Charter review; on the other, rights holders argue "that all aspects of government decision-making must be subject to Charter scrutiny and that broadly framed Charter guarantees should be read to include, rather than exclude, human rights violations experienced by disadvantaged individuals and groups."[18]

Critically, the *Tanudjaja* decision has far too narrow a scope to be positioned as settled law of such fundamental importance. After all, in that case, the Canadian and Ontario government litigation teams did not even engage with the question of Charter protections for people experiencing homelessness. Instead, they focused their motion to strike on limiting the role for the court in matters of social policy.

Tanudjaja is sometimes invoked by opponents of human rights claims for the principle that those experiencing homelessness may not invoke section 7 of the Charter (the section that protects people's security of the person) to impose positive obligations on governments. "Positive rights" refer to the idea that a government should take some action to protect someone, whereas "negative rights" refer to the idea that a government should restrain itself from interfering with a person. The Ontario Court of Appeal in *Tanudjaja* did not definitively rule out that section 7 might one day impose positive rights on governments. To read it otherwise misapprehends the decision. The Ontario Court of Appeal decision in *Tanudjaja* turned narrowly on the question of justiciability. Justice Lederer's broader reasons, which read section 7 as being limited to negative rights, were not dealt with by the Court of Appeal. That court therefore left the issue unsettled. What the majority of the court did find is that the claim as framed was not justiciable because it failed to identify a specific violation against which the government could defend itself.[19] The majority decision in fact has relatively narrow application to the claim as it was framed in that case. It therefore does not settle the question of the extent of governments' obligations to take particular measures to address homelessness in order to protect the rights to life and security of the person.

In contrast, the well-reasoned dissent of Justice Feldman might be more useful to courts considering substantive issues in future litigation related to homelessness and obligations under the Charter. Feldman found that the trial judge had erred in four ways:

> (1) he misunderstood the appellants' s. 7 claim and stated it in an overly broad manner; (2) he erred in stating that the s. 7 jurisprudence on positive obligations imposed on governments to address homelessness is settled; (3) he erred in purporting to define the law in a critical area of Canadian jurisprudence on a motion to strike; and (4) most importantly, he erred in concluding that the issue of whether the appellants had a potential claim under s. 7 could be decided without considering the full evidentiary record.[20]

The positive/negative rights paradigm privileges challenges to government "interference" with rights over claims of a failure to take the positive action necessary for the protection of the rights of those who are homeless. Essentially, a negative rights paradigm argues that Charter rights exist only to protect individuals from government actions and that a government can never be required to take action to ensure the rights of its people. There is a danger that this approach disadvantages those more likely to rely on positive rights (i.e., people experiencing poverty and holding other intersecting identities) and ignores the growing trend in international human rights law norms recognizing the interdependence of economic, social and cultural, and civil and political rights.[21]

In sum, the role of section 7 of the Charter in relation to homelessness is still unsettled in Canadian law, and over a decade later, at the core of this unsettled paradigm, is the reality that the world has changed significantly since *Tanudjaja* was argued – particularly in the contexts of the climate crisis and the COVID-19 health crisis.[22] The international human rights world itself is evolving to embrace indivisibility and interdependence of rights more fully.

International Human Rights and Jurisprudence on Homelessness and the Right to Life

As argued above, whether socio-economic rights are protected under the Charter remains unsettled law in Canadian courts. Yet, as Bruce Porter and Martha Jackman have argued, these rights "need not, however, be left exclusively to the courts to decide."[23] Rights holders and others asserting the right to life and security of the person for people experiencing homelessness have turned to the far more advanced international human rights legal systems. Indeed, there is much that we can learn from the application of the right to life for those experiencing homelessness in international human rights systems – which should have a significant influence on the domestic evolution of this area of unsettled law.

The Rights to Life and Housing: Interdependent and Indivisible

Interdependence and indivisibility are the principles in international human rights law that the full enjoyment of one set of rights (e.g., civil and political rights) cannot occur without the realization of another set of rights (e.g., economic, social, and cultural rights).[24]

The right to life is an international human rights law norm. Typically, we find it emerging in the context of civil and political rights, but it is nevertheless deeply indivisible from economic, social, and cultural rights, such as the right to housing. Some of the key UN documents that enshrine the right to life and the right to housing are the *International Covenant on Economic, Social and Cultural Rights* (ratified by Canada in 1976),[25] the *Convention on the Elimination of All Forms of Discrimination Against Women* (ratified by Canada in 1981),[26] the *Convention on the Rights of Persons with Disabilities* (ratified by Canada in 2010),[27] and the *United Nations Declaration on the Rights of Indigenous Persons* (accepted by Canada in 2010).[28]

General Comment No. 36 from the UN Human Rights Committee, adopted in 2019 after extensive consultations to replace an earlier general comment on the right to life,[29] articulates the modern consensus: a state party has a duty to protect life by taking appropriate measures to address the general conditions in society that can give rise to direct threats to life or prevent individuals from enjoying their right to life with dignity.[30] The "general conditions" to which the committee refers explicitly include homelessness, "degradation of the environment," and "deprivation of Indigenous peoples' land, territories and resources."[31] The measures that might be required include "strategic plans" and "social housing programmes."[32]

International human rights legal authorities have extensively examined the connection between the right to life and homelessness. In 2016, United Nations Special Rapporteur on the Right to Adequate Housing Leilani Farha explained that individuals experiencing homelessness and those in inadequate housing see their struggle for dignity and survival as a fight for human rights, feeling dehumanized and neglected by the government.[33] They consider being forgotten and left in intolerable conditions as a serious violation of human rights, indistinguishable in severity from the deprivation of life through direct government action.[34]

In 1999, while reviewing Canada's implementation of the *International Covenant on Civil and Political Rights*,[35] the UNHRC found that widespread homelessness in Canada had led to serious health problems and deaths, and it directed Canada to take positive measures to address homelessness as a violation of the right to life.[36] The effects of Canada's failure to act to prevent homelessness are perhaps most devastating for Indigenous women, girls, and 2SLGBTQQIA+ people. In the foreword to the Missing and Murdered Indigenous Women and Girls final report, Darlene Osborne, a member of the National Family Advisory Circle, decries the deaths and murders of

Indigenous women and girls as "shameful and preventable" because of the denial of the right to housing and adequate health care.[37]

Similarly, disability rights advocates have been raising concerns that persons with disabilities experiencing homelessness or inadequate housing are seeking medically assisted deaths to prevent suffering from experiences of rights violations.[38] Disability advocate David Fancy said that "[rights holders] would much prefer to be alive and there are simple social means such as housing or additional funding support that could reduce their suffering significantly to the point where they wouldn't need to try to reduce their suffering by having their life taken for them."[39]

The Path Less Travelled: The Optional Protocols

Many in the legal profession are unaware of the procedures available in international human rights systems. Indeed, this lack of familiarity with international human rights procedures can lead to hesitance among litigators to advance arguments that embrace a progressive interpretation of socio-economic rights or related right-to-life section 7 arguments for those experiencing homelessness. However, among rights holders, civil society advocates, and those bearing the brunt of the homelessness crisis, innovative applications of human rights authorities are commonly invoked. Perhaps one of the least understood systems of this nature – which holds some of the most salient jurisprudence – is the complaint or inquiry procedure under the Optional Protocols to human rights treaties and the resulting implications for the Charter.[40]

The Optional Protocol to the ICESCR

As a signatory to the *ICESCR,* Canada is obliged to ensure access to justice and effective remedies for violations of fundamental human rights under domestic law. Decisions under the Optional Protocol (OP-*ICESCR*) can be instructive in understanding interpretations of rights protected under the covenant and how Canada must ensure access to justice under domestic law – particularly for vulnerable and disadvantaged groups.

The Committee on Economic, Social and Cultural Rights (UNCESCR) has clarified that access to justice under domestic law need not always depend on courts. Alternative mechanisms such as tribunals or administrative bodies can be advantageous in some circumstances, but the committee has been clear that any "rigid classification" that places economic, social, and cultural rights beyond the reach of the courts would be incompatible with the indivisibility and interdependence of human rights and "drastically curtail the capacity of the courts to protect the rights of the most vulnerable and disadvantaged groups in society."[41] That concern is particularly relevant to the consideration of Charter claims to the right to life of vulnerable and disadvantaged groups in Canada.

However, Canada has not ratified the OP-*ICESCR.* Government lawyers have relied on this absence of ratification to argue that, despite the *NHSA,* Canada is under no obligation to ensure access to justice or effective remedies for socio-economic rights under domestic law or to engage genuinely with meaningful implementation of the *ICESCR.*

This position is at odds with jurisprudence from the UNCESCR and the consensus within the United Nations General Assembly affirming that access to justice and effective remedies must be equally available for rights under the *ICESCR* and that socio-economic rights must be placed on equal footing with civil and political rights.[42] The *ICESCR,* which Canada ratified in 1976, requires state parties to commit to ensuring access to justice and effective remedies, even if they have not ratified the OP-*ICESCR.* Therefore, the principle of indivisibility in economic, social, and cultural rights in international law showcases Canada's domestic obligation to the right to housing as a signatory to the *ICESCR.*

Related Optional Protocols

The decisions under optional protocols that Canada has ratified (e.g., the Optional Protocols to the *International Covenant on Civil and Political Rights*[43] and the *Convention on the Elimination of All Forms of Discrimination Against Women* [*CEDAW*][44]) reveal an emerging trend of vibrant jurisprudence that unequivocally and indivisibly connects economic and social rights with the rights to life and security of the person.

The UNHRC has rejected the idea that the right to life is a purely negative right and has affirmed both in its *General Comment No. 36* and in recent jurisprudence that states must adopt positive and strategic measures to address systemic violations of the right to life.[45] In the case of *Toussaint,* the UNHRC rejected Canada's arguments that positive obligations to ensure access to health care for irregular migrants are outside the scope of the right to life or that they relate exclusively to the right to health in the *ICESCR.* Canada's position, with respect both to the scope of the right to life and to the justiciability of the right to health, is increasingly at odds with jurisprudence from regional and international human rights bodies.

The ruling of the United Nations Committee on the Elimination of Discrimination Against Women (UNCEDAW) in the *Kell v Canada* complaint is an example of the indivisibility of the right to life, the right to housing, and the right to be free from gender-based discrimination.[46] Cecilia Kell, an Indigenous woman in the community of Rae-Edzo in the Northwest Territories, was removed from her assignment lease upon the request of her abusive partner (also a director of the Housing Authority Board) and subsequently evicted from her home. Kell fought for ten years to regain her home, and in 2008 she filed an individual complaint against Canada to the UNCEDAW. It accepted that she "was a victim of domestic violence, a fact which was not contested by the State party; that her partner tried to stop her from working, thus limiting her ability to lead an independent economic life; and that she was evicted from her home while seeking protection from domestic violence in a battered women's shelter."[47] The UNCEDAW found that Canada had failed to provide Kell with effective legal protections when seeking to regain her property rights.[48] The committee also recommended that Canada recruit and train more Indigenous women to provide legal assistance and that it review its legal system to ensure that Indigenous women have effective access to justice.[49]

It is important to recognize the significance of this decision by the UNCEDAW: an Indigenous woman in Canada turned to international human rights mechanisms because she was denied justice under Canada's domestic law. Although this case was decided on articles of *CEDAW* related to discrimination, those violations of *CEDAW* are directly connected to violations of the right to life and security of the person as it relates to the devastating impacts of homelessness.[50] Kell was escaping domestic violence, and because of the failure of government actors, "she and her three children became homeless for several years."[51] This bears repeating: a failure of government action resulted in a risk to the safety and security of Kell and her children. When domestic remedies were denied to her, she turned to international human rights mechanisms, which, instead of applying restrictive and exclusionary approaches to positive/negative rights, applied an approach of interdependence and indivisibility.

On December 2, 2018, Canada ratified the relatively new *Optional Protocol to the Convention on the Rights of Persons with Disabilities*.[52] The recent ratification means that we do not yet have a set of jurisprudence on which to rely. However, it is anticipated that, in the coming years, some of the most cutting-edge jurisprudence related to socio-economic rights and the right to life will be developed under it.

ESCR and the Right to Life in the Post-Pandemic World

The world has changed significantly since the Ontario Court of Appeal decided *Tanudjaja*. For example, *General Comment No. 36* highlighted interdependence in the right to life, environmental degradation, and climate crisis. It noted that "environmental degradation, climate change and unsustainable development constitute some of the most pressing and serious threats to the ability of present and future generations to enjoy the right to life."[53] The UNHRC further articulated in *General Comment No. 36* that "implementation of the obligation to respect and ensure the right to life, and in particular life with dignity, depends, inter alia, on measures taken by States parties to preserve the environment and protect it against harm, pollution and climate change caused by public and private actors."[54]

The committee then applied this intersection of the right to life and positive measures in relation to the environment in an Optional Protocol decision, *Portillo Cáceres v Paraguay*.[55] In this decision, the UNHRC recognized the state's duty to protect the right to life, and the requirement "to adopt positive measures that are needed to ensure the effective exercise of this right, in the light of interference by the State authorities and physical or legal persons."[56]

During the COVID-19 crisis, the intersection of the right to life and homelessness became increasingly evident.[57] As a recent study found, people experiencing homelessness had 2.7 deaths per 100 person years compared with 0.7 deaths per 100 person years among the study's two unexposed groups, and persons experiencing homelessness who died were seventeen years younger on average.[58] In litigation against the City of Toronto, for example, a group of advocates alleged that the city had violated both the Charter and the Ontario *Human Rights Code* by failing to ensure that shelter beds were two metres apart.[59]

The realities of the past few years have revealed that, without a more progressive approach to Canada's understanding of the intersection of the right to life and economic and social rights (particularly in the context of homelessness), Canada is staring down the precipice to a bleak future.

International Human Rights Obligations and Domestic Law in Canada

The context of the evolution of international human rights law, increasingly embracing the interdependence of the right to life and economic and social rights, is very relevant to domestic interpretations of the Charter. Canadian case law affirms that Canada's international human rights norms must be embedded in interpretations of the Charter.

Alex Neve has described international human rights as "*indivisible and interdependent and interrelated*," and a "robust understanding of dualism" can integrate more effectively Canada's international human rights obligations with domestic law:

> By ratifying UN treaties, Canada commits to implementing their provisions through domestic law and making the changes required to ensure access to effective remedies for any violations of these rights (Government of Canada, 2019a). *The* Charter *is a primary vehicle for implementing those rights and Canada's Supreme Court has determined that it should be presumed to provide at least the same level of protection as ratified treaties.* All domestic law, in fact, should be interpreted and applied by decision-makers in accordance with Canada's international commitments.[60]

As Supreme Court Justice Abella noted in *Nevsun Resources Ltd v Araya,*[61] international human rights norms are "the phoenix that rose from the ashes of World War II ... These norms were not meant to be theoretical aspirations or legal luxuries but moral imperatives and legal necessities."[62] The interpretation of the right to life in the Charter plays a central role in ensuring that international human rights norms are treated as legal necessities.

Conversely, litigators, particularly those representing governments, are continually pushing the erroneous idea that international human rights cannot possibly support a more progressive interpretation of the right to life (as indivisible from the right to housing) in the Charter. This is partly because of the prevalence of the positive/negative rights paradigm, which privileges challenges to government "interference" with rights (e.g., evicting people who are housed) over challenges for failing to take the positive action necessary for the protection of the rights of those who are homeless. Litigators representing rights holders and their advocates are more inclined to take forward negative rights claims because they believe that they are more likely to win.

But in reality the negative/positive rights paradigm ignores the indivisibility of rights at the core of international human rights law norms – as described in applications above – and instead adopts a negative rights paradigm at odds with international human rights law, and the paradigm tends to disenfranchise those who need positive measures and programs to address systemic violations of their rights. Advocates for homeless, disabled, and impoverished individuals argue that the Charter should scrutinize all government decisions and broadly interpret government guarantees to include protections against human rights violations experienced by disadvantaged groups.[63] They assert that the Charter must mandate proactive government measures to ensure rights to life, security, equality, and essential services, aligning with Canada's obligations under the *ICESCR*.[64]

The *NHSA*

I have argued thus far that *Tanudjaja* – a case with limited scope – did not settle the question of positive obligations under section 7 of the Charter for persons experiencing homelessness. However, even if this case were to be relied on as settling a question of such fundamental importance, that was before Parliament exercised its legislative authority to bring commitments under the *ICESCR* into domestic law by passing the *NHSA*.[65]

The *NHSA* was passed in 2019, after decades of advocacy from civil society. As Bruce Porter and Elizabeth McIsaac wrote at the time, "the lack of effective judicial response to homelessness as a human rights violation echoed into the void that was federal housing policy."[66] The *NHSA* recognizes the right to adequate housing as a "fundamental human right affirmed in international human rights law" and commits to "further the progressive realization of the right to adequate housing as recognized in the [*ICESCR*]."[67] Critically for rights holders, including persons with first-hand experience of the housing and homelessness crisis, the *NHSA* provides a pathway to claim rights through a parallel access-to-justice mechanism in the form of a National Housing Council and federal housing advocate.[68]

Perhaps the most powerful mechanism of the *NHSA* is the ability of the advocate to require the National Housing Council to appoint a three-person review panel[69] to hold a hearing with participation by members of affected communities, as well as human rights and housing experts, on a systemic housing issue under section 13.1 (1) and (2) of the *NHSA*. These participatory hearings will result in findings and recommended measures sent to the minister of housing, infrastructure, and communities. The federal housing advocate can also conduct a review of a systemic issue and report findings and make recommendations. In both cases, the minister is required to respond within 120 days. In the case of a review panel, the minister must table the response in both the House of Commons and the Senate.

As noted by Biss and co-authors, fundamentally, "the NHSA recognizes homelessness and inadequate housing in so affluent a country as Canada as a human rights problem, rooted not only in policy failures but in systemic failures to recognize some members of society as equal in dignity and rights."[70] They argue further that, "as with other human rights issues like systemic racism or colonization, the first step in addressing them is to recognize them as human rights issues and empower rights holders to claim their rights, ensuring meaningful accountability, and participation in decision-making."[71]

In December 2022, the federal housing advocate issued a formal request that the first review panel be on the topic of the financialization of purpose-built rental housing.[72] The panel held written and oral hearings throughout 2023. Critically for this chapter, the second review panel was on the topic of the failure to prevent and eliminate homelessness among women and gender-diverse persons, including Two-Spirit persons and Indigenous women.[73] The second panel was in response to two human rights claims under the *NHSA* launched by the Women's National Housing and Homelessness Network (WNHHN)[74] and the National Indigenous Women's Housing Network (NIWHN).

In the claim by the WNHHN, the authors noted that

> we are single moms trying to make rent. We are women and gender-diverse persons living the sheer terror of homelessness. We are women with disabilities trapped in housing that undermines our health and threatens our life. We are gender-diverse and 2SLGBTQIA+ people surviving on minimum wage and checking our mailboxes for eviction notices each morning. We are Indigenous and racialized women facing race-based discrimination in housing markets and public systems. We are young women enduring harassment and violence because we cannot afford our own place. We are newcomers being renovicted by corporate landlords. We are children being removed from our mothers' care because of poverty and homelessness. We are allies, housing and social service providers, and researchers whose decades of work ... [are] overshadowed by the enormity of the housing crisis and policy failures. We are living proof that the housing system in Canada is broken.
>
> We are here to claim a better future for ourselves, our children, our communities, and the planet. We will no longer accept the unacceptable. We call on the Government of Canada to fully realize our human right to housing and be held accountable for the human rights violations being perpetrated against us.[75]

As the panel conducts the review under its duties in section 16.3 of the *NHSA*, it is tasked with a new exercise of human rights implementation that could result in concrete policy recommendations. This process has incredible implications for some of those most affected by homelessness as a violation of the right to life and security of the person.

The Federal Court of Appeal recently interpreted the Ontario Court of Appeal's decision in *Tanudjaja* in a promising light. It held that challenges to inadequate policy or programmatic responses to social issues are not always beyond the scope of section 7; rather, such Charter challenges must have a sufficient legal standard against which to measure policy responses and be anchored in legislation. The Federal Court of Appeal was examining a challenge to climate change policy, but consider how it applies in the housing context. Where Parliament or a legislature has affirmed in legislation a commitment to adopt a strategy with targets to meet internationally agreed-upon norms, as has been done in the *NHSA,* failure to meet that legislative commitment in accordance with international norms can and should be reviewed to consider whether Charter rights have been infringed.[76]

Good Faith Obligations of Governments and *Toussaint v Canada (Attorney General)*

A recent decision by the Ontario Superior Court of Justice in *Toussaint* similarly demonstrates a new path forward to claim Charter protections under section 7 in relation to the right to life and economic and social rights. In this case, the government of Canada argued that it could disregard a decision from the UNHRC,[77] which determined that Canada must ensure that irregular migrants are no longer denied access to essential health care when their lives are at risk. In his decision, Justice Perell rejected the government's position.

Government lawyers argued that Ms. Toussaint was claiming a right to "free health care," but Justice Perell rejected that argument, characterizing it as "a dog whistle argument that reeks of the prejudicial stereotype that immigrants come to Canada to milk the welfare system."[78] Although the UNHRC's decision is not legally binding as such, Perell found that Canada's response can still be reviewed by the court with a view to ensure that it did not violate the Charter or the requirement that Canada implement its treaty obligations in good faith.

Justice Perell further described the historical context of good faith with Canada's accession to the *Vienna Convention on the Law of Treaties,*[79] in which Canada agreed to "perform its obligations under international treaties in good faith and not to invoke any provisions of its domestic system as a justification for its failure to perform its obligations."[80] He further noted that the *Vienna Convention* codified the "rule of customary international law known as *pacta sunt servanda*"[81] (meaning that agreements must be kept): namely, "the principle that all treaties are binding and must be performed in good faith is a principle of *jus cogens* [meaning the norms that govern international law] and a central unifying principle of the international legal system."[82] This means that, though treaty obligations are not directly enforceable under domestic law in Canada, unless incorporated into domestic law, courts can nevertheless review whether they have been implemented in good faith.

Importantly, in this context, Justice Perrell further wrote that "the purpose of modern international human rights law is to identify and remedy breaches of internationally accepted norms in a global war on human rights' abuses. Canadian courts have an important role to play and have a responsibility to participate and to contribute to the ongoing development of international law."[83]

Domestically, the principle of good faith is most prevalent in contract law and perhaps best contrasted to the application of the concept of "bad faith."[84] In looking to international examples of the application of good faith under the framework of the *Vienna Convention,* the International Court of Justice has explained that "the principle of good faith obliges the Parties to apply [the treaty] in a reasonable way and in such a manner that its purpose can be realized."[85]

For legal advocates in the right-to-housing sector, the principle of good faith provides a basis for arguing that the Charter must evolve to protect better the right to life for persons experiencing homelessness. With the domestic implementation mechanism of the *NHSA,* it could mean that the government must take the processes seriously and that – in responding (vis-à-vis the minister of housing, infrastructure, and communities) to findings and recommendations from the advocate, National Housing Council, or review panels – the government must implement international human rights obligations in good faith and respect the Charter rights of those affected.

Remedies for Rights Holders

The recent settlement in *Disability Rights Coalition*[86] is a beacon of hope that human rights can lead to great change and that perhaps, after all, there is an appetite for change in Canada's legal systems. The Nova Scotia Court of Appeal found that there was a case of systemic discrimination in the provincial government's failure to provide adequate financial assistance for supports, services, and housing for persons with disabilities to live with dignity in the community, instead forcing the claimants to live in totally unsuitable institutional settings.

The subject matter of this court challenge has been reflected in treaty recommendations to Canada for decades by international human rights bodies. The decision resulted in a settlement for a binding systemic remedy by which, in three years, any person with a disability currently on a wait-list and not receiving services will have access to full supports and services required to live in the community with dignity.[87] By the fifth year, the wait-list must be eliminated, providing immediate access to necessary supports and services for anyone who needs them. This form of remedy, by which the government must work collaboratively with rights holders and present a plan to the court, is an important reminder of how legal systems can work creatively to require the government genuinely to meet urgent human rights obligations for the most marginalized people.

Conclusion

In 2014, I sat in the overflow room at the Ontario Court of Appeal as the *Tanudjaja* case was argued. I was a new lawyer and energized to watch history in the making – an unprecedented exercise of justice by people who had experienced homelessness in Canada. It was a powerful moment to witness.

I remember the buzz in the room – the energy as intervenors across the spectrum of civil society came forward to argue that the case should proceed. I remember the devastation when the decision came down and the ruling that the case be dismissed without any of the 9,000 pages of evidence being read. I remember the visceral disappointment when the Supreme Court of Canada denied leave on the appeal from the Ontario Court of Appeal. This has left a decade of misinterpreted rulings related to section 7 Charter rights and the experience of homelessness in Canada.

Outside legal spaces, in engaging with rights holders, this case has been a focal point that illustrates the systemic exclusion of people experiencing homelessness from accessing their human right to life, which has been denied through Canada's Charter. In reality, *Tanudjaja* did not settle anything other than whether that particular claim was justiciable as framed. Far more salient jurisprudence is still evolving – the application of which should be heavily influenced by the will of Parliament as represented in the 2019 *NHSA*.

As the Supreme Court of British Columbia noted in the 2020 decision in *Cambie Surgeries* (a case that challenged the *Medicare Protection Act*,[88] which prohibited health-care practitioners from charging patients already recipients of Canada's universal health-care system),

> there is some discussion in the authorities and among scholars about the scope of the rights in s. 7 of the *Charter.* Some have criticized Tanudjaja and other s. 7 authorities ... because they did not acknowledge the rights to life, liberty and security of the person as providing positive rights to housing and healthcare. In addition, Justice Arbour in her dissent in *Gosselin v Quebec (Attorney General)*, 2002 SCC 84, concluded that s. 7 rights have a positive dimension for basic issues of health and security ... While the majority of the Supreme Court of Canada in *Gosselin* disagreed with her reasoning, I note they also said that "[o]ne day s. 7 may be interpreted to include positive obligations" ... Accordingly, the scope of the rights under s. 7 may be considered unsettled.[89]

In working with rights holders across the country, I perceive a tremendous feeling of hopelessness and outrage against the rising tide of Canada's housing and homelessness crisis. Some communities face near-constant loss. As a lawyer working in policy spaces with many people outside traditional legal practice, and in engaging in discussions with rights holders about legal challenges, human rights, or constitutional protection, I note a deep cynicism that the "law" is not for them. They feel as though it has left them behind. Exacerbating this divide is the fact that most lawyers, policy makers, and bureaucrats are part of the middle class and wealthy class who benefit from deeply entrenched systems of inequality.

Housing justice is possible in Canada, but to get there the legal profession needs to be braver in advancing progressive legal arguments. So many students enter law school with a desire to make the world a better place, but somewhere along the way many of us develop a cynicism that law is a vehicle that constrains creativity and innovation for the most marginalized. As an advocate who bears responsibility for upholding the human rights of those experiencing homelessness, I leave you with this call: If we are not fighting to safeguard the rights and lives of the most marginalized in Canada, then why are we here? The wind is shifting, and the living tree of Canada's constitutional framework can shift with it. It was always meant to grow. We see these changes rapidly advancing in international human rights jurisprudence, in legislative commitments, and in slowly emerging case law in Canada. And perhaps that day envisioned in *Gosselin,*[90] when positive rights are recognized under section 7, is drawing nearer.

Acknowledgments

I would like to express my deep gratitude to Bruce Porter (Social Rights Advocacy Centre) for his invaluable guidance and support. I would similarly like to acknowledge Raiha Shareef (2024 law student at McGill University's Faculty of Law) for her research and editing support.

Notes

1 There is no shortage of evidence that the experience of homelessness can lead to outcomes affecting life expectancy. See, for example, Centre for Equality Rights in Accommodation and National Right to Housing Network, *The Rights to Life, Protection of the Home, and Non-Discrimination in Canada* (2021), https://housingrights.ca/wp-content/uploads/ICCPRSubmission-NRHN-CERA-2021.pdf [perma.cc/Y29Q-SZUE].

2 Part I of the *Constitution Act, 1982*, being Schedule B to the *Canada Act 1982* (UK), 1982, c 11 [Charter].

3 *Tanudjaja v Canada (Attorney General)*, 2014 ONCA 852 [*Tanudjaja*]. See the discussion of this case in Chapter 9 of this collection.

4 *Edwards v Canada* (Attorney General), [1930] AC 124, [1930] 1 DLR 98 (JCPC).

5 *National Housing Strategy Act*, SC 2019, c 29, s 313 [*NHSA*].

6 *Toussaint v Canada (Attorney General)*, 2022 ONSC 4747 [*Toussaint*].

7 *Disability Rights Coalition v Nova Scotia (Attorney General)*, 2021 NSCA 70 [*Disability Rights Coalition*].

8 *Tanudjaja v Attorney General of Canada and Attorney General of Ontario* (2010), Toronto CV-10-403688 (Amended Notice of Application) [*Tanudjaja* Amended Notice of Application].

9 *Tanudjaja v Canada (Attorney General)* (December 5, 2012), Toronto CV-10-403688 (ONSC) (Factum, Respondent); *Tanudjaja v Canada (Attorney General)* (May 27, 2013), Toronto CV-10-403688 (ONSC) (Motion to Strike, Appellant).

10 *Tanudjaja v Canada* (Attorney General), 2014 ONCA 852.

11 Tracy Heffernan, Fay Faraday, and Peter Rosenthal, "Fighting for the Right to Housing in Canada" (2015) 24 *Journal of Law and Social Policy* 10–45 at 13, citing *Tanudjaja* Amended Notice of Application at 13.

12 Ibid.

13 See, for example, *The Regional Municipality of Waterloo v Persons Unknown and to Be Ascertained*, 2023 ONSC 670 at para 125.

14 Alexandra Flynn, Heidi Kiiwetinepinesiik Stark, and Estair Van Wagner, *Canada's Human Rights Obligations and Jurisprudence Regarding Encampments: Report for Lawyers and Advocates* (2024), https://homelesshub.ca/resource/encampments-and-legal-obligations-evolving-rights-and-relationships/ [perma.cc/Y4KZ-R3GZ] at 24.

15 *Tanudjaja*, leave to appeal to SCC refused, 36283 (June 25, 2015).

16 Margot Young, "Charter Eviction: Litigating out of House and Home" (2015) 24:3 *Journal of Law and Social Policy* 46–67.

17 Martha Jackman and Bruce Porter, "Social and Economic Rights in Canada," in *The Oxford Handbook of the Canadian Constitution,* ed. Peter Oliver, Patrick Macklem, and Nathalie Des Rosiers (New York: Oxford University Press, 2017), 843–62 at 858.

18 Ibid.

19 *Tanudjaja* at para 36.

20 Ibid at para 52.

21 World Conference on Human Rights in Vienna, *Vienna Declaration and Programme of Action,* A/CONF.157/23 (1993), OHCHR, https://ap.ohchr.org/documents/dpage_e.aspx?si=A/CONF.157/23 [perma.cc/3PXN-5P9Q].

22 See *Cambie Surgeries Corporation v British Columbia (Attorney General),* 2020 BCSC 1310 at para 2052 (in which Justice Steeves finds that, in light of SCC jurisprudence and academic criticism of the majority decision in *Tanudjaja,* "the scope of the rights under s. 7 may be considered unsettled"). This decision was upheld on appeal, though it did not address this point. See also *Mathur v Ontario,* 2020 ONSC 6918, dismissing a motion to strike, in which the court distinguished the *Tanudjaja* claim from a claim anchored in an explicit international commitment.

23 Jackman and Porter, "Social and Economic Rights," at 859.

24 Bruce Porter, "Interdependence of Human Rights," in *Research Handbook on Economic, Social and Cultural Rights as Human Rights,* ed. Jackie Dugard, Bruce Porter, Daniela Ikawa, and Lilian Chenwi (Cheltenham, UK: Edward Elgar, 2020), 302–27.

25 *International Covenant on Economic, Social and Cultural Rights,* December 16, 1966, 993 UNTS 3 (entered into force January 3, 1976) [*ICESCR*].

26 *Convention on the Elimination of All Forms of Discrimination Against Women,* December 18, 1979, 1249 UNTS 1 (entered into force September 3, 1981) [*CEDAW*].

27 *Convention on the Rights of Persons with Disabilities,* December 13, 2006, 2515 UNTS 3, art 28(1) (entered into force May 3, 2008) [*CRPD*].

28 *United Nations Declaration on the Rights of Indigenous Peoples,* UNGA, 61st Sess, UN Doc A/RES/61/295 (2007) GA Res 61/295 [*UNDRIP*].

29 United Nations Human Rights Committee (UNHRC), *General Comment No. 6: Article 6: Right to Life,* UNHRC, 16th Sess, https://www.refworld.org/legal/general/hrc/1982/en/32185 [perma.cc/94FG-GAJN].

30 UNHRC, *General Comment No. 36: Article 6: Right to Life,* UNHRC, 124th Sess, UN Doc CCPR/C/GC/36, https://documents.un.org/doc/undoc/gen/g19/261/15/pdf/g1926115.pdf [perma.cc/K5N7-J6VN] [UNHRC, *General Comment No. 36*].

31 Ibid.

32 Ibid.

33 Leilani Farha, *Report of the Special Rapporteur on Adequate Housing as a Component of the Right to an Adequate Standard of Living, and on the Right to Non-Discrimination in This Context,* UNGA, 71st Sess, UN Doc A/71/310 (2016).

34 Ibid.

35 *International Covenant on Civil and Political Rights,* December 16, 1966, 999 UNTS 171 (entered into force March 23, 1976, accession by Canada May 19, 1976) [*ICCPR*].

36 *Consideration of Reports Submitted by States Parties Under Article 40 of the Covenant,* UNHRC, 65th Sess, UN Doc CCPR/C/79/Add.105 (1999).

37 National Inquiry into Missing and Murdered Indigenous Women and Girls, *Reclaiming Power and Place: The Final Report of the National Inquiry into Missing and Murdered Indigenous Women and Girls,* vol. 1a (Ottawa: Privy Council Office, 2016) at 21.

38 Ontario, Ministry of the Solicitor General and Office of the Chief Coroner, *MAiD Death Review Committee Report 2024 – 3: Navigating Vulnerability in Non-Reasonably Foreseeable Natural Deaths* (Toronto: Government of Ontario, 2024), https://s3.documentcloud.org/documents/25238359/canada-euthanasia-3.pdf [perma.cc/23VD-R4PC].

39 Matthew P. Barker, "St. Catharines Man Facing Homelessness Considers Assisted Death an Option," *Standard* [St. Catharines] (October 21, 2022), https://www.stcatharinesstandard.ca/life/2022/10/21/st-catharines-man-facing-homelessness-considers-assisted-death-an-option.html [perma.cc/FRR2-MSSF].

40 An Optional Protocol may provide procedures for redress with regard to a treaty, though it is a treaty in its own right and open to signature, accession, or ratification. An Optional Protocol may provide for a communications procedure in which individual rights holders can make petitions directly to the treaty body. The complaints procedure under the OP-*ICESCR* provides an opportunity to seek recommendations from the CESCR for remedy and compensation in individual cases when a state is found to have violated economic, social, and cultural rights (ESCR). The procedure provides rights claimants with the opportunity to seek justice at the international level when access to it at the national level has been denied; the CESCR with an opportunity to advance new jurisprudence (legal interpretation of the content of a state's obligations) on ESCR; and a legal mechanism within which contributions of claimants, states, third parties, and the committee itself can help to define and clarify the nature and scope of the ESCR protected under the *ICESCR.* As a second procedure, the CESCR can conduct inquiries into grave or systemic violations of the rights protected in a treaty. See *Optional Protocol to the International Covenant on Economic, Social and Cultural Rights,* UNGA, A/RES/63/117 (2008).

41 UNCESCR, *General Comment No. 9: The Domestic Application of the Covenant,* UNESCOR, 19th Sess, UN Doc E/C.12/1998/24 (1998) at 4, https://documents.un.org/doc/undoc/gen/g98/148/36/pdf/g9814836.pdf [perma.cc/EP8U-QUSE].

42 UNGA, 63rd Sess, UN Doc A/63/PV.66 (2008) 66th Mtg.

43 *Optional Protocol to the International Covenant on Civil and Political Rights,* December 16, 1966, 999 UNTS 302.

44 *Optional Protocol to the Convention on the Elimination of All Forms of Discrimination Against Women,* October 6, 1999, 2131 UNTS 83.

45 UNHRC, *General Comment No. 36;* Nell Toussaint, *Views Adopted by the Committee Under Article 5(4) of the Optional Protocol, Concerning Communication No. 2348/2014,* UNHRC, CCPR/C/123/D/2348/2014 (2018) [Toussaint, UNHRC].

46 *Views of the Committee on the Elimination of Discrimination Against Women Under Article 7, Paragraph 3, of the Optional Protocol to the Convention on the Elimination of All Forms of Discrimination Against Women (Fifty-First Session),* UNCEDAW, 51st Sess, UN Doc CEDAW/C/51/D/19/2008 (2012) Annex [UNCEDAW, *Kell Decision*].

47 Ibid.

48 Ibid at 17.

49 Ibid at 18.

50 I do not examine the intersection of the right to life with discrimination under s 15 of the Charter or in light of *R v Sharma,* in which the majority stated that "s. 15(1) does not impose a general, positive obligation on the state to remedy social inequalities or enact remedial legislation" and that, "were it otherwise, courts would be impermissibly pulled into the complex legislative domain of policy and resource allocation, contrary to the separation of powers" (see *R v Sharma,* 2022 SCC 39 at para 63). I encourage readers to review Jackman and Porter, "Social and Economic Rights," at 843–66, which argues that, like s 7, jurisprudence on s 15, positive obligations, and socio-economic rights, remains unsettled in Canada.

51 UNCEDAW, *Kell Decision,* at para 9.1.

52 *Optional Protocol to the Convention on the Rights of Persons with Disabilities,* December 13, 2006, 2518 UNTC 283 (entered into force May 3, 2008, accession by Canada December 3, 2018); see also Chapter 10 of this collection.

53 UNHRC, *General Comment No. 36.*

54 Ibid.

55 *Views Adopted by the Committee Under Article 5(4) of the Optional Protocol, Concerning Communication No. 2751/2016,* UNHRC, 126th Sess, UN Doc CCPR/C/126/D/2751/2016 (2019).

56 Ibid at para 7.8.

57 See Leilani Farha and Kaitlin Schwan, "The Front Line Defence: Housing and Human Rights in the Time of COVID-19," in *Vulnerable: The Law, Policy and Ethics of COVID-19,* ed. Colleen M. Flood, Vanessa MacDonnell, Jane Philpott, Sophie Thériault, and Sridhar Venkatapuram (Ottawa: University of Ottawa Press, 2020), 355–66.

58 Lucie Richard, Brooke Carter, Linda Wu, and Stephen W. Hwang, "Disparities in All-Cause Mortality Among People Experiencing Homelessness in Toronto, Canada, During the COVID-19 Pandemic: A Cohort Study" (2024) 12 *Frontiers in Public Health* 1–9.

59 *Sanctuary et al v Toronto (City) et al,* 2020 ONSC 6207; Muriel Draaisma, "Homeless Advocates Head to Court in Fight with City over Physical

Distancing in Shelters," *CBC News* (September 29, 2020), https://www.cbc.ca/news/canada/toronto/lawsuit-homeless-shelters-physical-distancing-advocates-city-compliance-1.5742635 [perma.cc/YG2E-WQQG].

60 Alex Neve, *Closing the Implementation Gap: Federalism and Respect for International Human Rights in Canada,* Institute for Research on Public Policy (IRPP) Study No. 90 (Montreal: IRPP, 2023) at 15 (emphasis added).

61 *Nevsun Resources Ltd v Araya,* 2020 SCC 5 at para 1 [*Nevsun*].

62 Ibid.

63 Jackman and Porter, "Social and Economic Rights," at 844.

64 Ibid.

65 If the *Tanudjaja v AG* claim had been brought forward after the passing of the *NHSA,* then it could be argued that it would now be "anchored in legislation," which includes a commitment to an international norm. See *La Rose v Canada,* 2023 FCA 241 at paras 36–38.

66 Bruce Porter and Elizabeth McIsaac, "Housing Rights," *Literary Review of Canada* (November 2019), https://reviewcanada.ca/magazine/2019/11/housing-rights/ [perma.cc/ZW7R-YBTP].

67 *NHSA,* s 4(d).

68 A limitation of the *NHSA* is that its application is only to matters of federal jurisdiction.

69 For a fuller explanation of the review panel mechanism, see National Right to Housing Network, "Review Panels," https://housingrights.ca/review-panels/ [perma.cc/VDC6-WJRK]; also see the introduction to this collection.

70 Michèle Biss, Bruce Porter, Sahar Raza, and David DesBaillets, *Progressive Realization of the Right to Adequate Housing: A Literature Review* (National Right to Housing Network, 2022), https://housingrights.ca/wp-content/uploads/NHC-Progressive-Realization-Paper_EN.pdf [perma.cc/7HCT-8DUP].

71 Ibid.

72 Office of the Federal Housing Advocate, "Federal Housing Advocate Asks National Housing Council to Launch Public Hearing on Corporate Investment in Housing" (September 23, 2022), housingchrc.ca/en/federal-housing-advocate-asks-national-housing-council-to-launch-public-hearing-on-corporate-investment-in-housing [perma.cc/HF3R-EQ8H].

73 Office of the Federal Housing Advocate, "Federal Housing Advocate Requests Review into the Failure to Eliminate Homelessness Amongst Women and Gender-Diverse People" (May 11, 2023), housingchrc.ca/en/federal-housing-advocate-requests-review-into-the-failure-to-eliminate-homelessness-amongst-women-and-gender-diverse-people [perma.cc/KEV8-DG2Z].

74 WNHHN Human Rights Task Force, *The Crisis Ends with Us: Request for a Review into the Systemic Denial of the Equal Right to Housing of Women and Gender-Diverse People in Canada* (WNHHN, 2022), https://womenshomelessness.ca/wp-content/uploads/WNHHN-Claim-15-June-2022.pdf [perma.cc/9EBP-R862].

75 Ibid at 6.

76 *Mathur v Ontario,* 2024 ONCA 762 at para 5; *La Rose* at paras 36–38; Sophia Clare D'Souza, "Section 7 Revisited: A Critical Examination of Legislative

Objectives and Positive Rights in *Mathur v Ontario*" (2024) 45 *Windsor Review of Legal and Social Issues* 125–35; Joel Bakan, "Negating Positive Rights: A Note on *Mathur v Ontario*" (2025) 33:3 *Constitutional Forum* 1–14.

77 Toussaint, UNHRC.

78 *Toussaint* at para 134.

79 *Vienna Convention on the Law of Treaties,* May 23, 1969, 1155 UNTS 331 (entered into force January 27, 1980), https://www.refworld.org/legal/agreements/un/1969/en/73676 [perma.cc/P2S7-JKYQ].

80 *Nevsun* at para 1.

81 *Toussaint* at para 28.

82 Ibid at para 181; John H. Currie, *Public International Law,* 2nd ed. (Toronto: Irwin Law, 2008) at 154; Robert Kolb, *Good Faith in International Law* (Oxford: Hart Publishing, 2017) at ch 4. This argument was presented by the Charter Committee on Poverty Issues in its factum in the Motion to Strike in *Toussaint v Canada (Attorney General),* ONCA Court File No CV-20-00649404-0000 (Factum of the Interveners), https://socialrights.ca/2022/ccpi%20factum%20optimized.pdf [perma.cc/CDK4-3UVT].

83 *Toussaint* at paras 180–82.

84 Edward P. Belobaba, "Good Faith in Canadian Contract Law," in *Special Lectures of the Law Society of Upper Canada 1985 – Commercial Law: Recent Developments and Emerging Trends* (Toronto: De Boo, 1985), 73ff at 73.

85 *Gabčíkovo-Nagymaros Project (Hungary-Slovakia) (Merits),* [1997] ICJ Rep at 7, 78–79.

86 *Disability Rights Coalition* and see further discussion of this case in Chapter 10 of this collection.

87 Disability Rights Coalition of Nova Scotia, "Interim Agreement Reached on a Systemic Human Rights Remedy for Persons with Disabilities," news release (April 26, 2023), https://www.disabilityrightscoalitionns.ca/wp-content/uploads/2023/04/Rev-DRC-Media-Release-April-26-2023-130pmwith-links.pdf [perma.cc/YWR4-A7WJ].

88 *Medicare Protection Act,* RSBC 1996, c 286.

89 *Cambie Surgeries Corporation v British Columbia (Attorney General),* 2020 BCSC 1310.

90 *Gosselin v Quebec (Attorney General),* 2002 SCC 84.

Part 1

Legal Unhousing of Renters

2

The Banality of Eviction

Strategic Ignorance in Eviction Decision Making

SARAH BUHLER

Introduction

In their study of eviction in Canada, Sarah Zell and Scott McCullough shared stories of tenants who had experienced eviction from rental housing. One tenant said that they were still "living through the ramifications of this [eviction]" months after it had happened.[1] Another asked, "[H]ow do I get my life back?"[2] Zell and McCullough observed that many tenants used the language of trauma to describe the impacts of eviction on their lives and families.[3] Tenants who participated in the study spoke about the importance of home – a place that provided stability, safety, security, and well-being. They talked about how the loss of housing through eviction disrupted their sense of home and caused negative impacts that reverberated for a long time. Several participants became, and remained, homeless following their evictions.[4] A housing support worker who participated in the study said the following about the impacts of eviction: "We know what happens when people are evicted. They don't generally go to a better place – it's always a step away from something that's adequate ... to further instability, or insecurity. And that costs all of us."[5]

Eviction in Canada takes place in a social and economic context characterized by serious housing unaffordability, rising rents, deepening income inequality, and increased financialization of housing – meaning that housing is viewed primarily as a commodity or vehicle to generate profits for investors rather than a fundamental human need and right.[6] In many parts of the country, landlords evict tenants in order to convert their dwelling places into condominiums or more expensive rental units. Everywhere tenants are evicted because they are unable to afford the rent, often because of job loss, health problems, family crises, inadequate social assistance supports, or simply insufficient income. Tenants are also evicted for "behavioural" reasons, including when they are victims of domestic violence, have experienced a mental health or addiction crisis, or have become mistaken targets of police investigations.[7] Among tenants, eviction is not evenly distributed. Rather, we know that tenants who already face the highest levels of discrimination and oppression in society are most likely to be evicted: they include Indigenous women, Black women, trans and gender-diverse people, people with disabilities, people with histories of child welfare involvement, newcomers, and youth.[8]

Meanwhile, residential tenancy tribunals in Canada churn out thousands of eviction orders each year. It appears that landlords are overwhelmingly successful in receiving eviction orders (e.g., in Saskatchewan, landlords who apply for an eviction are successful over 90 percent of the time).[9] For the most part, eviction decisions read like mundane legal documents, listing the names of landlords and tenants, reproducing sections of legislation, reciting the monthly rent payable by the tenant and the amount of rent owing, and sometimes briefly setting out additional evidence.[10] The decisions are often brief, imbued with a sense of a routine, technocratic process with little room for variation. In particular, many decisions are characterized by an absence of any discussion of the circumstances of the tenant, the hardships that eviction might unleash, or why eviction is an appropriate remedy in the circumstances.[11] In this way, eviction decisions often read as if they are disconnected from the current social context described earlier – the ongoing financialization of housing, the affordability crisis, the homelessness crisis, and the fact that eviction reflects societal patterns of discrimination and marginalization. Rather, these decisions seem to exist in a different world altogether – a world where residential tenancy relationships are purely transactional and where everyone has commensurate choices. In such a world, it is a routine matter to evict a tenant who owes five dollars to a corporate landlord or a mother of five with a newborn in the hospital.[12]

In this chapter, I engage with the rift between the lived experience of eviction as a deeply impactful process entangled with larger social and economic forces and the often mechanistic, acontextual outputs of tribunals that adjudicate landlord eviction applications. Drawing from literature that critically analyzes eviction processes, I posit that eviction law and decision making are characterized by a form of "strategic ignorance" that encourages the avoidance of certain knowledge while actively reproducing meanings that uphold existing property and power relations. This strategic ignorance allows eviction to be seen as banal and unremarkable rather than disruptive and harmful. I urge lawmakers and eviction tribunals to reject this approach and instead embrace a commitment to the human right to housing, which requires seeing eviction as a grim outcome and a last resort.

The first two sections of the chapter discuss the literature on the importance of home and security of tenure and the research that documents the impacts of eviction on tenants and communities. The third section provides background on current eviction laws and practices. The chapter then introduces the concept of strategic ignorance, showing how it is not about an "absence" of knowledge but functions as a particular form of knowledge production within eviction law and practice. This section explores how actively "not knowing" about the impacts of eviction and the social forces that produce tenant vulnerability and landlord power allows eviction decision makers to see eviction as routine or even inevitable and how, in turn, it reproduces existing power relations. This part of the chapter also explores systemic and institutional factors that combine to create the conditions for this strategic ignorance to take hold. The final section proposes that eviction law and decision making be transformed to take account of current research on the impacts and contexts of eviction and that a human rights–informed proportionality analysis be implemented and taken seriously by decision makers. With this approach, an eviction decision would never be routine but always understood as a grave act of "legal unhousing."

The Importance of Home

As outlined in the introduction to this book, it is difficult to overstate the importance of "home" to human beings. Home encompasses a material place and a physical structure ("housing") but also holds complex emotional, cultural, and social meanings. Lorna Fox O'Mahony explains that home represents a "complex and multi-dimensional amalgam of financial, practical, social, psychological, cultural, politic-economic and emotional interests to its occupiers."[13] Fundamentally, a sense of home is a central requirement for human flourishing. We spend most of our time in our homes, and our ability to feel secure at home is central to our health and well-being. Homes are sites of identity formation and places where people can connect with family and culture. They are repositories of "essential psychological and cultural processes."[14] Having a place to call home is a fundamental determinant of health and well-being as well as an essential precondition of employment, integration into community, and custody of children. O'Mahony explains that home is simultaneously a physical structure and something more than that, describing the concept as "home = house + *x*."[15] Bronwyn Bate explains that home is not only a place but also a "process," meaning that it is actively created through various homemaking practices. She writes that homemaking practices "involve embodied interactions with social and material objects, and this creates social meaning, turning a dwelling into a home."[16]

Although home ownership is often held up in dominant discourses as the "dream," such that ideas of home are often linked to ownership,[17] large and growing numbers of people rent their homes in Canada and beyond. Researchers have documented the homemaking activities of tenants, demonstrating how they create a sense of home through their relationships and practices despite sometimes difficult conditions, including the spectre of eviction. Tenants actively work to create a sense of home within their dwelling places, often with additional challenges that homeowners do not face because of the need to navigate the inherent insecurity and "relational subjugation" that accompany many rental relationships.[18] Eviction shatters a tenant's sense of home and ability to create it. In so doing, eviction asserts the landlord's power over the tenant's home while unleashing great precarity into the life of the tenant. The next section outlines the impacts of eviction on tenants and considers how eviction increases tenant vulnerability while shoring up landlord power.

The Impacts of Eviction

The impacts and harms of eviction are almost never acknowledged by eviction decision makers. Yet a growing body of empirical research documents the harsh and often devastating impacts of eviction on tenants, families, neighbourhoods, and society more generally. The loss of home through eviction can lead to "intense personal suffering" for those who experience it.[19] As noted earlier, tenants in Zell and McCullough's study spoke of their eviction experiences using the language of trauma.[20] They attributed anxiety, fear, depression, a sense of loss, and being overwhelmed and exhausted to their experiences of eviction.[21] One tenant spoke of the huge amounts of energy required to cope with eviction and its fallout, including efforts to find alternative housing on short notice in difficult markets, to rearrange schooling for children, and to make other logistical arrangements.[22]

Eviction has been identified as a significant pathway to homelessness. In a recent point-in-time homelessness count in Saskatoon, more than half of respondents experiencing homelessness reported that eviction was a cause of their housing loss.[23] Homelessness is a major social determinant of health and is associated with poor physical and mental health outcomes and increased chances of death.[24] As one example, people who were homeless faced double the mortality rate during COVID-19 compared with the general population.[25] People who are homeless also face greater risks of being criminalized and higher levels of violence.

Eviction is also associated with child apprehension and therefore can cause specific suffering for children and their parents.[26] It is important to point out that eviction and child welfare systems have a bidirectional relationship. That is, eviction can trigger the apprehension of children by child welfare authorities who deem evicted parents unable to provide adequate housing for their children. In turn, parents whose children are apprehended are often cut off from social assistance, which can trigger eviction and create extreme barriers to finding future housing and family reunification.[27]

Eviction is associated with loss of employment and difficulty gaining employment as well as the loss of educational opportunities.[28] It is also bad for one's health: researchers have found that eviction is associated with adverse physical health outcomes, including poor self-reported health, higher rates of cardiovascular disease, poor maternal and child health, more emergency room visits, and higher risk of death.[29] This research has also explored the relationship between eviction and mental health, finding that eviction is associated with higher rates of depression, anxiety, and psychological distress.

Tenants who are evicted also often have trouble finding other adequate and secure housing and can find themselves in increasingly unstable and undesirable housing situations, thus facing more evictions in the future.[30] One explanation for this is that landlords might be reluctant to rent to tenants with a previous history of eviction. Indeed, in the American context, tenants with a history of eviction have been described as being marked with a "Scarlet E" because landlords routinely screen for eviction histories.[31] Remarking on the ways that eviction creates long-term hardship for those who experience it, Matthew Desmond has written that eviction thrusts people "onto a difficult, and much more difficult, path." Desmond concludes that eviction is therefore "a cause, not just a condition, of poverty."[32]

Eviction can also be violent. An eviction order legally authorizes a sheriff or other state-authorized agent to forcibly remove a tenant and their belongings. As Nicholas Blomley writes, eviction "legally realises the absolute expulsion of people and their possessions from a space to which they cannot return without permission."[33] In other words, even though eviction is often viewed as a private or civil law matter, eviction orders are backed by the force of the state. As Kathryn Sabbeth concludes, eviction enforcement can therefore manifest as the "violence of economic force."[34]

It is clear that eviction negatively affects individuals and families subjected to it. But it is important to emphasize that eviction also affects neighbourhoods and communities. Researchers have established that eviction, often concentrated in lower-income neighbourhoods, has a detrimental impact on neighbourhood stability and cohesion.[35] Eviction is also expensive for the public because it is associated with high health and other public expenditures.[36]

Eviction is not distributed neutrally among tenants. Rather, certain groups experience higher rates of eviction than others. As reported by Kaitlin Schwan and coauthors, in Canada, the groups most vulnerable to eviction are those most likely to experience the highest rates of poverty and discrimination in all aspects of life. They include "those living at the cross sections of oppression and discrimination," including Indigenous women, Black women, trans and gender-diverse peoples; persons with disabilities; and newcomers.[37]

Tenants in Emily Paradis's study of tenant experiences at the Ontario Landlord and Tenant Board (ON LTB) revealed that those facing eviction experienced deep poverty and had past experiences of housing insecurity and homelessness.[38] More than one-third of tenants reported that they or someone in their household had a disability, most lived in poverty, half identified as racialized, and many were single parents.[39]

Eviction has consequential impacts for landlords too. Despite frequent mythologizing of "mom and pop" landlords in media accounts, the landlords who undertake the majority of evictions are members of what Ricardo Tranjan calls "the landlord class" – primarily wealthy families, corporations, and financial investors in the business of building equity and making profit from their rental relationships.[40] Although some commentators lament the costs of eviction for landlords, eviction has been shown to be profitable for some landlords who may add extra fees and charges when evicting tenants. But the institutional availability of eviction itself is the real benefit, especially for large corporate landlords in the business of extracting profits by renting homes to tenants. Increasingly large swaths of rental properties are generating significant profits for corporations and investors in Real Estate Investment Trusts: the institutional availability of eviction clearly plays a significant role in the ability of these corporate landlords to ensure that tenants prioritize their rent payments over their obligations to other creditors. Indeed, researchers have shown that many landlords engage in "serial eviction" filing as a way to assert discipline over tenants and force those in financial distress to prioritize rent payments over all other needs, sometimes also using eviction processes to squeeze additional fees and charges from tenants.[41]

Eviction benefits all landlords (not just those who actually evict tenants) because it symbolically asserts the power of landlords and the subordinate status of tenants in the landlord-tenant relationship. Indeed, Blomley points out that the institutional availability of eviction as a remedy for landlords reveals the "power relations operative in any property context."[42] This performance of power affects tenants who are directly affected and also puts all tenants on notice of their precarious position. Studies have shown that tenants discipline themselves accordingly, taking pains to ensure that they are "good tenants," which can mean accepting unfair or exploitative behaviour by landlords.[43] Thus, eviction has the effect of simultaneously subordinating tenants and reinforcing the power of landlords in an uneven and precarious property landscape.

"Eviction Machines": Eviction Law and Processes

In Canada, evictions happen within a profoundly uneven field. As we have seen, research shows how harmful evictions can be for tenants, their children, and their communities. Eviction functions to reinforce landlords' power. Yet, rather than protect tenants from these harms, law and legal processes are designed to facilitate eviction.[44] Although a substantial number of evictions are enacted outside formal legal processes (e.g., through a simple landlord request or threat that a tenant leave, with an unaffordable rent increase, or when a landlord illegally locks a tenant out), the formal eviction law system helps to create the attitudes and conditions that make informal evictions seem natural and inevitable.

Each Canadian province and territory has its own legislation and institutional approach to eviction. Although there are many differences, some general observations can be made. Evictions can be handled by courts in some jurisdictions (e.g., Alberta), but it is most common for evictions to be handled by specialized administrative tribunals. Each province's or territory's residential tenancy statute sets out grounds under which landlords can evict a tenant. They include for "own use" or renovation, nonpayment of rent or rental arrears, and behavioural reasons – for example, when a tenant disrupts neighbours or has damaged the unit. Typically, a landlord must give a specified amount of notice to a tenant of a pending eviction application. The parties are able to exchange and submit relevant evidence, and then there is a dispute resolution or adjudicative process by which a decision maker considers the legality of the eviction. Hearings are held in person, by telephone, or online, depending on the jurisdiction. At a hearing, tenants and landlords have the opportunity to present evidence, to question the evidence presented by the other party, and to set out their positions. Decision makers must weigh evidence, apply the law, and render a fair decision. Most jurisdictions include some sort of appeal process to a higher level of decision maker.

In some (but not all) jurisdictions, the legislation and case law provide that decision makers have discretion to consider relevant circumstances and make an order other than eviction.[45] In other words, in these jurisdictions, decision makers can consider the circumstances and fairness of an eviction order beyond merely ensuring that technical or procedural requirements have been met. Other jurisdictions are primarily concerned with ensuring that evictions are not arbitrary and that technical requirements are met.[46] As noted above, an eviction order can be enforced by a sheriff or another state agent empowered to use force to remove a tenant.

Numerous American researchers have concluded that eviction tribunals and courts systematically favour landlords' interests and subordinate the rights and interests of tenants. Matthew Desmond concluded that the huge number of evictions that he observed "comes down to a system that provides landlords with a lot of power over low-income tenants."[47] Kathryn Sabbeth observed that eviction courts in the United States systematically work to entrench landlord power and tenant vulnerability.[48] American research on eviction law and processes resonates in Canada. Here residential tenancy tribunals have been described as "eviction factories"[49] and "eviction machines."[50] In one recent study, landlords were shown to win over 90 percent of the time.[51] And they often win quickly. In Alberta, for example, the average wait time between a landlord applying for an eviction order and having the matter heard is thirteen days.[52] Although some tribunals, including Ontario's Landlord and Tenant Board, faced heavy backlogs of cases following the COVID-19 pandemic, it seems that once the backlogs were cleared, the process would continue as before.

Power, Practice, and Strategic Ignorance in Eviction Law and Processes

Eviction decisions are a window into the "structures of the imagination"[53] inhabited by eviction decision makers as well as the priorities and values of the institutions within which they operate. How eviction decisions are written, which information they prioritize, and which information they omit give us insights into institutional priorities of eviction tribunals and show us how law and legislation are deployed to address day-to-day struggles within landlord and tenant relationships. In this section, I turn to the literature on "strategic ignorance" to explore how eviction decision makers are able to approach eviction as routine and transactional and turn their attention away from the harms and complications of eviction.

Eviction decisions are released by tribunals at a high volume and often appear to be highly patterned and routine in their formatting and language. This chapter focuses particularly on the jurisprudence of one eviction tribunal, the Saskatchewan Office of Residential Tenancies. Saskatchewan is one of the Canadian jurisdictions where the governing legislation mandates that hearing officers analyze whether an eviction would be "just and equitable in all the circumstances."[54] The Saskatchewan Court of King's Bench has stated that this requires the hearing officer not to take a highly legalistic approach but to consider all of the facts of the case and what is "just, fair, and right" with regard to those facts.[55] However, despite this clear direction by the Court, a review of eviction decisions in Saskatchewan reveals that most are highly formulaic. Many include identical wording, leading to a sense either that there is a pre-existing template in which decision makers simply fill in the blanks or that hearing officers routinely "cut and paste" large portions of their decisions. Indeed, evidence of the latter practice is found in decisions with identical, and apparently mistaken, descriptions of fact scenarios or replicated names of parties.[56] This patterned and repetitive nature of the jurisprudence suggests that outcomes are encoded in a fundamental way; after all, the template or cut-and-paste function, as well as the conceptual frames and structures visible in the decisions, predate each hearing and provide an easily traversed path for the decision maker.

A typical eviction decision in Saskatchewan is a page or two long and includes the names of the parties, the date of the hearing, a statement about the format of the hearing (usually telephone), and a statement about who appeared or failed to appear.[57] Most decisions are about rental arrears. The substance of the decision is usually distilled into a short paragraph or two. Typically, there is a sentence about the evidence brought forward by the landlord – this is usually a sentence or two noting that the hearing officer accepted the landlord's evidence and that the landlord proved their claim. Indeed, where questions of credibility are concerned, landlords are typically believed. Because tenants are not in attendance much of the time, the hearings usually proceed quickly to conclude that landlords have proven their claims and are entitled to an order of possession. When tenants are in attendance, many decisions do not refer to their evidence, and others include a sentence or two summarizing their circumstances but often do not mention them again. In terms of the legislatively mandated obligation to consider whether an eviction is "just and equitable," most decisions dispense with this requirement in one quick sentence, usually with the following wording: "Given the circumstances before me, I am satisfied that the decision accords with justice and equity." The vast majority of decisions end with an immediate eviction order – meaning that the sheriff can immediately take steps to remove the tenant, their family, and their belongings from the rental unit.

Missing from most of these decisions is any careful consideration of a tenant's circumstances, any examination of the likely impacts of eviction on a tenant, or any meaningful weighing of whether eviction is a proportionate or equitable outcome given the circumstances. In one case, for example, a tenant had not been paid by his employer and thus could not pay his rent. The hearing officer made an eviction order.[58] In another, the Ministry of Social Services had made a mistake leading to nonpayment of the tenant's rent. The tenant was evicted.[59] In another example, the tenant was a single mother of three children and had just gotten out of a bad relationship. The tenant had been in rental arrears but had paid all arrears by the time of the hearing. The landlord insisted that he wanted to proceed with the eviction, and the hearing officer ordered an immediate eviction.[60] What explains these decisions? I draw from the scholarship on strategic ignorance to posit that the tribunal's approach demonstrates knowledge practices designed to ignore or put aside considerations about the harms of eviction on tenants and instead to prioritize landlords' claims of possession.

A growing field of scholarship focuses on the dynamics and functions of ignorance within institutions and societies. "Ignorance studies" scholars draw attention to the social, cultural, and political aspects of knowledge practices and interrogate how ignorance can be deployed to fortify the status quo and reproduce power relations. That is, this field of research identifies ignorance not as the absence of knowledge but as a particular knowledge practice in itself – one with material consequences. Scholars have identified that often "not knowing" can be deployed strategically as a tool for maintaining status quo practices and relations. For example,

Scott Frickel writes that the "absence of knowledge clearly advantages some groups and disadvantages others."[61] And Judith Bovenspieven and Mathijs Pelkmans write that ignorance and awareness are "entangled with complex power relations."[62]

Scholars point out that strategic ignorance is usually a product of institutional practices and cultures rather than deficits of specific individuals within institutions. That is, institutions develop conventional patterns in terms of what to pay attention to, and what to ignore, and people working within these institutions adopt those frameworks. Linsey McGoey notes that patterns of "micro" (personal) and "macro" (institutional) ignorance thus work together. McGoey explains that ignorance among individuals becomes sedimented into policies and institutional perspectives that in turn "obscure their own mistaken assumptions from adherents, leading to new patterns of individual micro-ignorance."[63] Eviatar Zerubavel explains it this way: "Noticing and ignoring are not just personal acts, since they are always performed by members of particular social communities with particular social conventions of attention and communication."[64] We all learn what to notice, what to see, what to hear, and what to ignore from our colleagues and our institutional norms and practices. Thus, where and how knowledge holders are situated have key influences on which kinds of knowledge and information they have access to and what they ignore.

The critical literature on ignorance focuses extensively on how practices around knowledge and ignorance function to maintain power relations and hierarchies. These practices can be intentional or unintentional and are always affected by structural or institutional factors. McGoey refers to this as the "power" of strategic ignorance.[65] She writes that the "powerful have long had the ability to ignore inconvenient facts and voices. Indeed ... power functions *through* strategic ignorance – through the ability to select which voices to acknowledge and which to dismiss."[66]

This chapter identifies in eviction decision making a pattern of not engaging with the impacts or harms of eviction on tenants, even in jurisdictions such as Saskatchewan, where the Court of King's Bench has specifically directed hearing officers to consider tenants' circumstances. Thus, in Saskatchewan, it is not possible to claim that hearing officers are somehow required by law or the force of legal precedent to ignore the circumstances of tenants or the impacts of eviction on them – indeed, as outlined earlier, reviewing courts have explicitly required the opposite. Drawing from the literature discussed above, we can surmise that eviction decision making is deeply embedded within institutional norms and influenced by institutional knowledge practices, many of which function to maintain existing approaches. In other words, structural and institutional factors and knowledge practices work together to create the conditions for day-to-day tribunal decision-making practices in eviction matters.

So what are some of these norms and practices? We can start with examining the messages sent by governing legislation. For the most part, residential tenancy legislation can be described as depicting the landlord-tenant relationship as contractual and transactional; certainly, Canadian residential tenancy statutes do not explicitly acknowledge underlying power imbalances or larger societal housing inequities, nor do they evince an acknowledgment that rental housing engages tenants' fundamental human rights. Blomley describes this attitude of the "mythologizing" of landlord-tenant relationships as an "egalitarian form of horizontal mutuality."[67]

One way that the governing legislation promotes this underlying attitude toward the landlord-tenant relationship is by its reference to tenants' dwelling places. Rather than referring to a tenant's home as such, residential tenancy legislation typically uses the term "rental unit." This term helps to produce dwelling places as commodifiable sources of rent and monetary value. Another way that the legislation mythologizes a relationship of horizontal mutuality is by setting up ideas about reciprocal or mutual "rights" and "responsibilities" that suggest that landlords' interests in making profits can be evenly balanced with tenants' interests in having a home.

Residential tenancy legislation is often thought of as functioning to limit the rights of property owners to do whatever they please with their properties. After all, it provides tenants with various rights and limits owners' rights to exclude tenants arbitrarily. Accounts that focus on restrictions to landlords' rights seem to emphasize that there is a diminishment of property owners' power in residential landlord-tenant relationships. But as Blomley points out, residential tenancy law in practice functions explicitly to set the stage for the extractive and sometimes exploitative landlord-tenant relationships that feature so prominently in today's rental market. It does so primarily, he points out, by setting up accessible and responsive state institutions to manage and enforce evictions: "There is no eviction without the sheriff's deputies who carry it out, and no extractive market without the law that protects a landlord's right to maximum profit on a decaying apartment."[68]

Thus, residential tenancy legislation sends messages to hearing officers about how they should "see" the disputes about eviction before them. The legislation suggests that the relationship between landlords and tenants is contractual, that it concerns a commodifiable interest, and that both parties have "rights" and "responsibilities" that are able to be balanced. Significantly, it also protects landlords and their property interests by providing the remedy of eviction.

But there are other systemic and institutional reasons why landlords' property rights are routinely valued over tenants' security of tenure and why the impacts and harms of eviction are so opaque to decision makers. Multiple, mutually reinforcing institutional practices and patterns, themselves influenced by wider power relations, function to foster strategic ignorance of the harms of eviction by eviction decision makers.

First is the reality that, in a significant number of cases (e.g., more than half of the time in Saskatchewan), tenants do not show up at their eviction hearings. There are likely myriad systemic reasons for their nonattendance. We know that many tenants find the process overwhelming and intimidating.[69] Others are unaware of their rights, and many simply assume that they will be evicted regardless of whether they appear at a hearing. Most Canadian jurisdictions offer no or only limited legal aid for tenants who face eviction, meaning that those who do appear at their hearings almost always navigate the legal process without assistance.[70] We know that tenants who face eviction hearings are already among the most marginalized and oppressed members of society and can face numerous barriers to advocating for themselves in such hearings.

The high rate of tenant nonattendance at eviction hearings means that, in a huge number of cases, officers do not hear about the circumstances of tenants' lives or have an opportunity to consider the impacts that eviction might have on tenants and their families. The lack of legal representation and barriers to self-representation for those who do attend hearings mean that the law and jurisprudence develop in a lopsided manner, emphasizing landlords' rights to possession and de-emphasizing tenants' experiences and interests. Sabbeth points out that tenants' rights law is vastly underdeveloped because of the historical and ongoing lack of legal representation for tenants. Sabbeth writes that tenants' rights as a whole "atrophy" when they are not pushed forward through the day-to-day arguments in individual cases: "We can only imagine how the law and court culture might look if [tenants] had enjoyed decades of equality of representation."[71] Financial and logistical barriers to appeals of tribunal decisions further entrench this pattern. Meanwhile, though landlords in Canadian eviction proceedings do not typically have lawyers, many are represented by sophisticated agents and employees who accumulate expertise advocating for eviction orders in tribunals.[72] The fact that they are often "repeat players" in the system gives landlords clear advantages, including knowledge of the system, credibility, and informal relationships and social capital. Russell Engler's research showed that these compounding factors worked to tilt outcomes in favour of landlords regardless of whether they were represented by lawyers.[73] Thus, high rates of tenant nonattendance and absence of legal representation for tenants combine to make it harder for hearing officers to see, and easier to ignore, the impacts and harms of eviction.

Then there is the issue of hearing officer training and positionality. Little information is available about the training provided to residential tenancy hearing officers, so it is unclear whether they receive training about the impacts of eviction, social contexts of eviction, or strategies for eviction prevention. In addition, the positionality of hearing officers can influence how they understand situations before them. We know that such officers are usually lawyers. As such, they are more likely to have higher incomes and less likely to occupy marginalized social locations than many tenants facing eviction. They are also likely to be property owners and therefore more likely to identify with the interests of landlords than with those of tenants. Indeed, they might also be influenced by dominant discourses that position tenants as "irresponsible" or "less deserving" citizens because of their "failure" to achieve property ownership.[74]

In addition, there are practical and material constraints within which tribunals operate. Hearing officers have huge caseloads and often hear multiple cases in a day. Yet tribunals such as the Saskatchewan Office of Residential Tenancies consider speedy decision making as a primary metric of success. For example, a 2021 auditor general's report noted that decisions of this office are released on average 3.4 days after hearings.[75] This is a remarkable turnaround when we think about the backlogs and delays common in other parts of the civil and criminal justice systems. In other jurisdictions, such as Ontario, where there is a considerable backlog of residential tenancy tribunal cases that emerged as a result of COVID-19, it appears that decision makers are also highly constrained in terms of the time that they can spend on individual decisions.[76] It seems, then, that decision makers operate under challenging conditions, with significant caseload pressure and insufficient time to consider the situations that come before them. Significantly, scholars have pointed out that an emphasis on speed and efficiency in eviction decision making almost always benefits landlords, not tenants, who would benefit from a longer timeline to enable them to assert their rights and, if necessary, pack, move, and find alternative housing.[77]

Finally, we return to the incommensurability of landlord and tenant interests. Landlords seek to protect their property interests, build equity, and especially, in the case of financialized landlords, make profits. They do so by entering into a contract with a tenant that engages the latter's fundamental human need for shelter and a home. When facing an eviction application, rushed decision makers in busy tribunals have to make a determination that somehow makes sense of these deeply incommensurate interests. As Lorna Fox points out, it is easy to quantify the harms to a landlord of unpaid rent, lost opportunity, or other claims that the landlord might make. Indeed, these claims usually have a clear monetary value attached to them. It is much harder to quantify the "intangible" value of what Fox calls the "home interests" of tenants[78] or the harms that eviction might unleash. In other words, it is relatively easy for eviction decision makers to see and quantify economic impacts on landlords: unpaid rent and damage to property have numbers attached to them. Economic harm to landlords easily rises to the surface, but harms to tenants are much more complex to quantify.

Eviction is made possible by law. I would add that eviction decisions are the results of complex and interrelated institutional structures and knowledge practices that shape how decision makers apprehend the claims and situations that come before them, including which harms they see clearly (economic harms to landlords) and which harms are obscured to them (impacts of eviction on tenants). If this is the case, then laws, policies, and practices can also be transformed to reduce evictions and the harms that flow from them.

Conclusion

Given the fundamental importance of housing to human well-being and health, and given the harms of eviction, governments and societies in general should strive to prevent and reduce eviction whenever possible. One way to do so is by ensuring that eviction tribunals are unable to ignore the importance of housing and the harms of eviction in each decision that they make.

In jurisdictions where tribunals have little or no discretion to consider alternatives to eviction, legislation should be amended to ensure that hearing officers can fully consider tenants' circumstances and alternatives to eviction whenever possible. In all jurisdictions, legislation should explicitly acknowledge that rental housing engages the human right to housing and that eviction is harmful and should be ordered only as a last resort. This means that tribunals should be required to engage in a much more genuine balancing of the interests of landlords and tenants. As Fox argues, this kind of balancing exercise is a much more complicated process and requires exposing unstated "pro-creditor, pro-commercial interests" policies, subjecting landlord actions and interests to scrutiny, and looking carefully at what she calls the "value" of home to tenants, as well as the potential harms of eviction for tenants, against the monetary interests of landlords.[79]

This approach draws from international human rights frameworks for eviction. The European Court of Human Rights developed the requirement for a proportionality analysis in international law. This approach has since been adopted by the United Nations Committee on Economic, Social and Cultural Rights as a way to ensure that eviction laws and practices do not contravene the human right to housing.[80] The Canadian Centre for Housing Rights has explained that a proportionality framework applied in eviction matters would mean that a tenant can be evicted only if eviction is necessary to achieve the landlord's legitimate objective, that there are no reasonable alternatives to eviction, and that the consequences of eviction are proportionate to the objective.[81]

Other initiatives to ensure that the importance of tenants' security of tenure and the harms of eviction are placed at the centre of eviction decision making include policies that promote greater access to justice for tenants. One approach that has worked elsewhere to reduce evictions is to ensure that tenants have access to legal representation and advice in eviction matters. Other initiatives include making eviction processes less appealing to landlords, for example, by increasing application fees.[82] Tribunals and hearing officers should be provided with adequate resources and time to enable clear and careful decision making.

It is crucial for eviction tribunals to grapple with the reality that eviction can unleash great harm in the life of a tenant and is a gravely impactful legal outcome that engages basic human needs and rights. These insights should not be ignored or set aside in order to produce convenient or efficient outcomes for landlords. But taking seriously the harm of eviction also means that society as a whole must cease to ignore and tolerate the reality that too many people are living in unstable, unaffordable, and inadequate housing. We need broad and preventative approaches, far beyond the purview of residential tenancy tribunals, to get to the crux of the issue. We need human rights–centred, multi-system approaches that undo legacies of "organized abandonment" of marginalized communities and that support safe, affordable, and adequate housing as a human right for all.[83] This means investments in supportive and appropriate housing, health, social services, and community amenities. As Sarah Swan puts it, we need to "explore and implement policies that strengthen familial, social, and community ties, and promote stable housing, rather than policies that lead to ... destabilization, disruption, and broken familial and social connections."[84] We need to build a society where no one can look away or strategically ignore the harms of eviction and poor housing, or treat eviction as a banal or unremarkable event, and where we work together to ensure that the human right to housing is a reality for all.

Notes

1 Sarah Zell and Scott McCullough, *Evictions and Eviction Prevention in Canada* (Winnipeg: Institute of Urban Studies, University of Winnipeg, 2020) at 79.

2 Ibid.

3 Ibid at 78.

4 Ibid.

5 Ibid at 59.

6 See Martine August, *The Financialization of Multi-Family Rental Housing in Canada: A Report for the Office of the Federal Housing Advocate* (Ottawa: Office of the Federal Housing Advocate, Canadian Human Rights Commission, 2022).

7 See the discussion in Sarah Buhler, "Crim-eviction: Eviction and Social Control at a Residential Tenancies Tribunal" (2025) 62:1 *Osgoode Hall Law Journal* 109–52; see also Jonnette Watson Hamilton, "Reforming Residential Tenancy Law for Victims of Domestic Violence" (2019) 8 *Annual Review of Interdisciplinary Justice Research* 245–76.

8 Kaitlin Schwan, Mary-Elizabeth Vaccaro, Luke Reid, and Nadia Ali, *Implementation of the Right to Housing for Women, Girls, and Gender Diverse People in Canada*, prepared for the Office of the Federal Housing Advocate (Women's National Housing and Homelessness Network, 2021) at 15, https://housingrights.ca/wp-content/uploads/CHRC-WNHHN-Schwan-4-May-2021.pdf [perma.cc/S7VD-WNBZ].

9 Sarah Buhler, "Pandemic Evictions: An Analysis of the 2020 Eviction Decisions of Saskatchewan's Office of Residential Tenancies" (2021) 35 *Journal of Law and Social Policy* 68–99 at 83.

10 Note that in some jurisdictions written reasons for eviction are not provided. See Hamilton, "Reforming Residential Tenancy Law" at 249.

11 Some jurisdictions explicitly do not allow this type of proportionality analysis, part of the landlord-centric structural regime addressed and critiqued later in this chapter. See Canadian Centre for Housing Rights (CCHR), *Proportionality: A Legal Framework to Make Eviction a Last Resort in Canada* (Toronto: CCHR, 2023).

12 See ibid at 3; Buhler, "Pandemic Evictions," at 69.

13 Lorna Fox O'Mahony, *Conceptualising Home: Theories, Laws, and Policies* (Oxford: Hart Publishing, 2007) at 178.

14 Irwin Altman and Carol M. Werner, "Introduction," in *Home Environments*, ed. Irwin Altman and Carol M. Werner (New York: Plenum Press, 1985) xix–xxii at xix.

15 O'Mahony, *Conceptualising Home,* at 139.

16 Bronwyn Bate, "Understanding the Influence Tenure Has on Meanings of Home and Homemaking Practices" (2017) 12 *Geography Compass* 1–15 at 3.

17 Ibid at 1.

18 See the discussion in ibid at 5. Nicholas Blomley discusses "relational subjugation" in "Precarious Territory: Property Law, Housing, and the Social Spatial Order" (2020) 52:1 *Antipode* 36–57 at 46. See also Cayce C. Hughes, "'A House but Not a Home': How Surveillance in Subsidized Housing Exacerbates Poverty and Reinforces Marginalization" (2021) 100:1 *Social Forces* 293–315.

19 See O'Mahony, *Conceptualising Home,* at 110.

20 Zell and McCullough, *Evictions and Eviction Prevention,* at 78.

21 Ibid.

22 Ibid.

23 Niloofar Nili, Isobel M Findlay, and Rosmary Martinez Rueda, *2024 Saskatoon Point-in-Time Homelessness Count* (Saskatoon: Community-University Institute for Social Research, 2024) at 32.

24 See Stephen W. Hwang, "Homelessness and Health" (2001) 164:2 *Canadian Medical Association Journal* 229–33.

25 Lucie Richard, Brooke Carter, Linda Wu, and Stephen Hwang, "Disparities in All-Cause Mortality Among People Experiencing Homelessness in Toronto, Canada, During the Covid-19 Pandemic: A Cohort Study" (2024) 12 *Frontiers in Public Health* 1–9.

26 See Zell and McCullough, *Evictions and Eviction Prevention,* at 37–38. See also Lisa Berg and Lars Brannstom, "Evicted Children and Subsequent Placement in Out-of-Home Care: A Cohort Study" (2018) 13:4 *PLoS One* 1–13.

27 Kaitlin Schwan, Mary-Elizabeth Vaccaro, Luke Reid, Nadia Ali, and Khulad Baig, *The Pan-Canadian Women's Housing and Homelessness Survey* (Toronto: Canadian Observatory on Homelessness, 2021) at 34.

28 See Zell and McCullough, *Evictions and Eviction Prevention,* at 37–43 for a discussion of the literature on the impacts of eviction. See also Mary Clare Kennedy, Ryan McNeil, MJ Milloy, Huiru Dong, Thomas Kerr, and Kanna Hayashi, "Residential Eviction and Exposure to Violence Among People Who Inject Drugs in Vancouver, Canada" (2017) 41 *International Journal of Drug Policy* 59–64.

29 Yael Cannon, "Injustice Is an Underlying Condition" (2020) 6 *University of Pennsylvania Journal of Law and Public Affairs* 201–66 at 240–42; Emily Benfer, David Vlahov, Marissa Y Long, et al., "Eviction, Health Inequality, and the Spread of Covid-19: Housing Policy as a Primary Mitigation Strategy for Covid-19" (2021) 98:1 *Urban Health* 1–12; Hugo Vasquez-Vera, Laia Palencia, Ingrid Magna, Carlos Mena, Jaime Neria, and Carme Borrell, "The Threat of Home Eviction and Its Effects on Health Through the Equity Lens: A Systemic Review" (2017) 175 *Social Science and Medicine* 199–208; Gracie Himmelstein and Matthew Desmond, "Eviction and Health: A Vicious Cycle Exacerbated by a Pandemic" (April 1, 2021), https://www.healthaffairs.org/do/10.1377/hpb20210315.747908/full/; Robert Collinson and Davin Reed, "The Effects of Eviction on Low-Income Households" (2018), https://www.law.nyu.edu/sites/default/files/upload_documents/evictions_collinson_reed.pdf [perma.cc/AM6X-XQXX], at 25–26.

30 See Zell and McCullough, *Evictions and Eviction Prevention,* at 43 (referring to the work of Matthew Desmond).

31 Kathryn A. Sabbeth, "Erasing the 'Scarlet E' of Eviction Records" (April 21, 2021), https://theappeal.org/the-lab/report/erasing-the-scarlet-e-of-eviction-records/ [perma.cc/LSM2-W2MS].

32 Matthew Desmond, *Evicted: Poverty and Profit in the American City* (New York: Crown Publishers, 2016) at 299.

33 Blomley, "Precarious Territory," at 46.

34 Kathryn A. Sabbeth, "Simplicity as Justice" (2018) 2018:2 *Wisconsin Law Review* 287–304 at 297.

35 Kathryn A. Sabbeth, "Housing Defense as the New Gideon" (2018) 41:1 *Harvard Journal of Law and Gender* 55–117 at 87.

36 Ibid at 68–69; see also Lisa Moore, Ab Currie, Nicole Aylwin, and Trevor CW Farrow, *The Cost of Experiencing Everyday Legal Problems Relating to Loss of Employment and Loss of Housing* (Toronto: Canadian Forum on Civil Justice, 2017).

37 Schwan et al., *Implementation of the Right to Housing,* at 15. See also Scott Leon and James Iveniuk, *Forced Out: Evictions, Race, and Poverty in Toronto* (Toronto: Wellesley Institute, 2020), https://wellesleyinstitute.com/wp-content/uploads/2020/08/Forced-Out-Evictions-Race-and-Poverty-in-Toronto-.pdf [perma.cc/J29C-DB3H].

38 Emily Paradis, *Access to Justice: The Case for Ontario Tenants: Final Report of the Tenant Duty Counsel Review* (Toronto: Advocacy Centre for Tenants Ontario, 2016) at 55.

39 Ibid at 57.

40 Ricardo Tranjan, *The Tenant Class* (Toronto: Between the Lines, 2023) at 39–40.

41 See Lillian Leung, Peter Hepburn, and Matthew Desmond, "Serial Eviction Filing: Civil Courts, Property Management, and the Threat of Displacement" (2021) 100:1 *Social Forces* 316–44.

42 Blomley, "Precarious Territory," at 45.

43 See Emma Power and Charles Gillon, "Performing the 'Good Tenant'" (2020) 37:3 *Housing Studies* 459–82.

44 See the discussion in Kathryn A. Sabbeth, "Eviction Courts" (2022) 18:2 *University of St. Thomas Law Journal* 359–404. Sabbeth discusses American eviction court design and function, but many of her observations are applicable in the Canadian context.

45 See CCHR, *Proportionality.*

46 Ibid.

47 Quoted in Kevin Nance, "Matthew Desmond's 'Evicted' Details Costs of Evictions on Milwaukee's Poor," *Chicago Tribune* (March 10, 2016), https://www.chicagotribune.com/2016/03/10/matthew-desmonds-evicted-details-cost-of-evictions-on-milwaukees-poor/ [perma.cc/8YTA-MXWC].

48 Sabbeth, "Eviction Courts."

49 Tom Cardoso and Shane Dingman, "Eviction Factories: How Ontario's Tenants Get Trapped in a Never-Ending Cycle with Landlords," *Globe and Mail* (December 19, 2019), https://www.theglobeandmail.com/canada/toronto/article-toronto-ontario-housing-rental-eviction-data-landlords-tenants/ [perma.cc/MT6M-X4GH].

50 Ron Ellis, *Unjust by Design: Canada's Administrative Justice System* (Vancouver: UBC Press, 2013) at 107.
51 Buhler, "Pandemic Evictions," at 83.
52 Residential Tenancy Dispute Resolution Service, *RTDRS Annual Report* (April 2022–March 2023) (Edmonton: Government of Alberta, 2023), https://open.alberta.ca/dataset/01e0066a-c12f-4278-bfc4-2c807d50304d/resource/e8c4c0b5-1ab3-4bdb-b758-7a62863a7ff6/download/sartr-rtdrs-annual-report-2022-2023.pdf [perma.cc/CR76-M372] at 7.
53 "Structures of the imagination" are discussed in David Graeber, *The Utopia of Rules: On Technology, Stupidity, and the Secret Joys of Bureaucracy* (New York: Melville House, 2015) at 81.
54 *Residential Tenancies Act, 2006*, SS2006, c R-22.0001, s 70(6).
55 *Williams v Elite Property Management Ltd*, 2021 SKQB 46.
56 See the discussion in Buhler, "Pandemic Evictions," at 89.
57 Saskatchewan eviction decisions are available on CanLII.
58 *ICR Commercial Real Estate v Whiteman*, 2020 SKORT 144.
59 *Janzen v Fleing*, 2020 SKORT 102.
60 *Centurion Apartment Properties v Gartner*, 2020 SKORT 662.
61 Scott Frickel, "Not Here and Everywhere: The Non-Production of Scientific Knowledge," in *Routledge Handbook of Science, Technology, and Society*, ed. Daniel Lee Kleinman and Kelly Moore (Abingdon, UK: Routledge, 2014), 263–76 at 266.
62 Judith Bovenspieven and Mathijs Pelkmans, "Dynamics of Wilful Blindness: An Introduction" (2020) 40:4 *Critique of Anthropology* 387–402 at 398.
63 Linsey McGoey, *The Unknowers: How Strategic Ignorance Rules the World* (London: Zed Books, 2019) at 12.
64 Eviatar Zerubavel, *The Elephant in the Room: Silence and Denial in Everyday Life* (Oxford: Oxford University Press, 2006) at 20.
65 McGoey, *The Unknowers*, at 12.
66 Ibid at 315.
67 Blomley, "Precarious Territory," at 40.
68 Ibid at 41. A.J. van der Walt, *Property in the Margins* (Oxford: Hart Publishing, 2009) at 71, explains that landlord power in practice is not necessarily diminished by restrictions in residential tenancies legislation.
69 Sarah Buhler and Rachel Tang, "Navigating Power and Claiming Justice: Tenant Experiences at Saskatchewan's Housing Law Tribunal" (2019) 36 *Windsor Yearbook of Access to Justice* 210–30 at 222, 225.
70 Sarah Buhler, *The Right to Counsel for Tenants Facing Eviction: Security of Tenure in Canada* (Ottawa: Office of the Federal Housing Advocate, Canadian Human Rights Commission, 2022).
71 Kathryn A. Sabbeth, "(Under)Enforcement of Poor Tenants' Rights" (2019) 27:1 *Georgetown Journal on Poverty Law and Policy* 97–145 at 136.
72 David Wiseman, "Paralegals and Access to Justice for Tenants: A Case Study," in *The Justice Crisis: The Cost and Value of Accessing Justice*, ed. Trevor C.W. Farrow and Lesley A. Jacobs (Vancouver: UBC Press, 2020), 173–91 at 173.

73 Russell Engler, "Connecting Self-Representation to Civil Gideon: What Existing Data Reveal About When Counsel Is Most Needed" (2010) 37:1 *Fordham Urban Law Journal* 37–92 at 48.
74 See the discussion in Power and Gillon, "Performing the 'Good Tenant.'"
75 Provincial Auditor of Saskatchewan, *2021 Report – Volume I: Report of the Provincial Auditor to the Legislative Assembly of Saskatchewan* (Regina: Provincial Auditor of Saskatchewan, 2021) at 125.
76 See Ombudsman Ontario, *Administrative Justice Delayed, Fairness Denied: Investigation into Whether the Ministry of the Attorney General, Tribunals Ontario and the Landlord and Tenant Board Are Taking Adequate Steps to Address Delays and Case Backlogs at the Landlord and Tenant Board* (Toronto: Ombudsman Ontario, 2023) at 52–53.
77 See Sabbeth, "Simplicity as Justice," at 294.
78 O'Mahony, *Conceptualising Home,* at 13.
79 Ibid at 40.
80 See the overview in CCHR, *Proportionality* at 4.
81 Ibid. On a similar proportionality analysis in foreclosure proceedings, see Chapter 5 of this collection.
82 See Henry Gomory, Douglas S Massey, James R Hendrickson, and Matthew Desmond, "The Racially Disparate Influence of Filing Fees on Eviction Rates" (2023) 33 *Housing Policy Debate* 1463–83.
83 See Taylor Riley, Julia P Schleimer, Jacquelyn L Jahn, "Organized Abandonment Under Racial Capitalism: Measuring Accountable Actors of Structural Racism for Public Health Research and Action" (2024) 343 *Social Science and Medicine* 1–13.
84 Sarah Swan, "Home Rules" (2015) 64:5 *Duke Law Journal* 823–900 at 898.

3

Legal Unhousing and Landlords' Unenforced Duty to Accommodate Tenants with Disabilities

JONNETTE WATSON HAMILTON

Introduction

The focus of this chapter is on the intersection of human rights law and the termination of residential tenancies across Canada. More specifically, my focus is on evictions in which tenants' disabilities, particularly mental or psychological disabilities, appear to have been a factor in landlords' decisions to terminate tenancies. Examples include tenants with hoarding disorders evicted for failing to keep their rental premises in reasonably clean condition and tenants with alcohol or drug addictions evicted for interfering with other tenants' peaceful enjoyment of their premises. Of all the grounds protected by human rights legislation, disability is the one that appears most commonly in residential tenancy cases about evictions, and the vast majority of those cases involve tenants with mental disabilities. Yet, as far as can be determined, decision makers typically ignore or downplay legal protections against disability discrimination in eviction cases.

Persons with disabilities are more vulnerable than those without disabilities to unhousing through eviction because they are more likely to be tenants. The 2017 *Canadian Survey on Disability: Persons with Disabilities* found that of the 18.1 percent of the Canadian population fifteen years or older living with at least one disability, 32 percent or just over 2 million Canadians lived in rented premises, with 5.4 percent of persons with disabilities living in subsidized housing.[1] Among persons with disabilities, those with mental health and cognitive disabilities were the most likely to live in rented premises (41.7 percent and 40 percent, respectively).[2]

Sarah Buhler's chapter in this collection discusses the many harms of eviction, and harms to mental health are included in that lengthy list.[3] Eviction is often a traumatic experience; indeed, the perceived risk of eviction itself is associated with elevated mental health problems.[4] And housing is crucial for those tenants with mental disabilities who need regular contact with doctors, social services, and other treatment providers and the stability to stay on medications.[5] Tenant evictions are also a major cause of homelessness in Canada.[6] This is particularly true if a tenant is evicted from public housing, which is often "last resort" housing.

Evictions of tenants with disabilities are usually resolved by administrative tribunals or government branches created for the purpose of adjudicating landlord-tenant disputes quickly, inexpensively, and informally.[7] The claims usually arise after a landlord applies to evict a tenant for breaching a term or condition of their rental agreement. In response, the tenant raises facts about their inability to comply with the term or condition because of their disability or about their need for an accommodation.

Much of what residential tenancy decision makers do in Canada lacks transparency, and the available evidence suggests that the vast majority of these decision makers do not engage substantively with human rights law in their eviction decisions. In about half of the Canadian jurisdictions, we do not know what happens in eviction hearings; there is no publicly available record of the proceedings. In other jurisdictions, either adjudicators are not allowed to hear human rights complaints arising in eviction proceedings, or they pay little or no attention to human rights law, including to landlords' duty to accommodate tenants with disabilities to the point of undue hardship. There is only one jurisdiction – Ontario – where the Landlord and Tenant Board (ON LTB) adjudicators sometimes conduct at least a partial human rights analysis when disability appears to be a factor in an eviction. However, even in Ontario, human rights issues tend to be subsumed under an analysis that focuses on whether, in light of all the circumstances, refusing the landlord's application to evict a tenant would be unfair.[8] The tenant's human rights become just one factor among many to be weighed in determining fairness.

This lack of attention means that the primacy of human rights legislation is not being respected in the residential tenancy context. And, when there is no human rights analysis in eviction proceedings, there is little to counter the stigmas, stereotypes, and prejudices that people with disabilities such as mental illness face in Canada.[9]

The focus of this chapter is on whether and how adjudicators of residential tenancy disputes deal with the possibility that mental disability is a factor in an eviction. Answers depend on the province or territory in which the rental premises are located. In the second section, I review the relevant human rights and residential tenancy law. I discuss the different types of residential tenancy adjudicators in Canada and the lack of information on how evictions involving human rights are resolved. In the third section, I look at how adjudicators in Ontario, the Northwest Territories, and Saskatchewan approach evictions in which mental disability might be a factor. In the fourth section, I offer some conclusions.

Systemic barriers to the use of human rights law in eviction dispute resolution forums and processes are important. However, they are not the only relevant barriers. Tenants are often unaware that their human rights are protected in the context of an eviction. They might know that landlords cannot refuse to rent to them based on race, disability, family status, or other protected grounds, but they are rarely aware that the same protection against discrimination applies to the terms and conditions of their tenancy, such as requirements about cleanliness and noise. In addition, tenants often have limited time, energy, and money, and what they do have needs to be spent on finding replacement housing, not on defending themselves against landlords' eviction claims or pursuing human rights claims. As well, because of the stigma around many disabilities, tenants might be reluctant to disclose their disabilities to others. Alternatively, the nature of a mental disability might leave tenants unable to identify their accommodation needs.[10]

Human Rights and Residential Tenancy Law Intersections

Human Rights Legislation and Analytical Framework

All Canadian jurisdictions have human rights legislation that prohibits discrimination based on disability in the provision of rental housing, usually in two different situations. The first situation arises when a landlord refuses to rent to a prospective tenant based on a ground protected in the legislation. Discriminatory refusals to rent to someone are not within the scope of this chapter because my focus is on evictions.

The second situation protected by human rights legislation arises in the enforcement of terms and conditions of tenants' occupation of the rental premises. The Saskatchewan legislation is fairly typical, with a provision that no one shall "discriminate against any person or class of persons with respect to any term of occupancy of any commercial unit or any housing accommodation."[11] Under residential tenancy legislation, tenants must comply with the terms and conditions of their rental agreements and may be evicted for cause if they do not. This is the context in which landlords' duty to accommodate tenants' disabilities to the point of undue hardship arises.

All jurisdictions include physical disability and mental disability as protected human rights grounds. The terms are undefined in some jurisdictions.[12] Where they are defined, the ground of mental disability typically includes three elements: an intellectual or developmental disability, a learning disability, and a mental disorder.[13] Nova Scotia's and Nunavut's legislation expressly include dependency on drugs or alcohol,[14] but whether or not explicitly included in legislation, substance use disorders are recognized by all Canadian courts and tribunals as disabilities under human rights law.[15]

In ten of the thirteen jurisdictions, the applicable human rights legislation provides that it prevails in the event of any conflict between it and other legislation, such as residential tenancy acts.[16] In the other three jurisdictions in which the human rights legislation is silent, the administrative law principles set out by the Supreme Court of Canada in *Tranchemontagne* ensure that human rights legislation prevails in the absence of an express statutory provision to the contrary.[17] This means that residential tenancy decision makers should not decline jurisdiction over human rights matters unless the authority to decline is given to them explicitly. They usually have both the power and the duty to look beyond their residential tenancy statutes "in order to apply the whole law to a matter properly in front of them."[18]

Because the legislation in each province and territory is so similar, a framework guiding how all types of human rights claims should be analyzed by all types of decision makers has become standardized. The leading case is the Supreme Court of Canada decision in *Moore v British Columbia (Education).*[19] Claimants must first establish prima facie discrimination by proving three things on the balance of probabilities.[20] They must prove that they have a characteristic protected from discrimination under the applicable human rights legislation, that they have experienced an adverse impact within an area protected by the legislation, and that the protected characteristic was a factor in the adverse impact. If this framework is applied in the residential tenancy context for tenants with disabilities, then tenants need to prove that they have a mental or physical disability, that they were about to be or had been evicted from a residential tenancy, and that their disability was a factor in their eviction.

In certain circumstances, a respondent who provides the service or goods will have a duty to inquire about the claimant's protected characteristics as part of the analysis in the first step.[21] For example, where the evidence indicates that a landlord is aware or reasonably ought to be aware that there might be a relationship between a disability and a tenant's ability to fulfill their duties as a tenant, the landlord would have a duty to inquire into that possible relationship before making a decision that would adversely affect the tenant.[22] That duty includes providing an opportunity to the tenant to identify a disability as the reason for the conduct that the landlord has claimed is a breach of the residential tenancy agreement and to ask for accommodation.

If a claimant establishes a prima facie case of discrimination, then the burden shifts to the respondent to provide a defence.[23] In the landlord-tenant context, the typical defences for landlords are that their policies (e.g., a "no pet" clause in a lease) are justifiable and that they provided reasonable accommodation to the claimant or that they could not provide accommodation without undue hardship. If the conduct or practice cannot be justified, then discrimination will be found to have occurred.

The duty to accommodate to the point of undue hardship has both a procedural and a substantive component.[24] The first involves a consideration of the procedure adopted by the respondent to assess the issue of accommodation before taking action. The second looks at the substantive content or reasonableness of the accommodation, an individualized assessment of the measures offered, or the respondent's reasons for not providing accommodation. Some human rights acts define undue hardship. The Yukon and Nunavut legislation, for example, specifies that safety, disruption to the public, impact on contractual obligations, cost, and business efficiency are to be balanced.[25] The ON *HRC* specifies that "the cost, outside sources of funding, if any, and health and safety requirements, if any," are to be considered.[26] In jurisdictions without a definition, the same types of factors are used.[27]

If discrimination is found to have occurred, then the decision maker must order appropriate remedies.[28] Evictions are rarely the subject of human rights complaints because of the delays involved in having matters heard by human rights tribunals, and, if they are heard in that forum, then the usual remedy is damages. Remedies granted by a residential tenancy decision maker during an eviction hearing might include more time to comply with a term or condition of the lease or the suspension of the eviction as long as the tenant agreed to do certain things. Modifications of lease terms or conditions are also possible, such as when a "no pets" clause is changed to a "pet deposit" clause. Because human rights issues normally arise in eviction hearings before a residential tenancy tribunal, I turn to the legislation relevant to those hearings next.

Residential Tenancy Legislation

Three aspects of residential tenancy legislation are relevant to my analysis of the unhousing of persons with disabilities: rules on evictions for cause, designations of dispute resolution forums and whether they can consider human rights issues, and whether decisions by the adjudicators in those forums are published.

Evictions for Cause

A landlord can give a notice of termination or a notice to vacate in response to a breach of the relevant legislation or a tenancy agreement, but only a court or other adjudicator can order an eviction. An eviction order cannot be given until a tenancy is terminated, either by a notice from the landlord or by a court order, because until termination a tenant has a right to exclusive possession of the rental premises.

"No-fault" evictions are uncommon in most Canadian jurisdictions.[29] Most evictions are for nonpayment of rent,[30] and they are one type of "at-fault" eviction. All jurisdictions list other causes in their legislation that can justify evictions based on tenants' failure to fulfill their responsibilities. One commonly found in cases involving tenants with mental disabilities is breach of a statutorily implied covenant of quiet enjoyment: that is, a promise not to "disturb the landlord's or other tenants' possession or enjoyment of the rental premises or residential complex."[31] There are also statutorily implied promises requiring tenants to "maintain reasonable health, cleanliness and sanitary standards,"[32] and not to cause "extraordinary damage to the residential property,"[33] both of which might be raised in instances of hoarding. The last type of covenant often used as a reason for eviction in cases involving mental disabilities relates to the safety of persons, such as an implied covenant not to seriously jeopardize "the health or safety or a lawful right or interest of the landlord or another occupant."[34]

Adjudication Forums

Depending on the jurisdiction, landlord-tenant disputes are heard by one of three types of adjudicators at first instance: government departments, specialized administrative tribunals, or courts. The forum available to hear residential tenancy disputes differs by jurisdiction, but specialized administrative tribunals are the most common type, with government branches a distant second and courts even rarer. In all but two jurisdictions – British Columbia and Alberta – tenants must present any human rights issues connected to their evictions to these residential tenancy adjudicators if they want to stop their evictions. Not all of these adjudicators have legal backgrounds or human rights expertise.[35]

In Alberta and British Columbia, tenants cannot have their human rights issues decided by the residential tenancy adjudicators. The Residential

Tenancy Dispute Resolution Service (RTDRS) in Alberta is statutorily precluded from considering human rights issues.[36] Landlords who bring eviction applications then have a choice to withdraw them or designate either the Alberta Court of Justice or the Court of King's Bench of Alberta to hear them.[37] In British Columbia, human rights issues cannot be addressed by the arbitrators employed by the director of the Residential Tenancy Branch of the Ministry of Housing to adjudicate tenancy disputes in that province.[38] Instead, the human rights claim must be heard by the BC Human Rights Tribunal.

In British Columbia and Alberta, the bifurcation of jurisdiction between adjudicators who decide eviction applications and those who decide human rights claims likely means that landlords' failures to accommodate tenants with disabilities cannot stop evictions.[39] At best, tenants might be compensated monetarily years later for any breach of their human rights.[40] The obvious solution is to change the legislation in both provinces to allow the residential tenancy adjudicators to determine any human rights issue and then give them training and guidance on how to do so. However, because the adjudicators who determine evictions are not allowed to hear tenants' claims that their landlords might have a duty to accommodate them, I will not consider British Columbia or Alberta further in this chapter.

Availability of Decisions

Data gaps in both formal and informal evictions have been continually cited as barriers to more effective prevention of evictions and better support measures for tenants.[41] As of the end of 2023, six jurisdictions did not make the decisions made by adjudicators of landlord and tenant disputes publicly and freely available. Typically, these adjudicators provide oral decisions with reasons, usually at the end of the hearing, to the parties to the dispute and no one else. No decisions are available from any of the four Atlantic provinces or from Nunavut. Manitoba's Residential Tenancy Branch maintained a registry of orders that could be searched if an application to become a subscriber for a specified purpose was approved and an annual fee of $250 was paid.[42]

Yukon and Quebec did make some decisions publicly available. However, Yukon started to do so only in 2021 and has not published many decisions.[43] In the case of Quebec, a sample of ninety-seven eviction decisions by the Tribunal administratif du logement that mentioned "*handicap*" – the French term for the relevant ground in that province – revealed only one that might have involved a mental disability.[44]

As a result, evictions in Yukon, Quebec, Manitoba, Nunavut, New Brunswick, Nova Scotia, Prince Edward Island, and Newfoundland and Labrador are also not considered further. However, there is no reason to think that the residential tenancy adjudicators in these eight jurisdictions are better at applying human rights legislation in eviction proceedings than those in the three jurisdictions that I discuss in the third section. It seems likely that they also approach human rights issues in less than acceptable ways, given that tenants are usually unrepresented in eviction hearings, might not be aware of their ability to make human rights claims or able to make those claims, and often fail to attend their hearings. However, jurisdictions that do not yet make their anonymized decisions publicly available should be doing so for research, educational, and transparency purposes.

Of the remaining three jurisdictions that have residential tenancy administrative tribunals or government departments that do consider human rights issues, the Saskatchewan Office of Residential Tenancies (SKORT) and the Northwest Territories Rental Officer (NTRO), part of the Department of Justice, publish almost all of their decisions.[45] The ON LTB publishes a small percentage of its decisions, but they constitute a large number of decisions overall because of the high volume of residential tenancy cases heard every year in that province.[46] I consider all three jurisdictions in the third section.

Human Rights in Residential Tenancy Eviction Proceedings

This section begins with a brief discussion of my qualitative research approach to the Ontario, Northwest Territories, and Saskatchewan CanLII databases. I then turn to Ontario's approach to cases in which mental disability is or might be a factor in tenants' evictions. Based on the available cases, the ON LTB adjudicators are the decision makers who most often conduct a human rights analysis in such circumstances, compared with those in the Northwest Territories and Saskatchewan. I discuss the approach in the Northwest Territories next; although the NTRO rarely incorporated a human rights analysis when the facts and law appeared to require it, the Rental Officer has done so more often than the Saskatchewan adjudicators at SKORT. Some members of Saskatchewan's tribunal not only ignored human rights law but also denied that they had the authority or the duty to apply it.

Research Methods

In each of the three jurisdictions discussed in this section, I was looking for a large enough number of cases in which a tenant's mental disability was or might have been a factor in their eviction to be able to discuss their respective general approaches to human rights issues.

All searches were conducted in the relevant CanLII databases: ON LTB, for the Landlord and Tenant Board of Ontario; SKORT, for the Office of Residential Tenancies in Saskatchewan; and NTRO, for the Rental Office in the Northwest Territories. In addition to searching each of the three databases for "human rights" and "undue hardship" – both of which returned very few cases[47] – each of the other searches was composed of two elements.

The first element was a term or phrase used in the jurisdiction's legislation for the termination of tenancies, because all tenancies must be terminated before a tenant can be evicted, necessitating a two-step process. In Ontario and the Northwest Territories, "terminat*" was the search term for this element. The equivalent phrase in Saskatchewan's legislation was "end the tenancy"; however, because that phrase returned too many irrelevant decisions, I used the phrase "order for possession" from the landlord's second step in the eviction process.

The second element of each search term was a word or phrase intended to identify cases involving persons with disabilities. The search terms that returned a relatively high proportion of unique and relevant cases were "disab*," "mental health," "addict*," "mental illness," "hoard," "clutter," "fire inspect," "treatment program," and "schizophren*." The first and most general search for "terminat* disab*" or "order for possession disab*" returned the largest number of relevant decisions in the databases.

I reviewed decisions in which disability was inferable from the facts (e.g., an allegation by the landlord that a tenant was a "heavy drinker" who stole the landlord's liquor[48]), disability was claimed (e.g., a tenant applying for a disability pension, or a landlord testifying about "extensive hoarding and uncleanliness," and "numerous complaints from neighbouring tenants of a strong odour of cat urine and garbage" coming from the tenant's apartment[49]), or disability was proven (e.g., a tenant receiving a disability pension, a social housing landlord testifying that a tenant had a disability). I excluded decisions if tenants were simply said to be hospitalized or ill or if their conduct was attributed to unspecified medical conditions.

The start date for the reviewed decisions depended on the coverage in the CanLII databases: from 2009 for the ON LTB database, from 2002 for NTRO, and from 2006 for SKORT. The end date for the Ontario and Saskatchewan searches was the end of 2019 because this research was initially conducted in 2019–20 and because, once the pandemic began and hearings became exclusively or predominantly tele- or video-conference hearings, conditions affecting the likelihood of recognizing disability issues worsened.[50] Search results were sorted by relevance, and I read the most relevant decisions. However, in the case of the Northwest Territories, because the Rental Officer had experience with tele- and video-conferencing hearings long before 2020, and the number of eviction applications in the Northwest Territories was relatively small, I extended my search in the NTRO database to the end of 2022 and read all of the returned decisions. The patterns and trends observed before and after 2020 were the same.

As a result of those searches and parameters, 325 ON LTB decisions, 107 SKORT decisions, and 84 NTRO decisions were relevant to the question of how mental disabilities are dealt with in eviction proceedings.

Ontario's Landlord and Tenant Board

The approach of the ON LTB is clearly set out in the "Interpretation Guidelines" that it created to help landlords and tenants understand its usual interpretation of the law, provide guidance to LTB adjudicators, and promote consistency in decision making. Guideline 17 on human rights advises that the ON LTB must interpret the Ontario *Residential Tenancies Act* (ON *RTA*) in light of section 47 of the ON *HRC,* which provides that the ON *HRC* has primacy over other legislation.[51] In doing so, Guideline 17 relies on *Walmer Developments v Wolch,* an eviction case in which the Divisional Court held that adjudicators must consider and apply the ON *HRC* in its decision making, particularly when exercising its authority to grant relief from eviction under section 83 of the ON *RTA*.[52] That section states:

> 83 (1) Upon an application for an order evicting a tenant, the Board *may,* despite any other provision of this Act or the tenancy agreement,
>
> (a) *refuse to grant the application unless satisfied, having regard to all the circumstances, that it would be unfair to refuse;* or
>
> (b) order that the enforcement of the eviction order be postponed for a period of time.
>
> (2) If a hearing is held, the Board shall not grant the application unless it has reviewed the circumstances and considered whether or not it should exercise its powers under subsection (1).

Because of the court's direction in *Wolch,* reinforced by Guideline 17, the ON LTB adjudicators tend to apply all or a part of the human rights analytical framework when considering the landlord's duty to accommodate tenants with disabilities. They also do so almost exclusively when considering section 83 despite *Wolch*'s more general requirement that they consider the human rights law in their decision making.

In *Wolch,* the court held that the tribunal had erred in evicting a tenant because the adjudicator had not considered the tenant's disability and the possibility of a reasonable accommodation.[53] The adjudicator who first heard the landlord's eviction application ordered an eviction because the tenant had disrupted the reasonable enjoyment of the landlord and other tenants by screaming loudly and letting food on her stove catch on fire. The tenant applied for a review of that order, and the second tribunal adjudicator concluded that it was "not a serious error for a member not to apply the *Human Rights Code*."[54] The three District Court judges who heard the appeal in *Wolch* noted that the first adjudicator's sparse reasons did not refer to the ON *HRC* even though it was argued by the tenant, and only mentioned the tenant's "health problem," without considering the implications of the tenant having a disability.[55] The District Court disagreed with the second adjudicator, holding that there were two legislative sources for an adjudicator's duty to consider the ON *HRC*. The ON *HRC* states that it prevails if other legislation appears to authorize conduct that violates the ON *HRC*, unless the other legislation expressly says that it is to apply despite the ON *HRC*.[56] The tenancy legislation in force at the time of the decision said that it prevailed in the event of a conflict with any other legislation *except* the ON *HRC*. As a result, adjudicators could not permit an eviction that would contravene the ON *HRC* and had to consider whether any breach by a tenant of the lease or implied covenants "may be sufficiently alleviated by a reasonable accommodation of the disabled tenant without undue hardship to the landlord."[57] *Wolch* continues to be applied by both courts and the ON LTB in eviction decisions in Ontario.[58]

A review of the 325 relevant ON LTB decisions revealed that, in applying the human rights framework for analysis discussed earlier, the tenant rarely had to prove that they had experienced an adverse impact within an area protected by the legislation. The residential tenancy area is clearly protected by the legislation, and eviction is accepted as having an adverse impact on a tenant. Proving that the disability was a factor in the eviction was also seldom discussed, although the reason for this absence varied. The ON LTB's focus was usually on the need for the tenant to prove that they had a characteristic protected from discrimination under the human rights legislation: that is, proof of a disability. As a result, in most cases in which a disability was proven, the discussion immediately turned to the question of whether the landlord had accommodated the tenant up to the point of undue hardship.[59]

When considering proof of disability, the approach of the ON LTB was unpredictable. In one case, the tenant's lawyer urged the adjudicator "to consider that Tenant PW has schizophrenia, and is a recovering alcoholic," and the response from the adjudicator was simply that he had "considered this, and I am sympathetic to his plight."[60] Being "sympathetic" to someone's "plight" is not the same as recognizing that a person has disabilities and discussing whether they were factors in the tenant's eviction for "drunken aggression"[61] or relevant to his "failure to take the steps his doctor recommended so that he can get better and behave more appropriately."[62] There was no discussion of whether the tenant had proved prima facie discrimination or whether the landlord had a duty to accommodate the tenant. There was only consideration of the impact of the tenant's behaviour on the neighbours and a determination that it would be unfair to grant relief from eviction.

In ON LTB cases, tenants were usually required to produce supporting medical evidence to prove that they had a disability.[63] However, medical evidence was not always required. For example, a thorough human rights analysis was conducted for a tenant who did not attend the hearing of her eviction application. That analysis was based on her failure to keep the rental unit up to the level of ordinary cleanliness, an issue raised by the landlord's witness.[64] Based on their testimony the adjudicator determined that the tenant was likely a person with a disability – a drug addiction – and that her failure to maintain the standard of cleanliness was likely the result of her disability.[65] Nevertheless, because the tenant did not attend the hearing or request relief from eviction, and she owned a house, the adjudicator held that "it would be unfair to grant relief from eviction pursuant to subsection 83(1) of the Act beyond the Board's standard eleven day eviction order."[66]

Decisions discussing the relationship between the disability and the conduct complained of were relatively uncommon.[67] In one fairly typical example, a tenant established that she suffered from mental health issues, including bipolar affective disorder and ADHD, but whether or not those issues were factors in her disruptive behaviour that led to her eviction was not discussed. Instead, the focus was on whether her medication and support group could control her behaviour.[68] Usually, adjudicators' reasons moved immediately from a finding of disability to a consideration of whether the landlord had accommodated the tenant to the point of undue hardship.[69] This approach appears to put the burden on whether the tenant could prove that her behaviour likely would not cause problems in the future if she received accommodation, but a tenant does have a duty to facilitate accommodation, and it might be seen in that light.

On the question of the landlord's accommodation, the landlord must prove that they have accommodated the tenant up to the point of undue hardship. If they cannot, then an eviction will be denied.[70] This is reinforced by section 17 of the ON *HRC*, a disability-specific version of the general rule that a landlord may demonstrate that the challenged term or condition in the lease is reasonable and that the tenant cannot be accommodated without undue hardship. Section 17(2) provides that, if the landlord proves that the tenant cannot be accommodated without undue hardship, then under section 17(1) there is no violation of the ON *HRC* because the tenant is unable, because of a disability, to "act as is reasonably required of a tenant."[71] Section 17 is rarely mentioned, but its approach to finding no violation of the ON *HRC* is followed.[72]

What is counted as an accommodation by the landlord sometimes seems to be perverse. Recall that the duty to accommodate has both procedural and substantive elements. One example of a finding of procedural accommodation involved a notice of termination that could be voided if the tenant refrained from the behaviour complained of in the notice, because it gave the tenant notice of the conduct expected of them in order to avoid eviction.[73] When landlords send warning letters and present lists of behavioural requirements to tenants,[74] or even when they call the police, these actions have been described as "accommodation[s]."[75] Even if they are considered as procedurally satisfying the landlord's duty, there still needs to be an analysis of substantive accommodation.[76]

Which factors matter when an ON LTB adjudicator is deciding whether a landlord has accommodated a tenant to the point of undue hardship? Or – because the human rights analysis is most often conducted within the "just and equitable" framework of section 83 of the ON *RTA* – what weighs the most in the balancing of interests? Violence by a tenant, or even the threat of violence, appears to be a determinative factor: eviction almost always follows.[77] Other common determinative factors include a tenant's failure to request accommodation and their failure to cooperate in the search for reasonable accommodation, as required of tenants by law.[78] Relatedly, a tenant's failure to attend their hearing may also be a deciding factor, described by one adjudicator as a failure "to satisfy me that she is willing and able to correct her behaviour and continue her tenancy."[79] An indication by either the landlord or the tenant that the tenant had a place to go seemed to make it easier to grant an eviction order, as did a landlord's willingness to help the tenant find another place to live.[80] The last factor that seemed to matter was how long a tenant had been in the rental premises from which the landlord wanted to evict them; the longer they had called the rental premises home, the less likely they would be evicted.[81]

If this list of relevant factors is compared with the definitions of undue hardship discussed in the second section, then it appears that a wider range of factors is being considered by the ON LTB. Safety tops the list in both cases, but the length of a tenancy and having a place to go support a conclusion that the ON LTB approach is pragmatic rather than attentive to a human rights framework. This might be the result of considering the tenant's human rights within section 83 of the ON *RTA* with its focus on fairness.

Northwest Territories Rental Office

The requirement for a fairness assessment in the Ontario legislation appears to have a counterpart in the Northwest Territories. Under section 63(4) of the Northwest Territories *Residential Tenancies Act* (NWT *RTA*), evictions must be shown to be "justified." However, adjudicators usually interpreted "justified" to mean that there was a breach of the tenancy agreement serious enough, in frequency and/or severity, to warrant an eviction. When the focus is exclusively on tenants' breaches and not on all of the circumstances surrounding those breaches, the requirements for eviction orders are treated the same as the section 54(4) NWT *RTA* requirements for terminations, which do not include the need for termination orders to be justified beyond finding a breach of the act or tenancy agreement. No meaning is given to the word *justified* in section 63(4). There is no consideration of human rights issues as part of determining whether an eviction is justified.

The NTRO has claimed that its adjudicators are aware that "the *Human Rights Act* applies to tenancy agreements between landlord and tenants and establishes protected grounds including 'disability.'"[82] However, the application of human rights law has been restricted to a small number of cases involving service animals.[83] The awareness that human rights are relevant to "no pets" terms in leases might stem from a Northwest Territories Human Rights Adjudication Panel decision on accommodations for service animals that established a precedent for the jurisdiction.[84] Tenants might also be more aware of their rights with respect to service animals than other disability-related matters.

Addiction, hoarding, and nondisclosed but inferable mental illness were the most common types of disabilities mentioned in the NTRO decisions. Addiction and hoarding were discussed in quite a few cases, but neither was identified as a disability that might raise human rights issues. This was so even if medical evidence was introduced, landlords acknowledged the disability, or adjudicators' summaries of the facts recited actions by landlords that could be characterized as accommodations.[85] However, the language of accommodations was not used, and human rights were not mentioned.[86] Instead, details of landlords' efforts to accommodate tenants' disabilities were often described in NTRO decisions, perhaps because a much larger percentage of applications in the Northwest Territories involved tenants in subsidized public housing than was the case in southern jurisdictions. In 2021–22, they made up almost 60 percent of all applications to the NTRO, and these landlords might have been aware of their human rights obligations.[87]

One typical example of the general NTRO approach to human rights issues involved a long-term tenant with repeated failures to maintain the cleanliness of the rental premises.[88] The landlord was unable to install high-speed internet in the premises because of "a complete state of disarray, with garbage, clothes, food, and other items cluttered throughout the apartment ... [No] walking paths were identifiable and the odour was extreme."[89] Instead of discussing a landlord's duty to accommodate a tenant, the adjudicator noted that the landlord had been "very generous and patient with the Respondent in this situation ... [by giving] him more than two years to resolve the issue, with little to no effective results."[90] The adjudicator was satisfied that both termination of the tenancy and eviction of the tenant were justified but made both orders conditional on the tenant not bringing the rental premises into a state of ordinary cleanliness within seven weeks. There was no mention of a disability or the landlord's duty to accommodate the tenant and no assessment of the conduct of the landlord that might have amounted to efforts to accommodate the tenant up to the point of undue hardship.

In addition to illustrating the typical approach of the NTRO to the duty to accommodate tenants, that case included a conditional order.[91] Conditional orders that give tenants one last chance to rectify breaches were more common in the Northwest Territories than in Ontario and Saskatchewan. Tenants often agreed to them and were also likely to attend hearings, with tenants present in two-thirds of the NTRO cases reviewed. A conditional order can be seen as a type of accommodation, in much the same way that warning letters and notices of termination were seen as accommodations in Ontario. However, if the conditions in the NTRO eviction order are not met, then the eviction can proceed.

The Saskatchewan Office of Residential Tenancies

In eviction cases in Saskatchewan, adjudicators may only grant a landlord an order for possession if they consider it to be "just and equitable in the circumstances."[92] Thus, like the legislation in Ontario and the Northwest Territories, Saskatchewan's residential tenancy legislation has a general requirement for fairness. However, unlike Ontario but like the Northwest Territories, that statutory requirement is not used to consider human rights issues.

Only three SKORT decisions mentioned the *SK HRC,* but even then there was no human rights analysis conducted in any of them. Similar to the situation in the Northwest Territories, two of those three decisions involved service animals. One of them relied on the Saskatchewan Human Rights Commission's policy on service animals to resolve the dispute.[93] The other found that it would not be just and equitable to evict a tenant when the landlord had not enforced its "no pets" policy for the previous four and a half years.[94]

The third case involved an ongoing dispute between a landlord and tenant concerning the allegedly excessive noise that the tenant made during the night that disturbed other tenants.[95] The tenant claimed that the noise was the result of health issues that caused her to trip and fall, but the evidence concerned loud and disruptive noise made by her television, her cat, and her throwing things into boxes.[96] A human rights analysis was not conducted. Instead, the adjudicator held that she saw "nothing in the evidence to suggest that the Landlord brought its application seeking to evict the Tenant because she has health issues ... [Rather,] the Landlord's claim is with respect to excessive noise disruptive to the other tenants' right to quiet enjoyment,"[97] a holding not responsive to the legal requirement to decide whether the tenant's disability was a factor in the eviction.

Even when disability was proven or accepted – in about one-quarter of the cases – there was no analysis of whether the disability was a factor in the eviction. Most tenants' claims of disability were simply not given much weight.[98] In my sample of cases, SKORT adjudicators seemed to be unaware of their obligations to consider human rights issues. And most tenants with disabilities caught up in eviction proceedings seemed to be unaware that they could argue that their landlords had a duty to accommodate.

This conclusion is reinforced by three SKORT decisions published after the end date of my searches of the database. Between 2021 and the end of 2023, there were three reported SKORT decisions denying that SKORT adjudicators have the jurisdiction to apply the *Human Rights Code: Fortugno v Valois & Anor,*[99] *Carrot River Housing Authority v Buyaki,*[100] and *Broadstreet Properties Ltd v Muhawenimana.*[101] There was also apparently a King's Bench decision upholding *Fortugno,* but it is not reported.[102]

In *Fortugno,* the landlord sought damages for cleaning and repair costs as well as rent in arrears. The parties had concurrent matters before the Human Rights Commission and SKORT, but there was no indication of whether the commission had accepted the tenant's complaint. The heart of both legal disputes seemed to be the tenant's acquisition of an emotional support animal. The SKORT adjudicator, Tyler Young, accepted that the tenant had serious physical and mental disabilities.[103] Young also recognized that some of the tenant's claims were human rights issues. He invited the parties' submissions on whether SKORT has jurisdiction to determine such matters. He provided them with his own unreported decision in *Wakaw Housing Authority v Ewart,*[104] quoted at length in *Fortugno.*[105] In *Ewart,* Young had relied on a case in Nova Scotia in which the adjudicator had held that "tenancy officers, who are not obligated to have legal experience, should not be required to interpret the [Nova Scotia] Human Rights Act" and noted that the power to interpret the *Human Rights Act* was not expressly granted to him in the residential tenancy legislation.[106]

The tenant's lawyer in *Fortugno* argued that SKORT did have jurisdiction, either under the primacy provision in section 52 of the *SK HRC* or based on the 2010 decision of the Supreme Court of Canada in *R v Conway.*[107] With respect to the latter, Young decided to "extend" the holding in *Conway* to reach a conclusion contrary to the one reached in that case:

> *Conway* posits that unless there is an explicit prohibition within the establishing legislation, then an administrative tribunal has jurisdiction to address issues of Charter breaches. It is true that the Residential Tenancies Act does not specifically prohibit such consideration. However, I am of the view that as an extension of *Conway,* if the same legislators of the authorizing statute issued other legislation which explicitly provides jurisdiction to another administrative tribunal, then it is reasonable to infer the intent of the legislation is that there is an effective exclusion within the one tribunal and inclusion in the other.[108]

In other words, Young's reasoning was that because the Human Rights Commission could deal with enforcement of discriminatory terms and conditions in a tenancy agreement, SKORT could not. Young backed up this opinion by noting that an unreported BC adjudicator's decision was determined on the basis of residential tenancy law and not on its human rights issues, according to a summary in a Human Rights Tribunal decision.[109] He failed to note that BC legislation expressly states that residential tenancy adjudicators cannot decide human rights issues. He also failed to consider *Tranchemontagne,* which directly contradicts his "extension" of *Conway.*

Young's is the wrong approach to the jurisdiction question given the primacy provision in section 52 of the *SK HRC*[110] and the Supreme Court of Canada decision in *Tranchemontagne* that ensure that human rights legislation prevails in the absence of an express statutory provision to the contrary.[111] Residential tenancy decision makers cannot decline jurisdiction over human rights matters unless the authority to decline it is given to them explicitly.

Nevertheless, at least one other SKORT adjudicator was convinced that refusing to hear human rights issues was the correct approach. *Buyaki,* a decision by adjudicator Randall King, involved an application by a public housing landlord to evict a tenant for behaviour alleged to have damaged the rental premises, disturbed the quiet enjoyment of other tenants, and affected the safety of the landlord and those providing maintenance services. The tenant was under the care of mental health professionals and being treated by medication.[112] King stated that he "acknowledge[d] the Landlord has a duty to do what is reasonable to accommodate the Tenant."[113] However, when the tenant's lawyer raised what she described as human rights issues, he said that "I am not qualified or mandated to make such a determination. There are other forums for that. I can only do what I feel is just and equitable under the circumstances."[114] Apparently, the "circumstances" did not include the landlord's human rights obligations.

The final decision of the three denying human rights jurisdiction was a second decision by adjudicator Young. *Muhawenimana* was a SKORT case from 2023. It was similar to *Fortugno* in that both the tenant and the landlord were claiming damages, and eviction was not an issue. Young stated his position clearly and outrageously: "I do not accept that the provisions of the [Human Rights] Code are to inform the scope of the Landlord's duties as provided by the Act."[115] This statement seems to deny not only his jurisdiction but also that the *SK HRC* applies to residential premises, despite the existence of section 11 of the *SK HRC.*[116] Young provided the same reason as in *Fortugno:* "The fact that the Code exists and provides for these breaches would imply, to my mind, a separate jurisdiction to address these complaints through that Human Rights tribunal."[117] This reasoning ignores the fact that the Human Rights Commission does have the power to decline human rights matters in favour of proceeding before another tribunal under section 30(3) of the code.

These three SKORT decisions ignore the primacy clause in section 52 of the code and fail to apply the Supreme Court of Canada decision in *Tranchemontagne.* They also fail to note the Saskatchewan Court of Queen's Bench appeal decision in *Crosby v Pasklar,*[118] in which the court held that the SKORT adjudicator properly gave effect to the *SK HRC,* as well as *Wolch,* the leading Ontario case on why residential tenancy adjudicators should determine human rights issues if their home statutes allow them to do so. These three SKORT decisions were wrongly decided. On the basis of the failure to note the applicable law, the three decisions could simply be categorized as *per incuriam* and ignored. But they do exist, and the issue that they purport to deal with still needs to be resolved.

Conclusion

A landlord's eviction application normally get decided by specialized residential tenancy adjudicators, but they fail to apply human rights law effectively or at all. Human rights forums are not an alternative because they take too long to hear matters and cannot stop evictions that happened months or years earlier. Overall, human rights are not being enforced in evictions from residential tenancies. This is unacceptable for many reasons, chief among them being that the eviction of people with mental disabilities from rental housing, particularly from public housing, too often results in people ending up unhoused.

We do not know just how ineffective the enforcement of landlords' human rights duties to accommodate persons with disabilities is because seven jurisdictions did not make residential tenancy adjudicators' reasons for decisions publicly available: Manitoba, New Brunswick, Nova Scotia, Prince Edward Island, Newfoundland and Labrador, and Nunavut.

Of the six jurisdictions where we do have some idea of what happens, the results are underwhelming. In two of them – British Columbia and Alberta – the adjudicators who decide evictions cannot deal with human rights issues because of legislative restrictions. That legislation needs to be changed to allow those who decide eviction applications to hear human rights issues. Because eviction applications are heard relatively quickly, but human rights hearings can take years to decide whether to award tenants damages or other remedies for rights violations, this bifurcation strongly favours landlords.

Of the remaining four jurisdictions – Saskatchewan, Northwest Territories, Ontario, and Quebec – it seems that most adjudicators are either unaware of or ignore human rights issues and the duty of landlords to accommodate tenants with mental disabilities up to the point of undue hardship when it comes to enforcing the terms and conditions in rental agreements. Except in Ontario, and aside from the handful of service animal cases in which human rights issues do seem to be recognized, no one is enforcing this particular human right. In Saskatchewan, some adjudicators even claim that human rights provisions do not inform the interpretation of landlords' duties as set out in residential tenancy legislation.[119] Amending the legislation to tell residential tenancy adjudicators explicitly that they must apply human rights law would help to some extent. However, even in Ontario, breaches of human rights – quasi-constitutional legislation that should be interpreted in a liberal and purposive manner to advance the policy considerations underlying it[120] – tend to be just one factor to be considered in determining whether an eviction would be unjust, making it easier to forgo a thorough human rights analysis.

Human rights legislation often benefits tenants only if they are aware of their right to be accommodated, able to engage their landlords in discussions of accommodation, and able to enforce that right if their landlords refuse accommodation. The law as it currently stands places too much of the burden of enforcement on the rights holders. In instances of tenants with mental disabilities, those most in need of these human rights might be the least likely to ask that they be enforced.[121] Providing legal aid or legal clinics focused on residential tenancy issues would help. So would educating landlords and residential tenancy tribunals about their duties. Having an explicit policy guide available to landlords, tenants, and adjudicators – as the ON LTB does – would help to ensure awareness and a uniform approach to applying the law.

Tenants with mental disabilities are required to make their accommodation needs known to the best of their abilities and cooperate in the search for appropriate accommodations. However, because of the extreme stigma of certain types of mental health disabilities, many tenants might be very reluctant to disclose their disabilities. The evictions of many of these tenants might be informal, with no engagement with the legal system. But for formal evictions within the legal system, this reluctance might be partially addressed if adjudicators looked into whether the landlord in a particular case had a duty to inquire whether (i.e., to be alert to the possibility that) the tenant might need an accommodation even if a specific or formal request for it has not been made. Currently, the duty to inquire is rarely addressed even when it appears to be triggered by the facts. Better training on how to apply the human rights analytical framework might help.

All residential tenancy decision makers should make a significant portion of all of their judgments publicly available. In the tribunals' annual reports to the government ministries in charge of housing, they should track disability issues and how they are resolved. Tribunals should be evaluated periodically for their compliance with the law.

The impoverished state of the enforcement of the law in the intersection of residential tenancy and human rights legislation is far from the main cause of homelessness in Canada. But it is a cause. The application of human rights law in the residential tenancy context, as envisioned in every human rights act in the country, should no longer be ignored or denied.

Acknowledgments

I want to acknowledge and thank the Canadian Foundation for Legal Research for providing the initial funding to begin this research and the Faculty of Law, University of Calgary, for providing additional support in the form of student research assistance. I also want to express my gratitude to the following law students who helped to shape as well as conduct some of the research: David Kim, Tyler Anthony, Jordan Kadach, and Gregory Radisic. And a special thank you goes to my colleague Jennifer Koshan for sharing her human rights law expertise.

Notes

1 Zach Thurston and Jeff Randle, *Housing Experiences in Canada: Persons with Disabilities,* Statistics Canada Catalogue No. 46280001 (Ottawa: Statistics Canada, June 10, 2022) at 3–4. Of the total population (including those with disabilities), 26 percent lived in rented dwellings in 2016, and 3 percent lived in subsidized rented dwellings.

2 Ibid at 12.

3 See Chapter 2 of this collection.

4 Binod Acharya, Dependra Bhatta, and Chandra Dhakal, "The Risk of Eviction and the Mental Health Outcomes Among the US Adults" (2022) 29 *Preventative Medicine Reports* 101981.

5 Molly Hayes, "Code Z59.0: Diagnosing the Toll of Homelessness on Health Care," *Globe and Mail* (January 14, 2023), https://www.theglobeandmail.com/canada/article-experts-look-to-diagnose-the-toll-of-homelessness-on-health-care/ [perma.cc/Y66D-SFBW].

6 Formal evictions that engage the legal system are only part of the evictions picture, and informal evictions are probably more common. See Sarah Buhler, "Pandemic Evictions: An Analysis of the 2020 Eviction Decisions of Saskatchewan's Office of Residential Tenancies" (2021) 35 *Journal of Law and Social Policy* 68–99 at 73; Canada Mortgage and Housing Corporation (CMHC), *Housing Research Report: Evictions and Eviction Prevention in Canada* (Ottawa: CMHC, 2020) at iii, https://eppdscrmssa01.blob.core.windows.net/cmhcprodcontainer/sf/project/archive/research_6/evictions-and-eviction-prevention-in-canada.pdf [perma.cc/VRE9-VUZY].

7 For example, between April 2019 and March 2022, the Alberta Residential Tenancy Dispute Resolution Service (RTDRS) typically heard landlords' eviction applications within eleven to twenty-four business days of being filed on payment of seventy-five dollars as a filing fee. RTDRS, *RTDRS Annual Report: Fiscal Year 2021–2022* (RTDRS, 2022), https://open.alberta.ca/publications/rtdrs-annual-report [perma.cc/B26F-MHEZ], at 7.

8 *Residential Tenancies Act, 2006*, SO 2006, c 17, s 83 [ON *RTA*].

9 *Ontario (Attorney General) v G*, 2020 SCC 38. "People with mental illnesses face persistent stigma and prejudicial treatment in Canadian society, which has imposed profound and widespread social, political, and legal disadvantage on them. In particular, discriminatory perceptions that those with mental illnesses are inherently and indefinitely dangerous persist. These perceptions have served to support some of the most unjust treatment of those with mental illnesses" (at para 1).

10 Ontario Human Rights Commission (OHRC), *Minds that Matter: Report on the Consultation on Human Rights, Mental Health and Addictions* (Toronto: OHRC, 2012), ohrc.on.ca/en/minds-matter-report-consultation-human-rights-mental-health-and-addictions [perma.cc/7T3N-N7QA]; Natalie A. MacDonnell, "Disability Disclosure in the Digital Age: Why the Human Rights Tribunal of Ontario Should Reform Its Approach to Anonymized Decisions" (2016) 25:1 *Journal of Law and Social Policy* 109–49 at 112.

11 *The Saskatchewan Human Rights Code*, SS 1979, c S-24.1, s 11(1)(b) [*SK HRC*].

12 *Human Rights Code*, RSBC 1996, c 210 [BC *HRC*]; *The Human Rights Code*, CCSM c H175, s 9(2)(l) [MB *HRC*]; *Charter of Human Rights and Freedoms*, CQLR c C-12 [Quebec *Charter*]; *Human Rights Act*, RSPEI 1988, c H-12 [PEI *HRA*].

13 *Alberta Human Rights Act*, RSA 2000, c A-25.5, s 44(1)(h) [*AB HRA*]; *SK HRC*, s 2(1)(.1); *Human Rights Code*, RSO 1990, c H.19, s 10(1)(b), (c), (d) [ON *HRC*]; *Human Rights Act*, RSNB 2011, c 171, s 2 [NB *HRA*]; *Human Rights Act*, 2010, SNL 2010, c H-13.1, s 2(c) [NL *HRA*]; *Human Rights Act*, RSY 2002, c 116, s 37 [YK *HRA*]; *Human Rights Act*, SNWT 2002, c 18, s 1(1) [NWT *HRC*].

14 *Human Rights Act*, RSNS 1989, c 214, s 3(l) [NS *HRA*]; *Human Rights Act*, SNu 2003, c 12, s 1 [NU *HRA*].

15 See, for example, *Stewart v Elk Valley Coal Corp*, 2017 SCC 30; *Tranchemontagne* v *Ontario (Director, Disability Support Program)*, 2006 SCC 14 [*Tranchemontagne*].

16 See BC *HRC*, s 4; *AB HRA*, s 1(1); *SK HRC*, s 44; MB *HRC*, s 58; ON *HRC*, s 47(2); Quebec *Charter*, art 52; PEI *HRA*, s 1(2); NL *HRA*, s 5; YK *HRA*, s 39; NU *HRA*, s 5(1). Most of these acts allow individual statutes to declare expressly that they operate notwithstanding the human rights legislation, but no residential tenancy legislation does so.

17 *Tranchemontagne* at para 44. The issue before the Supreme Court of Canada in *Tranchemontagne* was whether Ontario's Social Benefits Tribunal, a provincially created statutory tribunal, was required to follow the province's human rights legislation in its decision making (at para 1).

18 Ibid at para 14. *Tranchemontagne* has been critiqued on the basis that it did not take the lack of tribunal capacity to deal with human rights issues seriously, a critique equally applicable in the residential tenancy tribunal context. See Lorne Sossin, "Jurisdiction or Access to Administrative Justice? How the Supreme Court of Canada Missed the Point in *Tranchemontagne*" (March 4, 2015), CanLII Connects, https://canliiconnects.org/en/commentaries/36099 [perma.cc/MB47-Y6A2].

19 *Moore v British Columbia (Education)*, 2012 SCC 61 [*Moore*].

20 Ibid at para 33.

21 *Robdrup v J Werner Property Management*, 2009 HRTO 1372 at paras 26–28; *TSL-70657-16 (Re)*, 2016 CanLII 71321 (ON LTB) at paras 26–29; *Stewart v Jordan*, 2023 AHRC 4 at paras 31–36.

22 *Kvaska v Gateway Motors (Edmonton) Ltd*, 2020 AHRC 94 at para 36.
23 *Moore* at para 33.
24 *British Columbia (Public Service Employee Relations Commission) v BCGSEU*, 1999 CanLII 652 (SCC) at para 66 [*Meiorin*].
25 YK *HRA*, s 8(2); NU *HRA*, s 1.
26 ON *HRC*, ss 11(2), 17(2).
27 In the employment context, see *Central Okanagan School District No 23 v Renaud*, 1992 CanLII 91 (SCC).
28 *Stewart v Jordan*, 2023 AHRC 4 at para 18.
29 These are evictions in which the reasons for terminating periodic tenancies are prescribed in provincial legislation but have nothing to do with tenants' conduct. No-fault evictions include those in which landlords want to sell, move into, or renovate the rental premises, and typically they make up 5.9 percent of all evictions across Canada, except in British Columbia, where the rate is 10.5 percent. See Silas Xuereb and Craig Jones, *Estimating No-Fault Evictions in Canada: Understanding BC's Disproportionate Eviction Rate in the 2021 Canadian Housing Survey* (Vancouver: Balanced Supply of Housing Research Partnership, 2023). There is a much smaller category of "no-cause" evictions that does not require a landlord to have any reason to evict a tenant from a periodic tenancy, but these evictions are confined to public housing. See, for example, *Residential Tenancies Act*, RSNWT 1988, c R-5, s 51(5) [NWT *RTA*].
30 See, for example, Adelle Guigon, *Annual Report on the Activities of the Rental Office, April 1, 2019 to March 31, 2020* (Yellowknife: NWT Rental Office, 2020), justice.gov.nt.ca/en/files/rental-office/2019-2020%20Rental%20Officer%20Annual%20Report.pdf [perma.cc/977Z-U24B], at 10; Tribunals Ontario, *Tribunals Ontario: Annual Report 2018–19* (Toronto: Tribunals Ontario, 2019), https://tribunalsontario.ca/documents/sjto/2019_11_19-Tribunals_Ontario_Annual_Report.html [perma.cc/S8HW-WUGD], at 51.
31 NWT *RTA*, s 43(1).
32 *Residential Landlord and Tenant Act*, SY 2012, c 20, s 33(2) [YK *RLTA*].
33 Ibid, s 52(1)(f).
34 *Residential Tenancy Act*, SBC 2002, c 78, s 47(1)(d)(ii) [BC *RTA*]. This covenant arises in cases that also involve domestic violence. For an analysis of the residential tenancy legislative provisions dealing with terminating leases in such cases, see Jonnette Watson Hamilton, "Reforming Residential Tenancy Law for Victims of Domestic Violence" (2019) 8 *Annual Review of Interdisciplinary Justice Research* 245–76.
35 See, for example, NWT *RTA*, s 72(2)(b), where qualification equivalent to those of five-year members of a law society or of an administrative tribunal or a court are acceptable.
36 An RTDRS tenancy dispute officer must "make an order that a matter cannot be heard by the Dispute Resolution Service where the tenancy dispute officer believes (a) the matter to be heard involves (i) the determination of a question of constitutional law or of human rights." See *Residential Tenancy Dispute Resolution Service Regulation*, Alta Reg 98/2006, s 17(1)(a)(i) [*RTDRS Reg*].
37 Ibid, s 17(2). In Alberta, it does not appear that a tenancy dispute officer can decline to hear a human rights issue raised as defence to an eviction but still proceed to hear

the eviction. Section 17 of the *RTDRS Reg* requires a tenancy dispute officer to make an order that a "matter" cannot be heard by the RTDRS if they believe that the matter involves the determination of a "question" of human rights. The regulation equates a matter with a party's entire "application" and specifies that, when a tenancy dispute officer makes such an order, the applicant can either withdraw their application or designate a court to which the matter will be transferred.

38 BC *RTA*, s 5.1, provides that s 46.3 of the *Administrative Tribunals Act*, SBC 2004, c 45, applies to the director as if the director were a tribunal and to dispute resolution proceedings under the *Residential Tenancy Act.* Section 46.3(1) of the *Administrative Tribunals Act* states that "the tribunal does not have jurisdiction to apply the *Human Rights Code.*" In British Columbia, the only alternative is usually the Human Rights Tribunal since courts do not have jurisdiction in most human rights disputes. See BC *RTA*, s 58(3).

39 In Alberta, there is also the possibility that the landlord will ask the RTDRS to refer the matter to one of the two levels of court, and a court would then hear both the eviction and the human rights matters. Based on reported cases, this rarely happens.

40 In late 2023, the BC Human Rights Tribunal advised that it takes more than eighteen months from complaint to decision in the event of a contested complaint. See BC Human Rights Tribunal, "FAQs About Complaints Process" (updated December 23, 2023), https://www.bchrt.bc.ca/law-library/faq/complaint-process/ [perma.cc/G8HF-VY84]. In Alberta, see *Miller v Alberta (Human Rights Commission)*, 2021 ABQB 696, in which a tenant whose claim against his landlord for denying him a housing subsidy was successful on the grounds of source of income, mental disability, and physical disability; the tenant later unsuccessfully sued the Human Rights Commission for taking too long to hear his complaint and grant him financial relief. *Miller v Capital Management Ltd*, 2021 AHRC 38.

41 CMHC, *Evictions: New Typologies and Analysis for the Canadian Landscape* (Ottawa: Research Insight, 2011) at 5. Formal evictions engage the province's legal processes. Informal evictions are far more numerous and include tenants who leave "voluntarily" when told that their tenancy is being terminated or are forced out after the landlord raises the rent or refuses to maintain the premises. See Sarah Buhler, "Pandemic Evictions: An Analysis of the 2020 Eviction Decisions of Saskatchewan's Office of Residential Tenancies" (2021) 35 *Journal of Law and Social Policy* 68–99 at 73.

42 Manitoba Residential Tenancies Branch, "Residential Tenancies Orders System," https://gov.mb.ca/cca/rtb/ot/rtos/index.html [perma.cc/R675-3PG3].

43 When the Yukon Residential Tenancies Office, part of the government's Department of Community Services, started adding some of its decisions to CanLII in 2021, its database contained decisions only only eighty-one decisions made between 2016 to 2023, an average of eleven and a half decisions each year.

44 The 97 decisions read were among the first 100 decisions located by searching the CanLII QCTAL database for the decisions of the Tribunal administrative du logement (formerly the Regie du logement) that included the search term "handicap*" or "invalid*" paired with the search term "resili*" or "expuls*" in order to show decisions mentioning disability in cases involving terminations of tenancies or evictions.

45 Buhler, "Pandemic Evictions," at 78*n*73. In the Northwest Territories, before July 2016, all orders and reasons for decisions except those containing personal medical

information or information about minor children were published. See Adelle Guigon, *Annual Report on the Activities of the Rental Office, April 1, 2016–March 31, 2017* (Yellowknife: NWT Rental Office, 2017), justice.gov.nt.ca/en/files/rental-office/2016-2017%20Rental%20Officer%20Annual%20Report%20.pdf[perma.cc/86EN-KUAR], at 4. Subsequently, written reasons for decisions became optional and dependent on the discretion of adjudicators if they stated their reasons for the oral record and if the matter was not complex. See NWT *RTA*, s 84.1, introduced by *Justice Administration Statutes Amendment Act*, SNWT 2019, c 21, s 9.

46 In the fiscal years 2016–17, 2017–18, 2018–19, and 2019–20, the ON LTB resolved between 61,868 and 78,783 disputes annually, and from 2016 to 2019 it published between 878 and 2,463 decisions annually – between 1 and 3 percent of its decisions.

47 A large majority of the searches for "human rights" only turned up cases of landlords who refused to rent premises to individuals on other protected grounds, including race, family status, and source of income. The results of searches for "undue hardship" either duplicated the results of the "human rights" search or were unrelated to the landlord's duty to accommodate a tenant.

48 *Avendano v Willing*, 2011 CanLII 94458 (NWT RO) at 3.

49 *NTHC v SW*, 2021 CanLII 83258 (NWT RO) at 5.

50 The pandemic in early 2020 resulted in hearings being postponed and eviction moratoriums. Most importantly, many jurisdictions, including both Ontario and Saskatchewan, stopped hearing disputes in person and, when hearings resumed, conducted almost all hearings by tele- or videoconferencing (see Buhler, "Pandemic Evictions," at 73). As a number of reports on access to justice during the pandemic have concluded, "adjudicators are less able to recognize and address vulnerabilities affecting a party's participation where that individual is participating by videoconference – and by phone of course it is that much harder." Kathy Laird, "The 'Digital Transformation' at Tribunals Ontario: The Impact on Access to Justice," Tribunal Watch Ontario Discussion Paper 29 (2021), tribunalwatch.ca/wp-content/uploads/2021/03/two-access-to-justice-and-the-digital-transformation-at-tribunals-ontario-march-28.docx.pdf/ [perma.cc/8DHA-6TTU], at 27. I therefore expect that the recognition of disability issues in eviction hearings since 2020 has decreased.

51 ON LTB, "Human Rights Interpretation Guideline 17" (December 5, 2018), https://tribunalsontario.ca/documents/ltb/Interpretation%20Guidelines/17%20-%20Human%20Rights.html [perma.cc/C56V-CRVQ] [Guideline 1].

52 *Walmer Developments v Wolch*, 2003 CanLII 42163 (ON SCDC) at para 35 [*Wolch*].

53 Ibid at para 35.

54 Ibid at para 9. Under the legislation in effect at the time, s 21.2 of the *Statutory Powers Procedure Act*, RSO 1990, c S.22, allowed a tribunal to review all or part of its own decision or order and to confirm, vary, suspend, or cancel the decision or order, if its rules dealt with the matter.

55 *Wolch* at para 8.

56 Ibid at paras 20–21; ON *HRC*, s 47(2).

57 *Wolch* at paras 22, 35.

58 See, for example, *Krishna v Alexandra Park Co-operative*, 2022 ONSC 92; *Ajax Municipal Housing Corporation v Vanleeuwen*, 2023 ONLTB 69982 (CanLII).

59 See, for example, *CEL-72371-17 (Re)*, 2018 CanLII 42727 (ON LTB) (the public housing landlord provided evidence of the tenant's disability and explained the accommodations agreed to by the tenant and health-care professionals, which the adjudicator adopted).

60 *EAL-57549-16 (Re)*, 2016 CanLII 72095 (ON LTB) at para 11 [*EAL-57549-16 (Re)*]. See also *SWL-13549-18 (Re)*, 2018 CanLII 86125 (ON LTB) at para 2; *TEL-72112-16 (Re)*, 2016 CanLII 72254 (ON LTB) at paras 3, 5.

61 *EAL-57549-16 (Re)* at para 10.

62 Ibid at para 13.

63 See, for example, *TSL-75125-16-RV-IN2 (Re)*, 2016 CanLII 100385 (ON LTB) at paras 22–23; *SWL-01016-17-RV (Re)*, 2017 CanLII 60757 (ON LTB) at paras 4–5, 10; *TSL-32669-12 (Re)*, 2014 CanLII 71668 (ON LTB) at paras 12, 14.

64 *TEL-72255-16 (Re)*, 2016 CanLII 88399 (ON LTB) [*TEL-72255-16*] at paras 19–20.

65 Ibid at paras 21–23. See also *EAL-59734-16 (Re)*, 2016 CanLII 88305 (ON LTB).

66 *TEL-72255-16* at para 30.

67 See, for example, *TSL-49899-14-RV (Re)*, 2016 CanLII 88392 (ON LTB); *EAL-59734-16 (Re)*, 2016 CanLII 88305 (ON LTB) at paras 1–4, 11–16; *TSL-02027-18-SA-AM (Re)*, 2019 CanLII 134429 (ON LTB) at para 13; *TSL-49899-14-RV (Re)*, 2016 CanLII 88392 (ON LTB) at paras 6–7, 9, 29–30, 40.

68 *TSL-52680-14-SA (Re)*, 2014 CanLII 58657 (ON LTB).

69 See, for example, *SWT-97811-16 (Re)*, 2017 CanLII 48795 (ON LTB) at paras 55–56.

70 See, for example, *SOL-94702-18-RV (Re)*, 2018 CanLII 141507 (ON LTB) at paras 23–26.

71 *Wolch* at para 34 (holding that the "limitation on the rights of a disabled person in s. 17 must be read narrowly, as befits the purpose of the Act"). See also *Hamilton-Wentworth District School Board v Fair*, 2016 ONCA 421.

72 See, for example, *TSL-46861-13 (Re)*, 2014 CanLII 23631 at paras 8–12; *TSL-57457-14-SA (Re)*, 2015 CanLII 59176 (ON LTB) at paras 17–21.

73 *TSL-02327-19 (Re)*, 2019 CanLII 87558 (ON LTB) at para 16.

74 *TSL-09593-19 (Re)*, 2019 CanLII 134678 (ON LTB) at para 8.

75 *EAL-59734-16 (Re)*, 2016 CanLII 88305 (ON LTB) at para 13 (the police attended at the tenant's rental unit on eleven occasions in four months in response to complaints from other tenants about her throwing things at them, chasing them down the hallways, and threatening them with violence).

76 *Meiorin* at paras 66, 78.

77 See, for example, *Joseph v Toronto Community Housing Corporation*, 2013 ONSC 413 at paras 8, 30; *Metropolitan Housing Authority v Owusu-Ansah*, [1995] OJ No 3864 at para 35, 59 ACWS (3d) 1193; *TSL-49899-14-RV (Re)*, 2016 CanLII 88392 (ON LTB) at paras 6–7, 9, 29–30, 40. But also see *TSL-57457-14-SA (Re)*, 2015 CanLII 59176 (ON LTB) at paras 8–10.

78 See, for example, *TEL-72255-16 (Re)*, 2016 CanLII 88399 (ON LTB) at paras 26–27.

79 *TSL-09593-19 (Re)*, 2019 CanLII 134678 (ON LTB) at para 10; *TEL-72255-16 (Re)*.

80 *TSL-52680-14-SA (Re)*, 2014 CanLII 58657 (ON LTB); *EAL-65158-17 (Re)*, 2017 CanLII 142944 (ON LTB) at paras 5, 8; *SWL-13871-18 (Re)*, 2018 CanLII 42924 (ON LTB); *CEL-75468-18 (Re)*, 2018 CanLII 88527 (ON LTB); *TSL-02327-19 (Re)*, 2019 CanLII 87558 (ON LTB).

81 *TNL-24324-11 (Re)*, 2011 CanLII 91397 (ON LTB); *TEL-96313-18-SA (Re)*, 2019 CanLII 126882 (ON LTB); *TSL-99869-18 (Re)*, 2019 CanLII 87663 (ON LTB); *CEL-72695-18 (Re)*, 2018 CanLII 141452 (ON LTB).
82 *MPM v HO*, 2020 CanLII 114851 (NWT RO) at 4 [*MPM v HO*].
83 In addition to ibid, see *Yellowknife Housing Authority v Caisse*, 2014 CanLII 29029 (NWT RO).
84 *Lawson v 994486 NWT Ltd*, 2008 NWTRTA 8, cited in *MPM v HO* at 13–14.
85 See, for example, *Yellowknife Housing Authority v AD*, 2011 CanLII 94203 (NWT RO); *NTHC v DC*, 2020 CanLII 114826 (NWT RO) at 3–4.
86 See, for example, *NTHC v AG*, 2019 CanLII 59118 (NWT RO); *NTHC v MW*, 2016 CanLII 27519 (NWT RO); *NTHC v MA*, 2016 CanLII 101329 (NWT RO).
87 Adelle Guigon, *Annual Report on the Activities of the Rental Office, April 1, 2021–March 31, 2022* (Yellowknife: NWT RO, 2022), https://www.ntassembly.ca/sites/assembly/files/td_714-192.pdf [perma.cc/WG9Z-FWLC], at 16.
88 *JF and SF v TD*, 2022 CanLII 49816 (NWT RO).
89 Ibid at 2.
90 Ibid at 3.
91 The decision in ibid at 4 provided that an order would issue "terminating the tenancy June 30, 2022, unless the rental premises has been returned to a satisfactory state of ordinary cleanliness (p. 45(4)(e), ss. 83(2)); and evicting the Respondent from the rental premises July 1, 2022, if the termination of the tenancy becomes effective." For similar cases, see *NTHC v MA*, 2016 CanLII 101329 (NWT RO); *NTHC v MW*, 2016 CanLII 27519 (NWT RO); *NSHC v NG*, 2019 CanLII 37916 (NWT RO); *NTHC v KB*, 2018 CanLII 71432 (NWT RO); *NTHC v WH*, 2018 CanLII 39511 (NWT RO); *NTHC v MM*, 2022 CanLII 11182 (NWT RO).
92 *Residential Tenancies Act, 2006*, SS 2006, c R-22.0001, s 70(6) [SK *RTA*]. For a discussion of this proportionality analysis, see Chapter 2 of this collection.
93 *Roberts Properties Inc v OS*, 2018 SKORT 177 at paras 42–45.
94 *Bracken Financial Services Inc v MY*, 2016 SKORT 208 at paras 25–26, 37–38.
95 *Borden Housing Authority v NT*, 2015 SKORT 68.
96 Ibid at para 2.
97 Ibid at para 6.
98 See, for example, *Universal Realty Ltd v RL*, 2016 SKORT 460; *DFB Capital Ltd v EE*, 2017 SKORT 084.
99 *Fortugno v Valois & Anor*, 2021 SKORT 1704 [*Fortugno*].
100 *Carrot River Housing Authority v Buyaki*, 2021 SKORT 3206 [*Buyaki*].
101 *Broadstreet Properties Ltd v Muhawenimana*, 2023 SKORT 20236 [*Muhawenimana*].
102 Ibid at para 62 (stating that *Fortugno* was upheld on appeal by Justice H.D. MacMillan-Brown in an unreported decision of the Court of King's Bench (File QBG-SA-00766-2021), without specifying which of the issues or reasons in the 149-paragraph *Fortugno* decision had been upheld).
103 Ibid at para 55.
104 *Wakaw Housing Authority v Ewart*, ORT File 207708 (SKQB) [*Ewart*].
105 *Fortugno* at para 59.

106 Ibid, quoting *Ewart* at para 41, quoting *Killam Properties Inc v Frail*, 2009 NSSC 419 at paras 30–32. Young understood the *Ewart* decision "as establishing that a human rights complaint *per se* is outside of my jurisdiction" (at para 42).

107 Ibid at paras 61–63, citing *R v Conway*, 2010 SCC 22.

108 Ibid at para 65.

109 Ibid at para 50, quoting *Smith v Mohan*, 2018 BCHRT 207 at paras 24–26.

110 The *SK HRC* provides that

> 52. Every law of Saskatchewan is inoperative to the extent that it authorizes or requires the doing of anything prohibited by this Act unless:
> (a) that law falls within an exemption provided by this Act; or
> (b) that law is expressly declared by an Act to operate notwithstanding this Act.

111 *Tranchemontagne* at para 44.

112 Ibid at para 23.

113 Ibid at para 41.

114 Ibid at para 42. In determining what he thought was just and equitable in the circumstances, King stated that he could not take into account that the tenant has no place else to go. This refusal denies the statutory duty to consider the individual circumstances of the tenant and not simply whether a breach of an obligation allows a landlord to ask for an eviction, a duty often confirmed by the courts. See, for example, *Donnelly v Dupuis*, 2007 SKQB 481 at paras 19–22; *Unwin v Bender*, 2020 SKQB 116 at paras 31–34; *Williams v Elite Property Management Ltd*, 2021 SKQB 46 at paras 21–31.

115 Ibid at para 62.

116 *SK HRC*, s 11(1), provides that

> 11(1) No person, directly or indirectly, alone or with another or by the interposition of another, shall, on the basis of a prohibited ground:
> (a) deny to a person or class of persons occupancy of any commercial unit or any housing accommodation; or
> (b) discriminate against a person or class of persons with respect to any term or condition of occupancy of any commercial unit or any housing accommodation.

117 *Muhawenimana* at para 62.

118 *Crosby v Pasklar*, 2011 SKQB 229.

119 *Buyaki* at para 62.

120 See, for example, *Ontario Human Rights Commission and O'Malley v Simpsons-Sears Ltd et al*, [1985] 2 SCR 536 at 546–47, 52 OR (2d) 799; *B v Ontario (Human Rights Commission)*, 2002 SCC 66 at para 44; *New Brunswick (Human Rights Commission) v Potash Corporation of Saskatchewan Inc*, 2008 SCC 45 at para 19.

121 See, for example, Suzanne Fitzpatrick and Beth Watts, "The Right to Housing for Homeless People," in *Homelessness Research in Europe*, ed. Eoin O'Sullivan, Volker Busch-Geertsema, Deborah Quilgars, and Nicholas Pleace (Brussels: FEANTSA, 2010), 105–22 at 116.

4 Enabling and Resisting Financialized Legal Unhousing in Ottawa
Toward a "Righting" of Legal Frameworks

DAVID WISEMAN

Introduction: Evictions and Resistance in Heron Gate Village

People living in the Heron Gate Village community in Ottawa have been engaged in a years-long effort to resist legal unhousing associated with a residential rental property redevelopment project of the company Timbercreek (since renamed Hazelview), which owns the land and buildings that they call home. When Timbercreek purchased the property in 2012–13, it integrated the new "asset" into the broader property portfolio that it offers as an investment vehicle via local and global financial markets. In other words, Timbercreek "financialized" the property and, in turn, embarked on financialized legal unhousing. The ongoing redevelopment project began in 2015 and posed two types of threats of unhousing: one type was demolition-based evictions from two specific areas within Heron Gate Village; the other type was development-based evictions associated with Timbercreek's overall plan for redevelopment of Heron Gate Village. These threats were met with a mix of resistance strategies spanning social, political, and legal mechanisms that produced only limited successes. The demolition-based evictions were not prevented, but some additional supports were obtained, and an anti-discrimination human rights claim was launched. The redevelopment will go ahead but with a guarantee that remaining residents will not be displaced from the community as it progresses. In this chapter, I describe and analyze the efforts of the Heron Gate Village community as a case study in enabling and resisting financialized legal unhousing.

My analysis of these events will involve five main points. First, the legal frameworks relevant to redevelopment of urban residential rental communities in Ottawa – consisting of municipal, provincial, and federal components – operate more to enable than to prevent legal unhousing. Second, nevertheless, depending on the circumstances, a community can use a mix of resistance strategies – loosely falling into the categories of social action and legal engagement – to prevent, mitigate, and/or reform legal unhousing projects to achieve better individual and collective outcomes in the community. Third, the limited successes on some matters achieved through resistance by the community can be understood as implementing the normative benchmark of the right to adequate housing as guaranteed in international human rights law. Fourth, the extent of consensus among the various parties involved in the Heron Gate Village situation on the key matter of housing nondisplacement, consistent with that normative benchmark, can be understood as a potentially significant occurrence in the resistance to legal unhousing. And, fifth, the nondisplacement guarantee eventually integrated into the redevelopment plan ought to be both reinforced and expanded to tenants across Ontario and Canada by more meaningfully aligning the relevant legal frameworks with the right to adequate housing, both substantively and procedurally. As I address in the conclusion, this need for realignment is especially pronounced in circumstances in which individuals and communities grapple with the power imbalance inherent in resisting the nature and scale of operations of corporatized and financializing landlords such as Timbercreek.

Case Study Overview

The Herongate neighbourhood of urban Ottawa is almost entirely composed of the Heron Gate Village residential property area.[1] When Heron Gate Village was purchased in 2012–13 by Timbercreek, it consisted of approximately 1,750 residential rental units housing around 4,000 people, distributed among high-rise and low-rise apartment buildings and townhouses.

The residents of Herongate are racially diverse, and many live with inadequate income and in substandard housing. According to the 2016 census report, the residents of the Herongate neighbourhood were 70 percent visible minorities, and 52 percent were immigrants (i.e., not Canadian citizens by birth).[2] The immigrants were predominantly from Africa and Asia, and the majority came to Canada after 2000. Over 90 percent of the residents were renters, with 28 percent of households receiving some form of social assistance. Statistics Canada also reported that 27.6 percent of residents were living in housing categorized as "unsuitable," and 45.5 percent of residents were classified as living in "inadequate conditions" by reference to the Core Housing Need metric of the Canada Mortgage and Housing Corporation (CMHC). The Herongate census tract is one of the least affluent communities in Ottawa, having the second-highest proportion of low-income persons in the Ottawa-Gatineau region. As of 2015, 48.1 percent of the households in the census tract had incomes below the after-tax low-income measure of Statistics Canada.

Timbercreek was a subsidiary of Timbercreek Asset Management,[3] a Canadian-based investment firm that operates globally.[4] As mentioned, in purchasing Heron Gate Village, Timbercreek financialized the residential rental property.[5] The broader phenomenon of "the financialization of housing" has been defined as referring to "structural changes in housing and financial markets and global investment whereby housing is treated as a commodity or asset, a means of accumulating wealth, and often as security for financial instruments that are traded and sold on global markets."[6] Timbercreek's plans for demolition-based and redevelopment-based evictions can therefore be regarded as amounting to threats of financialized legal unhousing.

Timbercreek purportedly purchased Heron Gate Village without any particular plan for redevelopment,[7] yet just two years later, in 2015, an initial phase of redevelopment began in the form of demolition-based evictions. The first round of these evictions occurred in an area of the property that Timbercreek referred to as "Heron Gate 7" from November 2015 to February 2016.[8] This first round affected some eighty residential rental townhouses and displaced about 200 people across fifty-three families. A second round of demolition-based evictions occurred in an area referred to as "Heron Gate 5" from May to September 2018. This round affected about 150 residential rental townhouses (not all of which were then occupied) and affected over 500 people.

Each round of demolition-based evictions constituted an immediate and direct threat of unhousing for the residents of these two areas of townhouses. By 2018, a second phase of redevelopment had begun, constituted by the announcement of a broader vision of redevelopment encompassing Heron Gate Village. This broader vision raised the fear of an ongoing plan of unhousing potentially affecting many more residents over many years to come.

Members of Heron Gate Village undertook resistance along two partially contemporaneous paths, responding to these two types of threats.

The first path responded to the specific and immediate demolition-based evictions in the two areas of the community discussed above. The second path responded to the broader vision of redevelopment affecting the entire community over the longer term.

Along both paths, a mix of resistance strategies was used that can be categorized generally into two types: social action strategies and legal engagement strategies.[9] The former primarily involved collective mobilization of community members to participate in the use of social and political mechanisms for resistance based on claims of social/community justice and human rights. The latter also involved collective mobilization of community members, in different formations, but with a focus on using legal processes for resistance based on legal rights claims. Both types of strategies were used along both paths; however, since the relevant legal frameworks provided relatively few legal grounds to resist each type of unhousing, there was generally a greater use of social action strategies than legal engagement strategies along both paths of resistance.

Ultimately, and although some important resistance efforts are ongoing and unresolved, the efforts to resist the broader redevelopment plan along the second pathway can be regarded as more successful than those to resist the demolition-based evictions along the first pathway, at least in terms of the extent to which legal unhousing appears to have been prevented. It is not an objective of this case study to explore why the one path of resistance might have been more successful than the other,[10] partly because each path involved overlapping actors pursuing intertwined and interdependent strategies, so there would be an artificiality in drawing too clear a distinction between them.[11] For my present purposes, then, what should be noted is that a mix of strategies spanning all available mechanisms for resistance was used and that some limited positive outcomes were achieved. Overall, the case study illustrates how resistance activity across a range of mechanisms could not prevent legal unhousing, even though the outcome likely would have been worse if no resistance had been attempted or if it had been limited to just legal engagement strategies (given the general lack of legal grounds for resistance available in the applicable legal frameworks).

In terms of the methodology and positionality of this case study, I should note that I have been involved directly and indirectly in ongoing social action and legal engagement in Heron Gate Village since before Timbercreek purchased the property. My involvement arose from my position as a legal academic and an advocate for community-based access to justice and legal empowerment in the context of the right to housing.

More specifically, my involvement occurred via an experiential learning course ("The A2J Lab") that I have co-taught in the Faculty of Law at the University of Ottawa. The course has a core focus on supporting tenants' rights, and my co-teachers have been local lawyers (George Brown and Daniel Tucker-Simmons) who have also directly participated in action and advocacy with the Heron Gate Village community. Over the more than ten years of our involvement, the main community-based advocacy group with which we have worked is ACORN Ottawa, the local chapter of ACORN (Association of Community Organizations for Reform Now) Canada that describes itself as "a multi-issue, membership-based community union of low- and moderate-income people."[12] ACORN Ottawa has a neighbourhood chapter in Heron Gate. At the inception of the threatened second round of demolition-based evictions, another community-based advocacy group, the Herongate Tenant Coalition (HTC) sprang into being and became a key actor. We also worked closely with the HTC. Most of the events and activities described in this case study are therefore reported on the basis of first-hand involvement, knowledge, and recollection, aided by nonsystematic personal notes and records. I am not a licensed lawyer and so did not act in that capacity for any party, although both of my co-teachers have over the years. Tucker-Simmons is also the lead lawyer for the ongoing anti-discrimination human rights complaint that is one of the legal engagement resistance strategies undertaken by the community. I have not shared any confidential information to which I might have been privy throughout my involvement. I corroborate when possible from publicly available sources for my descriptions of events, activities, and viewpoints of the various parties. No interviews or other qualitative research activities were undertaken.

One corroborating source for this case study, which proceeds from a positionality similar to mine, is Andrew Crosby's recently published work *Resisting Eviction.*[13] Utilizing a methodological combination of institutional ethnography and political activist ethnography, his book-length treatment undertakes a close examination of the resistance efforts in Heron Gate Village, with a focus on the activities and strategies of the HTC, with whom he was directly involved. This focus means that some of the activities associated with ACORN Ottawa and the neighbourhood ACORN members described in my case study are not captured in Crosby's study. Similarly, but vice versa, my case study does not fully capture some of the legal engagement strategies used by the HTC as part of their resistance efforts, especially the important battles that they fought with Timbercreek and its lawyers in relation to attempts to have the HTC social media account disabled, to push back against threats by Timbercreek of a law suit for defamation, and to take Timbercreek itself to court for defaming HTC members as part of those actions.[14] As reported by Crosby, and in contrast to ACORN Ottawa, the HTC opted not to engage directly the mechanisms of the municipal planning approval process, based on a position that such an engagement could only serve to co-opt them into a "gentler form of domicide at Heron Gate."[15] One potentially significant legal engagement activity that involved HTC (but not ACORN Ottawa), and that is addressed in both case studies, is the anti-discrimination human rights complaint. Crosby's work addresses only the right to housing in international law to a limited extent and mainly in the contexts of discussing the general problem of the financialization of housing and the more specific details of the anti-discrimination complaint. His analysis is very informative and insightful. Importantly, Crosby applies a wider lens of analysis than I do, in the sense that he explores the problematic content and deployment of the socio-political and conceptual frameworks of settler-colonial urbanism, racial capitalism, and so-called community well-being, livability, and revitalization. Overall, the description of events and resistance activities is consistent between our studies, as is the conclusion that those events and activities did prompt limited positive changes.

In the following sections of this chapter, I describe in greater detail the resistance efforts along each pathway. To understand why certain resistance strategies were used, or not used, I explain the extent to which the most immediately relevant legal frameworks provided (or failed to provide) avenues for claiming legal rights or, in other words, for using legal engagement strategies. I then describe the broader landscape of legal frameworks potentially relevant to regulating unhousing. This leads to an explanation of how the right to housing offers a normative benchmark for both implementing and assessing the content and impact of those legal frameworks. I argue that this normative benchmark is not sufficiently reflected in the legal frameworks applicable in Ottawa, yet it is consistent with a key success of the resistance efforts – the nondisplacement guarantee – and somewhat better reflected in equivalent legal frameworks elsewhere in Ontario and Canada.

Resisting Demolition-Based Evictions

The demolition-based evictions ultimately were not prevented. In combination, the two rounds displaced about 700 people, over one-fifth (or over 20 percent) of the total number of about 4,000 residents of Heron Gate Village at the time that Timbercreek purchased the property.[16] Given that scale, it seems to be reasonable to refer to the combined rounds of demolition-based eviction as constituting a "mass eviction," although that is not a legal term.[17] In explaining the resistance strategies used against this mass eviction, I first address the efforts that engaged the legal framework for regulating evictions from residential rental housing for reasons of demolition, including a brief treatment of the unhelpful legal framework for regulating demolition of residential properties in Ottawa. (Later I consider alternative approaches in other jurisdictions that could be adopted and adapted as part of a revised legal framework to prevent unhousing in Ottawa, and I discuss the ongoing anti-discrimination human rights claim.)

The Legal Framework Regulating Demolition-Based Evictions

The legal framework for the regulation of demolition-based evictions in Ottawa is a combination of two components, neither of which provides meaningful grounds for resistance through legal engagement. The relevant provisions of the provincial legislation regulating residential tenancies, the Ontario *Residential Tenancies Act* (ON *RTA*), are one component.[18] The other component is the municipal demolition control bylaw of the City of Ottawa.[19]

That bylaw can be dealt with briefly. Timbercreek's demolition-based evictions exposed the fact that the bylaw did not provide residents with any meaningful ability to challenge such evictions on the basis that they would result in their unhousing. The Ottawa bylaw is narrowly drawn and essentially seeks only to ensure that public safety is not imperilled. There is no mechanism for making a demolition approval conditional on the prevention of housing displacement. This shortcoming stands in stark contrast to the regulatory framework in the City of Toronto (which will be discussed later).

Under the ON *RTA*, then, landlords are permitted to give notice to terminate a tenancy for a residential rental unit if they require possession of the unit in order to demolish it, to convert it to a use other than residential premises, or to conduct repairs or renovations extensive enough that a building permit and vacant possession are necessary.[20] In all of these situations, the landlord is required to give 120 days (four months) of notice and, with some exceptions, to offer the equivalent of three months of rent in compensation or an equivalent unit in the same residential complex (if applicable).[21] In addition, but only in the situation of repairs or renovations, the affected tenant has a right of first refusal to reoccupy the premises following the completion of repairs or renovations.[22] If the tenant gives notice that they wish to exercise their right of first refusal, then they will be entitled to reoccupy the rental unit at a rate that is no more than it lawfully could have been had the tenancy not been interrupted by the repair/renovation.[23] This protects the tenant against the general right of landlords to raise rent when a tenancy ends and a rental unit is vacated. There is no right of first refusal in the context of a demolition-based eviction, then, so in Heron Gate Village these provisions did not provide any basis for preventing the evictions.

The ON *RTA* does contain a separate general provision that empowers an adjudicator of an eviction application at the Ontario Landlord and Tenant Board (ON LTB) to refuse to grant it unless the adjudicator determines that it would be unfair to do so. This general provision compels adjudicators to refuse to grant an eviction application in a range of specified circumstances that either involve a serious breach of the landlord's obligations or are motivated by a tenant's attempt to claim their rights or organize a tenants' association. Beyond those specified circumstances, adjudicators have discretion to consider other arguments for refusal, but this discretionary power is typically exercised only narrowly, even when there is a risk of homelessness.[24] Given this discretion, the view of lawyers and other advocates supporting the tenants facing demolition-based evictions in Heron Gate Village was that the ON LTB would be highly unlikely to refuse to grant an application to evict them, despite the unhousing and other negative impacts that they would experience.

Resistance Efforts in the First Round of Demolition-Based Evictions

The first round of demolition-based eviction notices was issued by Timbercreek two years after it acquired Heron Gate Village, affecting residential rental units of about eighty townhouses and estimated to have housed over 200 people. The notices were issued in late September 2015, which meant that the tenants faced the prospect of having to move out in the middle of winter and during the school year. In apparent acknowledgment of this added inconvenience, Timbercreek provided five months of notice (one month more than required under the ON *RTA*). Even so, the affected tenants were upset at the prospect of having to find new housing, especially during winter. Both the prospect of the unhousing and the inconvenience of its timing prompted collective resistance strategies involving ACORN Ottawa.

Some of the tenants affected by the first demolition-based evictions were already members of a Heron Gate ACORN group that had existed since at least 2011 and undertaken both legal engagement and social movement activities in relation to successive prior corporate owners/landlords (the original builder/owner, the Minto Group, and then the subsequent purchaser/owner, TransGlobe). Most notably, the ACORN group had achieved significant success through the strategy of a mass filing of tenant applications for failure to undertake repairs and maintenance, along with associated applications for rent abatements.[25] At the same time, the ACORN group, along with other tenants and supporting groups, had held regular rallies in the community and lobbied the local councillor and Ottawa City Council more broadly to address disrepair and other tenants' rights problems in Heron Gate Village and similar residential rental properties. In late summer 2011, these social movement strategies prompted the mayor of Ottawa, Jim Watson, to express dissatisfaction with TransGlobe and to hold a stakeholder meeting to engage community concerns.[26] In late 2012, just a few months after Timbercreek became the new owner of Heron Gate Village, ACORN members announced that their mass filings, which constitute a legal engagement strategy, had collectively been awarded over $75,000 in repair costs and rent abatements.

Since the legal framework for the regulation of demolition-based evictions did not provide grounds for legal engagement to challenge the eviction notices issued in late summer 2015, the ACORN-member tenants and others resorted to protests and rallies at the Timbercreek office in Heron Gate Village[27] as well as rallies and lobbying at the office of the local city councillor and city hall. These social movement activities did not succeed in preventing the evictions, but they did prompt Timbercreek to offer each household an additional payment of up to $1,500 for the costs of relocation.[28] These activities also drew an expression of support from the local councillor, Jean Cloutier, reported as stating that "I agree with ACORN that having to move out at the end of February is very disruptive ... I have encouraged Timbercreek to be flexible in the moving date."[29] But in an affirmation of these evictions as an example of legal unhousing by Timbercreek, he was also reported as stating that the company was "completely in compliance with the law."[30]

The evictions in this first area of Heron Gate Village were completed in the winter of 2016, and the housing was demolished before the year was out. In the middle of the year, Timbercreek applied to the ON LTB for approval of an above-guideline rent increase for various residential buildings in Heron Gate Village to recoup the millions of dollars that it said it had spent on upgrades since it purchased the property.[31] Timbercreek expected approval of a 9 percent increase in rent phased in over three years.[32] Toward the end of the year, the company announced its redevelopment plan for this first area, and a public meeting was held in December. The plan proposed construction of a low-rise residential apartment building with over 300 units that a Timbercreek representative expressly described as seeking to advance an "alignment" between this area of Heron Gate Village and the neighbouring community of Alta Vista,[33] immediately to the north and socio-economically more wealthy and demographically less diverse.[34] The new residential rental buildings would provide a "premium" and "resort-style" community, which the representatives also acknowledged would "not meet any criteria for affordability."[35] The building, called Vista Local, was constructed and is now occupied. The current rent for a one-bedroom apartment in Vista Local is $2,139 per month,[36] more than $700 higher than the average market rent of $1,411 for a one-bedroom apartment in Ottawa as reported by the Canada Mortgage and Housing Corporation for October 2023.[37]

Resistance Efforts in the Second Round of Demolition-Based Evictions

Two years later a second area was slated for demolition that contained about 150 townhouses, of which approximately 105 were occupied by over 500 people. Some of them had relocated to this area as part of the demolition in the first area. A targeted survey of the households in this second area carried out by the HTC community group, which formed at this time, indicated that 93 percent of the residents were people of colour, with 49 percent of them identifying as of Somali origin or descent and a further 21 percent identifying as of Arab origin or descent. The HTC also found that a majority of those facing evictions were Muslim and that the average household size was 5.4 persons.[38]

Apparently informed by its experience with the social movement resistance strategies deployed in the previous evictions, this time Timbercreek issued the notices of tenancy termination in May, again with five months of notice, so that tenants would be relocating in the summer and between school years. Initially, an additional payment of up to $1,500 for relocation expenses was offered. As tenants, community members, and community advocates expressed their opposition to the evictions, this amount was raised to $2,000. Since the evictions were again compliant with the unhelpful legal framework of the ON *RTA,* the tenants did not seek to oppose this unhousing at the ON LTB. Instead, many of them engaged in social movement resistance efforts throughout the summer of 2018, and a group of tenants from about fifteen households launched a human rights complaint.

Ultimately, the evictions occurred, and the housing was demolished the following year.

In terms of social movement strategies, the members of the Heron Gate chapter of ACORN, as well as the community activists of the HTC, took a variety of actions.[39] The ACORN members staged a rally shortly after the issuance of the eviction notices and put forward three demands aimed at the City of Ottawa and Timbercreek: first, stop the evictions; second, if they did proceed, then replace the affordable housing that would be lost through the demolition and offer it to the evicted tenants at the same rent; third, implement an inclusionary zoning policy to increase the availability of affordable housing. By early July, the ACORN members had compiled a list of some thirty-five outstanding work orders for repairs and maintenance related to their homes and delivered it to Timbercreek as part of a push to demand better living conditions while also repeating their three demands. In August, ACORN Ottawa issued a report entitled *The State of Affordable Housing in Ottawa: Affordable for Who?*[40] It included a brief case study of the challenges of a long-time tenant of Heron Gate Village, who would be affected by the demolition-based evictions, in securing affordable housing. Among other things, the report noted that, though the City of Ottawa's housing policy sought to "encourage" the achievement of a target of 25 percent of all new residential rental development (or redevelopment) to be affordable, over the preceding decade the outcome had been less than 3 percent.[41] The report set out both short-term and long-term demands. In the short term, ACORN Ottawa demanded either that the evictions be stopped or that they be delayed for one year to allow for re-engagement with the community on its future. Other direct action rallies and marches were organized by the ACORN members throughout the summer, and there was ongoing outreach to local media that contributed to keeping the community's concerns about the evictions in the news.

The ability to draw media attention was partly attributable to the impending municipal elections scheduled for October 2018. ACORN Heron Gate members, and ACORN Ottawa staff, continuously lobbied the local councillor and mayor in an effort not only to have them intervene in the evictions but also to make the evictions, and the broader issue of the lack of affordable housing, an election issue. The resistance efforts were supported by Joel Harden, an NDP MPP first elected in the Ontario election in June 2018, and by Shawn Menard, challenging the incumbent councillor in the neighbouring municipal ward on a platform raising concerns about the city's approach to urban redevelopment in the upcoming municipal election.[42] The incumbent councillor of the municipal ward that included Heron Gate Village, Jean Cloutier, was also facing a tight re-election race, at least partly because of the resistance advocacy. Apparently feeling the pressure, the incumbent mayor, Jim Watson, had discussions with Cloutier and Timbercreek and in late September issued a message on social media in which he tagged Harden and Menard and took credit for Timbercreek's increase to the moving expense allowance from $1,500 to $2,000. Watson added that "I have also ensured that all residents can move back to their homes at the same rent."[43] Although this "move-back" guarantee did represent a step beyond what was required under the ON *RTA* (the "right of return" provided by the ON *RTA* for forced displacement of tenants covers only repair and renovation, not demolition), so far it has proven to be hollow, since no new construction has begun in Heron Gate Village since the razing of the houses in this second area.

Meanwhile, the HTC group undertook and publicized its community census, launched a *#DefendHerongate* website and a fundraising campaign, organized its own rallies in the local community, and engaged in a vigorous social media campaign to raise awareness of the situation and apply pressure to Timbercreek, the local councillor, and the mayor. In addition, the HTC collaborated with community reporters to research and report on the nature and structure of Timbercreek's business and redevelopment plans as well as the ongoing resistance efforts. A series of articles was published on *ricochet*, an online site for public interest journalism, and in *The Leveller* community newspaper. The HTC-associated social movement activities also attracted the attention of CBC Ottawa and the *Ottawa Citizen*, and numerous reports also appeared throughout the summer.

In response to the ongoing HTC advocacy activities on social media and in the community, Timbercreek regularly issued "cease and desist" letters, threatening to sue HTC representatives for libel and defamation as well as petitioning Twitter to shut down the HTC social media account.[44] These Timbercreek actions were characterized by the local lawyer representing the HTC activists as equivalent to a SLAPP threat: that is, a strategic lawsuit against public participation.[45] In Ontario, specific legislation was enacted in 2015 to address the problems of SLAPPs by providing a mechanism for the expedited consideration of whether a defamation lawsuit aimed at "public interest" expression should be summarily dismissed.[46] Timbercreek did not succeed in having the social media account disabled and ultimately did not sue for defamation, but, in an interesting twist described by Crosby, the HTC successfully turned the table on Timbercreek by suing it for defamation and then settling out of court.[47] Crosby argues that the HTC's participation in legal processes beyond the most immediate legal frameworks of demolition control and residential tenancy (given that they offered little) provides an important lesson in the potential strategic value of different avenues of legal engagement oriented toward protecting the expressive activity of community advocates, in the right circumstances.[48]

Enabling Legal Unhousing via Demolition-Based Evictions

In sum, then, a financialized landlord/owner undertook a large-scale eviction of predominantly low-income, racialized, immigrant, and minority-ethnic/religious renters in an inner neighbourhood of Ottawa, the capital city of Canada, a wealthy G7 nation, in the summer of 2018. Yet, as stated by the author of a long exposé in the *Ottawa Citizen,* the leading local newspaper, "legally, it doesn't appear Timbercreek has done anything wrong."[49]

Nevertheless, there were three main concrete short-term outcomes of the combined social movement activities primarily undertaken by ACORN members and HTC community activists. First, Timbercreek offered an additional $500 (for a total of $2,000) in a moving expense allowance to the affected tenants. Second, Timbercreek personnel and City of Ottawa staff worked more directly and proactively with the affected tenants to assist them in finding alternative housing, including rent geared to income for those who were part of that program. Third, community members became active and engaged, and their self-advocacy appeared to be a catalyst for prompting local politicians to encourage Timbercreek to be more responsive to community concerns. In particular, local politicians indicated their support for the community's demand that Timbercreek not repeat this type of mass demolition and displacement as it continued to redevelop the neighbourhood.

In addition to the social movement resistance activities described above, one legal engagement strategy against the demolition-based eviction was launched during the summer of 2018: that is, the anti-discrimination human rights complaint. I discuss that strategy later. In the next section, I describe the resistance strategies undertaken in relation to the unhousing threat posed by the broader redevelopment plan.

Resisting the Broader Redevelopment Plan

As the demolition-based eviction was unfolding, Timbercreek also unveiled a more formal redevelopment plan covering the Heron Gate Village community. This plan represented a new and broader unhousing threat and prompted a second pathway of resistance efforts.

The process for approval of future-oriented redevelopment plans by municipalities such as the City of Ottawa is legally defined but predominantly revolves around social and political decision-making mechanisms rather than mechanisms for claiming legal rights. Consequently, the strategies used along the resistance pathway to the broader plan of redevelopment for Heron Gate Village were more heavily oriented toward social action and advocacy than toward legal engagement. Timbercreek's redevelopment plan required approval of an amendment to Ottawa's *Official Plan* to allow increased building heights and more units.[50] The municipal approval process is multi-faceted and not always uniform, but in basic terms it requires submission of the redevelopment proposal; public consultations; review by staff of the Planning Department of the city and their report to the Planning Committee; consideration by that committee, with a recommendation to City Council; and, finally, consideration by City Council. Typically, written and oral submissions by the public can also be made to the Planning Committee and City Council, and city staff and the developer also participate. The ultimate decision of City Council can be challenged at the Ontario Land Tribunal (OLT) if there are appropriate grounds for doing so.

Through the early stages of the municipal approval process, culminating in the completion of the city staff report to the Planning Committee, the members of ACORN and the community activists of the HTC undertook activities to communicate tenants' concerns about the redevelopment plans. They held rallies in the community and attended the public consultation events in order to voice their concerns directly to Timbercreek, city staff, and local politicians. These efforts continued to draw the attention of local media.

One Step Forward? A Social Contract on Nondisplacement and Affordable Housing

These efforts yielded results. At a community meeting in early 2019, Timbercreek announced its commitment to a five-point "social contract," which included that 20 percent of the units in the redeveloped property would be "affordable" and that no existing residents would be displaced from their housing unless and until they were provided with equivalent units, at equivalent rents, elsewhere in Heron Gate Village.[51] Compared with what occurred in the demolition-based evictions, this "nondisplacement" undertaking was regarded as an important achievement for the community. Indeed, that this guarantee was offered at all seems to be a testament to the impact of the social movement and legal engagement strategies utilized to resist the demolition-based evictions. In other words, although those initial evictions went ahead, the efforts to resist them had a positive impact on the residents' ability to resist further unhousing via the redevelopment plan.

Subsequently, key provisions of the "social contract" related to affordable housing and nondisplacement were converted into a purportedly legally binding memorandum of understanding (MOU) between Timbercreek and the City of Ottawa. This MOU was integrated into the process of planning approval that culminated in an *Official Plan Amendment* (*OPA*) authorizing the broader redevelopment plan in 2021. Throughout that planning approval process, the community remained engaged in trying to ensure that the key undertakings provided in the social contract would be maintained and that their specification in greater detail would be appropriate. This primarily involved both social movement strategies engaging the City of Ottawa and its council, but it also involved an appeal to the legal mechanism of the OLT on some key deficiencies in relation to affordable housing guarantees identified by the community. The OLT appeal failed, but the terms of the MOU related to affordable housing and nondisplacement will guide the redevelopment going forward. However, the community and other concerned stakeholders continue to regard the terms of the MOU as deficient. In what follows, I describe the process for review and approval of the *OPA* and MOU, with a focus on the issue of affordable housing.

Two Steps Back? The Deficiencies of the Affordable Housing Plan

The broader redevelopment plan announced by Timbercreek required amendments to the City of Ottawa *Official Plan,* principally to allow for increased densification with additional and higher buildings. The public was invited to submit comments in the summer of 2019, and in the lead-up to that deadline, the local members of ACORN, supported by ACORN Ottawa, pushed for the creation of a community benefits agreement incorporating and elaborating the terms of the five-point social contract. Their intention was that the agreement would be signed by Timbercreek, the City of Ottawa, and community representatives to ensure its adequacy, transparency, and accountability. All of the suggested signatories and stakeholders initially indicated support for this proposal. Ultimately, though, Timbercreek and the City of Ottawa preferred to pursue the MOU as part of the *OPA* approval process, with only themselves as the parties to it. This meant that the community was denied a potential mechanism for holding Timbercreek and the city accountable for their undertakings.

An issue that the members of ACORN and other community members wanted clarified was the extent to which the redevelopment plan would preserve and increase affordable housing. This was a key issue because the initial redevelopment proposal did not adequately address affordable housing, even though it is a crucial element of the City of Ottawa *Official Plan.*[52] The initial redevelopment proposal acknowledged that affordable housing was an element of the *Official Plan,*[53] and it noted that "affordability and quality of life"[54] were factors in the city's Community Well-Being Framework.[55] Yet the proposal devoted barely any attention to the current status of or the intended future for affordable housing in Heron Gate Village and offered no details. The only mention appeared to be in the opening paragraph of the overview: "The variety of dwelling types proposed is anticipated to include a mix of 0, 1, 2 and 3+ bedroom units to meet a wide range of household structures, and support a range of affordability levels."[56] Thereafter, the proposal was silent on housing affordability.

Submissions to the planning approval process by ACORN Ottawa and others argued that the failure to address housing affordability adequately in the redevelopment plan should have been a significant concern to both the city and the Planning Committee, especially given the loss of affordable housing that had already occurred as a consequence of the two rounds of demolition-based evictions. It was pointed out that the city had expressed concerns about the negative impacts of redevelopment-motivated demolition on affordable housing in its *Official Plan.*[57] At the same time, though, the *Official Plan* established only an aspirational target in the following terms: "The City will encourage the production of affordable housing in new residential development and redevelopment to meet an annual target of ... 25% of all new rental housing ... to be affordable to households up to the 30th income percentile."[58]

Timbercreek's lack of specific plans for affordable housing became an increasing focus of attention as its *OPA* application continued through the review process over the next two years. Over that time, Timbercreek incrementally fleshed out its plans for affordable housing, partly in association with a parallel process for negotiating the terms of the MOU with the city meant to reflect the commitments of the social contract. ACORN Ottawa, the community activists of the HTC, and other concerned parties continued to apply pressure on the issue of affordable housing. For instance, in advance of public consultations scheduled for March 2021, ACORN Ottawa prepared a report,[59] which included a summary of results of a community survey conducted earlier that month. Drawing from those results, the report called for more than the minimal commitments that Timbercreek made in its social contract. Thus, though the social contract set out a goal of building up to 20 percent of the total units as affordable, nearly half of the survey respondents said that they wanted the community to have over 50 percent affordable units, and another quarter of respondents wanted at least 35 percent to 50 percent. The report further noted that it would be important to define affordability and to include a guarantee of a certain proportion of so-called deeply affordable units as well as accessible housing units.

The review process for the *OPA* application culminated in a report from the director of planning services and staff in the Planning, Infrastructure and Economic Development Department of the City of Ottawa (the PIEDD Report). The Planning Committee received the PIEDD Report in mid-August, in advance of its meeting to consider the *OPA* application in late August.[60] The PIEDD Report recommended approval of the *OPA* application and provided details on the updated redevelopment plan and its affordable housing component. By this time, per the PIEDD Report, Heron Gate Village consisted of 1,864 residential rental units, with 957 units across five apartment towers (ranging in height from eight to nineteen storeys), 252 units across numerous low-rise apartment buildings, 307 townhouse units, as well as 348 newly constructed units in the low-rise building built after the first round of demolition-based evictions. Together the first and second rounds of demolition-based evictions had removed 230 townhouse units, but the newly constructed apartment building added back 348 units. This meant an overall increase in the current total number of residential rental units, albeit with a loss of affordable units. Timbercreek's plan was that Heron Gate Village ultimately would consist of 6,427 residential units (representing almost a tripling in size). According to the PIEDD Report, based on current zoning and planning rules, including permitted building heights, Timbercreek could undertake redevelopment construction to achieve a total build-out of approximately 4,988 units. Under the *OPA* application, and more specifically because of the application for permission for higher building heights (and associated densification, also known as "density bonusing"), Timbercreek sought a total of 6,427 units at full build-out. In other words, the *OPA* application involved seeking permission to add 1,439 units over the total number of units that could be built "as-of-right" under the current rules. To achieve this number, though, Timbercreek's redevelopment plan required demolition of the remaining townhouses and low-rise apartment buildings, which would remove 559 of the existing residential rental units and, in so doing, displace hundreds of current residents.

The PIEDD Report elaborated how Timbercreek would preserve affordable housing. Timbercreek now proposed to designate 510 existing units, which would survive through the redevelopment, to remain available as affordable housing for twenty years. For these units, affordability would be defined as remaining at a rent at or below the Average Market Rent (AMR), calculated on a city-wide basis and by unit type. In addition, Timbercreek would designate a further 510 units of those to be constructed as affordable housing, but with a different definition of affordability, namely at a rent at or below 30 percent of the Average Income by Household Income Decile, guaranteed for ten years. The PIEDD Report also noted that the other 447 existing units that would survive the redevelopment process would remain subject to the ON *RTA*, by which it presumably meant that any rent increases would be limited and regulated in accordance with the act. According to the report, the ultimate total of 1,020 designated affordable housing units would constitute 16 percent of the total 6,427 units at full build-out. The 510 affordable units designated from the new units would constitute 10 percent of the total of 5,122 new units added through the redevelopment and 35 percent of the total of 1,439 units attributable to the density bonusing granted via the *OPA*. Finally, it was noted that Timbercreek would commit to a nondisplacement guarantee that there would be no future demolition of occupied units unless and until the affected tenants were offered the option to relocate to equivalent newly constructed units at the same rent or to relocate to newly renovated equivalent units at the same rent.

These details of the redevelopment plan and its affordable housing component left the community members and their advocates both angry and disappointed. The general view of these community stakeholders was that the city had used inappropriate measures of housing affordability and ultimately would oversee a loss of affordable housing. The community identified two key problems. First, ACORN and others opposed the use of AMR as a reference point for affordability. As the PIEDD Report itself noted, "a large number of the existing units are currently rented out at a rate that is below the Average Market Rent."[61] In other words, many of the existing 1,864 units already constituted affordable housing by reference to one of the measures of affordability applied by the city. But the AMR was calculated on a city-wide basis and thus failed to take into account the particularly low-income status of most households in Heron Gate Village. The AMR benchmark failed to take into account that existing rent for many households there was affordable only because it was significantly below the city-wide AMR (and there was no provision in the redevelopment plan for any deeply affordable housing). The guarantee that 510 existing units would remain at a rent at or below the AMR was therefore no guarantee that the rents could not significantly increase above current levels. In turn, there was no guarantee that they would remain affordable for the families who currently constituted the low-income community of Heron Gate Village. Second, similar concerns were raised about the inappropriateness of the measure of affordability that would be applied to the designated newly constructed units, specifically that rent would be pegged at or below 30 percent of the Average Income by Household Income Decile. The problem was that, as set out in the PIEDD Report, this yielded benchmark rent levels *higher*, and so even less affordable, than the AMR levels for equivalent unit sizes.

When these concerns were raised with the Planning Committee, a minority of its members pressed city staff to revisit the proposed plans and terms related to affordable housing. They sought not only more appropriate affordability measures but also longer periods of guaranteed affordability. City staff were resistant to these efforts, and ultimately they received cover from the incumbent councillor for the area, Jean Cloutier, who persuaded the committee to settle for a revision to the terms such that the affordable rent guarantee applicable to the newly constructed designated units would be extended from ten years to fifteen years.[62] On that basis, the Planning Committee also approved, by majority, the recommendation of the PIEDD Report that council approve the *OPA* application.

In the lead-up to the consideration by council the following month, the community stakeholders continued to lobby for a better result for affordable housing, and the issue remained a significant focus of discussion and debate at the council meeting. A group of concerned councillors again pressed city staff on the problems that had been raised with the appropriateness of the affordability measures and the duration of the affordability guarantees. The responses of the city planning director responsible for submitting the PIEDD Report to council revealed the very different lens through which she was looking to assess the suitability of the affordable housing deal. In a nutshell, her view was that the city ultimately had no power to force Timbercreek to maintain rents at or near the AMR and that it needed to be recognized that the company would be sacrificing profit in order to provide any affordable housing. So, according to this view, all that the city could do was leverage the opportunity provided by Timbercreek's *OPA* request to secure the best deal for protecting and securing some affordable housing, without jeopardizing the profitability of the overall redevelopment. From that starting point, the director of city planning claimed that securing a deal for just over 1,000 units as affordable housing should be seen as a "home run."[63] To continue the metaphor, from the point of view of the community, if this counted as a home run, then the game had already been lost.

A core group of concerned councillors, principally from inner-urban wards, presented motions at the council meeting requesting that city staff further review the affordable housing dimensions of the redevelopment plan and the MOU to achieve more appropriate and meaningful outcomes. Those motions were defeated by a solid majority that included the ward councillor (Cloutier), the mayor, and the suburban and outer-urban councillors.[64] On a similar division of votes, the council also carried a motion to approve the Planning Committee recommendation to approve the *OPA* application. Consequently, an MOU primarily related to the affordable housing commitments was executed on the terms as negotiated and revised through this process. Significantly, the MOU included a clause that purported to prohibit the city from seeking any additional affordable housing in the redevelopment area as part of any further planning approval process required. This was despite the fact that the redevelopment plan is to be implemented incrementally over an estimated period of twenty to twenty-five years, so Timbercreek will need to continue to engage with the City of Ottawa regarding more specific zoning law allowances and amendments. Not only was the community dissatisfied with the immediate outcome noted in the MOU, but also the city has purportedly tied its own hands in perpetuity.

Following council approval, ACORN appealed the decision to the Ontario Land Tribunal, primarily on the ground that the affordable housing guarantees, and the supporting analysis in the PIEDD Report, were insufficient to comply with the 25 percent target in the *Official Plan*. This appeal was dismissed at a summary hearing on the basis that the target in the plan was expressly aspirational.[65] At the same time, the OLT noted that the city had not yet opted to enact a bylaw to implement the power to require affordable housing as part of inclusionary zoning as allowed under the *Planning Act*. In other words, until the city empowered itself to impose mandatory requirements for affordable housing by enacting an inclusionary zoning regime, the OLT would not intervene.

In sum, then, along this second pathway of resistance efforts aimed at the redevelopment-based threat of unhousing, the Heron Gate Village community did achieve the potentially significant outcome of the nondisplacement guarantee. This guarantee, if upheld, will provide some protection against unhousing. However, another key threat of unhousing exists in the rent structure of the redevelopment and the potential for tenants to be driven out of Heron Gate Village over the longer term by a lack of affordability. The problems with the benchmarks used for defining affordability in the commitments that Timbercreek made on affordable housing make them more apparent than real. In combination with the general right of landlords to raise rents when units are vacated, and to seek above-guideline rent increases for capital improvements, a less obvious form of legal unhousing can occur throughout the duration of the redevelopment and beyond. Again, then, the relevant legal frameworks for decision making on the redevelopment plan (principally existing in the social-political mechanisms of municipal planning) have enabled legal unhousing.

"Righting" the Legal Frameworks

As set out above, the most immediately relevant legal frameworks of demolition control, the ON *RTA* and the municipal planning approval process applicable in Ottawa, failed to provide meaningful grounds for the Heron Gate Village community to pursue their demands in the form of legal rights claims. In other words, they were unable to use legal engagement strategies at that most immediate level of their resistance. This raises the question of whether immediate legal frameworks can be constructed in different ways to provide more meaningful legal rights to tenants facing the types of threats of unhousing that the Heron Gate Village community attempted to resist. Another question is whether more general and overarching legal frameworks, such as human rights law, do or could provide similarly meaningful rights to tenants. In this section, I consider each of these questions, with a focus on legal rights that could mitigate or prevent displacement, the common element of unhousing threats faced in Heron Gate Village. Ultimately, my argument is that the normative benchmark of the right to adequate housing as guaranteed in international human rights law can provide the basis for "righting" the relevant legal frameworks.

In what follows, I first describe examples from elsewhere in Ontario and Canada of alternative approaches to demolition control and residential tenancy regulation that, if available in Ottawa, would have provided a greater degree of protection. I then turn to an analysis of the extent to which more general legal frameworks based on protection of human rights were relevant to or consistent with the community's resistance efforts. After briefly considering the limited current relevance of the *Canadian Charter of Rights and Freedoms*,[66] I focus on explaining the connections between the community's demands and the right to adequate housing as guaranteed in international human rights law. I consider the recent outcome of the nonjudicial mechanism that the federal government ostensibly established to advance implementation of that right in Canada. Finally, I explain the community's use of the protection against discrimination provided by the Ontario *Human Rights Code*[67] as a legal engagement strategy.

Regulation of Demolition-Based Evictions

The absence of legal engagement mechanisms for resisting the unhousing associated with the demolition-based evictions in Heron Gate Village is not an inevitable or inherent limitation of legal regulation of that situation. Other Canadian jurisdictions offer examples of alternative approaches that highlight the constructed nature of the law's enablement of unhousing in Ottawa.

A key example of an alternative approach exists in the legal framework for demolition control in the City of Toronto in its municipal code.[68] Under those provisions, demolition or conversion of residential and rental properties of six units or more requires engagement with a city process for permit approval by City Council, which can impose conditions on a variety of grounds. The most relevant ground is the impact on the supply of rental housing. On the basis of this ground, the city can impose conditions requiring the replacement of demolished rental units with similar units at similar rents. The city can also set conditions requiring specific steps to be taken, and assistance to be provided, for tenant relocation during demolition and redevelopment displacement as well as terms for the right to return to the replacement housing. These provisions therefore allow the city to intervene in demolition-based redevelopment to protect affordable housing. In addition, the provisions require that notice of the approval process be provided to tenants and nearby landowners so that they can make submissions to City Council on potential conditions. Reports of the City of Toronto indicate that this legal framework has been very successful in preserving affordable housing. For the period 2013–18, the city reported the replacement of 99 percent of demolished affordable housing units.[69] This is not to say that this legal framework could not be improved, but it does provide an example of an existing legal framework that, if adopted in Ottawa, would have improved the ability of the City of Ottawa and the affected tenants of Heron Gate Village to achieve a better outcome. In a report of city staff submitted to City Council in October 2021, it was confirmed that the city has the power to enact a similar legal framework.[70]

Another example of an alternative approach is provided by the Tenant Assistance Policy (TAP) established by the City of Burnaby, British

Columbia.[71] The TAP sets out obligations for developers and landlords that must be met when they propose plans for renovation- or demolition-based redevelopment that also require applications for rezoning. Specifically, it requires that the landlord/developer subsidize the rent payable by the tenant for relocation housing to a level ensuring that the tenant is not paying more rent than in the unit from which they have been displaced.[72] In addition, the TAP includes provisions referring to general requirements for rental replacement imposed under a separate Rental Use Zoning Policy[73] framework and similar to those found in the City of Toronto municipal code on demolition control.

In the Burnaby bylaw, association of the protections for tenants with rezoning means that this regime would not be directly applicable to the demolition-based eviction situation in Heron Gate Village, though the broader redevelopment plan of Timbercreek does require rezoning approval. There are ways in which such a bylaw, if adopted in Ottawa, could be revised to apply in non-rezoning situations. The TAP is an important example because it provides more robust assistance to tenants facing displacement and relocation.

The Right to Adequate Housing

There are three types or levels of human rights frameworks potentially relevant to the situation of unhousing that occurred in Heron Gate Village: international human rights standards, the Charter, and provincial anti-discrimination codes. At the international level, a right to adequate housing has been elaborated comprehensively and provides a foundational legal framework. In accordance with Canadian domestic law, that legal framework is not automatically available for direct domestic legal enforcement via judicial means. However, a nonjudicialized mechanism of accountability was established not long after the Heron Gate Village unhousing events.[74] At the national level of the Charter, there is no express protection for a right to housing. But a more limited protection for the self-help erection of temporary and nonpermanent shelter has been recognized as arising from the section 7 right not to be deprived of life, liberty, or security of the person except in accordance with fundamental justice (reinforced to some extent by the section 15 Charter guarantee of equality).[75] (The very limited ambit of this protection is discussed in the introduction to this collection.) At the provincial level of the *Human Rights Code* in Ontario (as in all other provinces and territories in Canada), there is protection against discrimination in the provision of housing.[76] I will consider below the ambit of this protection in relation to unhousing since the lodging of a complaint under the ON *HRC* was one form of resistance that the community undertook. My focus here is on international human rights standards and the extent to which they informed and validated the Heron Gate Village community's demands, especially for nondisplacement.

At the international level, the right to adequate housing is recognized as a component of the broader right to an adequate standard of living in Article 25 of the *Universal Declaration of Human Rights*[77] and Article 11 of the *International Covenant on Economic, Social and Cultural Rights.*[78] The United Nations Committee on Economic, Social and Cultural Rights has elaborated the substance of the right to adequate housing in its *General Comment No. 4*,[79] which explains that there are a number of elements that must be satisfied for housing to be regarded as minimally adequate: security of tenure, including protection against forced eviction; availability of services and infrastructure, such as safe drinking water, sanitation, and energy for cooking; affordability; habitability; accessibility; suitable location, with reasonable proximity to employment, schooling, and social services; and culturally appropriate.

The *ICESCR* also places responsibilities on states to ensure nondiscrimination in relation to the right to housing.[80] Reinforcement of this responsibility is found in the *International Convention on the Elimination of All Forms of Racial Discrimination*,[81] which requires states to "eliminate racial discrimination in all of its forms,"[82] including by ensuring that individuals are treated equally under the law with respect to access to housing.

When considering how the international human rights framework can engage situations of unhousing, the protection against forced evictions and the related protection against development-based displacements require exploration. The UNCESCR has also issued a general comment on forced evictions, defining them as "permanent or temporary removal against their will of individuals, families and/or communities from the homes and/or land which they occupy, without the provision of, and access to, appropriate forms of legal or other protection."[83] Protection against forced eviction is based not only on the *ICESCR* but also on the *International Covenant on Civil and Political Rights*[84] and, more specifically, Article 12(1), which guarantees lawful residents of a state freedom to move within that territory and take up residence where they choose. The Committee on Civil and Political Rights has interpreted this right to include protection against internal displacement.[85]

Bringing these and other threads of protection together, Miloon Kothari, during his term as the UN special rapporteur on the right to adequate housing, issued *Basic Principles and Guidelines on Development-Based Evictions and Displacement* in 2007.[86] The norms related to forced eviction and displacement are typically associated with large-scale development and infrastructure projects sponsored by governments themselves, such as construction of dams or facilities for global sports events, or with "clearance" of large informal settlements (formerly "slums") for such purposes. But the *BPGs* defined "development-based evictions" as also including those motivated by "urban renewal" and "housing renovation."[87] In elaborating recommended procedural and substantive parameters for such displacement, the *BPGs* directed states to seek to prevent or mitigate the underlying causes of forced evictions, including land and real estate speculation.[88] The *BPGs* also called on states to "review the operation and regulation of the housing and tenancy markets and, when necessary, intervene to ensure that market forces do not increase the vulnerability of low-income and other marginalized groups to forced eviction."[89] In addition, the *BPGs* suggested that eviction impact assessments should be undertaken, including the "exploration of alternatives and strategies for minimizing harm."[90]

A more recent UN special rapporteur on the right to adequate housing, Leilani Farha, built upon the *BPGs* in issuing *Guidelines for the Implementation of the Right to Housing* in 2019.[91] These *Guidelines* extended the *BPGs* by devoting attention to the applicability of the right to adequate housing to contexts of housing insecurity, eviction, and displacement associated with high-income countries. Thus, Guideline 6 recognizes that forced evictions have occurred in order to clear "homeless encampments" or "to replace existing lower-cost housing with luxury housing." In addition, Guideline 12 draws attention to the need to regulate appropriately private businesses engaged in the housing sector and to address the financialization of housing. This guideline specifies that the obligations of states include "adopting planning and development approval criteria to ensure that any proposed housing development responds to the actual needs of residents, including affordable housing for low-income households and employment opportunities."[92]

The point of these international standards is not to prohibit outright forced evictions or eviction-based displacements. Rather, it is to ensure that evictions and displacements are appropriately justified and regulated in ways consistent with international human rights standards. Those standards include minimizing negative impacts and leaving people at least no worse off in terms of the right to adequate housing and its constituent elements.

As stated in the *Guidelines,* "all feasible alternatives to eviction must be explored, in consultation with affected persons. If, after meaningful engagement with those affected, relocation is deemed necessary and/or desired by the community, adequate alternative housing of similar size, quality and cost must be provided in close proximity to the original place of residence and source of livelihood."[93]

The comprehensive elaboration of the right to adequate housing in international human rights law can thus serve as a normative benchmark for assessing unhousing processes and events. And it is worth noting that this normative benchmark has both substantive and procedural dimensions. This outline of the right to adequate housing has focused primarily on its substantive dimension, but the procedural dimension is evident, for instance, in the passage above quoted from the *Guidelines,* which mentions the need to consult with affected communities, a consistent refrain in elaborations of the right to adequate housing. Similarly, a further report on *Access to Justice for the Right to Housing,*[94] issued by Farha during her mandate as special rapporteur, emphasized, among other things, the need to enable communities to participate in processes that might cause their displacement.[95] Her report also reiterated a call for public agencies to take responsibility for undertaking human rights impact assessments as part of the process for considering approval of development plans.[96]

Returning to the resistance efforts of the community members from Heron Gate Village, we can clearly see connections between the demands of the community and the content of the normative benchmark of the right to housing. These connections are not accidental, for community members and their advocates specifically referenced the right to adequate housing in the course of their resistance efforts. Indeed, Farha, who is Ottawa born and lives and works in the city, spoke at a community meeting held shortly after Timbercreek announced the second round of demolition-based evictions.[97] A connection between the community demands and the right to adequate housing is seen most clearly in the nondisplacement guarantee, which reflects the priority given to preventing displacement in the guidelines elaborated by successive UN special rapporteurs. In addition, the ongoing insistence of the community members that their voices and concerns be heard as part of the redevelopment process also reflects those guidelines. Furthermore, and turning to the recognized substantive components of the right to adequate housing, there is a clear connection in the emphasis that community members placed on the importance of maintaining the social, economic, and cultural supports available to them in Heron

Gate Village. Similarly, a connection exists in their demand that they not be worse off in terms of accessibility and proximity to their established sources of community services, education, and places of employment. Moreover, the community's demand that current levels of affordable housing be at least maintained and, ideally, improved clearly connects to the general principle of nonderogation in international human rights law. By virtue of that principle, states must first and foremost refrain from, and provide protection against, reductions in the level of attainment of human rights. In other words, at a minimum, no one should be made worse off as housing and other human rights are affected by redevelopment or other social processes.

The relevance of the right to housing to the situation in Heron Gate Village extends even further, though. Not long after the unhousing there, the federal government enacted the *National Housing Strategy Act*, which declares that the housing policy of Canada is based, among other things, on the recognition "that the right to adequate housing is a fundamental human right affirmed in international law."[98] As described in the introduction to this collection, the *NHSA* provides a nonjudicialized mechanism of accountability to the right to adequate housing, including a federal housing advocate and a National Housing Council. The utility of this new accountability mechanism has been tested through the establishment of a first review panel on the financialization of housing. Community advocacy emanating from the unhousing in Heron Gate Village, as well as legal analysis and academic research examining it and other examples of financialized unhousing, played a role in the federal housing advocate's initial investigation of the issue and the request for the review panel.[99] In addition, members of the Heron Gate Village community and associated advocates made submissions to the review panel and participated in its hearings.[100]

In late May 2024, in accordance with the nonjudicial accountability mechanism of the *NHSA*, the review panel submitted its report to the federal government's minister of housing, infrastructure, and communities.[101] The report included an opinion of the three-member panel that accepted a key concern of stakeholders such as the community of Heron Gate Village, as highlighted in the italicized portion of the following text:

> The panel contends that housing must be viewed through the same lens as the principle of universal access to adequate health care. Access to health care services is essential – so is access to adequate housing. *While most housing in Canada is financialized, the panel is concerned about the use of financialized strategies that aim to refinance existing affordable rental stock*

to increase profit.[*] It is the opinion of the panel that these strategies have an adverse impact on the right to adequate housing and significantly reduce affordable rental housing supply.[102]

This paragraph included a footnote (indicated by the [*] above) of particular salience to Heron Gate Village: "Eg, targeting affordable rental housing stock for redevelopment to increase profits from sales of rental properties, and/or from rent increases after renovations, demolitions, and/or tenant turnovers, etc."[103]

Beyond the endorsement of the key concern about the negative impact of the financialization of housing, the panel's opinion and recommendations can be regarded as a disappointment. Leilani Farha (who completed her mandate as UN special rapporteur in 2020) and Julieta Perucca expressed their disappointment in an opinion piece that framed the work of the review panel as a "missed opportunity" rooted in the "well-intentioned but misguided" comparison to Canada's health-care system.[104] As they argued, in keeping with this skewed self-direction toward a largely publicly funded system, the panel's recommendations focused on measures to increase the supply of nonmarket housing and in doing so largely let the private sector financializers of rental housing off the hook.[105]

Leaving aside the disappointing outcome of the review under the *National Housing Strategy Act* process, the preceding analysis points to a fundamental failing of the current legal framework relevant to unhousing in Ottawa: namely, a lack of integration of the clear normative parameters that characterize the right to housing in international human rights law. Yet this analysis, and especially the ultimate terms of the MOU agreed between Timbercreek and the City of Ottawa, point to the appropriateness and feasibility of using those normative parameters as a benchmark for revising applicable legal frameworks in Ottawa and Ontario to better regulate demolition-based evictions and redevelopment of residential rental housing. Alternative approaches in other jurisdictions incorporate those normative parameters, especially in relation to the attempt to provide protection against making anyone worse off. This nonderogation element can be seen in the more managed process for displacement and relocation in Burnaby and in the rental replacement standard of Toronto's demolition-control framework.

The limited successes of the Heron Gate Village residents also drew from normative parameters of international human rights law. The nondisplacement obligation of the right to housing matched not only a key demand made by the community of Heron Gate Village but also a key commitment in the MOU. Indeed, inclusion of the nondisplacement guarantee in the MOU can be regarded as representing an implicit consensus among the diverse group of stakeholders involved in the municipal process that the right to adequate housing is an appropriate and feasible benchmark. Understood in that way, although the resistance efforts of the Heron Gate Village community yielded only limited successes, the achievement of the nondisplacement guarantee, and the implicit consensus underlying it, are potentially groundbreaking for addressing unhousing.

Anti-discrimination

An anti-discrimination human rights complaint was launched as a further legal engagement strategy to resist the second round of demolition-based evictions. This invoked the remaining more general legal framework of human rights (the others being the Charter and international human rights law) potentially relevant to the situation of Heron Gate Village. If successful, then this complaint would also be groundbreaking.

The Ontario *Human Rights Code* provides "a right to equal treatment with respect to the occupancy of accommodation"[106] and, in turn, protection against discrimination in accommodation on a range of enumerated grounds (typically referred to as "prohibited grounds").[107] Such grounds are "race, ancestry, place of origin, colour, ethnic origin, citizenship, creed, sex, sexual orientation, gender identity, gender expression, age, marital status, family status, disability or the receipt of public assistance."[108] In addition to this protection against what is often referred to as "direct" discrimination, the code provides protection against what it categorizes as "constructive" discrimination. The latter type occurs when "a requirement, qualification or factor exists that is not discrimination on a prohibited ground but that results in the exclusion, restriction or preference of a group of persons who are identified by a prohibited ground of discrimination," except where "the requirement, qualification or factor is reasonable and *bona fide* in the circumstances."[109]

As it became clear that the legal framework applicable to demolition-based evictions did not provide any legal ground for resisting the unhousing, the community activists of the HTC, along with a group of affected tenants, began exploring with legal counsel and other human rights experts whether a complaint could be lodged under section 2 and/or section 11 of the *Human Rights Code*. Ultimately, a complaint was lodged, with the tenants who comprised the applicants alleging that the unhousing caused by Timbercreek was based on multiple violations of the code. First, it was claimed that Timbercreek had "systematically neglected its maintenance obligations towards the Applicants in a manner that amounts to systemic discrimination on prohibited grounds."[110] From the perspective of the applicants, this alleged systematic neglect had contributed to the ongoing dilapidation of their housing, which had three effects: first, in saving money on maintenance and repairs, Timbercreek gained more profit from the property in the short term; second, the dilapidated state of the housing made it less desirable for the tenants to fight to keep it; and, third, the state of the housing made its demolition more justifiable, which in turn paved the way for redevelopment that repositioned the property for a higher-income demographic of tenants. As mentioned in the complaint, scholars have labelled this multi-faceted process "squeezing" and identified it as a common business practice of financialized landlords.[111]

Second, it was claimed that Timbercreek's very model of redevelopment was discriminatory because it disproportionately affected people, such as the applicants, identified by a mix of code-prohibited grounds. The applicants alleged that Timbercreek was deliberately engaging in what they called "hyper-gentrification,"[112] "predatory redevelopment,"[113] and "demographic engineering."[114] In a nutshell, they argued that Heron Gate Village was selected for redevelopment because it was considered "undervalued" or, in other words, because there was significant potential "to generate and capture higher value and income from the property"[115] by upgrading it and replacing the existing low-income tenants with higher-income tenants. Typically, the new tenants would be different demographically from the old tenants in that they would tend to be white, be affluent, have no families or smaller families, and be nonimmigrants. The property was therefore "undervalued precisely because it was primarily inhabited by people of colour, immigrants, people receiving public assistance, and people with families" (and often large families).[116]

Third, it was also claimed that the applicants would be disproportionately affected by the redevelopment, in particular the displacement and unhousing that it produced, because they would lose the protective and supportive benefit of the "ethnic enclave"[117] in which they lived, which provided an important buffer against their vulnerability to discrimination in society at large. In addition, they would face the challenge of overcoming the broader pattern of discrimination known to exist in the residential rental market as they searched for alternative housing outside their supportive enclave.

A key point in the human rights complaint is that it expressly drew from the normative content of the right to adequate housing as a source for giving meaning to the scope of protection that ought to be offered by the code. This included identifying the connection between the benefits that the applicants derived from their ethnic enclave and the constituent elements of adequate housing as defined by the UNCESCR, in particular the elements of housing being suitably located, with reasonable proximity to employment, schooling, and social services, as well as culturally appropriate. In addition, the complaint expressly drew from the overarching guarantee of nondiscrimination in relation to the right to housing as well as the guarantees of nondisplacement and nonderogation (not making people worse off).

In its response to the complaint, Timbercreek denied that it had neglected maintenance obligations or taken prohibited grounds into account in its decision making on the demolition-based evictions. In addition, it sought to establish that most of the applicants ultimately relocated to equivalent housing within a few kilometres of Heron Gate Village and thus did not lose access to their community. The evidence presented by the applicants and Timbercreek will be important in determining each point of response. I will not speculate here on what might be presented or its potential persuasiveness. But I will offer a criticism of the legal coherence of the position that Timbercreek did not consider prohibited grounds in its decision making. That position does not seem to recognize or engage the extent to which the applicants' claim is based on an allegation of constructive, rather than direct, discrimination. As per the definition of constructive discrimination in the code, quoted above, the issue is whether there were disproportionate detrimental *impacts* on people identifiable by code-prohibited grounds resulting from the decision making, not whether those grounds or the impacts were *actually considered* in the decision making.

The human rights complaint was filed in early 2019 but has progressed very slowly, partly because of the backlog of cases at that time and partly because of the intervening impacts of the COVID-19 pandemic. In a disturbing recent development, the Ontario Human Rights Tribunal has granted Timbercreek's motion for a summary hearing of its application that the complaint be dismissed as having no reasonable prospect of success. The summary hearing is yet to be scheduled. Only time will tell if this legal engagement strategy proves to be effective. If the claim does succeed, then it will be a very significant legal outcome potentially providing strong protection against threats of financialized unhousing in Ottawa, across Ontario, and in other Canadian jurisdictions.

Conclusion: "Righting" and Financialized Unhousing

The people of Heron Gate Village, along with their community supporters and allies, engaged in an impressive and sustained range of resistance strategies against the two main types of financialized legal unhousing threats posed by Timbercreek. Ultimately, their efforts did not prevent the legal unhousing associated with the demolition-based evictions. The almost complete absence of grounds for opposing these evictions in the most immediately relevant legal frameworks of demolition control and residential tenancy regulation largely nullified the potential for pursuing legal engagement strategies. Leaving aside the unresolved anti-discrimination human rights complaint, the applicable legal frameworks offered only a touch of mitigation (in the form of three months of rent in compensation for demolition-based evictions) and not even an iota of prevention. The community achieved some success in further mitigating the impacts of the second round of demolition-based evictions, and in resisting the threat of unhousing posed by Timbercreek's redevelopment plans, through social action strategies. In relation to the demolition-based evictions, the community secured the additional measures of the enhanced moving allowances and the "move-back" guarantee. In relation to the redevelopment plans, although they do include commitments on affordable housing, those commitments are barely positive and deficient in important ways. In contrast, the commitment to the nondisplacement guarantee is a significant positive outcome that might have an important broader impact going forward.

As this case study shows, the right to housing as understood in international human rights law can be a key source for reforming applicable legal frameworks to incorporate substantive normative parameters such as, at a minimum, nonderogation, nondiscrimination, and nondisplacement. In other words, this is an argument for a substantive "righting" of the relevant legal frameworks in order to assist in correcting the current tilt toward enabling unhousing evident in the multi-level legal frameworks that apply in Ottawa. This argument follows the lead of the demands made by the Heron Gate Village community as part of their resistance efforts, which included express and implicit references to the substance of the right to adequate housing and manifested in the achievement of the nondisplacement guarantee. This argument is also consistent with the substantive elements that characterize the alternative approaches in other jurisdictions inside and outside Ontario. Moreover, as mentioned earlier in the overview of the right to adequate housing, that right can also be a source for procedural "righting" of that framework, in the sense that the right has been interpreted as validating the demands of communities to be able to participate in the social, political, and legal mechanisms by which proposals and threats of unhousing are formulated and regulated.

As a final reflection on this argument for both substantively and procedurally "righting" the legal frameworks applicable to regulating unhousing, I suggest that the need to do so is especially pressing in the specific context of financialized unhousing, given both the mass scale and the magnified power imbalances likely to be associated with that context. This case study of the resistance efforts mounted in Heron Gate Village illustrates the difficulty that such a community faces in effectively challenging the scale and nature of the operations of a corporate/financialized landlord. On the one hand, the mass scale of the demolition-based unhousing and redevelopment plans might have assisted in spurring the extent of community involvement both in the resistance strategies and in the media attention and other amplifying forces that ultimately contributed to achieving the positive outcomes. On the other hand, those outcomes ultimately were only modest, despite all of the community activism, media attention, and councillor scrutiny. This suggests that, in the absence of appropriate normative parameters instantiated in applicable legal frameworks, there is a significant imbalance of power between the community and the corporate/financialized landlord that will always be difficult to counter effectively. Incorporating substantive normative parameters into those legal frameworks is therefore potentially a necessary step in order to offer some rebalancing of legal and social/political power in these situations.[118]

The power imbalance between the community and Timbercreek existed not only in the lack of substantive protection against unhousing but also in the lack of support for the community as it engaged the legal and political processes of decision making. Timbercreek had access to significant financial and other resources to navigate the process of demolition-based eviction and redevelopment planning, including experienced planning consultants and legal counsel. The City of Ottawa could rely on its staff. In contrast, the community members needed to volunteer their time while relying on the capacity of the HTC activists to do likewise (although this included staging some relatively successful, if still modest, fundraising campaigns). ACORN Ottawa has a small and under-resourced office with rarely more than two or three staff members who focus on organizing in local communities and supporting their community-based members to advocate on their own behalf – it is stretched thin at the best of times. The local lawyer who filed the anti-discrimination human rights claim (Daniel Tucker-Simmons) invested significant pro bono hours (as did some other local lawyers and community allies) but did succeed in obtaining a grant from the test case funding program of Legal Aid Ontario for the human rights complaint. And, though a group of legal advocacy organizations and experts contributed their views on the development of that claim, none was in a position to offer sustained assistance to the community as it engaged decision-making processes.[119] This significant imbalance left the community with an ongoing disadvantage in terms of engaging and influencing the relevant processes.[120]

The impacts of these imbalances of resources and power experienced by the Heron Gate Village community in resisting unhousing ought to be addressed as part of a systemic improvement of access to justice in Ottawa and Ontario (and beyond).[121] In the absence of such systemic measures, I suggest that these imbalances add impetus to the main argument of this case study that the legal frameworks applicable to the regulation of unhousing ought to be substantively and procedurally "righted," in keeping with the normative benchmark of the right to housing in international law, at least in the context of financialized and other forms of threatened mass eviction and unhousing.

Acknowledgments

With many thanks to Anna Lund and Sarah Buhler for their vision and substantial work on convening the Legal Unhousing research workshop and editing this associated publication as well as for their more specific feedback on this chapter. Thanks also to the participants in the research workshop and the anonymous peer reviewer for feedback.

Notes

1 In this chapter, I use "Herongate" to refer to the entire neighbourhood area and "Heron Gate Village" to refer to the more particular area of residential rental property purchased by Timbercreek within that neighbourhood. It should be noted, however, that there is a lack of consistent usage of the labels "Herongate" and "Heron Gate" in official and other documents, and in news reporting and the like, so the usage I adopt is not always consistently reflected in titles of sources.

2 The Herongate neighbourhood forms one whole census tract of Statistics Canada: see Statistics Canada, *Census Profile, 2021 Census of Population – More Information: 505007.02 [Census Tract], Ontario,* Catalogue No. 98-316-X2021001 (Ottawa: Statistics Canada, February 9, 2022), https://www12.statcan.gc.ca/census-recensement/2021/dp-pd/prof/details/moreinfo-plusinfo.cfm?Lang=E&cdguid=2021S05075050007.02&SearchText=K1V%206A5&DGUIDlist=2021S05075050007.02&GENDERlist=1,2,3&STATISTIClist=1,4&HEADERlist=0 [perma.cc/QU4J-FDLA].

For data in the 2016 census, see Statistics Canada, *Census Profile, 2016 Census,* Catalogue No. 98-316-X2016001 (Ottawa: Statistics Canada, November 29, 2017), https://www12.statcan.gc.ca/census-recensement/2016/dp-pd/prof/details/page.cfm?Lang=E&Geo1=CT&Code1=5050007.02&Geo2=CMACA&Code2=505&SearchText=K1V6A5&SearchType=Begins&SearchPR=01&B1=All&TABID=2&type=1 [perma.cc/5US4-V2DW]. By the time of the 2021 census, the total population of the census tract had been slightly reduced. The visible minority population had risen to 77 percent, but the proportion of immigrants in the population remained unchanged. See Statistics Canada, *Census Profile, 2021 Census of Population,* Catalogue No. 98-316-X2021001 (Ottawa: Statistics Canada, February 9, 2022), https://www12.statcan.gc.ca/census-recensement/2021/dp-pd/prof/details/page.cfm?Lang=E&SearchText=5050007%2E02&DGUIDlist=2021S05075050007.02&GENDERlist=1,2,3&STATISTIClist=1,4&HEADERlist=0 [perma.cc/BC7S-E5DF]. A key demographic change over this five-year period appeared to be an increase in the overall number and proportion of Black-identifying members of the visible minority population (from around 30 percent to around 40 percent) and a similarly sized decrease in the overall number and proportion of the non–visible minority population (from around 30 percent to around 22 percent).

3 I refer to Timbercreek Asset Management for ease of reference since this was the general brand name of the overarching corporate group at the time of purchase of the Heron Gate Village property; see, for instance, Timbercreek Asset Management, *Consolidated Financial Statements of Timbercreek Mortgage Investment Corporation* (Toronto: Timbercreek Mortgage Investment Corporation, 2014), https://timbercreekfinancial.com/wp-content/uploads/2022/09/2013-financial-statements-tmic.pdf [perma.cc/9M2X-ABUD]. The precise corporate name and ownership structure of Timbercreek are not straightforward and were a matter investigated by supporters of the resistance efforts of the tenants. See Andrew Crosby, *Resisting Eviction: Domicide and the Financialization of Rental Housing* (Winnipeg: Fernwood, 2023) at 65–67, 72–74.

4 Crosby, *Resisting Eviction,* at 72–74.

5 Ibid. See also Andrew Crosby, "Financialized Gentrification, Demoviction, and Landlord Tactics to Demobilize Tenant Organizing" (2020) 108 *Geoforum* 184–93.

6 The SHIFT, *The SHIFT Directives: From Financialized to Human Rights-Based Housing* (Ottawa: The SHIFT, 2022) at 6–7, https://make-the-shift.org/wp-content/uploads/2022/12/Directives-Updated-Dec-9.pdf [perma.cc/27SW-PAAH]. See also Martine August, "The Financialization of Canadian Multi-Family Rental Housing: From Trailer to Tower" (2020) 42:7 *Journal of Urban Affairs* 975–97; Martine August and Alan Walks, "Gentrification, Suburban Decline, and the Financialization of Multi-Family Rental Housing: The Case of Toronto" (2018) 89 *Geoforum* 124–36.

7 At para 33 of its response to the HRTO claim, Timbercreek states that "Heron Gate Village was purchased in 2012 and 2013 as part of a portfolio transaction, and was therefore not individually identified for purchase as a result of its redevelopment potential." Timbercreek Asset Management Inc., "Response to an Application Under

Section 34 of the Human Rights Code (Form 2)" (September 27, 2019), https://herongatetenants.ca/wp-content/uploads/2021/01/Timbercreek-Response-to-Application-HRTO-et-al-Final_Redacted.pdf [perma.cc/XNT8-X3DK].

8 Images depicting the proposed stages of redevelopment of Heron Gate Village are accessible on the website of the Herongate Tenant Coalition. Herongate Tenant Coalition, "Hazelview's Plans for Herongate," (n.d.), https://herongatetenants.ca/hazelviews-plans-for-herongate/ [perma.cc/2JJA-SH8V].

9 The categories of "social action" and "legal engagement" can be linked to the broader and deeper concepts and strategies of "social movements" and "legal empowerment" and in turn to debates about the role and merits of litigation as a strategy for social change. It is not my purpose in this chapter to explore those concepts or to assess their relative success or failure in the Heron Gate context. There is a vast literature in this area. For a recent overview and analysis, see Whitney K. Taylor and Sidney Tarrow, *Law, Mobilization, and Social Movements: How Many Masters?* (Cambridge, UK: Cambridge University Press, 2024).

10 See the note above.

11 The social action activity of the Herongate Tenant Coalition has been considered in a report on the role that legal clinics can play in supporting community organizing and social action in relation to rights to the city and to housing. See Martine August and Cole Webber, *Demanding the Right to the City and the Right to Housing (R2C/R2H): Best Practices for Supporting Community Organizing* (Toronto: Parkdale Community Legal Services, 2019).

12 ACORN Canada, "About ACORN Canada" (n.d.), https://acorncanada.org/about/ [perma.cc/6KM3-JRXW].

13 Crosby defines domicide in this context as "the deliberate destruction of home, through gentrification, urban development, eviction, and displacement" (at 4), relying on Douglas Porteous and Sandra E. Smith, *Domicide: The Global Destruction of Home* (Montreal and Kingston: McGill-Queen's University Press, 2001).

14 Crosby, *Resisting Eviction,* at 104–13.

15 Ibid at 141.

16 The numbers provided here are not exact, in part because some people displaced by the first round of evictions were relocated to the area then affected by the second round of evictions, and in turn some people displaced by the second round were relocated to residential units in other areas of Heron Gate Village.

17 Anna Lund has defined "mass eviction" as occurring "when an entire building or rental complex is closed and all the tenants are forced to relocate." Anna Lund, "Intersections Between Precarious Housing and Residential Tenancy Law: A Review of *A Complex Exile* and Recent Legal Scholarship on Residential Tenancies" (2023) 36 *Journal of Law and Social Policy* 44–63 at 48. Although the demovictions in Heron Gate Village did not encompass the entire residential rental property (a huge area), they demolished entire areas of rental housing within that property.

18 *Residential Tenancies Act, 2006,* SO 2006, c 17 [ON *RTA*].

19 City of Ottawa, revised Bylaw No. 2012-377, *Demolition Control.*

20 ON *RTA*, s 50(1).

21 Ibid, ss 50(2), 52, 54.

22 Ibid, s 50(3). Note that this subsection will be amended by legislation awaiting proclamation. With the amendments, landlords will need to take additional steps to prove that proposed repairs or renovations necessitate vacant possession. See *Helping Homebuyers, Protecting Tenants Act*, SO 2023, c 10, Schedule 7, s 2 [*Helping Homebuyers*].

23 ON *RTA*, s 53(3). Note that part of s 53 will be amended by legislation awaiting proclamation. With the amendments, landlords will need to take additional steps to ensure that tenants are kept informed about timelines for the completion of repairs/renovations and for reoccupancy. See *Helping Homebuyers*, Schedule 7, s 3.

24 This statement about the narrow exercise of discretion is based on personal knowledge of unreported ON LTB decisions as well as opinions expressed by lawyers working in the legal aid clinic system in Ontario over many years. Further substantiation is challenging because only a selection of decisions of the ON LTB (since 2009) is available on CanLII, as determined by which decisions the ON LTB chooses to transmit to CanLII. Only four ON LTB decisions referring to s 83 were found on CanLII for the period 2009–16, and none mentioned a risk of homelessness. But more decisions of relevance are available for subsequent years, and they offer some substantiation. See, for instance, *TEL-02300-19 (Re)*, 2019 CanLII 89692 (ON LTB), in which a stay of eviction was refused on the grounds that there was no realistic prospect of paying arrears and no evidence of the tenant taking responsibilities seriously, despite an explicit risk of homelessness and a probationary job offer. See also *TNL-20735-19 (Re)*, 2020 CanLII 31135 (ON LTB), in which s 83 was relied on to defer the deadline for an eviction, but not to refuse the eviction, in circumstances of rent arrears in the context of family breakdown and risk of homelessness. In contrast, though, see *TNL-19665-19 (Re)*, 2019 CanLII 134459 (ON LTB), in which relief from eviction was granted amid mention of the risk of homelessness and instead a repayment plan was ordered. For discussion of a comparable proportionality analysis under Saskatchewan's residential tenancy legislation, see Chapter 2 of this collection.

25 This mass filing initiative marked the beginning of more systematic participation of law students from the Faculty of Law at the University of Ottawa in a project supporting tenants' rights advocacy and legal empowerment strategies of ACORN Ottawa. The law students participated under the legal supervision of George Brown, a local lawyer, former city councillor, and pro bono counsel to ACORN, with my assistance as an academic supervisor and liaison to the Faculty of Law. One of the first law students to be involved was Daniel Tucker-Simmons, who subsequently became a legal supervisor and co-teacher.

26 ACORN Canada, "Ottawa Tenants Celebrate Herongate Progress" (September 20, 2011), https://acorncanada.org/news/ottawa-tenants-celebrate-herongate-progress/ [perma.cc/4G6Q-QKRU]. Also reported on in the *Ottawa Citizen*, as archived on ACORN Canada's website, "Watson Wants Heron Gate Property Properly Managed," *Ottawa Citizen* (August 16, 2011), https://acorncanada.org/news/ottawa-citizen-watson-wants-heron-gate-property-properly-managed/ [perma.cc/SLK8-9DF6].

27 ACORN Canada, "Ottawa ACORN vs. Timbercreek" (November 24, 2015), https://acorncanada.org/news/ottawa-acorn-vs-timbercreek/ [perma.cc/Z8SJ-6NM7].

28 Eric Elliott, "Heron Gate Residents Protest Planned February Eviction," *Ottawa Citizen* (November 19, 2015), https://ottawacitizen.com/news/local-news/heron-gate-residents-protest-planned-february-eviction [perma.cc/JJZ7-MN94].

29 Ibid.

30 Ibid.

31 Erin McCracken, "'Treated Like Dirt': Herongate Tenants Oppose Above-Guideline Rent Hikes," *Ottawa Community News* (July 12, 2016), archived at https://acorncanada.org/news/ottawa-community-news-treated-dirt-herongate-tenants-oppose-above-guideline-rent-hikes/ [perma.cc/T5NG-S9JK].

32 Ibid.

33 Erin McCracken, "Alta Vista Residents Object to 'Three Monsters' Herongate Complex," *Ottawa Community News* (December 13, 2016), archived at https://acorncanada.org/news/ottawa-community-news-alta-vista-residents-object-three-monsters-herongate-complex/ [perma.cc/C7A8-4ASL].

34 The Alta Vista neighbourhood is much larger than the Herongate neighbourhood and includes several census tracts. Data for the Alta Vista census tract immediately north of the Herongate census tract are available from Statistics Canada, *Census Profile, 2016 Census – 5050007.03 [Census Tract],* Catalogue No. 98-316-X2016001 (Ottawa: Statistics Canada, February 8, 2017), https://www12.statcan.gc.ca/census-recensement/2016/dp-pd/prof/details/page.cfm?Lang=E&Geo1=CT&Code1=5050007.03&Geo2=CMACA&Code2=505&SearchText=K1H6M3&SearchType=Begins&SearchPR=01&B1=All&TABID=2&type=0 [perma.cc/72SF-ZLFQ].

35 McCracken, "Alta Vista."

36 As viewed on Vista Local, "Available Suites" (last accessed July 25, 2024), vistalocal.com/suites [perma.cc/43WL-FZTH].

37 CMHC, "Ontario – Rental Market Statistics Summary by Metropolitan Areas, Census Agglomerations and Cities," https://www03.cmhc-schl.gc.ca/hmip-pimh/en/TableMapChart/Table?TableId=2.1.31.2&GeographyId=35&GeographyTypeId=2&DisplayAs=Table&GeograghyName=Ontario#1%20Bedroom [perma.cc/3T3U-3PNS].

38 The results of the survey are reported at Herongate Tenant Coalition, "Herongate Eviction Census" (2018), https://herongatetenants.ca/herongate-eviction-census/ [perma.cc/R2ZV-AE22].

39 The HTC community activists took a somewhat hostile stance toward the actions of ACORN Ottawa and local ACORN members. HTC appeared to regard ACORN as being too willing to engage in dialogue with Timbercreek and municipal politicians, whereas HTC preferred more radical approaches.

40 ACORN Canada, *Affordable for Who? The State of Affordable Housing in Ottawa* (Ottawa: ACORN Canada, 2018), https://acorncanada.org/resources/affordable-who-state-affordable-housing-ottawa/ [perma.cc/2SLS-GU4M].

41 Ibid at 6, 8.

42 Menard won the election.

43 Picketing and protesting likely played a role in prompting Watson to engage with the situation. Jim Watson, "Aside from Picketing and Protesting What Have You Done?" [referring to Harden and Menard] (September 28, 2018), https://x.com/JimWatsonOttawa/status/1045777458052698112 [perma.cc/866N-JWTT].

44 Crosby, *Resisting Eviction*, at 104–14.
45 The local lawyer was Daniel Tucker-Simmons, who had been involved in tenants' rights legal advocacy in Heron Gate Village since the mass filing of repair/maintenance and abatement applications in 2012.
46 Bill 52, *Protection of Public Participation Act, 2015*, 1st Sess, 41st Leg, Ontario (assented to November 3, 2015), SO 2015, c 23.
47 Crosby, *Resisting Eviction*, at 111.
48 Ibid at 146.
49 Taylor Blewett, "Battle Lines Drawn in Heron Gate, Where an Evicted Community Doesn't Plan on Leaving," *Ottawa Citizen* (August 14, 2018), https://ottawacitizen.com/news/local-news/battle-lines-drawn-in-heron-gate-where-an-evicted-community-doesnt-plan-on-leaving [perma.cc/H77N-9W9A].
50 Crosby, *Resisting Eviction*, at 125.
51 Briefly stated, the five points were nondisplacement, proportion of affordable housing, mixed-size housing, training and employment opportunities for residents as well as community-use facilities, and enhanced green spaces.
52 City of Ottawa, *Official Plan Amendment No. 150* (Ottawa: City of Ottawa, 2017).
53 Antonio Gomez-Palacio, *Heron Gate Village Planning Rationale Report and Urban Design Study* (Ottawa: City of Ottawa, 2019) at 41.
54 Ibid.
55 For an explanation of the genesis of this framework and a critique of its content and application in the Heron Gate Village context, see Crosby, *Resisting Eviction*, at 115–16, 121–25.
56 Gomez-Palacio, *Heron Gate Village*, at 20.
57 City of Ottawa, *Official Plan Amendment 150*, s 2.5.2.
58 City of Ottawa, *Official Plan Amendment No. 10* (Ottawa: City of Ottawa, 2004).
59 ACORN Canada, *The Alternative Vision for Herongate: The Fight for the Right to Housing and No Displacement* (Ottawa: ACORN Canada, 2021), https://acorncanada.org/resources/alternative-vision-herongate/ [perma.cc/854P-QFX4].
60 City of Ottawa, Planning Committee, *Report 47 – Planning Services, Planning, Infrastructure and Economic Development*, ACS2021-PIE-PS-0081 (August 13, 2021) [PIEDD Report] (submitted to the Planning Committee meeting, September 8, 2021).
61 Ibid at 78.
62 City of Ottawa, Planning Committee, *Minutes 47*, Motion No. PLC 2021-47/2 (August 26, 2021).
63 Crosby, *Resisting Eviction*, at 134.
64 One of the amending motions (Motion 59/7) approved called on Timbercreek to engage with the tenants who had been displaced by the demolition-based evictions to inform them that they could apply for a designated affordable housing unit, when available.
65 *ACORN v Ottawa (City)*, 2022 CanLII 42275.
66 *Canadian Charter of Rights and Freedoms*, Part I of the *Constitution Act, 1982*, being Schedule B to the *Canada Act 1982* (UK), 1982, c 11 [Charter].
67 *Human Rights Code*, RSO 1990, c H.19 [ON *HRC*].

68 City of Toronto, *Toronto Municipal Code*, c 667, "Residential and Rental Property Demolition and Conversion Control" (April 29, 2024).

69 City of Toronto, *Toronto Official Plan Indicators (2017)* (Toronto: City of Toronto, 2017) at 22, https://www.toronto.ca/wp-content/uploads/2017/12/8e46-cityplanning-official-plan-indicators-09-22-2017.pdf [perma.cc/X34J-TCMC]; City of Toronto, *Official Plan Indicators (2018)* (Toronto: City of Toronto, 2018) at 30, https://www.toronto.ca/wp-content/uploads/2018/12/84a1-CityPlanning_OfficialPlanIndictors_2018_AODA.pdf [perma.cc/R7M8-URNH].

70 City of Ottawa, "Memo: Review of Tools to Prohibit or Prevent 'Renovictions'" (October 12, 2021) at 12 [copy on file with the author].

71 City of Burnaby, *Council Report – Finalized Tenant Assistance Policy* (March 4, 2020), https://pub-burnaby.escribemeetings.com/filestream.ashx?DocumentId=46014 [perma.cc/CS5X-5QST].

72 There are some limits on the amount of a subsidy or top-up payment when the tenant chooses to relocate to a unit significantly more expensive than the median market rent for the applicable type of unit.

73 City of Burnaby, *Council Report – Finalized Rental Use Zoning Policy* (March 9, 2020), https://pub-burnaby.escribemeetings.com/filestream.ashx?DocumentId=46009 [perma.cc/8Z3S-BT8A].

74 *National Housing Strategy Act*, SC 2019, c 29, s 313 [*NHSA*].

75 See, for example, the following line of cases: *Victoria (City) v Adams*, 2009 BCCA 563; *Abbotsford (City) v Shantz*, 2015 BCSC 1909; *Bamberger v Vancouver (Board of Parks and Recreation)*, 2022 BCSC 49; *Prince George (City) v Stewart*, 2021 BCSC 2089; *The Regional Municipality of Waterloo v Persons Unknown and to Be Ascertained*, 2023 ONSC 670; *The Corporation of the City of Kingston v Doe*, 2023 ONSC 6662.

76 ON *HRC*. The term "accommodation" is used in the code.

77 *Universal Declaration of Human Rights*, UNGA, 3rd Sess, UN Doc A/810 (1948) GA Res 217A (III) [*UDHR*].

78 *International Covenant on Economic, Social and Cultural Rights*, December 16, 1966, 993 UNTS 3 (entered into force January 3, 1976, accession by Canada May 19, 1976) [*ICESCR*].

79 United Nations Committee on Economic, Social and Cultural Rights (UNCESCR), *General Comment No. 4: The Right to Adequate Housing (Art. 11 (1) of the Covenant)*, OHCHR, 6th Sess, UN Doc E/1992/23 (1991).

80 Ibid, art 2.

81 *International Convention on the Elimination of All Forms of Racial Discrimination*, March 7, 1966, 660 UNTS 195 (entered into force January 4, 1969, accession by Canada October 14, 1970) [*ICERD*].

82 Ibid, art 5 (e)(iii).

83 *General Comment No. 7: The Right to Adequate Housing (Art. 11(1)): Forced Evictions*, UNCESCR, 16th Sess (1997) at para 3.

84 *International Covenant on Civil and Political Rights*, December 16, 1966, 999 UNTS 171 (entered into force March 23, 1976, accession by Canada May 19, 1976) [*ICCPR*].

85 *CCPR General Comment No. 27: Article 12 (Freedom of Movement),* OHCHR, 67th Sess, UN Doc CCPR/C/21/Rev.1/Add.9 (1999) (General Comments); see also *Guiding Principles on Internal Displacement,* UNOCHA, UN Doc E/CN.4/1998/53/Add.2 (2004).

86 *Basic Principles and Guidelines on Development-Based Evictions and Displacement,* OHCHR, 4th Sess, UN Doc A/HRC/4/18 (2007) Annex Agenda Item 1 [*BPGs*].

87 Ibid at para 8.

88 Ibid at para 30.

89 Ibid.

90 Ibid at para 32.

91 *Guidelines for the Implementation of the Right to Adequate Housing,* OHCHR, 43rd Sess, UN Doc A/HRC/43/43 (2019) Annex Agenda Item 3.

92 Ibid at para 69(b)(i).

93 Ibid at para 38(b).

94 *Access to Justice for the Right to Housing – Report of the Special Rapporteur on Adequate Housing as a Component of the Right to an Adequate Standard of Living, and on the Right to Non-Discrimination in This Context,* OHCHR, 40th Sess, UN Doc A/HRC/40/61 (2019).

95 Ibid at para 39. For a discussion of the consultation obligations arising under the *UNDRIP,* see Chapter 9 of this collection.

96 Ibid.

97 Crosby, *Resisting Eviction,* at 99.

98 *NHSA*, s 4(a).

99 See the research reports commissioned by the federal housing advocate, including one by ACORN: Bhumika Jhamb and Judy Duncan, *The Impact of Financialization on Tenants* (Ottawa: Office of the Federal Housing Advocate, Canadian Human Rights Commission, 2022), https://homelesshub.ca/resource/impact-financialization-tenants/ [perma.cc/Z9EY-D6ZD].

100 Information on the review panel process, including the hearing record documents, is available at National Housing Council, "Financialization of Purpose-Built Rental Housing" (January 30, 2024), https://nhc-cnl.ca/review-panels/review-2 [perma.cc/Z942-GLJW].

101 National Housing Council, *The Financialization of Purpose-Built Rental Housing Report* (Ottawa: National Housing Council, 2024), https://nhc-cnl.ca/publications/post/review-panel-the-financialization-of-purpose-built-rental-housing-report - [perma.cc/NRU8-598F].

102 Ibid at 13 (emphasis added).

103 Ibid at n20.

104 Leilani Farha and Julieta Perucca, "National Housing Council's Missed Opportunity," *The Hill Times* (June 10, 2024), https://www.hilltimes.com/story/2024/06/10/national-housing-councils-missed-opportunity/424530/ [perma.cc/4TGQ-D5EU].

105 Indeed, and worse, Farha and Perucca, ibid, argue that, "incredulously, the Council then proceeds to make a series of recommendations that benefit financialized landlords."

106 ON *HRC*, s 2(1).

107 Ibid.

108 Ibid.

109 Ibid, s 11(1).

110 *Mohamed Yussuf et al v Timbercreek Asset Management, Mustang Equities Inc, TC Core LP, TC Core GP and the City of Ottawa* (now *Ali v Timbercreek Asset Management Inc*, 2019 HRTO 1058) (Schedule A to Form 1, Applicants at para 145(i)) [*Timbercreek*].

111 See August and Walks, "Gentrification."

112 *Timbercreek* at para 142.

113 Ibid at para 141.

114 Ibid at 36.

115 Ibid at para 141.

116 Ibid at para 145(iii).

117 Ibid. The concept of an "ethnic enclave" was based on Joseph Mensah and Christopher Williams, *Boomerang Ethics: How Racism Affects Us All* (Halifax: Fernwood, 2017), and was applied to Heron Gate Village in expert evidence provided by Mensah for the human rights complaint.

118 Inclusionary zoning is an example of a more systemic mechanism for substantively "righting" applicable legal frameworks in this way since it allows municipalities preemptively to require that a certain proportion of new residential rental housing will be affordable. This mechanism has been introduced only recently in Ontario, and thus far only taken through the steps necessary for implementation in Toronto, but it has existed for some time in many other jurisdictions in the United States and Canada, including Vancouver and Montreal. At the same time, though, the effectiveness of inclusionary zoning can depend on the details of the implementing regulations, and concerns have been raised about ongoing revisions in Ontario. See, for example, Canadian Centre for Housing Rights (CCHR), *Submission to the Ontario Ministry of Municipal Affairs and Housing on Proposed Amendment to O. Reg 232/18: Inclusionary Zoning* (Toronto: CCHR, 2022), https://housingrightscanada.com/wp-content/uploads/2022/12/CCHR-Submission-Ontario-IZ-Reg.-232-18-December.9.2022.pdf [perma.cc/RU5N-QDDH].

119 Staff lawyers at the local community legal clinics were unable to provide much contribution because they were largely unable to justify devoting time to community housing defence campaigns that do not have a sufficient foothold in the legal framework of the *RTA*. The Advocacy Centre for Tenants of Ontario, a specialist legal aid clinic meant to be engaged in systemic legal cases and law reform, did provide consultative advice on the development of the human rights test case but was not able to contribute beyond that given competing priorities (especially once the COVID-19 pandemic arrived and there was a need to address more immediate systemic concerns about introducing a moratorium on evictions and otherwise protecting tenants as a group). The Centre for Equality Rights in Accommodation (now the Canadian Centre for Housing Rights) also provided input on the human rights claim and, together with the Social Rights Advocacy Centre (which also consulted on the claim), produced a detailed report in 2019 on the applicability of international human rights standards to interpretating and applying the duty to accommodate

under the Ontario *Human Rights Code.* Again, these contributions were useful and important, and significant in terms of the organizational time devoted to them, but they remained modest compared with the human and other resources that could be marshalled and applied by Timbercreek.

120 Interestingly, and illustrating the extent to which this access to justice imbalance is also constructed, in February 2019 the new government under Doug Ford shut down a fledgling government agency that had a mandate to provide legal information and other legal assistance to residents seeking to engage development-based changes in their communities. This agency, named the Local Planning Appeal Support Centre, had been established only the preceding April, by what turned out to be the outgoing government under Kathleen Wynne, as part of a broader suite of reforms that sought to address the tendency of the Ontario Municipal Board to side with developers. See Mike Crawley, "Ford Government Shuts Down Agency that Helps People Fight Zoning Appeals," *CBC News* (February 23, 2019), https://www.cbc.ca/news/canada/toronto/doug-ford-closing-local-planning-appeal-support-centre-1.5029624 [perma.cc/2U5J-VZRA].

121 A more systematic approach is illustrated to some extent by the policy framework established by the City of Toronto that is reviewed, and critiqued, from the perspective of access to justice in Right to Housing in Toronto, *Access to Justice for the Right to Housing – Rights Review* (Toronto: Right to Housing in Toronto, 2022), https://right2housingto.ca/wp-content/uploads/2022/01/Rights-Review-Access-to-Justice-full.pdf [perma.cc/KGU5-2FLM].

Part 2

Legal Unhousing of Homeowners

5

The Right to Housing in Mortgage Enforcement Proceedings

Lessons for Canada from South Africa

ANNA JANE SAMIS LUND

A Right to Housing in Mortgage Enforcement Proceedings?

It might seem that there is little scope for the right to housing to make a difference in how lenders enforce mortgages against residential properties, a legal process colloquially referred to as foreclosure. Mortgage enforcement is a form of debtor-creditor law. If a debtor fails to perform their obligations under a contract, then the creditor is entitled to enforce their rights, including their right to sell the house to satisfy the debt. In a mortgage, the creditor's rights are both contractual and proprietary, and this latter status – as a property rights holder – is afforded significant protection in Canadian law. Creditors defend the need for straightforward, inexpensive enforcement mechanisms as foundational to a functioning credit market because they will be reluctant to loan money if they are uncertain about their ability to collect it.[1]

Yet mortgage enforcement proceedings are not merely a form of debt collection. When a debtor has used their house as collateral for a loan, they risk losing that house if they default on the loan. The involuntary loss of a home has significant, negative impacts on the dispossessed residents. They experience stress as they look for a new place to live. Their work lives might be disrupted. Children living in the home might need to relocate to a different school, which disrupts their education.[2] The loss of a home has been associated with mental and physical health problems, including death by suicide.[3] People who undergo foreclosure experience stigma, shame, and ostracism.[4] A forced relocation severs the relationships that a person has with neighbours, depriving them of social supports and eroding the broader community's sense of cohesion and security.[5]

Foreclosures have other impacts on the broader community. They can depress the value of nearby properties, making it more difficult for highly leveraged neighbours to refinance their homes or reducing the prices at which they can sell them.[6] Foreclosures can limit consumer spending and thereby put recessionary pressure on the economy.[7] American research indicates that neighbourhoods with high numbers of foreclosures have lower voter turnout.[8]

Mortgage finance plays a central role in Canada's housing policy. Home ownership has been a significant focus of the Canadian government's housing strategy, and the government has promoted home ownership by encouraging lenders to offer mortgage financing for residential purchases.[9] The home ownership rate in Canada has exceeded 60 percent since 1971, peaking at 69 percent in 2011.[10] Rising consumer debt is driven by rising levels of mortgage debt, attributable in turn to rising housing prices and innovations in mortgage financing, such as reverse mortgages and home equity lines of credit.[11] Many Canadians are highly leveraged, and any disruption to their finances – an illness, a job loss, a relationship breakdown – can trigger financial defaults on their mortgages and put them at risk of losing their homes.

Because foreclosures cause significant individual and collective harm, guardrails are warranted in the process. The law governing mortgage enforcement proceedings – as written by legislators and applied by courts – should ensure that individuals are not unnecessarily unhoused following a mortgage default. Avoiding unnecessary unhousing means, at a minimum, ensuring that a borrower can remain in their house when there is a financial solution that will allow them to bring their mortgage into good standing.

South Africa offers a model for Canada to learn from regarding how a lender's enforcement rights can be qualified to avoid unnecessary unhousing.[12] When the Republic of South Africa adopted its modern, post-apartheid constitution in 1996, it included the "right to have access to adequate housing."[13] South African courts and legislators have considered how mortgage enforcement proceedings can be carried out in a manner consistent with the borrower's constitutional right to have access to adequate housing. The resulting case law and statutory interventions point toward general guidelines that can be used to evaluate mortgage enforcement proceedings and specific aspects of foreclosure practice that warrant careful consideration. This chapter canvasses the lessons that Canada might take from South Africa. I argue that the South African experience is relevant in Canada, even in the absence of comparable constitutional protections, because the South African legal developments engage with two issues that arise in Canadian foreclosure proceedings: the negative impacts of unhousing on the residents of the home, and the power imbalance that exists between lenders and borrowers.

The South African Constitution and the Right to Housing

In the 1990s, South Africa transitioned from a racially segregated apartheid state, governed by a white minority, into a multiracial democracy. As part of this transition, South Africans drafted two constitutions: an interim constitution, which came into effect on April 27, 1994, and a subsequent final constitution, which came into effect on February 4, 1997, and remains in force.[14] The final constitution contained a *Bill of Rights* that provides for a number of socio-economic rights: to food and water, health care, social security, education, and, of particular interest for this chapter, housing.[15] The socio-economic rights in the South African *Bill of Rights* were modelled on those contained in the *International Covenant on Economic, Social and Cultural Rights* (*ICESCR*)[16] but have a long history of development by successive generations of the anti-apartheid activists in South Africa.[17]

The *Bill of Rights* declares that everyone has the right "to have access to adequate housing."[18] Importantly, the right is to *access* housing, not to housing per se. Geoff Bundlender, who acted as counsel for amicus in the first South African case to consider the right to adequate housing, argues that this declaration places an obligation on the state not to deprive people of access to housing.[19] Lufuno Nevondwe and Kola Odeku indicate that this wording means the state must create "an enabling environment in which individuals are able to realize the right for themselves."[20]

This general declaration is accompanied by two additional provisions, which impose both positive obligations and negative restrictions on the state and private parties.[21] The *Bill of Rights* obliges the state to "take reasonable legislative and other measures, within its available resources, to achieve the progressive realisation" of the right to housing.[22] It also restricts the state and private parties, including financial institutions, from evicting someone from their home "without an order of court made after considering all relevant circumstances."[23] This negative right creates procedural and substantive protections for occupiers: procedurally, an eviction cannot occur without "judicial authorization"; substantively, the court tasked with authorizing the eviction must first take account of all the "relevant circumstances."[24]

It is permissible for parties to infringe the rights contained in the South African *Bill of Rights,* including the right to housing. The South African Constitution contains a section, based on Section 1 of the *Canadian Charter of Rights and Freedoms,* providing that the rights in the *Bill of Rights* can be limited by "a law of general application to the extent that the limitation is reasonable and justifiable in an open and democratic society based on human dignity, equality and freedom."[25] The provision includes a nonexhaustive list of five factors that a court should consider when deciding whether a limitation is justifiable, including "the nature of the right, the importance of the purpose of the limitation, the nature and extent of the limitation, the relation between the limitation and its purpose, and less restrictive means to achieve its purpose."[26] These factors were derived, in part, from Supreme Court of Canada jurisprudence on Section 1 of the Charter.[27]

The Right to Housing Applied to Mortgage Enforcement Proceedings

The right to housing has led courts and legislators in South Africa to think differently about mortgage enforcement proceedings. Writing in 2015, Reghard Brits described a radical shift that "changes the traditionally unqualified right of the [lender] ... into one that is qualified by a human-rights norm that is external to the agreement between the parties and the private-law rules governing their relationship."[28] Brits was referring to the effect of a pair of cases in South Africa's highest court, the Constitutional Court. This section starts with a brief introduction to these two foundational cases: *Jaftha v Schoeman*[29] and *Gundwana v Steko Development CC.*[30]

Foundational Cases

Jaftha v Schoeman was not about mortgage enforcement but dealt with the related area of judgment enforcement law.[31] A judgment is a court order requiring one party (a debtor) to pay another (a creditor). The debtor has not specifically pledged their house to pay the debt; however, if the debtor does not comply with the order to pay, then the creditor has tools to forcibly recover the debt. In South Africa, the judgment enforcement rules allowed creditors to sell a debtor's house without court oversight.[32] The court was asked whether these rules violated the debtor's right to access adequate housing.

The Constitutional Court held that court oversight is required when a judgment creditor forces the sale of a debtor's home. The oversight ensures that sales are not allowed when the harm to the debtor would be disproportionate to any benefit to the creditor. For example, in the *Jaftha* case, the debtors were both impoverished women and would have been rendered homeless if the creditors were allowed to take their homes. Not only would the debtors have lost their current homes, they would not have been able to acquire replacement housing. The benefit to the creditor was likely meagre: the initial debts that the women owed were small, under CAD$100.[33] The court held that the existing judgment enforcement rules infringed the debtor's right to access adequate housing to the extent that they allowed creditors to sell homes in such circumstances.

The court revised the applicable rules to require judicial oversight of the judgment enforcement process. Under the revised rules, before a court allows a creditor to sell a debtor's home, it must weigh the impacts on the debtor against the benefits to the creditor.[34] A court needs to consider relevant factors, including whether there are other ways for the creditor to collect the debt (e.g., through an instalment payment plan), whether the sale will render the debtor "completely homeless," how significant or trifling the debt is to the creditor trying to collect it, and how the debt arose, including whether the debtor acted recklessly in incurring it.[35]

It was not initially obvious how *Jaftha* would apply to mortgage enforcement proceedings because of an important difference between judgments and mortgages. A judgment creditor has a court order requiring the debtor to pay a debt, and the creditor is entitled to recover the amount owing from the debtor's property and income, including the debtor's house. However, the debtor has not specifically pledged their house as collateral for the debt, which is what a debtor does in a mortgage transaction. In a mortgage transaction, the borrower commits to repaying a debt and provides the lender with additional assurance by granting the lender property rights to their home, including the right to sell it if the borrower defaults on their repayment obligations. The court in *Jaftha* suggested that the connection between the house and the debt in mortgage enforcement proceedings is important:

> If the judgment debtor willingly put his or her house up in some or other manner as security for the debt, a sale in execution should ordinarily be permitted where there has not been an abuse of court procedure. The need to ensure that homes may be used by people to raise capital is an important aspect of the value of a home which courts must be careful to acknowledge.[36]

In *Gundwana v Steko Development CC,* the Constitutional Court clarified that the requirement for judicial oversight set out in *Jaftha* also applied to mortgage enforcement proceedings. A judicial officer had to consider the specific facts of each case and ensure that the harm to the debtor was not disproportionate to the benefit to the creditor. The court identified which considerations might be relevant, and there was significant overlap with the list from *Jaftha:* whether the property was the debtor's primary home, whether the debtor was indigent to such a degree that selling their home would render them homeless, and whether there was another reasonable way for the creditor to collect the amount owed.[37]

The court in *Gundwana* addressed the distinction that *Jaftha* had drawn between judgment enforcement and mortgage enforcement proceedings. It held that even when a person has voluntarily encumbered their home with a mortgage, they have not waived their right to housing, including the requirement for court oversight of any legal process that might result in eviction.[38] But the right to access adequate housing did not bar creditors from enforcing against a home. The court characterized execution (i.e., enforcement against homes) as part of "normal economic life" and indicated that the court should prevent a creditor from carrying out an execution only where there was a disproportionate impact between the method of execution and alternative means of extracting payment.[39] This focus on the proportionality of the impact of the foreclosure flows from the structure of the South African Constitution, which allows for infringements of a constitutionally protected right if they are reasonable and justifiable.[40]

The impact of the right to housing on mortgage enforcement proceedings extends beyond the requirement for judicial oversight. South African courts have articulated principles that apply when assessing existing mortgage enforcement practices against the right to housing. They have considered what that right means in the context of specific issues such as the creditor's right to accelerate a mortgage debt or charge their legal expenses to the debtor. In the balance of this section, I consider, first, the general principles articulated by the South African courts and, second, the specific aspects of mortgage practice that have been evaluated against the right to housing. The cases discussed below have been decided by the following courts, listed in ascending order of authority: the High Courts (of which there are nine divisions, covering nine provinces in South Africa), the Supreme Court of Appeal, and the Constitutional Court.[41] Legislators have also acted to protect homeowners in foreclosure proceedings, and I describe the relevant statutory interventions below.

General Principles

Three general principles emerge from the South African cases on how the right to housing applies to mortgage enforcement proceedings: (1) foreclosures of residential homes require processes different from foreclosures of other properties; (2) courts need to be sensitive to the specific facts of each case when deciding whether a foreclosure is warranted; and (3) courts need to make decisions about foreclosures in the context of a significant power imbalance between creditors and debtors. I consider each of these principles in turn.

Greater Care Is Required when Foreclosing Against a Home

A key insight flowing from South African law is that not all mortgage enforcement proceedings require the same level of procedural protections for borrowers: greater care is required when the property in question is the residence of the borrower.[42] The right to access adequate housing is implicated only when a debtor is at risk of losing their primary residence, and thus the courts draw a distinction between enforcement proceedings against a primary residence and foreclosures against other properties. Of course, an owner's income property might be a tenant's home, and foreclosure on it can have significant, negative impacts on the tenant. The question of which protections tenants should be afforded in foreclosure proceedings is important and warrants further analysis.

Whether a Foreclosure Sale Is Justifiable Is Fact Specific

Under South African law, foreclosures are not inconsistent with the constitutional right to housing; rather, courts must determine whether a foreclosure is justified *in this case.* By asking courts to analyze "all relevant circumstances," the South African *Bill of Rights* invites courts to compare the relative impacts of the mortgage enforcement proceedings on both debtor and creditor.

Not all debtors are equally affected by foreclosure proceedings against a home, and there are different types of impacts that a court might evaluate. British academic Susan Bright distinguishes between two types of impacts of home loss on debtors. She describes them in terms of the stories that debtors can tell in legal unhousing proceedings: a personal financial story and a home story. The former explains why a person has "fallen into debt" and describes their prospects for bringing the debt into good standing.[43] The latter is broader and accounts for the "emotional, social and practical" consequences of losing a home.[44] For example, an elderly resident who loses a home might be forced to move away from their support network, or a child whose family is unhoused might be forced to switch schools, disrupting their education.

The Constitutional Court in *Jaftha* invited courts to consider the personal financial stories of debtors but allowed that other factors might be relevant. It summed up the potentially relevant factors as follows:

> the circumstances in which the debt was incurred; any attempts made by the debtor to pay off the debt; the financial situation of the parties; the amount of the debt; whether the debtor is employed or has a source of income to pay off the debt and any other factor relevant to the particular facts of the case before the court.[45]

South African courts can use the open-ended category of "other relevant factors" to take account of the personal home stories of borrowers. And they do. Courts pay attention to whether a foreclosure will result in an individual being completely homeless, meaning that they lose the foreclosed property and are unable to find "suitable alternative accommodation."[46] By considering this factor, courts look beyond whether individuals have financial solutions to their defaults. However, courts are limited in their ability to take account of the emotional, social, and practical consequences of a foreclosure on a debtor, because borrowers are infrequently before the courts, and evidence of these impacts is usually primarily or exclusively in their control.

The courts consider the impacts on creditors too. Both the amount owing to a creditor and the impact of nonpayment on the creditor are relevant considerations. The court in *Jaftha* recognized that part of this analysis was subjective to the creditor: "What might seem trifling to an affluent observer might not be trifling to a poor creditor reliant on his or her ability to recover debts."[47] Reflecting this subjective assessment, the High Court in *Ntsane* characterized the R18.46 (approximately CAD$3.32 in 2023) owed to the lender a "piffling" amount, especially given that the lender was "part of a multibillion Rand international financial conglomerate."[48] Forcing a debtor out of their home is less justifiable when the lender can easily absorb the losses stemming from nonpayment of the mortgage debt.

Foreclosure Proceedings and the Power Imbalance Between Creditors and Debtors

South African courts strive to balance the rights of creditors and debtors, but they are also alive to the power imbalance between these two parties.

Lenders are commonly more legally sophisticated and better resourced than borrowers. Thus, to strike a fair balance, courts must first address this power differential. One way in which this imbalance manifests itself is that debtors are often absent from foreclosure proceedings because of the various barriers to participation, including borrowers' lack of awareness of their legal rights and lack of resources.[49]

South African courts have addressed the power imbalance between creditors and debtors by taking active steps to protect the latter's interests. This active judicial stance is a departure from the traditional approach to adversarial litigation, premised on party autonomy and party prosecution.[50] In the adversarial model, "courts function as impartial arbiters ... They depend on the parties to present the evidence and relevant arguments fully and skillfully."[51] If a party is provided with adequate notice of the hearing and does not attend it, then the court assumes that the decision was deliberate and does not advance arguments on behalf of the absent party.[52] However, to the extent that this model is premised on a contest between two parties with equal capacity to advance their cases, in practice it benefits the "wealthier, more experienced and better organized party."[53]

The assumption that litigants make deliberate choices about which defences to advance does not hold in foreclosure proceedings in South Africa. The reality is that debtors are frequently absent because of their lack of power, resources, and knowledge. Courts respond to a debtor's absence in at least three ways. First, they recognize that they must often act of their own accord (*mero moto*) to ensure that constitutionally protected rights are not infringed.[54] Contrary to the role of the judge in a purely adversarial system, South African judges raise issues not raised by litigants. Second, they may appoint amicus to argue a debtor's case or grant public interest standing to organizations prepared to represent debtors in foreclosure litigation.[55] Third, creditors have been directed to treat the proceedings as de facto without notice proceedings with concomitant heightened disclosure obligations. The absence of the defendant means that the lender is "duty bound" to disclose all relevant facts in their materials.[56]

Because of the barriers to debtors actively engaging in court processes, South African courts have recognized that giving debtors the ability to revisit a decision after it has been made is not equivalent to having the decision made properly in the first instance. In both *Jaftha* and *Gundwana,* the creditors had argued that judicial oversight was not required for every warrant or order making property executable because a dissatisfied borrower could always return to court to have the warrant or order reconsidered once they became aware of it.[57] The Constitutional Court disagreed with this argument in both cases, holding that it was important for courts to evaluate prospectively the propriety of each sale because many borrowers would be unaware of the provisions allowing them to have a warrant or order reconsidered or "too poor to make proper use of them."[58] The benefit of judicial oversight is that it "takes place invariably without prompting by the debtor."[59]

Specific Issues

In addition to general themes, South African case law can be read for insights into how specific aspects of foreclosure practice can be modified to prevent unnecessary unhousing. Many of the issues addressed by South African courts are relevant to the issues that arise in mortgage enforcement practice in Canada, including overseeing the fees and costs claimed by the lender, limiting the lender's right of acceleration, allowing insolvency law to provide debt relief to borrowers, and ensuring the adequacy of the sale price.

Overseeing the Lender's Fees and Costs

The amount owing on a mortgage usually increases as mortgage proceedings unfold. Over time, the principal accrues interest, the borrower can incur penalty fees, and the borrower might be liable for the lender's costs of enforcement. In South Africa, as in Canada, borrowers are commonly required by the terms of the mortgage to pay any cost that the lender incurs to enforce its rights after a default by the borrower.[60] As the amount owing increases, it becomes more difficult for the borrower to avoid foreclosure by paying down the debt. For example, in the *Jaftha* case, one of the debtors initially borrowed R250, made a number of payments toward the principal over the years (including payments of R300 and R200), but lost her house in a foreclosure sale after being advised that she owed an additional R7,000.[61]

One way that foreclosure law can ensure that borrowers are not unnecessarily unhoused is to guard against excessive claims for costs or other fees by lenders. The relatively disempowered position of many borrowers makes them ill suited to challenge excessive claims for costs or other fees, and thus other oversight mechanisms are necessary.

In South Africa, courts have performed an oversight function to protect debtors from losing their homes based on excessive claims for costs and fees. In the 2006 case of *ABSA Bank v Ntsane,* the High Court dealt with the question of penalty fees. It criticized the lender for not providing a breakdown of how much of the balance owing comprised penalty fees. The court wanted to know whether the credit arrangement had been profitable for the lender because of the default fees collected.[62] The question of whether the creditor was losing money or had profited factored into whether it was proportional for the court to allow execution against a residence.

In the 2015 case of *Nkata v First Rand Bank*, the Constitutional Court held that there must be an oversight process for ensuring that any costs that a lender added to a mortgage were "reasonable." The defendant's property had been sold, and the defendant had turned to the courts for relief. The High Court raised (of its own volition) the question of whether the defendant had reinstated the mortgage, thus precluding sale of the property.[63] The defendant had paid, at one point, all of the arrears owing on the mortgage but not the additional enforcement costs incurred by the lender in the proceedings. To reinstate the mortgage, a debtor must pay the reasonable costs of enforcement. Thus, the case that eventually reached the Constitutional Court turned on what amounted to reasonable costs of enforcement.

In a 7:2 decision, the Constitutional Court held that, for costs to be reasonable, the lender must provide notice of them to the borrower and then either have the quantum of costs agreed to by the borrower or reviewed using the court's taxation process.[64] The lender in *Nkata* had not taken these steps, but rather had merely added the costs of enforcement onto the debtor's mortgage account. These steps were insufficient to satisfy the reasonableness test, and the court held that the debtor had reinstated the mortgage even though they had not paid the lender's enforcement costs.[65]

Limiting the Creditor's Right to Acceleration and Safeguarding the Debtor's Right of Reinstatement

In addition to costs, fees, and interest, the amount owing on a mortgage can be affected by a creditor's right of acceleration. Consider how that right operates. Some mortgages are payable on demand, meaning that the lender can ask the borrower to pay the full amount of the mortgage immediately. Other mortgages are structured such that the borrower only owes periodic payments over the term of the loan, with the full amount being owed on the maturity date of the mortgage. However, if the borrower defaults on the periodic payments, then typically the lender will have a contractual right of acceleration, allowing them to claim the full amount owing. When a lender can rely on this right, they will significantly increase how much is owing on a mortgage and how much a borrower needs to pay to avoid losing their home (i.e., unpaid arrears versus the full balance of the loan).

The right of acceleration can affect how courts evaluate the impacts of foreclosures on creditors. Recall that the amount owing is one of the "relevant factors" that a court will consider when determining whether the sale of a residence is justifiable. Courts have to determine whether the amount owing on a periodic mortgage means the unpaid arrears only or the full balance owing after the creditor exercises their right of acceleration. Initially, the courts offered conflicting answers. In the 2006 case of *ABSA Bank v Ntsane,* the High Court held that it should take account of the arrears only.[66] Where the borrower's arrears were not very sizable, it would ordinarily violate the borrower's right to housing for a court to grant an order for execution against the home because small amounts could be collected through other means.[67] Conversely, in the 2011 case of *Nedbank Limited v Fraser,* the High Court took account of the full balance of the loan.[68] Brits and Van Der Walt criticized the court in *Fraser* as being inconsistent with the constitutional requirement of "develop[ing] the common law so as to promote the spirit, purport and object of the *Bill of Rights.*"[69]

A creditor's ability to rely on the right of acceleration has been affected by legislative developments. In 2007, the *National Credit Act, 2005,* came into force, and it applies to mortgages.[70] The act provides debtors with the right of reinstatement, which enables them to reinstate a mortgage by paying the arrears plus default charges and reasonable costs of enforcement.[71] Prior to this provision coming into force, a debtor could redeem their mortgage right up to the time of sale but had to pay the entire accelerated amount.[72] The new legislation resolved the issue that the courts tackled in *Ntsane* and *Fraser,* but the courts then needed to determine how long the statutory right of reinstatement lasted or, put differently, at what stage in the foreclosure proceedings this right was terminated.

The South African courts interpreted the statutory right of reinstatement generously, ensuring that borrowers can avoid the loss of a home up to a late point in the foreclosure process: when the property is sold and the proceeds of the sale are realized. The Constitutional Court adopted this approach in the 2016 case of *Nkata.*[73] This holding means that the right continues to exist even once a lender has been granted a monetary judgment for the amount outstanding on a mortgage and an order declaring the property to be specifically executable. The right to housing was not implicated in the *Nkata* case because the property subject to foreclosure was not the debtor's residence (and the debtor owned other properties); however, the majority judgment was attuned to the power imbalance between creditors and debtors and noted that the *National Credit Act* was designed to address that imbalance.[74]

In 2014, the legislature changed the wording in the *National Credit Act* to allow the consumer to "remedy a default" rather than "reinstate an agreement."[75] These amendments were not considered in the *Nkata* case because the underlying facts preceded them. It was unclear whether the holding in *Nkata* had been changed by the amendments. In the 2018 case of *Absa Bank Limited v Mokebe,* a three-member bench of the High Court reconfirmed the *Nkata* holding.[76] The court held that interpreting the provision to preserve the right of reinstatement until the time of sale best aligned with the borrower's constitutional right to access adequate housing.[77]

Allowing Insolvency Law to Provide Debt Relief to Borrowers

A debtor at risk of losing their home through foreclosure can turn to insolvency law. In Canada, personal insolvency law generally does not provide a debtor with any relief from their mortgage obligations, but they can use it to reduce other debts and thereby make it easier to pay their mortgage. In South Africa, personal insolvency law provides some relief to debtors from their mortgage obligations. South African courts have held that foreclosure should be a last resort, and one way to ensure this is to give debtors the opportunity to use personal insolvency proceedings before lenders are allowed to sell their homes.

To understand how South African insolvency law interfaces with foreclosure proceedings, it helps to know the manner of debt relief provided to mortgage holders by South African insolvency law. Under the *National Credit Act,* a borrower can apply to a debt counsellor to rearrange debt payments to avoid foreclosure.[78] The counsellor makes a proposal to the debtor and their creditors about how the debtor's payment obligations should be rearranged.[79] The debtor and creditors can accept the counsellor's proposal, or the counsellor can refer it to the court to be imposed on the affected parties.[80] If a debtor applies for debt relief before a lender starts mortgage enforcement proceedings, then the lender is stayed from taking enforcement steps until the debt relief process concludes.[81] After a mortgage enforcement proceeding is commenced, a borrower can raise their overindebtedness as an issue in the enforcement proceedings, or the court can take account of the borrower's overindebtedness of its own volition. Once the debtor's overindebtedness has been raised, the court can either grant a rearrangement order or refer the debtor's case to a debt counsellor.[82] If a court makes a referral to a counsellor, then the court would stay the mortgage proceedings while the counsellor is working out a rearrangement.[83]

In the 2009 case of *Firstrand Bank v Maleke,* the High Court indicated that borrowers might be entitled to access debt relief proceedings prior to losing their homes through foreclosure. The case involved multiple applications by lenders to sell the homes of four disadvantaged borrowers, all but one of whom owed small sums in arrears on their mortgages.[84] The defendants had not appeared to defend the claims. The court declined to grant the lenders their requested orders, noting instead that the defendants had been paying the mortgages for long periods of time (thirteen to nineteen years), likely had significant equity in their homes, and owed relatively minor arrears.[85] The court determined that the borrowers should be afforded opportunities to pay off their arrears in some other manner. The court also noted that the borrowers' cases were "ideally suited" for referral to a debt counsellor.[86] At the time, courts could not refer a matter to a counsellor directly, but subsequent amendments to the *National Credit Act* empowered them to make such a referral.[87]

Brits and Van Der Walt argue that the *Maleke* approach is the preferable way to reconcile the housing rights of borrowers with the property and contractual rights of lenders. Borrowers should be referred to debt counselling; if they are unable to come up with a debt rearrangement, then a court can safely assume – absent exceptional circumstances – that no alternative method of payment is possible and that execution against the home is justified as a collection measure of last resort.[88]

Ensuring an Adequate Sale Price

A perennial concern in mortgage enforcement proceedings is to guard against a borrower's property being sold for less than it is worth. If a borrower has equity in the home, then selling it below its market value deprives the borrower of that equity. If a borrower is in a deficiency position (i.e., the amount owed exceeds the value of the home), then selling the property below its market value will increase the deficiency for which they might be liable.[89] A borrower who loses equity or incurs an inflated deficiency judgment because of an improvidently low sale price is in a worse position financially than one whose house is sold at a reasonable price, and the resulting financial hardship can make it difficult for them to secure replacement housing.

In mortgage enforcement proceedings, the home is sold by the lender rather than the borrower/owner. There is a risk that the lender will not take sufficient steps to maximize the sale price because many of the costs of a sale below market value are borne by the borrower and not the lender. For example, if the amount owing on the mortgage ($300,000) is less than the value of the home at a reasonable sale price ($500,000), then the lender has little economic motivation to try to sell the home for more than the balance of the mortgage. Here, if the lender sells the home for $350,000, they recover the full amount owing on the mortgage, and the lost equity ($150,000) is borne by the borrower.

In the 2018 case of *Absa Bank Limited v Mokebe*, the High Court was asked whether courts should be setting a reserve price when a borrower's primary residence is sold in foreclosure proceedings. A reserve price is a minimum amount that a purchaser must offer for the home to be sold, and it guards against a sale at an improvidently low price. The High Court held that generally courts should set reserve prices. It allowed that there can be exceptional circumstances in which a court would be justified in not setting a reserve price but noted that such circumstances would be rare.[90] It connected the idea of setting a reserve price to the constitutional right to access adequate housing, noting that the "relevant circumstances" that a court must consider include "a proper valuation of the property (under oath)."[91] It also noted that setting a reserve price protected borrowers against the unjust outcome of losing equity that they had built up in their homes or being held liable for a deficiency.[92]

Applying the Lessons from South Africa in Canada

Canadians can draw concrete lessons from South Africa regarding how foreclosure practice can be modified to protect borrowers from being unnecessarily unhoused. None of the South African modifications has prevented lenders from selling the collateral when there is no alternative way to collect the amount owing. However, the modifications ensure that other financial solutions – including reinstatement and insolvency – are explored before a home is sold, and they protect debtors from the unfairness that can arise from excessive costs and fees, premature acceleration, and inadequate sale prices. Judicial oversight plays a central role in ensuring that debtors are treated fairly because of the barriers that they face in advocating for themselves during the foreclosure process.[93] This last point is particularly salient in Canada, where some provinces require judicial oversight of foreclosure proceedings and others allow for sales without such oversight.

Canadian courts have evidenced reluctance to apply South African case law on the right to housing, noting that Canada does not have a constitutionally protected housing right.[94] The Charter's section 7 protection of "life, liberty and security of the person" has been interpreted by courts to provide a right to shelter in cases such as *Victoria (City) v Adams* and *Regional Municipality of Waterloo v Persons Unknown and to Be Ascertained*, but so far courts have held that this right is limited to erect shelters in public spaces when there are insufficient alternative housing options in a municipality.[95]

Canada is a signatory to international agreements that protect a more robust right to housing, including the *ICESCR.* Article 11 of the covenant recognizes that all people have a right to adequate housing, including limits on when and how a person can be evicted.[96] The South African case law reflects principles applicable to Canada as a signatory of the covenant. The courts' proportional weighing of harm to creditors and debtors coheres with the general principle of proportionality that state parties to the covenant must ensure govern evictions.[97]

Yet the " 'transmission belt' model of international human rights" requires states to implement these legal protections by transposing them to state law.[98] The federal government has incorporated a right to housing into the *National Housing Strategy Act,* but this provision is not self-evidently justiciable.[99] Moreover, this federal legislation is not binding on provincial and territorial governments, which are largely responsible for the laws governing mortgage enforcement proceedings.[100]

To complicate matters further, South Africa and Canada have different social, historical, and political contexts. The history of apartheid and arbitrary evictions of Black South Africans plays a role in the South African jurisprudence on the right to access adequate housing.[101] Residential segregation was a key element of the apartheid regime in South Africa and was achieved through laws that restricted where Black South Africans could own land and then facilitated their eviction from land that they were deemed incapable of owning.[102] The drafters of the post-apartheid constitution included protection from arbitrary evictions as a response to this "shameful history."[103] Many of the cases that have considered the right to housing in South Africa have arisen in response to the rapid urbanization that followed the relaxation of apartheid controls on where Black South Africans can live.[104] Canada has its own history of settler colonialism and dispossession of Indigenous Peoples that must be accounted for when analyzing housing in this country.[105] One must proceed cautiously when engaging with constitutional concepts from another country where the context is different.[106]

Despite the differences between Canada and South Africa, they share a constitutional heritage. The Charter and the case law interpreting it were used as models for some of the provisions in the *Constitution of the Republic of South Africa,* and subsequent Canadian case law has been influential in the Constitutional Court's interpretation of the constitution.[107] Additionally, the South African courts have produced a robust body of case law that addresses mortgage enforcement practices that will be familiar to those involved in foreclosures in Canada. Given these similarities in constitutional principles and mortgage practices, Canadians considering how the right to housing should inform mortgage enforcement proceedings can look to South African courts for direction. Canadian courts and legislators need not blindly follow the South African model but can use it to "test [our] understanding of [our] own traditions and possibilities by examining them in the reflection of [South Africa's experience]."[108]

The lessons from South Africa have purchase beyond the question of how we might implement a right to housing in Canada. The rights in South Africa's *Bill of Rights* invite courts and legislators to pay attention to the important individual interests at stake in legal disputes.[109] By focusing attention on the individual, the *Bill of Rights* invites South African courts to consider the personal circumstances and the relative power or powerlessness of litigants when granting judicial remedies against them. Legislators in South Africa have responded too, passing legislation such as the *National Credit Act* designed to address the power differential and avoid unnecessary foreclosures. This focus on individual experience and litigants' relative power has enabled South African courts and legislators to reshape foreclosure practice to be more responsive to the lived realities of borrowers and lenders rather than the theoretical abstractions for whom the adversarial model works well. This careful contextual approach is warranted in Canada because similar considerations apply in foreclosure proceedings here: there is a power imbalance between creditors and borrowers, and the latter experience serious, negative impacts following the involuntary loss of a house. For decades, the federal government has afforded a central role in its housing policy to home ownership through mortgage financing; however, unless sufficient attention is paid to how Canadians fare when they cannot meet their mortgage obligations, the overall impact of this system will be to undermine the dignity and well-being of Canadians. By drawing on the lessons from South Africa, Canadian courts and legislators can minimize the harms that result when people default on their mortgages.

Acknowledgments

This chapter has benefited immensely from the research and editorial contributions of Rukayat Edidi, Jessica Csandl, and Eli Ziff and feedback from many people, including Reghard Brits, Sarah Buhler, Jessica Eisen, the participants in the 2023 Canadian Commercial Law Symposium, and the anonymous peer reviewers. All errors are my own.

Notes

1 On a variation of this argument in the insolvency context, see Anna Lund, "Engaging Canadians in Commercial Law Reform: Insights and Lessons from the 2014 Industry Canada Consultation on Insolvency Legislation" (2016) 58:2 *Canadian Business Law Journal* 123–64 at 155–56.

2 Matthew Desmond, *Evicted: Poverty and Profit in the American City* (New York: Crown Publishing Group, 2016) at 296.

3 In the context of foreclosures, see Jason N. Houle and Danya E. Keene, "Getting Sick and Falling Behind: Health and the Risk of Mortgage Default and Home Foreclosure" (2015) 69:4 *Journal of Epidemiology and Community Health* 382–87; Theresa L. Osypuk, Cleopatra Howard Caldwell, Robert Platt, and Dawn Misra, "The Consequences of Foreclosure for Depressive Symptomatology" (2012) 22:6 *Annals of Epidemiology* 379–87. In the context of other unhousing processes, see Anna Lund, "Tenant Protections in Mobile Home Park Closures" (2021) 53:3 *University of British Columbia Law Review* 753–834 at 780; Esther Sullivan, *Manufactured Insecurity: Mobile Home Parks and Americans' Tenuous Right to Place* (Oakland: University of California Press, 2018) at 8, 122–24, 147, 150.

4 Kathryn Marie Dudley, *Debt and Dispossession: Farm Loss in America's Heartland* (Chicago: University of Chicago Press, 2000) at 129–36.

5 David H. Kaplan and Gail G. Sommers, "An Analysis of the Relationship Between Housing Foreclosures, Lending Practices, and Neighborhood Ecology: Evidence from a Distressed County" (2009) 61:1 *Professional Geographer* 101–20. See also Lund, "Tenant Protections," at 780–81; Sullivan, *Manufactured Insecurity,* at 117–18, 145; Desmond, *Evicted,* at 70.

6 Atif Mian and Amir Sufi, *House of Debt: How They (and You) Caused the Great Recession, and How We Can Prevent It from Happening Again* (Chicago: University of Chicago Press, 2014) at 27.

7 Ibid at 39–43.

8 Andrew Hall, Jesse Yoder, and Nishant Karandikar, "Economic Distress and Voting: Evidence from the Subprime Mortgage Crisis" (2017), Working Paper, https://doi.org/10.31235/osf.io/9ptqc; Vanesa Estrada-Correa and Martin Johnson, "Foreclosure Depresses Voter Turnout: Neighbourhood Disruption and the 2008 Presidential Election in California" (2012) 93:3 *Social Science Quarterly* 559–76.

9 Anna Lund, "Uncertainty over the Scope of Borrower Protections in Mortgage Enforcement Proceedings in Alberta: The Problems and Potential Solutions" (2023) 60:4 *Alberta Law Review* 905–31 at 913 (describing some of these initiatives). See also Jason Stuart Leslie, "The Financialization of Housing in Canada and Federally-Backed Mortgage Securitization: Public Risks, Private Benefits" (PhD diss., University of British Columbia, 2022) [unpublished]; Chapter 6 of this collection.

10 Statistics Canada, "The Homeownership Rate in Canada Is Beginning to Decline from its Peak in 2011" (November 21, 2022), https://www150.statcan.gc.ca/n1/daily-quotidien/220921/cg-b001-eng.htm [perma.cc/XL8H-9V5C]; Statistics Canada, "Homeownership Rate Declines from 2011 to 2021 in All Provinces and Territories, Except in the Northwest Territories" (November 21, 2022), https://www150.statcan.gc.ca/n1/daily-quotidien/220921/mc-b001-eng.htm [perma.cc/U3BH-ZG3P].

11 Statistics Canada, *What Do We Know About Homeownership and Mortgage Debt in Canada?*, Catalogue No. 11-627-M (Ottawa: Statistics Canada, August 8, 2019), https://www150.statcan.gc.ca/n1/en/pub/11-627-m/11-627-m2019054-eng.pdf?st=vzfJ863V [perma.cc/4HYG-KJF5]; Lawrence L. Schembri, "The Long-Term Evolution of House Prices: An International Perspective" (August 25, 2015), https://www.bankofcanada.ca/2015/08/long-term-evolution-house-prices/ [perma.cc/6YPD-648Y]; Stephen S. Poloz, "Canada's Economy and the Household Debt: How Big Is the Problem?" (May 1, 2018), https://www.bankofcanada.ca/2018/05/canada-economy-household-debt-how-big-the-problem/ [perma.cc/GX8G-J7E7]; Raj K. Chawla and Sharanjit Uppal, *Household Debt in Canada,* component of Catalogue No. 75-001-X (Ottawa: Statistics Canada, March 23, 2012), https://www150.statcan.gc.ca/n1/en/pub/75-001-x/2012002/article/11636-eng.pdf?st=DwjLazPh, at 4 [perma.cc/QCZ3-2KTF]. For a discussion of how mortgage securitization is connected to household indebtedness, see Chapter 6 of this collection.

12 The approach suggested here is one of engagement – Canadian courts and legislators can be "informed but not controlled" by South African law. See Vicki C. Jackson, "Constitutional Comparisons: Convergence, Resistance, Engagement" (2005) 119:1 *Harvard Law Review* 109–28 at 112.

13 *Constitution of the Republic of South Africa, 1996*, No 108 of 1996, s 26 [*Constitution of South Africa*]; Sandra Liebenberg, *Socio-Economic Rights: Adjudication Under a Transformative Constitution* (Claremont, South Africa: Juta, 2010).

14 For a concise overview of this process, see Eric C. Christiansen, "Adjudicating Non-Justiciable Rights: Socio-Economic Rights and the South African Constitutional Court" (2007) 38:2 *Columbia Human Rights Law Review* 321–86 at 325–28. For a comprehensive description of the process, see Hassen Ebrahim, *The Soul of a Nation: Constitution-Making in South Africa* (Cape Town: Oxford University Press, 1998).

15 *Constitution of South Africa*, ss 26–27, 29. Children are also provided with enhanced socio-economic rights in a stand-alone provision (s 28). There were fewer socio-economic rights in the Interim Constitution as a result of the National Party's greater influence on the content of that document (see Christiansen, "Adjudicating Non-Justiciable Rights," at 335).

16 *International Covenant on Economic, Social and Cultural Rights*, December 16, 1966, 993 UNTS 3 (entered into force January 3, 1976) [*ICESCR*].

17 Lufuno Nevondwe and Kola Odeku, "Challenges to Housing Delivery in South Africa: Lessons Learnt from Jurisprudence" (2012) 6:45 *African Journal of Business Management* 11327–41 at 11328; Christiansen, "Adjudicating Non-Justiciable Rights," at 341. The language of progressive realization is drawn from s 2.1 of the covenant; see Daniel Schneider, "The Constitutional Right to Housing in South Africa: The Government of the Republic of South Africa v. Irene Grootboom" (2004) 2:2 *International Journal of Civil Society Law* 45–62 at 57. Christiansen, "Adjudicating Non-Justiciable Rights," at 331, traces the history of socio-economic rights in the South African anti-apartheid movement back to the 1955 *Freedom Charter.*

18 *Constitution of South Africa*, s 26(1).

19 Geoff Bundlender, "Justiciability of the Right to Housing: The South African Experience," in *National Perspectives on Housing Rights,* ed. Scott Leckie (The Hague: Kluwer Law International, 2003), 207–19 at 208.

20 Nevondwe and Odeku, "Challenges to Housing Delivery in South Africa," at 11329.

21 Bundlender, "Justiciability of the Right to Housing," at 207–8. On positive and negative rights in the *Constitution of South Africa,* see Schneider, "The Constitutional Right to Housing in South Africa," at 47. For critiques of the dichotomy, see Christiansen, "Adjudicating Non-Justiciable Rights," at 346–47; Richard J. Goldstone, "A South African Perspective on Social and Economic Rights" (2006) 13:2 *Human Rights Brief* 4–7 at 4.

22 *Constitution of South Africa,* s 26(2).

23 Ibid, s 26(3).

24 Michael Dafel, "The Negative Obligation of the Housing Right: An Analysis of the Duties to Respect and Protect" (2013) 29:3 *South African Journal of Human Rights* 591–614 at 603. For a discussion of a similar proportionality analysis under residential tenancy law, see Chapter 2 of this collection.

25 *Constitution of South Africa,* s 36; *Canadian Charter of Rights and Freedoms,* Part I of the *Constitution Act, 1982,* being Schedule B to the *Canada Act 1982* (UK), 1982, c 11, s 1 [Charter].

26 *Constitution of South Africa,* s 36.

27 Heinz Klug, "The Canadian Charter, South Africa and the Paths of Constitutional Influence," in *Canada in the World: Comparative Perspectives on the Canadian Constitution,* ed. Richard Albert and David R. Cameron (Cambridge, UK: Cambridge University Press, 2017), 397–417 at 405.

28 Reghard Brits, "Protection for Homes During Mortgage Enforcement: Human-Rights Approaches in South African and English Law" (2015) 132:3 *South African Law Journal* 566–95 at 593.

29 *Jaftha v Schoeman and Others, Van Rooyen v Stoltz and Others,* [2004] ZACC 25 (SAFLII) [*Jaftha*].

30 *Gundwana v Steko Development CC,* [2011] ZACC 14 (SAFLII) [*Gundwana*].

31 See Chapter 7 of this volume, which examines the loss of a home in Canadian judgment enforcement law.

32 *Jaftha* at paras 13, 15–16.

33 One had borrowed R250 in 1998 and the other R190 in 1995. In 2023, these amounts would be worth R963.13 and R904.40, respectively, as calculated to January 1, 2023. See Renier Crause, "South African Inflation Adjustment Calculator" (last modified September 2024), https://inflationcalc.co.za [perma.cc/Z8JF-DHWJ]. In Canadian dollars, these amounts would be $68.14 and $63.98, respectively, as calculated on July 5, 2023 using the XE Currency Converter, https://www.xe.com/currencyconverter/ [perma.cc/5QS2-3W8W].

34 *Jaftha* at para 55.

35 Ibid at paras 41 (reckless conduct), 56 (other reasonable ways for debt to be paid, "completely homeless"), 57 (debt trifling or significant to creditor), 58 (manner in which debt arose), 59 (instalment payments).

36 Ibid at para 58.

37 Ibid at paras 43, 53.
38 Ibid at para 44.
39 Ibid at para 54.
40 Brits, "Protection for Homes During Mortgage Enforcement," at 585–86. See also notes 25–27 and accompanying text.
41 Office of the Chief Justice of South Africa, *The South African Judiciary* (Midrand, South Africa: Office of the Chief Justice, 2017) at 25–27, judiciary.org.za/index.php/documents/publications/category/55-judiciary-publications [perma.cc/V3TB-6RQZ].
42 Corlia van Heerden, André Borai, and Lienne Steyn, "Perspectives on Protecting the Family Home in South African Insolvency Law," in *International Insolvency Law: Reforms and Challenges,* ed. Paul Omar (Farnham, UK: Ashgate, 2013), 247–95 at 292. See also *Absa Bank Limited v Mokebe,* [2018] ZAGPJHC 487 (SAFLII) at para 70 (the court distinguished one of the four cases before it because the property being foreclosed against was a rental property and not the debtor's primary residence).
43 Susan Bright, "Dispossession for Arrears: The Weight of Home in English Law," in *The Idea of Home in Law: Displacement and Dispossession,* ed. Lorna Fox O'Mahony and James A. Sweeney (Farnham, UK: Ashgate, 2011), 13–40 at 17.
44 Ibid at 13.
45 *Jaftha* at para 60. For other examples of courts considering personal financial histories, see the list of factors cited by the court in *ABSA v Ntsane,* [2006] ZAGPHC 115 (SAFLII) at para 72 [*Ntsane*].
46 In *Jaftha* at paras 3, 5, 12, the evidence was that losing their homes would disqualify the debtors from receiving state-aided subsidies. See also *Ntsane* at para 62 (where the court explains that state housing subsidies are limited to first-time home buyers).
47 *Jaftha* at para 40. Dafel, "The Negative Obligation of the Housing Right," at 611–12, has described this decision as placing an obligation on nonstate actors to "tolerate financial losses."
48 *Ntsane* at para 18. The amount of $3.32 was calculated using an inflation calculator from the date of debt cited in the decision (February 24, 2006) to January 1, 2023 (Crause, "South African Inflation Adjustment Calculator") and then converted to Canadian dollars on July 10, 2023.
49 *Firstrand Bank v Maleke,* [2009] ZAGPJHC 41 (SAFLII) at para 6 [*Maleke*]. In the Canadian context, the Alberta Law Reform Institute speculated that borrowers might also not appear because they feel embarrassed or intimidated; see Alberta Law Reform Institute, *Mortgage Remedies in Alberta,* Report No. 70 (Edmonton: Alberta Law Reform Institute, 1994) at 178. In other research, I found that in Canadian mortgage enforcement proceedings, homeowners were absent in 72 percent of all court hearings; see Anna Lund, "Security of Tenure in Foreclosure Proceedings: The Judicial Role when Borrowers Are Absent or Self-Represented" (2025) 56:2 *Ottawa Law Review* 211–46 at 224.
50 Neil Brooks, "The Judge and the Adversary System," in *The Canadian Judiciary,* ed. Allen Linden (Toronto: Osgoode Hall Law School, 1976), 89–133 at 93.

51 *Canada v Downtown Eastside Sex Workers United Against Violence*, 2012 SCC 45 at para 29.
52 Janet Walker and Lorne Sossin, *Civil Litigation* (Toronto: Irwin, 2010) at 17–19; Brooks, "The Judge and the Adversary System," at 93.
53 Marc Galanter, "Why the 'Haves' Come Out Ahead: Speculations on the Limits of Legal Change" (1974) 9:1 *Law and Society Review* 95–160 at 121.
54 *Ntsane* at paras 72, 76; *Maleke* at para 6; *Absa Bank Limited v Mokebe*, [2018] ZAGPJHC 487 (SAFLII) at para 59 [*Mokebe*].
55 The court requested an organization to serve as amicus in *Ntsane* at para 26. In *Campus Law Clinic (University of KwaZulu-Natal Durban) v Standard Bank of South Africa Ltd*, [2006] ZACC 5 (SAFLII) at paras 4, 22, the Constitutional Court held that the legal clinic had standing to advance arguments on behalf of the debtors but with limits on the matters to which it could make representations (at paras 24, 26).
56 *Ntsane* at para 50 (specifically referring to the affidavit filed in support of an application for default judgment).
57 *Jaftha* at para 19; *Gundwana* at para 50.
58 *Gundwana* at para 50; *Jaftha* at para 47.
59 *Jaftha* at para 55.
60 *Nkata v First Rand Bank*, [2016] ZACC 12 (SAFLII) at para 155 [*Nkata*].
61 *Jaftha* at para 4.
62 *Ntsane* at paras 43–44, 91.
63 *Nkata* at para 20.
64 Ibid at paras 121, 124.
65 Ibid at para 121. The two dissenting judges held that the borrower must pay the costs before they could have their mortgage reinstated. One focused on how the obligation to have costs taxed should fall to the borrower, not the bank, because it is the borrower who wishes to reinstate the mortgage; the other suggested that the reasonableness of the costs was an objective question separate from whether the costs had been agreed to or taxed (at paras 55, 153).
66 *Ntsane* at paras 92–93.
67 Ibid at paras 81, 85.
68 *Nedbank Limited v Fraser*, [2011] ZAGPJHC 35 (SAFLII) at paras 35–42.
69 *Constitution of South Africa*, s 39(2), as discussed in Reghard Brits and A.J. Van Der Walt, "Application of the Housing Clause During Mortgage Foreclosure: A Subsidiarity Approach to the Role of the National Credit Act (Part 1)" (2014) 2 *Journal for South African Law* 288–305 at 304.
70 *National Credit Act, 2005*, No 34 of 2005, ss 8(1)(b), 8(4)(d) (S Afr) [*National Credit Act*].
71 Ibid, s 129(3)(a), as discussed in David Marais, "Mortgage Foreclosures and the National Credit Act: Balancing the Rights of the Creditor and the Rights of the Debtor in Light of *Jaftha v Schoeman*" (2013) *Responsa Meridiana* 98–114 at 106.
72 Zamanguni Sithabile Mazubane, "Balancing the Rights of Creditors and Consumers When a Home Is Sold in Execution: What Procedures Should Be Followed?" (LLM thesis, University of KwaZulu-Natal, 2020) [unpublished] at 70–72; *Nkata* at para 59.

73 *Nkata* at paras 108, 131.
74 Ibid at paras 93–94.
75 Compare the old wording of the reinstatement provision in s 129(3) of the *National Credit Act,* contained in *Mokebe* at para 36, with the new wording in *Mokebe* at para 48.
76 *Mokebe.*
77 Ibid at paras 46, 49.
78 *National Credit Act,* s 86(1); Reghard Brits and A.J. Van Der Walt, "Application of the Housing Clause During Mortgage Foreclosure: A Subsidiarity Approach to the Role of the National Credit Act (Part 2)" (2014) 3 *Journal for South African Law* 508–19 at 509 [Brits and Van Der Walt, "Part 2"].
79 *National Credit Act,* s 86(7).
80 Ibid, ss 86(7)–(9).
81 Ibid, s 88(3); Stefan Renke and Hermie Coetzee, "The Circumstances Under Which Section 85(a) of the National Credit Act 34 of 2005 Can Be Utilised as an Avenue to Access or Re-Access the Debt Relief Measures in Terms of the Act" (2018) 51:2 *De Jure* 234–50 at 246–48.
82 *National Credit Act,* s 85; Mazubane, "Balancing the Rights of Creditors and Consumers," at 79–80, discussing the amendments in *National Credit Amendment Act, 2019,* No 7 of 2019, s 11 (S Afr) [*National Credit Amendment Act*].
83 *National Credit Act,* s 130(4)(c); Marais, "Mortgage Foreclosures and the National Credit Act," at 108.
84 *Maleke* at para 5.
85 Ibid at para 8.
86 Ibid at para 17.
87 *National Credit Act,* s 85, as amended by *National Credit Amendment Act,* s 11; Mazubane, "Balancing the Rights of Creditors and Consumers," at 80.
88 Brits and Van Der Walt, "Part 2," at 518.
89 Some Canadian jurisdictions protect some debtors from personal liabilities for deficiency judgments; see Ronald CC Cuming, "Mortgage Obligation Deficiency Recovery" (2018) 81:2 *Saskatchewan Law Review* 113–31 at 114–15; Lund, "Uncertainty over the Scope of Borrower Protections," at 911–12. On concern about deficiency judgments in the South African context, see *Mokebe* at para 53.
90 *Mokebe* at para 66.
91 Ibid at para 57.
92 Ibid at paras 51, 56, 65. In *Ntsane* at para 83, the court expressed its concern about the possibility that "the sale in execution [will] render a price less than the reasonable value of the immovable property, [allowing] some speculator [to] score a handsome profit."
93 Lund, "Security of Tenure."
94 *Abbotsford (City) v Shantz,* 2015 BCSC 1909 at para 174; *Abbotsford (City) v Shantz,* 2014 BCSC 1817 at paras 78–79.
95 *Victoria (City) v Adams,* 2009 BCCA 563 at para 10 [*Victoria*]; *The Regional Municipality of Waterloo v Persons Unknown and to Be Ascertained,* 2023 ONSC 670 at para 105. On the development of the right to shelter in Canada in *Victoria* and

subsequent cases, see Scott McAlpine, "More than Wishful Thinking: Recent Developments in Recognizing the Right to Housing Under S 7 of the Charter" (2017) 38 *Windsor Review of Legal and Social Issues* 1–19; Sarah E. Hamill, "Caught Between Deference and Indifference: The Right to Housing in Canada" (2018) 7 *Canadian Journal of Human Rights* 67–95; Mark Zion, "Making Time for Critique: Canadian 'Right to Shelter' Debates in a Chrono-Political Frame" (2020) 37:1 *Windsor Yearbook of Access to Justice* 88–116; Stepan Wood, "Reconsidering the Test for Interlocutory Injunctions Affecting Homeless Encampments: A Critical Assessment of BC Case Law" (2024) 61:1 *Osgoode Hall Law Journal* 161–222; Estair Van Wagner and Alexandra Flynn, "Human Rights Cities: Realizing the Right to Housing at the Municipal Scale" (2024) 57:1 *University of British Columbia Law Review* 235–94.

96 *ICESCR*, art 11.

97 Martin Gallié, *Eviction and International Obligations: Security of Tenure in Canada* (Ottawa: Office of the Federal Housing Advocate, 2022) at 17–19.

98 Padraic Kenna, "Can International Housing Rights Based on Public International Law Really Impact on Contemporary Housing Systems?," in *The Idea of Home in Law: Displacement and Dispossession*, ed. Lorna Fox O'Mahony and James A. Sweeney (Farnham, UK: Ashgate, 2011), 133–63 at 149.

99 *National Housing Strategy Act*, SC 2019, c 29, s 313, s 4.

100 *Constitution Act, 1867* (UK), 30 & 31 Vict, c 3, s 92(13), reprinted in RSC 1985, Appendix II, No 5.

101 See Klug, "The Canadian Charter," at 412, noting that the Constitutional Court has "repeatedly noted the legal system, history and culture of South Africa ha[ve] to be taken into account when interpreting the Constitution."

102 *Port Elizabeth Municipality v Various Occupiers*, [2004] ZACC 7 (SAFLII) at paras 8–10 (Sachs J) (discussing the *Prevention of Illegal Squatting Act*, No 52 of 1951 (S Afr)).

103 Ibid at para 10; Stuart Wilson, Jackie Dugard, and Michael Clark, "Conflict Management in an Era of Urbanisation: 20 Years of Housing Rights in the South African Constitutional Court" (2015) 31:3 *South African Journal of Human Rights* 472–503 at 476.

104 Wilson, Dugard, and Clark, "Conflict Management in an Era of Urbanisation," at 473.

105 See, for example, the encampment eviction case of *Prince George v Stewart*, 2021 BCSC 2089 at para 70, where the court noted that the homeless population in Prince George was 79 percent Indigenous and cited *R v Ipeelee*, 2012 SCC 113 at para 60, for the proposition that courts must "take judicial notice of such matters as the history of colonialism, displacement, and residential schools." See also Chapters 8, 9, and 11 of this collection.

106 On the importance of context when looking to foreign legal sources, see Jackson, "Constitutional Comparisons," at 122. On recontextualizing borrowed constitutional ideas in the host jurisdiction, see Günter Frankenberg, "Constitutional Transfer: The IKEA Theory Revisited" (2010) 8:3 *International Journal of Constitutional Law* 563–79 at 575. On the importance of culture in the receiving jurisdiction of a legal transplant, see Toby S. Goldbach, "Why Legal Transplants?" (2019) 15 *Annual Review of Law and Social Science* 583–601 at 592–93.

107 Klug, "The Canadian Charter," at 412, notes that in its first twenty years Canadian law was the second most frequently cited source of foreign law by the Constitutional Court, which often "embraced the jurisprudence of the Canadian Supreme Court." See also Daniel Hoadley, Max Bartolo, Robin Chesterman et al., "A Global Community of Courts? Modelling the Use of Persuasive Authority as a Complex Network" (2021) 9:665719 *Frontiers in Physics* 1–19 at 17 (Figure 11), https://doi.org/10.3389/fphy.2021.665719. The Supreme Court of Canada has been a less active participant in this judicial dialogue, having cited South African law only seventeen times in the period 2000–16; see Klodian Rado, "The Use of Non-Domestic Legal Sources in Supreme Court of Canada Judgments: Is This the Judicial Slowbalization of the Court?" (2020) 16:1 *Utrecht Law Review* 57–85 at 65 (Figure 3).

108 Jackson, "Constitutional Comparisons," at 114; Sujit Choudhry, "Migration as a New Metaphor in Comparative Constitutional Law," in *The Migration of Constitutional Ideas,* ed. Sujit Choudhry (Cambridge, UK: Cambridge University Press, 2009), 1–35 at 22.

109 There is a risk that the individualistic focus of rights discourse can undermine progressive social change; see Mark Tushnet, "The Critique of Rights" (1994) 47:1 *SMU Law Review* 23–34 at 26–27.

6

Does Mortgage Securitization in Canada Affect the Right to Housing?
Some Cause for Concern

JASON LESLIE

Introduction

In the past few years, it has become common to say that Canada is in a housing crisis.[1] Despite the enactment of a federal *National Housing Strategy Act* in 2019, accompanied by a significant commitment of federal funds, many cities in Canada remain in a state of acute housing unaffordability.[2] Market forces remain, by far, the dominant force in the housing system. Yet housing is not a mere market commodity: it has been recognized internationally as a fundamental human right since at least 1948, included in several international human rights treaties, including the *Universal Declaration of Human Rights,* the *International Covenant on Economic, Social and Cultural Rights,* the *Convention on the Elimination of All Forms of Discrimination Against Women,* and the *Convention on the Rights of the Child.*[3] If housing systems that centre homeownership, market rentals, and private mortgage financing are not adequate to ensure that the human right to housing is met, then governments have a positive obligation to find other means of safely, comfortably, and affordably housing everyone within their borders.

Canada is not the only country experiencing housing challenges, and in the wake of the 2008 financial crisis, the tight interplay between residential property and the financial sector requires greater scrutiny. Housing scholars worldwide are starting to examine the effects of financialization on the affordability and quality of housing.[4] Drawing from the work of David

Harvey, Manuel Aalbers identifies a "global wall of money" arising from the concentration of capital in the financial sector that puts pressure on housing markets. This pressure financializes housing assets by finding ways to drive up housing prices and rents and saddling owners with large debts, all in order to provide a large and relatively low-risk ocean of assets within which to secure wealth.[5] The results are distorted housing markets, threats to tenure security, and increased risks to the overall economic system as the "fate of homeowners is increasingly tied to the fate of financial markets."[6]

In Canada, where housing prices have skyrocketed in recent years, the literature on housing financialization has focused on Real Estate Investment Trusts (REITs).[7] REITs enable investors to pool capital together and acquire residential real estate to secure wealth and engage in speculation. However, another pervasive form of financialization in Canada deserves attention: mortgage securitization. In this chapter, I aim to open the complex world of securitization to further academic scrutiny and make the literature on the financialization of housing in Canada more complete.

In Canada, mortgage securitization takes two forms. I am concerned with the first form, publicly guaranteed securities issued through the *National Housing Act* Mortgage Backed Securities (*NHA* MBS) and Canada Mortgage Bond (CMB) programs. The second form is privately secured "covered bonds," enabled and protected through federal legislation but not guaranteed by the government. Both programs involve hundreds of billions of dollars in residential mortgage debt and cover a substantial portion of the total consumer debt outstanding across the country. Here I bring to light some of the issues raised by the first form of securitization, which is older than the covered bonds program and directly implicates the state in a way that the covered bonds program does not. Nevertheless, covered bonds can also pose similar risks and cause similar effects, and they deserve similar attention at a later date.

My research for this chapter is based largely on documents released from a series of *Access to Information Act* requests (ATIP materials) to the Canada Mortgage and Housing Corporation (CMHC), the Canadian Department of Finance, and other federal government actors.[8] As a result, some of the material cited is not publicly available. Such material is identified in the notes as "CMHC Release Material." Copies can be made available upon request.

In the second section, I provide a cursory overview of the history and structure of the *NHA* MBS and CMB programs. In the third section, I outline some of the programs' significant financial risks and discuss how the federal government provides legally binding financial guarantees so that the public, rather than private investors, mostly bears those risks. I focus mostly on the CMB program, which creates unusual and hard-to-measure financial risks through the extensive use of two derivative instruments: payment swap agreements and repurchase agreements. In the fourth section, I review some of the broader impacts that the securitization programs can have in the financial and housing sectors. I discuss the potential impacts on housing prices, the reliance of financial institutions on these securities for capitalization, and the diversion of capital away from affordable housing programs and general public spending into private home purchases and equity loans. In the fifth section, I discuss how securitization feeds into the ideology of private home ownership, assists privileged segments of the population while sidelining those in acute housing need, and entrenches patterns of generational and class inequality. Finally, in the sixth section, I outline how this chapter fits into a broader research agenda for the financialization of housing and call for further investigation of the concerns that it raises.

Mortgage Securitization in Canada

Mortgage securitization solves a problem for lenders that arises from the nature of mortgage debt. Traditionally, banks and other financial institutions fund mortgage loans with capital obtained from their investors and creditors or from their customers' deposit accounts. Funding mortgages in this way leaves the lending institutions with large, long-term, slowly amortizing debts on their books, tying up capital for many years. In theory, an institution could sell its mortgage debt and obtain more cash on hand to issue more debt or for other purposes, such as capitalization or hedging. However, mortgage debt is not an attractive investment to most investors because of the long amortization terms and the substantial risks of default or prepayment posed by any one mortgage. In other words, mortgage debt is generally "illiquid."

Securitization provides a means of repackaging mortgage debt for sale on the secondary market so that an institution can obtain capital from additional sources. Through securitization, institutions pool mortgage loans together and transfer the underlying debt to new investors in the form of securities. Rather than purchasing mortgage loans directly, these investors purchase a share in the mortgage loan pool. Generally speaking, shares in this pool are less risky and provide a more predictable cash flow than individual mortgages. For the seller, the transaction brings in fresh capital with which to make further mortgage loans. Moreover, the selling institution can continue to service the underlying mortgage debt by collecting and maintaining records of loan payments, managing arrears and defaults, and communicating regularly with the borrower. By doing so, it can make a profit on the difference between the mortgage loan interest rates that it charges to borrowers and the slightly lower interest rates that it pays to investors in the securities. With this system, mortgage lenders can get mortgage debt "off their books," obtain more funding, and support much higher volumes of mortgage lending than would be possible from traditional funding sources.

Mortgage securitization has the potential to flood mortgage-lending markets with capital. It also enables policy makers to promote home buying as a staple of citizenship and the key to a middle-class lifestyle without requiring any up-front public expenditure. For this reason, mortgage securitization became prominent in societies with a homeowner mindset, especially in the Anglo-American world, during the latter half of the twentieth century. However, mortgage securitization can also increase risks and spread them widely through the financial system. The securitization of "subprime" loans – which pose risks because of small minimum down payments, lower credit scores and income requirements for borrowers, fewer financial document requirements, and other factors – was a major contributor to the financial crisis of 2008. Dividing mortgage securities into complex risk structures, a process called "tranching," was also an important factor, along with the widespread use of complex financial derivative products for risk hedging, resulting in opaque risk profiles and unreliable valuations. The crisis showed that to make mortgage securitization safe and effective, it must be subject to limits and public oversight.

In Canada, mortgage securitization was first introduced in 1987 through the CMHC in the form of *NHA* MBS.[9] These securities remain in widespread use today and form the backbone of mortgage securitization in Canada.[10] *NHA* MBS are a relatively simple form of securitization, using a straightforward "pass-through" structure. Investors who purchase *NHA* MBS obtain a share of a mortgage debt pool. As mortgagors make their monthly payments, funds are passed directly through to the holders of the *NHA* MBS in proportion to their ownership shares in the pool. *NHA* MBS cannot be tranched into different risk categories, and the principal used to purchase the securities is returned to the investors according to the amortization schedules of the underlying mortgage loans. Generally speaking, when a mortgage is prepaid, that payment is also forwarded on to the investors.[11]

To create *NHA* MBS, a financial institution assembles a pool of mortgage debt that meets certain criteria, arranges for itself or another institution to service the loans during the term of the *NHA* MBS, applies to the CMHC for approval, and pays the CMHC a guarantee fee. The pool criteria include certain conditions to help manage potential default risk. Importantly, all loans in a pool must be insured by the CMHC or an approved private insurer, the mortgaged properties must be spread out geographically, and the difference in interest rates on all of the loans cannot exceed 2 percent. CMHC-approved insurance is available on mortgage loans only for properties with a value of less than $1 million, so the loans used for securitization are aimed squarely at middle-class buyers. Only institutions approved by the CMHC can create *NHA* MBS. The CMHC also imposes an annual limit on the total amount of *NHA* MBS that can be created, and it issues equal allotments to all institutions that want to participate in each offering.[12]

Through these mechanisms, the federal government exercises tight control over how many *NHA* MBS are created, the risk profiles of the mortgage loans and pools used to create them, and their distribution throughout the mortgage-lending sector. In return for complying with these requirements, the issuing institutions and the purchasers of the *NHA* MBS receive a "Timely Payment Guarantee" from the CMHC. With this guarantee, the purchasers are protected against delays or defaults by mortgagors or the institutions that service the underlying mortgage debts. If a servicer does not forward the underlying mortgage payments on time, then the CMHC, as the agent of the federal Crown, is liable to make those payments and ensure that the investors are made whole. Because of this guarantee, the credit ratings of *NHA* MBS are extremely high, comparable to standard government of Canada bonds.

Despite government backing, the *NHA* MBS market failed to take off when it was first introduced in the late 1980s and collapsed during the recession of the early 1990s. Around this time, the new Liberal government implemented some of the most austerity-minded policies in Canadian history, including "commercialization" of the CMHC. Beginning with amendments in 1999 to the *National Housing Act,*[13] the CMHC was expected to abandon nearly all support for social and co-op housing, focus its efforts on supporting private borrowing and home ownership, compete directly with the private sector in the mortgage insurance market, and turn a profit.[14]

In this new environment, the CMHC turned to mortgage securitization. At the request of the banking sector, it developed a new product, the CMB, as an alternative to *NHA* MBS. The stated purpose of the CMB is to reduce mortgage borrowing costs – that is, interest rates – for home buyers in two ways: by providing lenders with a ready source of funds for mortgage lending and by increasing competition within the mortgage-lending sector.[15] This new form of mortgage securitization, unique to Canada, takes pools of *NHA* MBS and converts them into a bond-like instrument. Unlike the amortizing *NHA* MBS, the CMB behaves just like a government of Canada bond. An investor purchases a CMB, collects interest payments during the life of the bond, and then receives the principal in full when the bond matures.[16]

Creating the issue of a CMB requires several steps. First a mortgage lender assembles pools of mortgage loans to create a pool of *NHA* MBS in the manner described above. Then the lender transfers the *NHA* MBS pool to the Canada Housing Trust No. 1 (CHT or the Trust), a private trust acting as a special purpose investment vehicle. The CHT holds the *NHA* MBS pool in trust for the CMHC. The CHT then creates a series of CMBs, secured by the *NHA* MBS pool, and sells the CMB instruments on international credit markets. The proceeds of these sales are then forwarded to the original mortgage lender, which can use the funds to fuel more lending.

After the transaction is complete, the original mortgage lender (or, in some cases, a third party) continues to service the loans, receiving the amortizing loan payments from the original mortgage loan pool. This lender enters into an agreement with the CHT as a "swap counterparty." The lender forwards funds to the CHT to cover the interest payments due to the CMB investors and gradually accumulates funds in a trust account to cover the return of principal to those investors when the bonds mature. In exchange, the lender keeps whatever proceeds remain after the payment to the CHT. If the funds received are not enough to cover the interest payments and the required accumulation of principal, then the lender must make up the difference from its own funds.

In effect, the swap counterparty arrangement is a modified form of an interest rate swap with the CHT. The legal agreements governing these transactions use an amended version of a standard international interest rate swap contract. The swap acts as an interest rate hedge for the CHT, guaranteeing that it will be able to make the required bond interest payments, and gives the counterparty an opportunity to make a profit (and risk a loss) on the collection of mortgage interest payments.

The issue of how to handle the return of principal from the mortgagees is complex. As the amortizing mortgage payments come in, the counterparty must find a safe way to reinvest the returning principal on behalf of the CHT so that the full principal can be returned to the CMB investors on maturity. Because the legal authority for the CMB program rests on a provision of the *National Housing Act* that authorizes the CMHC to guarantee securities issued specifically on the basis of *housing* loans, most of these reinvestment assets must involve such loans.[17] Furthermore, only assets that mature close to the date that a CMB series matures can be used as reinvestment assets for that CMB series. This requirement ensures that there will be sufficient cash on hand to provide the CHT with the funds necessary to return the CMB principal to investors on the CMB maturity date.

Early on in the program's operation, participating financial institutions found that it was impossible to obtain enough additional *NHA* MBS or other eligible housing-related assets for reinvestment that matured at the right time. They proposed to the CMHC to use repurchase agreements, a financial instrument using *NHA* MBS as collateral that could be crafted to mature exactly when needed, as an approved reinvestment asset. Consequently, shortly after the CMB program was rolled out, the CMHC introduced a new policy allowing the widespread use of such agreements.

Repurchase agreements, or "repos," are effectively short-term secured loans. The borrower, or "seller," provides collateral to the lender, or "buyer," and the buyer provides cash to the seller. The collateral is usually a financial instrument such as a bond or security. A short time later the seller "repurchases" the collateral from the buyer with a cash payment, usually slightly higher than the original purchase price. Thus, though the agreement is called a repurchase agreement, because the seller repurchases the collateral from the buyer, the agreement is effectively a short-term secured loan from the buyer to the seller.

Repo agreements provide a way for the buyer to park cash temporarily with the seller and for the seller to convert financial assets quickly and temporarily into cash. Because repo terms are short, often days or even hours, they can be flexibly structured and quickly rolled over. A buyer can create a secured, on-demand bank account with a seller by continuously swapping collateral from one repo term to the next. As long as asset values remain stable, the arrangement is very low risk. However, if asset values change quickly for some reason, then the buyer can have a significant unsecured debt that the seller owes.

To create a repo in the CMB program, a swap counterparty sells an additional pool of *NHA* MBS to the CHT by transferring those *NHA* MBS to its CHT trust account. In exchange, the counterparty takes funds from the trust account that have accumulated from previous mortgage payments. In so doing, the swap counterparty also becomes a repo counterparty. During the life of the CMB, the repo counterparty will roll over the repo collateral at least once a month, legally entering into a new repurchase agreement every time that it does so. Through this system, the CMHC, through the CHT, effectively maintains a secured bank account with the repo counterparty in which to deposit the returning principal. When the associated CMB series matures, the counterparty stops turning over the repo agreements, collects the currently outstanding *NHA* MBS collateral, and returns funds to the CHT for distribution of principal for the investors.

The CMHC provides a government guarantee on the CMB payments. Thus, the credit ratings of the CMB are extremely high and, like *NHA* MBS, very similar to standard government of Canada bonds. Because of this, and because of their bond-like, predictable payment structure, CMBs became very popular upon their introduction in 2001. By the time of the financial crisis in 2008, CMBs had subsumed a substantial portion of the overall mortgage debt market, about one-sixth of the total.[18] The predictability of the payment flows, together with the robust federal guarantee, made them a highly desirable, extremely low-risk asset for the financial sector. In essence, they constituted a better alternative to government of Canada bonds, carrying the same level of risk while paying a slightly higher interest rate. The result, as the CMHC had hoped, was a large influx of capital into Canada's mortgage finance markets.

However, the CMB program introduced substantial new risks to the federal government in the Canadian mortgage securitization system, particularly through the use of the payment swaps and repos. It also increased the reliance of the Canadian banking sector on mortgage securities and changed the overall shape of the mortgage financing markets. In the rest of this chapter, I outline some of these additional risks and effects and consider how they might be distorting housing markets and contributing to the Canadian housing affordability crisis.

Risks Created by the Securitization Programs

Creation of the *NHA* MBS and CMB programs introduced additional layers of risk to the Canadian financial system. The CMHC recognized that it was introducing such risks and that the federal government was taking legal responsibility for some of those risks through the timely payment guarantee.[19] As compensation, the CMHC charges a guarantee fee upon the creation of both *NHA* MBS and CMBs. The CMHC commissioned a risk analysis when it first introduced the CMB program in 2001, and it has revisited that risk when reviewing the adequacy of the guarantee fees and other aspects of the programs from time to time.[20]

I found it impossible to discern exactly what the CMHC has concluded about the risks of its mortgage securitization programs because much of the relevant information was redacted from the ATIP release materials. However, some troubling patterns were evident. In particular, the CMHC analyses all assume that the risk to the government posed by the mortgage debt underlying the securities is nil because those debts are insured.[21] Such assumptions are not warranted because the federal government assumes the overwhelming majority of the risks of insurance payouts. Moreover, these analyses ignore the possibility of a broad financial crisis such as the one in 2008–09, focusing on the possibility of only one program participant going into default and the potential losses that can arise in that case. Such analyses assume that other program participants remain in good standing and that a functional, healthy financial market remains in order to contain and manage any fallout. The failure to address the possibility of catastrophic risk means that the securitization programs might not have been properly assessed in terms of uncertainty and focus instead on predictable housing market risks that occur in the ordinary course of mortgage lending.

A partially external review of the CMB program was completed by KPMG and a number of other third-party contractors in 2008.[22] However, the review was set up as an "attribution analysis" aimed at finding potential benefits and attributing them to the program.[23] No full cost/benefit analysis was conducted, and the issues of financial and systemic risk were largely ignored. Moreover, the review was finished right before the onset of the financial crisis in 2008 and thus did not consider the impacts of the crisis on the CMB program in any detail, though a short "discussion paper" appended to the report expressed the views of a few industry insiders that the CMB program had been a stabilizing force, enabling mortgage loan lenders to continue with business as usual and letting smaller lenders stay competitive during the turmoil.[24]

The KPMG report as a whole presented its results in the best possible light for the CMB program. Those results were nevertheless tepid. The report concluded that the major banks had obtained a small saving of about eighteen basis points on their wholesale mortgage funding, that smaller lenders probably experienced some savings (though no small lender reported any saving), and that some of the savings had probably been passed on to consumers (though there was no concrete evidence of this).[25] Furthermore, the presumed savings were limited to sophisticated buyers procuring a new mortgage loan who actively shopped around for a deal and "may have been in the range of 5 to 10 basis points."[26] To date, the KPMG report remains the only comprehensive review of the CMB program's potential benefits to home buyers.

Given little evidence of benefits to the Canadian public, any risk that the securitization programs pose seems to be hard to justify. This is especially true if the risks are not fully understood or potentially catastrophic. Although the full details of the CMHC's risk assessments are not publicly available, it is possible to look at the programs' general operation, and at some of the unredacted material, to piece together a tentative risk profile for the programs and to identify reasonable concerns.

Much of the base risk for these programs is set by the qualifications for mortgage insurance. When mortgage insurance criteria are relaxed, the risk of default increases, as does the pressure on the system. In recent years, mortgage criteria have been loosening, and the CMHC has lost much of its in-house mortgage insurance business to private companies, which have accelerated the development of a robust subprime market.[27] Furthermore, private mortgage insurance is subject to a 90 percent federal government guarantee, which means that if private insurers fail, then the CMHC is obligated to step in. The 90 percent guarantee is required under the legislation that authorizes private mortgage insurance, and it was introduced to enable private insurers to compete fairly with the CMHC.[28] The latter holds tiny reserves to cover these insurance claims: at the end of 2022, it held $318 million in reserve on $399 billion of CMHC in-house insurance in force.[29]

In the event of widespread mortgage loan defaults, insurance claims could fail. Because of the *NHA* MBS system, the CMHC would be called on not only to make good on the insurance claims over and above its reserves and those of private insurers but also to draw directly from federal funds in order to make *NHA* MBS investors whole. Failure to do so – or even just the perception by investors that doing so would not happen fully and immediately – could lead to destabilization of *NHA* MBS valuation. Because the CMB program relies on *NHA* MBS as security for the bond offerings and for reinvestment assets, and because the large banks use *NHA* MBS as a principal pillar of their capitalization portfolios, *NHA* MBS value destabilization could cause ripples throughout the Canadian banking system and make any existing crisis worse.[30]

The CMB program creates two additional, complex categories of risk. The first category arises from the payment swap system that, in part, converts *NHA* MBS interest rates into CMB interest payments. The most significant risk here arises from potential interest rate mismatches. In many cases, the *NHA* MBS interest rates are floating, whereas the CMB interest rates are fixed. In an environment of rapidly falling interest rates, that could quickly cause *NHA* MBS payments to be insufficient to cover the CMB payments, leading to counterparty defaults and calls on the timely payment guarantee. During the life of the CMB program, interest rates have been at historical lows, so the program has not yet been tested within this kind of financial environment.

The second category of CMB risks arises from the large volumes of reinvestment assets. The most significant risk in this category relates to the extensive use of *NHA* MBS and repos of them. If there were a crisis leading to widespread mortgage loan defaults, then *NHA* MBS values could destabilize. Moreover, the secondary market for *NHA* MBS is illiquid, making it difficult to sell large volumes quickly in order to raise funds to make the required payments of principal to CMB investors on time. This could be especially true if the crisis prompted all of the large lenders to attempt to sell their *NHA* MBS simultaneously. To make matters worse, destabilization of *NHA* MBS values could lead repo counterparties to default on their obligation to repurchase the *NHA* MBS at the end of the repo terms, leaving the CHT with large volumes of illiquid, depreciating assets. In these scenarios, investors would call on the federal government's timely payment guarantee, potentially costing billions of dollars overnight.

The CMB program includes a number of measures to mitigate the risk of calls on the guarantee. For example, it requires counterparties to post collateral when they are in a position of loss on the payment swaps, and it requires a "haircut" on repo collateral to ensure that the collateral value is slightly higher than the repurchase payment that it secures. However, the system is not perfect. Because there is no robust, active secondary market for *NHA* MBS, their valuation is uncertain even in normal economic times, so their use as collateral for both payment swaps and repos carries significant valuation risk. Furthermore, during serious economic turbulence, positions of loss on payment swaps and *NHA* MBS valuations can change rapidly, and it might not be possible for financial institutions to keep up with their collateral requirements to match. In fact, having to post additional collateral quickly could make already stressed lenders even worse off, creating a positive feedback loop that could accelerate a default and make any crisis even worse.

The guarantee fee, charged on the creation of both *NHA* MBS and CMBs, is intended to compensate the government for these risks to the federal treasury. This raises two questions. The first question is whether the current guarantee fee adequately compensates the government for the risk that it is taking. This is impossible to answer precisely without confidential financial information about both the CMHC's internal operations and the private financial institutions involved in the securitization programs. It might be possible to derive upper or lower bounds on reasonable fee amounts based on the overall structure of the programs, the financial information publicly accessible (as in the CMHC's annual reports and ATIP releases), and reasonable assumptions about information not publicly accessible. However, it is incumbent on the CMHC to conduct a full evaluation and reassure the public that its guarantee fees are adequate, even if it cannot release all of the relevant information.

The second question is whether it is even possible to set a guarantee fee that both adequately compensates for government risk and allows the CMHC to achieve its policy objective of reducing costs for home buyers. Any increase to the guarantee fee is an additional cost to mortgage lenders that will be passed on to mortgage debtors, reducing the programs' intended benefits. This question gets to the heart of the justification for the securitization programs in the first place. Moreover, the fees are set not only to compensate the federal government for the financial risks that it is taking but also to generate a targeted return on capital, as required by the amendments in 1999 to the *National Housing Act.*[31] It is possible that having a target for the return on capital functions as a mitigating factor for risk, for charging a higher fee would generate more funds that could be used to offset losses in case of program failure. At the same time, aiming to make a profit works counter to the programs' stated goal of reducing borrowing costs for Canadian consumers by introducing an additional financing cost. As with the first question, answering this question precisely would require access to confidential financial information, so it is vital that the public be able to see that the CMHC has analyzed and answered this question and released all of the information that it reasonably can to public scrutiny.[32]

Broader Economic Impacts of Securitization

The direct effects of mortgage securitization in Canada happen deep within the mortgage financing system. As KPMG found, these effects reduce the cost of wholesale capital for mortgage lending slightly, possibly resulting in a small reduction in mortgage interest rates for some home buyers.[33] However, given the size and scope of the securitization programs, it is reasonable to ask whether their impacts might extend beyond these immediate effects and to ask further who benefits, and who does not, as a result of those impacts. In particular, if the impacts include decreasing housing affordability, then the programs would act in opposition to their stated purpose and justification.

One preliminary question that has not received enough attention is whether reducing interest rates would even be a net benefit for home buyers. Reduced interest rates have been identified as a factor in causing house prices to rise.[34] Lower rates enable borrowers to borrow more money and make higher bids for home purchases, leading to higher prices overall. If the mortgage securitization programs are effective, as claimed, then the resulting upward pressure on housing prices could remove any overall benefit to home buyers or even make the overall cost more expensive. And, even if home buyers see some benefits, the housing price increase could put upward pressure on rental rates, further exacerbating housing affordability and imposing additional costs on people who receive no benefit from the securitization programs and, in many cases, are from economically disadvantaged populations that suffer most from housing insecurity. Unfortunately, I have yet to find any economic studies analyzing or addressing this issue with respect to mortgage securitization in Canada.

Although the impacts of the programs on mortgage funding and interest rates are unclear, their benefits to the financial sector are clear. Financial institutions use CMBs and *NHA* MBS extensively in managing their financial portfolios and capitalization. In 2014, during a guarantee fee review, the CMHC flagged overreliance on *NHA* MBS to fulfill capitalization requirements as a problem.[35] The CMHC was concerned that the largest banks were holding nearly all of the then-outstanding *NHA* MBS for capitalization purposes, so the failure of even one presented a huge liability for the federal government under its timely payment guarantee. To promote diversification of capitalization assets, the CMHC introduced a higher guarantee fee for *NHA* MBS issued above a $9 billion annual limit per issuer.[36] It is unclear whether this has reduced reliance on *NHA* MBS, though tellingly their volumes have risen since then, from $422 billion in 2014 to $471 billion in 2022.[37] The risk remains that the major banks will rely extensively on *NHA* MBS, and thus on direct financial guarantees from the government of Canada, to bolster their capitalization and support other lending. It seems to be likely, too, that the ability to convert mortgage debt readily into secured, government-backed capital provides the financial sector with a strong incentive to create as much mortgage debt as possible, overselling the idea of home purchasing to the public and working against any policy initiatives that might provide affordable housing alternatives.

Another issue is the extent to which CMBs have replaced traditional government of Canada bonds in the bond markets and what impact it could have on the capacity of the federal government to borrow money. Since their introduction in 2001, CMBs have taken over a substantial amount of total government-backed borrowing. When considered alongside *NHA* MBS volumes, the proportion of capital backed by government guarantee that has been directed into private mortgage lending is substantial. After CMBs were introduced in 2001, their total volume rose rapidly, whereas government of Canada bonds fell proportionately. Indeed, until the start of the crisis in 2008, CMBs replaced government bonds at a rapid pace, and for a time their volumes were nearly equal.[38] As of the end of 2022, the value of outstanding CMBs and *NHA* MBS (approximately $461 billion) totalled over one-third of the value of outstanding treasury bills and bonds (approximately $1.19 trillion).[39] Such volumes could reduce demand for standard government bonds, driving up interest rates and making government borrowing more expensive.

This history of replacing government of Canada bonds with mortgage securities is troubling. The overall picture shows that the federal government has actively diverted capital away from traditional government borrowing into private mortgage markets. Although the interest on *NHA* MBS and CMBs is paid by private home borrowers, not tax revenues, these instruments are backed by the Canadian government just like traditional bonds. If a mortgage or banking crisis were to occur, then the government could be on the hook for interest payments and returning principal to investors. As a consequence, *NHA* MBS and CMBs are considered extremely safe investments. They pay interest rates slightly higher than regular government bonds and can be used in the same manner for the purposes of capitalization. Even after recent increases in direct government borrowing because of the COVID-19 pandemic, *NHA* MBS volumes remain over one-third of government of Canada bond volumes. This is capital that could be tapped to fund affordable housing instead of single-family, detached homes and condominium units.

Some *NHA* MBS pools are indeed used to securitize mortgages for purpose-built multi-unit rentals and nonmarket housing.[40] Although this is potentially a better use of government-guaranteed borrowing, it provides an incentive for the financial sector to push private mortgages instead of public investments. Furthermore, *NHA* MBS and CMB mortgage pools include second mortgages and collateralized mortgage loans.[41] Securitization is thus being used to fuel homeowner access to equity, a benefit that accrues only to those who already have substantial wealth embedded in their homes and are not in acute housing need.

Securitization has also enabled the federal government and the banking sector to keep Canadians at record levels of household debt. As revealed in a recent CMHC report, debt levels in Canada are the highest in the G7 and exceeded among peer countries only by Australia.[42] Although many other countries experienced a contraction in household debt after the 2008 financial crisis, Canada did not. Instead, household debt totals rose from 80 percent of GDP in 2008 to 107 percent of GDP in 2021.[43] Government-backed mortgage securitization is central to the maintenance of this debt. The CMHC report notes that about three-quarters of total household debt constitute mortgage loans, and during the crisis the federal government was able to use the *NHA* MBS and CMB programs to keep the mortgage taps flowing. The total amount of CMBs outstanding rose from about $117 billion at the end of 2007, to $147 billion at the end of 2008, and to $177 billion at the end of 2009 as investors turned to low-risk assets during the height of the crisis.[44] Additionally, in October 2008, the Department of Finance announced a new program, the Insured Mortgage Purchase Program (IMPP), under which the CMHC purchased *NHA* MBS pools from troubled financial institutions in order to inject them with funds.[45] Under the IMPP, $69 billion of illiquid mortgage debt was converted into cash for the banks between October 2008 and March 2010 in order to maintain lending.[46]

In its 2009 annual report, the CMHC proudly touted Canadian Imperial Bank of Commerce Senior Economist Benjamin Tal, who described the CMHC and its securitization programs as the "secret weapon" that enabled Canada to weather the crisis and avoid a bank bailout.[47] Yet the federal government did purchase billions of dollars of assets to keep the financial system afloat. One estimate is that the total amount of cash injected into the banking system through securitization was approximately $138 billion, half from IMPP purchases and half from new CMBs.[48] Whether these actions constituted a "bailout" is arguable since the assets purchased were relatively low-risk mortgage pools that the government had guaranteed already, and CMBs were not purchased, only guaranteed.[49] But in any event, they allowed Canadians to maintain record high levels of debt. John Loxley claims that the scale of state support throughout the crisis represents a "massive socialization of the private debt problem, which is the way global financial crises have always been dealt with," and he notes with irony that increasing liquidity and continuing the flow of credit exacerbate the extensive lending that originally led to the crisis.[50] Nathan Hume argues that the IMPP, though not a bailout per se, nevertheless distorted mortgage finance markets, enabling Canadians to put off reckoning with record high levels of household debt and capital being sunk into housing.[51] These latter observations led one financial writer to suggest that maybe it was individual Canadian debtors who in fact were the ones being bailed out, rather than the banks, enabling our collective borrowing spree to continue unabated.[52]

The Ideology of Securitization

Publicly backed mortgage securitization is not inevitable, and the original development of these programs, especially the CMB program, looks like a solution in search of a problem. In anticipation of a new era of balanced budgets and market-oriented policy, and in the wake of financial deregulation in the 1990s, the federal government commissioned a report from the Task Force on the Future of the Canadian Financial Services Sector. The report, known commonly as "the MacKay Report," was published in September 1998.[53] It favoured a "facilitative" framework for financial regulation, opening the financial sector to foreign actors and relying largely on competition for efficiency and effectiveness. The MacKay Report did not address housing finance, but its tone matched the government's commercialization plans for the CMHC.

Anticipating changes in the CMHC's mandate, and inspired by the MacKay Report, an internal CMHC Task Force drafted its own report entitled "Future of CMHC's Housing Finance and Related Functions" in November 1998.[54] Its report took the MacKay Report's favourable view of competitive markets, its willingness to engage foreign investors, its observation that traditional bank deposit volumes were decreasing, and a short passage supporting securitization for small-business loans as support for a renewed focus on mortgage securitization.[55] Even though mortgage markets were "healthy," and there was sufficient funding to meet demand and real competitive pressure on lenders to attract borrowers,[56] the CMHC focused on increased mortgage lending through securitization as its primary means of helping Canadians to access housing.

In 1999, as the CMHC expected, Parliament gutted support for public, cooperative, and rental housing in the amendments to the *National Housing Act*.[57] Decision-making power over housing finance policy devolved from Parliament to the CMHC through a change in mandate and removal of operational restrictions. The CMHC was to be run on a commercial basis while, paradoxically, determining public policy. Support for nonmarket housing was nearly eliminated, whereas support for housing insurance and mortgage-backed securities was expanded. As noted in the legislative summary, it was hoped that the bill would "give CMHC the necessary tools to compete effectively and fairly in the loan insurance marketplace[,] ... simplify the NHA by removing unnecessary restrictions and permit CMHC to respond quickly to shifts in consumer demand and market conditions."[58]

The CMHC thus rolled out CMBs during an ideologically charged period in which privatization and markets were the only acceptable answers to any policy question. Indeed, a third-party risk assessment commissioned by the CMHC at the time noted that it would be cheaper overall for the CMHC to issue mortgage loans directly using federal money, as it had done decades previously. However, as noted in the assessment, "the Canadian government does not want to participate as a principal in the mortgage arena ... The primary reason for this is the government's stated philosophy of avoiding competition with the private sector."[59]

The federal government could sidestep private banking entirely and set up a mortgage loan securitization system internally. For example, the CMHC could issue housing bonds directly and then issue mortgage loans using the proceeds raised from the housing bonds. If the CMHC wanted to enter into interest rate swaps with third parties to hedge its financial risks, then it could do so. Creating such a public system would be expensive and intrusive, effectively requiring the CMHC to nationalize a portion of the mortgage loan system. However, it is worth considering whether such a program, once in place, might exceed any saving generated through the current private system, especially if done on a cost-recovery rather than a for-profit basis.

More broadly, the idea of home ownership as the primary way, and perhaps the only legitimate way, of providing Canadians with housing is the real ideological elephant in the room. The *NHA* MBS and CMB programs reinforce the common cultural assumption that home ownership is the best way for all Canadians to obtain housing and that renters, co-op members, and the like are just temporarily embarrassed future homeowners or people who have failed in life and deserve second-class status. Purchasing a first home is often seen as a rite of passage and a necessary step toward a middle-class lifestyle, and in societies with a high rate of home ownership, such as Canada, failing to purchase a home can be stigmatized.[60] It is also touted as a form of investment and a means to grow household wealth, though its effectiveness in doing so is not clear, and depending on a number of factors it can be better to rent a home and invest in other assets.[61]

It is worth considering whether the *NHA* MBS and CMB programs do more than simply assist Canadians to access housing by also shaping housing markets and class structures. Mortgage securitization fosters a society in which households clamour to enter a saturated home-ownership market, are willing to take on historical levels of debt to do so, and are providing financial institutions with a source of government-backed assets for their convenience.

Moreover, though it might seem that facilitating home purchases should decrease demand for rental units, leading to lower rents and more affordable rental housing, this does not appear to be happening. Despite a small dip during the COVID-19 pandemic, average asking rents in Canada rose from $1,796 per month in June 2019 to $2,042 in June 2023.[62] The higher profitability of housing sales over rentals in a market fuelled by securitized mortgage capital provides incentives to take rental units off the market to be sold as condos and reduces incentives to create new purpose-built rental units. Indeed, data suggest that from 2006 to 2019 the stock of purpose-built rental units across Canadian cities "remained virtually unchanged."[63] Meanwhile, the stock of individual condominium units offered as "secondary rentals" increased. These secondary rentals are generally more expensive and provide less tenure security than purpose-built rentals. Increasing reliance on secondary rentals disproportionately affects disadvantaged segments of the population without the means to obtain a mortgage loan and provides incentives to those who do buy larger properties and become landlords of a "mortgage helper" secondary rental unit in order to avoid having to rent themselves. Although recent initiatives such as the federal government's National Housing Strategy are supplying new nonmarket capital for housing, it remains to be seen whether they will have appreciable impacts on the availability, affordability, and quality of purpose-built rental units.[64]

Finally, as Jim Kemeny and others suggest, and as discussed in the more recent literature on the financialization of housing, the structure of housing tenure affects the distribution of wealth across class and generational divides.[65] A robust home-ownership regime embeds capital in the private housing system, requires younger generations to incur and service large, long-term debts in order to obtain and secure middle-class status, and discourages a more flexible system of tenure that might better serve various needs, lifestyles, and economic circumstances. The *NHA* MBS and CMB programs entrench this system by committing the federal government to five- and ten-year financial obligations and encouraging the banking sector to arrange its affairs with reliance on a continuing supply of these securities. By focusing its efforts on securitization, the CMHC provides assistance to families who have enough wealth to enter into the residential property market. In doing so, it might be sidelining those with acute housing needs while providing significant benefits to the financial sector. Moreover, if there was ever a push to go beyond programs that merely provide supplementary funding for affordable housing, and truly to reform Canadian housing to promote a more equal and more generationally fair society, then the securitization programs could present a significant hurdle.

Conclusion

Mortgage securitization is a form of financialization that has been underexamined in the Canadian context. I have aimed to provide the general outlines of how these unique programs work and to raise red flags for further consideration and investigation. In particular, I have highlighted the complex financial risks created by the securitization programs, the potential distorting effects on housing prices and on mortgage markets, and the reinforcement of cultural and economic norms around home purchasing that exacerbate wealth inequality across generations and social classes. The programs might also be contributing to the rental housing crisis by increasing reliance on secondary rentals, driving up rents, and increasing tenure insecurity. Meanwhile, the clearest benefits of the programs accrue to the financial sector and to people not in acute housing need while risking government funds and diverting capital away from affordable housing initiatives and other social programs.

This chapter contributes to a research agenda proposed by Gertjan Wijburg to "de-financialize" housing.[66] Wijburg draws from a 2018 report by the special rapporteur of the United Nations that placed housing financialization, including mortgage securitization, at odds with the internationally recognized human right to adequate housing.[67] That report recommended that states "reclaim the governance of housing systems from global credit markets" in order to "redesign housing finance and global investment in housing around the goal of ensuring access to adequate housing for all by 2030."[68] To further this purpose, Wijburg calls for research on "financial market reforms aimed at dismantling finance-led housing accumulation," taking a closer look at financial innovations such as mortgage-backed securities to ask whether and how they could be structured to reduce financial risks rather than increase them.[69]

Such a research agenda requires the cooperation of, and the insight from, a multidisciplinary approach that includes economics, finance, law, geography, and housing policy. My hope is that, by uncovering the details of Canadian mortgage securitization and identifying issues of concern, scholars and other analysts might find inspiration and a starting point for examining the details of, understanding the effects of, and recommending potential changes to these large and consequential government programs.

Acknowledgments

I would like to acknowledge the gracious mentorship of my PhD supervisor, Doug Harris, as well as my committee members, Cristie Ford and Tom Davidoff. I would also like to thank the Law Foundation of British Columbia, which provided much-needed funding to finish my PhD research. The views in this chapter are expressed from my capacity as an independent scholar and do not represent the position of British Columbia.

Notes

1 As one example, see the series of articles collected by the Canadian Real Estate Association, "How Does Canada Fix the Housing Crisis?" (November 2023), https://policyoptions.irpp.org/magazines/november-2023/fix-housing-crisis/ [perma.cc/6SAZ-XBVJ].

2 *National Housing Strategy Act*, SC 2019, c 29, s 313 [*NHSA*].

3 *Universal Declaration of Human Rights*, UNGA, 3rd Sess, UN Doc A/810 (1948) GA Res 217A (III), art 25(1); *International Covenant on Economic, Social and Cultural Rights*, December 16, 1966, 993 UNTS 3, art 11(1) (entered into force January 3, 1976) [*ICESCR*]; *Convention on the Elimination of All Forms of Discrimination Against Women*, December 18, 1979, 1249 UNTS 13, art 14 (entered into force September 3, 1981); *Convention on the Rights of the Child*, November 20, 1989, 1577 UNTS 2, art 27 (entered into force September 2, 1990).

4 See, especially, Manuel B. Aalbers, *The Financialization of Housing: A Political Economy Approach* (New York: Routledge, 2016). See also Manuel B. Aalbers, "The Variegated Financialization of Housing" (2017) 41:4 *International Journal of Urban and Regional Research* 542–54; Manuel B. Aalbers, "Housing and Financialization," in *A Research Agenda for Housing*, ed. Markus Moos (Cheltenham, UK: Edward Elgar Publishing, 2019), 31–46. Other academic works focusing on financialization of housing include Rod Hick and Mark Stephens, "Housing, the Welfare State and Poverty: On the Financialization of Housing and the Dependent Variable Problem" (2022) 40:1 *Housing, Theory and Society* 78–95; Erlend Fikse and Manuel B. Aalbers, "The Really Big Contradiction: Homeownership Discourses in Times of Financialization" (2021) 36:10 *Housing Studies* 1600–17; Martine August, "Financialization of Housing from Cradle to Grave: COVID-19, Seniors' Housing, and Multifamily Rental Housing in Canada" (2021) 102:3 *Studies in Political Economy* 289–308.

5 Aalbers, *The Financialization of Housing*, at 134.

6 Ibid at 44.

7 See, especially, August, "Financialization of Housing."

8 *Access to Information Act*, RSC 1985, c A-1.

9 The CMHC obtained authority to create *NHA* MBS through *An Act to Amend the National Housing Act*, RSC 1985, c 8 (1st Supp).

10 Details on current volumes of government-backed housing securities and current securities program guides are available at CMHC, "Securitization," https://www.cmhc-schl.gc.ca/professionals/project-funding-and-mortgage-financing/securitization [perma.cc/A8GR-HGAN].

11 Publicly available details on the operation of the *NHA* MBS program can be obtained at CMHC, *The* NHA *Mortgage-Backed Securities Guide 2018* (Ottawa: CMHC, 2018), https://eppdscrmssa01.blob.core.windows.net/cmhcprodcontainer/sf/project/cmhc/pdfs/content/en/nha-mbs-guide-2018-en.pdf [perma.cc/33MN-KR8Y] [*NHA* MBS Program Guide].

12 However, if an institution does not use all of the amount allocated to it in a round, then its left-over amount can be reallocated to other lenders.

13 *National Housing Act*, RSC 1985, c N-11 [*NHA*].

14 For a detailed discussion of the change in Canadian public policy during the 1990s, see Timothy Lewis, *In the Long Run We're All Dead: The Canadian Turn to Fiscal Restraint* (Vancouver: UBC Press, 2003). For a similar discussion focused specifically on changes to housing policy, see Greg Suttor, *Still Renovating: A History of Canadian Social Housing Policy* (Montreal and Kingston: McGill-Queen's University Press, 2016).

15 CMHC and Canada Housing Trust, *Canada Mortgage Bonds Program (CMB Program) User Guide 2018* (Ottawa: CMHC, 2018), https://www.cmhc-schl.gc.ca/professionals/project-funding-and-mortgage-financing/securitization/canada-mortgage-bonds/cmb-program-guide [perma.cc/W3AE-N9FY], at 1.1 [CMB Program Guide]. The 2018 version is current as of July 2023.

16 Publicly available details can be found in ibid. Further details were obtained through ATIP release documents, available from the author upon request.

17 *NHA*, s 14(a).

18 The total amount of Canadian residential mortgages at that time was approximately $900 billion. See Parliamentary Information and Research Service, *The Insured Mortgage Purchase Program*, by Jean-François Nadeau (Ottawa: Library of Parliament, March 13, 2009) at 2. In comparison, the total CMB amount at the end of 2008 was $147 billion. See CMHC, *CMHC Annual Report 2008* (Ottawa: CMHC, 2008), https://publications.gc.ca/collections/collection_2010/schl-cmhc/nh1-1/NH1-1-2008-eng.pdf [perma.cc/4XMG-VB6D].

19 CMHC, "Memo to Management re: Mortgage Backed Bonds" (September 20, 2000) [CMHC Release Material].

20 The initial analysis of risk, completed in 2000, could not be found by my ATIP requests and appears to have been lost; Daphne Gentillon, Senior Analyst ATIP, Archival and Operational Records Unit, Library and Archives Canada, email to the author (August 5, 2021) [on file with the author]. However, I was able to obtain several partial risk analyses conducted or commissioned by the CMHC for specific purposes, including Andrew Kalotay Associated, "Canada Mortgage Bond (CMB) Program Final Report on Financial Risks Faced by CMB Trust" (January 8, 2001) [CMHC Release Material]; CMHC, "NHA MBS Guarantee Fee Analysis"

(November 21, 2007) [CMHC Release Material]; CMHC, "CMB Guarantee Fee Adequacy Assessment" (November 27, 2007) [CMHC Release Material]; CMHC, "Memo to ALCO Members re: Guarantee Fee and Related Collateral Requirements for the 10-Year CMB" (June 23, 2008) [CMHC Release Material]; CMHC, "Memo to Management re: Revisions to the MBS Repo Policy in the CMB Program" (February 23, 2009) [CMHC Release Material]; CMHC, "Submission to Management re: Adequacy of NHA MBS and CMB Guarantee Fees" (January 7, 2013) [CMHC Release Material]; CMHC, "Submission to Management re: NHA MBS and CMB Guarantee Fee Review" (May 21, 2014) [CMHC Release Material]; and others, all part of the CMHC Release Material.

21 See, for example, Nadeau, *The Insured Mortgage Purchase Program;* Andrew Kalotay Associated, "Canada Mortgage Bond (CMB) Program Final Report."

22 KPMG LLP and CMHC, *Canada Mortgage Bonds Program Evaluation Final Report* (Ottawa: CMHC, June 2008), https://silo.tips/download/audit-and-evaluation-services [perma.cc/TUJ8-8X28].

23 CMHC, "Memo to Management re: Scope of Work for the Evaluation of Benefits to Canadians as a Result of the Canada Mortgage Bonds Program" (June 16, 2005) [CMHC Release Material] at 1–2.

24 KPMG and CMHC, *Canada Mortgage Bonds Program Evaluation Final Report,* at C-20.

25 Ibid at ii, 29, 34.

26 Ibid at 34.

27 See, for example, Geoff Zochodne, "CMHC's Loss is Sagen's Gain, as Private-Sector Mortgage Insurer Sees Market Share Grow," *Financial Post* (April 6, 2021), https://financialpost.com/real-estate/mortgages/cmhcs-loss-is-sagens-gain-as-private-sector-mortgage-insurer-sees-market-share-grow [perma.cc/MY7T-FJCR]; Peter Evans, "CMHC Urges Lenders to Stop Offering So Many High-Risk Mortgages," *CBC News* (August 12, 2020), https://www.cbc.ca/news/business/cmhc-mortgage-insurance-1.5683506 [perma.cc/GP8P-GQRV].

28 *Protection of Residential Mortgage or Hypothecary Insurance Act,* SC 2011, c 15, s 20, by operation of ss 16, 22.

29 CMHC, *2022 Annual Report* (Ottawa: CMHC, 2022), https://publications.gc.ca/collections/collection_2023/schl-cmhc/NH1-1-2022-eng.pdf, at 103–4 [perma.cc/5K2Z-67NN].

30 See the fourth section for a discussion of the use of *NHA* MBS in bank capitalization.

31 Bill C-66, *An Act to Amend the National Housing Act and the Canada Mortgage and Housing Corporation Act,* 1st Sess, 36th Parl, 1999 (assented to June 17, 1999), SC 1999, c 27 [Bill C-66].

32 The discussion in this section has identified some of the most significant risks created by the securitization programs. However, there are other risks involved, including those arising from the selection and supervision of participating financial institutions, those arising from possible delays caused by default grace periods and notification delays in the programs' legal documents, those from delays and debt discharges resulting from bankruptcy and insolvency proceedings, and those

resulting from special measures taken to support the participation of smaller lenders. Ultimately, the risk profiles of the programs are large and complicated, calling for more attention and analysis than either the CMHC or the public has given them to this point.

33 KPMG and CMHC, *Canada Mortgage Bonds Program Evaluation Final Report.*

34 Kamila Sommer, Paul Sullivan, and Randal Verbrugge, "The Equilibrium Effect of Fundamentals on House Prices and Rents" (2013) 60:7 *Journal of Monetary Economics* 854–70.

35 CMHC, "Submission to Management re: NHA MBS and CMB Guarantee Fee Review" (May 21, 2014) [CMHC Release Material].

36 See *NHA* MBS Program Guide at C4-4.

37 Data from CMHC annual reports.

38 Data from CMHC annual reports show that government of Canada bonds and *NHA* MBS amounts were nearly equal in 2008, with government bonds at $274 billion and *NHA* MBS at $234 billion. *NHA* MBS amounts then remained above 80 percent of government bond amounts until COVID-19 hit in 2020, at which point government bond amounts increased dramatically in order to handle the extraordinary government spending necessary to manage the pandemic.

39 CMHC, *Housing at the Heart of Our Accomplishments: CMHC Annual Report 2022* (Ottawa: CMHC, May 4, 2023), https://www.cmhc-schl.gc.ca/media-newsroom/news-releases/2023/housing-heart-our-accomplishments-cmhc-annual-report-2022 [perma.cc/JD5Q-4V4Y].

40 The current *NHA* MBS users' guide notes that there are two categories of "Multiple-Family Pools," which can include social housing projects, and one special category for "Social Housing Loans." See *NHA* MBS Program Guide at C5-5–C5-6.

41 Ibid at C5-2–C5-3; CMB Program Guide at 6-1.

42 Aled ab Iorwerth, "Risks to Canada's Economy Remain High as Household Debt Levels Continue to Grow" (May 23, 2023), https://www.cmhc-schl.gc.ca/blog/2023/risks-canadas-economy-remain-high-household-debt-levels-continue-grow [perma.cc/8FS7-AUY6].

43 Ibid.

44 CMHC annual reports.

45 Nadeau, *The Insured Mortgage Purchase Program,* at 1–2.

46 David MacDonald, *The Big Banks' Big Secret: Estimating Government Support for Canadian Banks During the Financial Crisis* (Ottawa: Canadian Centre for Policy Alternatives, 2012) at 18. See also the CMHC reports on the IMPP auctions, CMHC, "NHA MBS Auction Operations," archived at Wayback Machine Internet Archive, https://web.archive.org/web/20130610210018/https://www.cmhc-schl.gc.ca/en/hoficlincl/mobase/auop/.

47 CMHC, *CMHC 2009 Annual Report* (Ottawa: CMHC, 2010), https://publications.gc.ca/collections/collection_2010/schl-cmhc/nh1-1/NH1-1-2009-eng.pdf, at 18 [perma.cc/A65D-CC7W].

48 Alan Walks, "Canada's Housing Bubble Story: Mortgage Securitization, the State, and the Global Financial Crisis" (2014) 38:1 *International Journal of Urban and Regional Research* 256–84 at 269.

49 John Kiff, Steven Mennill, and Graydon Paulin, "How the Canadian Housing Finance System Performed Through the Credit Crisis: Lessons for Other Markets" (2010) 16:3 *Journal of Structured Finance* 44–64.

50 John Loxley, "Financial Dimensions: Origins and State Responses," in *Bankruptcies and Bailouts,* ed. Julie Guard and Wayne Antony (Black Point, NS: Fernwood, 2009), 62–75 at 72–73.

51 Nathan Hume, "Canada's Very Own Mortgage Mess: The Laws and Programs Behind a National Dilemma" (2010) 89:1 *Canadian Bar Review* 111–40.

52 Scot Blythe, "Canadian Banks Got Bailed Out in 2008: Critics" (November 11, 2011), uat-cumulus.benefitscanada.com/expertpanel_/scot-blythe/did-the-cmhc-bail-out-banks-in-2008/ [perma.cc/UB7V-KP9S].

53 Task Force on the Future of the Canadian Financial Services Sector, *Report of the Task Force* (Ottawa: Department of Finance, 1998) [the MacKay Report].

54 CMHC, "Task Force Report on Future of CMHC's Housing Finance and Related Functions" (November 17, 1998) [CMHC Release Material].

55 Ibid at 2–3.

56 Ibid at 5.

57 Bill C-66.

58 House of Commons, Parliamentary Research Branch, Economics Division, *Bill C-66: An Act to Amend the National Housing Act and the Canada Mortgage and Housing Corporation Act,* by Jean Dupuis (Ottawa: Library of Parliament, February 16, 1999).

59 Andrew Kalotay Associated, "Canada Mortgage Bond (CMB) Program Final Report," at 4.

60 Steve Huebl, "Homeownership Rates in Canada Still Among Highest Globally" (March 4, 2019), https://www.canadianmortgagetrends.com/2019/03/homeownership-rates-in-canada-still-among-highest-globally/ [perma.cc/HX73-EEL8].

61 See, for example, Eli Beracha, Alexandre Skiba, and Ken H. Johnson, "Housing Ownership Decision Making in the Framework of Household Portfolio Choice" (2017) 39:2 *Journal of Real Estate Research* 263–89 at 284–85, concluding that households with homeownership as part of their financial profiles outperform households without homeownership only in terms of "risk-adjusted" rather than "raw" wealth creation and then "only for households for which the down payment they apply toward housing is substantial and, at the same time, not an overwhelmingly high portion of their overall wealth."

62 Rentals.ca, "July 2023 Rent Report," https://rentals.ca/national-rent-report.

63 Social Innovation Canada, *Financialization and Housing: A Social Innovation Approach to a Better Housing System, Housing Lab Report December 2021* (Toronto: Social Innovation Canada, 2021), https://sicanada.org/wp-content/uploads/2021/12/Financialization_of_Housing_Report.pdf, at 34 [perma.cc/HP9W-2EYY].

64 Government of Canada, "National Housing Strategy, Funding Programs," https://placetocallhome.ca/funding-programs [perma.cc/FSQ3-QNDN].

65 Jim Kemeny, *The Myth of Home Ownership: Private Versus Public Choices in Housing Tenure* (London: Routledge, 1981). See also Aalbers, *The Financialization of Housing;* Hick and Stephens, "Housing, the Welfare State and Poverty."

66 Gertjan Wijburg, "The De-Financialization of Housing: Toward a Research Agenda" (2021) 36:8 *Housing Studies* 1276–93.

67 *Report of the Special Rapporteur on Adequate Housing as a Component of the Right to an Adequate Standard of Living, and on the Right to Non-Discrimination in This Context,* UNHRC, 34th Sess, UN Doc A/HRC/34/51 (2017).

68 Ibid at 21–22.

69 Wijburg, "The De-Financialization of Housing," at 1278.

7

Full Home Exemption
Justifiable or Overreach?

RONALD CC CUMING

Introduction

The long-standing problem of providing Canadians with adequate housing has been exacerbated in recent years by several factors, including an inadequate supply of modestly priced housing, dramatically increased interest rates, the failure of income sources to match inflationary increases in housing costs, and a significant increase in the Canadian population resulting from immigration. The magnitude and complexity of the problem require the implementation of a wide range of short- and long-term measures designed to address it. This chapter focuses on prophylactic measures that prevent home loss in the context of debt collection proceedings.

As detailed in the introduction to this collection, security of tenure is a key component of the right to housing. This security requires that a person not be forcibly evicted from their home without first being provided with "appropriate forms of legal or other protection."[1] The other two chapters in this section examine how secured lending can undermine a homeowner's security of tenure.[2] Secured lending refers to an agreement in which a lender has acquired rights to a borrower's property to ensure the repayment of a loan. This chapter examines the relationship between unsecured debt collection and security of tenure. Unsecured debt collection refers to when a creditor is owed money but does not have property rights to the debtor's home or other assets. This area of law is often called judgment enforcement because the creditor ordinarily must get a court order memorializing their

Table 7.1: **Ascending value of home exemptions by jurisdiction**

Jurisdiction	*Amount of exemption applicable to home*
Yukon	$3,000
British Columbia	$9,000–$12,000 depending on whether the debtor resides within or outside the Capital Regional District or the Metro Vancouver Regional District
Newfoundland	$10,000
Ontario	$10,783
Alberta	$40,000
Nunavut	$50,000
Northwest Territories	$50,000
Saskatchewan	$50,000, but an active residence cannot be seized and sold

Sources: Court Order Enforcement Act, RSBC 1996, c 78, ss 71.1–71.2; *Court Order Enforcement Exemption Regulation,* BC Reg 28/98, s 3; *Civil Enforcement Act,* RSA 2000, c C-15, s 88 [*Civil Enforcement Act*]; *Civil Enforcement Regulation,* Alta Reg 276/1995, s 37(1)(e); *The Enforcement of Money Judgments Act,* SS 2010, c E-9.22, ss 93(1)(l), (2) [*EMJA*]; *The Enforcement of Money Judgments Regulations,* RRS, c E-9.22, Reg 1, s 23(4) [*EMJA Reg*]; *Judgment Enforcement Act,* SNL 1996, c J-1.1, ss 131(1)(h), (i) [*Judgment Enforcement Act*]; *Executions Act,* RSO 1990, c E.24, ss 2(2)–(3); *Exemptions,* O Reg 657/05, s 1(2); *Exemptions Act,* SNWT 2010, c 4, s 2(1)(f) [*Exemptions Act*]; *Exemptions Act,* RSMWT (Nu), 1988, c E-9, s 2(1)(f); *Exemptions Act,* RSY 2002, c 80, ss 2(3).

right to payment (i.e., a judgment) before they can take steps to force the debtor to pay. Creditors holding judgments can seize and sell the debtor's home, albeit subject to a range of legal protections.

Eight Canadian jurisdictions provide for some measure of protection for debtor-homeowners and their dependants from loss of possession of their homes through judgment enforcement proceedings.[3] However, there is no uniformity in approach, as evident in Table 7.1.

The variations across the jurisdictions result, in part, from a failure to update exemptions law to reflect current economic circumstances. The two approaches contained in provincial and territorial law are exempting the interest of a judgment debtor's home up to a specified amount[4] and making a full exemption. In two jurisdictions, there is a different approach depending on whether the home is owned by a farmer or nonfarmer.[5]

The focus of this chapter is on the home exemption provisions of Saskatchewan's *Enforcement of Money Judgments Act* (*EMJA*), which protects an occupied home of a judgment debtor, regardless of the value of the debtor's interest in the home.[6] This exemption provision protects the security of tenure of debtors yet in a calibrated manner ensuring that creditors can still recover their money when the home is voluntarily sold or the underlying debt results from the debtor's serious misconduct. The second section of this chapter describes the history of Saskatchewan's provision, the arguments for and against it, and how it has been calibrated to address some of the most trenchant critiques of a full home exemption. The third section considers how the exemption operates once a debtor commences bankruptcy proceedings. Bankruptcy creates practical hurdles to enforcing against a debtor's nonexempt equity in a home, and creditors can use bankruptcy proceedings to undermine the exemption provision. When designing an effective home exemption, drafters and legislators must take careful account of how provincial judgment enforcement law interacts with federal insolvency legislation.

The Saskatchewan Home Exemption

Evolution of the Exemption

Saskatchewan fully exempts houses from sale in judgment enforcement proceedings if the debtor is using the home as an active residence. Historically, it fully exempted farmsteads, but for the homes of nonfarmers there was a limit on how much value would be treated as exempt. The full exemption for nonfarmer debtors arose through judicial interpretation and then was codified in the *EMJA*.

The first statutory measure related to exemption from execution against land in the North-West Territories (part of which became Saskatchewan in 1905) was *An Ordinance Exempting Certain Property from Seizure and Sale Under Execution.*[7] The ordinance exempted from execution a rural "homestead"[8] of 160 acres[9] or an urban house and buildings occupied by the defendant and the lot or lots on which they were situated to the amount of $1,500.[10] The pattern established by the 1888 Ordinance was replicated in all exemption acts of Saskatchewan until 2012, when the *EMJA* came into effect.

The exemption for nonfarmer-owned homes has always been limited to a specified value. What happens when the debtor's interest in the home exceeds that value? Courts initially interpreted the limitation on the value of the nonfarmer exemption as providing that, after sale by the sheriff, the judgment debtor could retain the proceeds from the sale up to the specified amount.[11] Any proceeds in excess of the exemption amount would be distributed to the creditors. This interpretation of the exemption was later reversed, and courts interpreted the exemption as prohibiting the sale of a debtor's property, even when the proceeds of the sale would exceed the exempted amount.[12] The result of this revised interpretation was full exemption of debtors' homes. The exemption was not lost when the land was sold to enforce a mortgage, but it was lost if the judgment debtor voluntarily disposed of it.[13]

The *EMJA* codified much of the policy of prior law related to exemptions from judgment enforcement against land, with some additional refinements.[14] The *EMJA* exempts from judgment enforcement an interest in one home, house trailer, or equivalent facility and the land on which it is permanently situated with a value that does not exceed $50,000.[15] However, the full exemption feature results because the legislation bars judgment creditors from selling a debtor's home as long as it is maintained by the judgment debtor, or one of their dependents, as an active residence.[16] If an otherwise exempt home is damaged, destroyed, or expropriated, then any insurance proceeds, indemnity payments, or compensation payments may be retained by the judgment debtor as exempt for the purpose of repairing the home. However, if the house is totally destroyed or expropriated, then the judgment debtor is entitled to retain an amount not exceeding $50,000.[17] If the judgment debtor sells the home, then the proceeds of the sale up to $50,000 may be retained and used to acquire replacement accommodation.[18] The judgment debtor is entitled to any surplus proceeds resulting from the enforcement of a security interest (mortgage) on the home up to the amount of $50,000.[19]

The Arguments for an Occupied Home Exemption

Underlying all home exemption legislation is the policy that judgment enforcement or bankruptcy proceedings (which incorporate provincial property exemptions)[20] should not result in a judgment debtor or bankrupt homeowner being deprived of a home or the capacity to acquire an interest in a home.[21] The policy provides protection from the disruption and extra cost of having to find a replacement for a home seized and sold in judgment enforcement or bankruptcy proceedings. Instead of incurring these extra costs, homeowners can direct available income to mortgage payments or property tax obligations, thereby reducing the risk of loss of the home through mortgage or tax enforcement measures. The social disruption and negative psychological effects on the debtor and the debtor's family resulting from forced eviction from their home are avoided.[22] A home exemption eliminates the need to terminate employment and otherwise disrupt family arrangements as might be required if the debtor and their dependants must move to another community where there is employment available and in which the home real estate market is more accommodating to persons with few spare resources.

Full implementation of this policy would address only peripherally the current problem of the lack of affordable housing, but it can limit the number of persons who become homeless as a result of judgment enforcement or bankruptcy proceedings and enhance security of tenure for all homeowners who become overburdened with unsecured debt.[23] However, even in this narrow context, the policy is not being effectively implemented in most Canadian jurisdictions.

These jurisdictions provide limited home exemptions based on dollar value. If the judgment debtor's interest in a home falls within or below the value of the exemption, then it cannot be seized and sold. For example, in Alberta, the maximum exemption for a principal residence of a nonfarmer is $40,000.[24] If the value of a home owned by the debtor (e.g., the proceeds remaining after any mortgage is paid) is $35,000, then the home cannot be seized.[25] However, if as a result of inflation or home improvements the debtor's equity increases to $50,000, then the home can be seized and sold (subject to the mortgage), and the excess over $40,000 ($10,000) is applied to the judgment being enforced.

The values of the exemptions are rarely reviewed and increased to reflect the current real estate market for homes. The result is that even modest equity in a home is likely to exceed the permissible dollar limit because of the appreciation of a debtor's equity through inflation in real estate values, payments toward the mortgage, or home improvements. None of the provinces provides a dollar exemption that reflects the rising costs of homes in Canada's real estate market.[26] In comparison, a full home exemption – like the one in place in Saskatchewan – guarantees a measure of economic and social stability to debtors rarely available where a dollar value approach is implemented.

Arguments Against a Full Home Exemption

A range of arguments calls into question the economic and social desirability of any home exemption, especially full home exemption. The first argument that comes to mind is the lack of fairness to unsecured creditors of judgment debtors or bankrupt homeowners resulting from exemptions. This argument is usually graphically presented in a scenario in which a Saskatchewan judgment debtor protects significant equity (e.g., $1 million) in a home, thereby precluding creditors from collecting debts incurred by the judgment debtor in regular contractual arrangements with the creditors. The scenario, although not totally fanciful, is not representative of the great bulk of judgment debtors or bankrupt homeowners, very few of whom have financial interests in their homes that come close to this value.[27] In any event, enforcement of a judgment against a home is not the only method of recovery permitted by law. Seizure or garnishment of wages and bank accounts is another tool commonly used by unsecured creditors to collect judgments.[28] Furthermore, when a debtor becomes bankrupt, the court has power under the *Bankruptcy and Insolvency Act* (*BIA*)[29] to require the debtor to make payments to their creditors if they have an exempt house or other asset of dubiously high value.[30]

A more nuanced version of the argument against full home exemption is that it is unfair and commercially unreasonable for the law to protect an interest in a judgment debtor's home in excess of an amount sufficient to obtain replacement accommodation, either rented or purchased. This argument, though sound in theory, is dependent on two factors: first, the willingness of Canadian legislators to ensure that the maximum equity exemption in judgment debtors' homes is adequate for these purposes; second, the availability of alternative accommodation that the debtor can access. Too often these factors do not prevail.[31] For example, the value of the exemption provided in Alberta legislation is $40,000. When the judgment debtor's home exceeds this amount, it is sold, and the person is entitled to $40,000 from the proceeds of the sale. Under current market circumstances, the cost of a replacement home is likely to be much more than this amount. This amount might be sufficient for a down payment on a replacement house, but it is unlikely that the debtor subject to enforcement proceedings or bankruptcy will be able to obtain a mortgage to finance the balance of the price of the replacement home. This amount would be enough, however, to pay for rental accommodation for a period of time if it is available.

Another argument against full home exemption is that it provides a method through which debtors can "shelter" assets that otherwise would be available to creditors. A debtor who has nonexempt liquid assets can use them to acquire an interest in a home, thereby removing the value of the assets from the reach of creditors or the trustee in bankruptcy. For example, a debtor could avoid having funds in a bank account garnished or seized by using them to purchase an exempt residence. This risk also exists in jurisdictions that provide realistic dollar value home exemptions.[32] Where, as in Saskatchewan, there is no dollar limit on the amount of the debtor's interest in a home, the debtor can protect a large sum of otherwise nonexempt assets.

A policy under which a debtor is prevented from converting nonexempt assets into an exempt asset in the form of an interest in a home (or any other exempt asset) is intuitively attractive.[33] However, it would be difficult to administer and has a fundamental weakness. It would be necessary to identify a time after which the conversion becomes objectionable.[34] Take the example of the debtor who uses otherwise sizable funds to purchase an exempt home. The purchase cannot be objectionable if it occurs before a person incurs unsecured debts. Does it become objectionable when the debtor incurs an unsecured debt, when the debtor defaults in paying an unsecured debt, when a creditor sues to recover an unsecured debt, when the creditor is awarded a judgment, when the debtor becomes insolvent, or when the debtor starts formal bankruptcy proceedings?[35] There is not a moment when the purchase of the home clearly becomes blameworthy.

Alternatively, maybe timing does not matter. If, as a matter of public policy, the legislature has decided that the homes of judgment debtors are to be exempt from judgment enforcement, then should it be objectionable for a debtor who does not have a home to use nonexempt assets to obtain an interest in one? Should it matter when or how a judgment debtor acquired a home?

The unfairness argument against full home exemption also ignores the reality of the credit market. An aspect of voluntary credit granting is the need to assess the legal risk associated with a proposed transaction. Full home exemption law is an aspect of this assessment. Where it prevails, a potential credit granter must take it into account when assessing the risk of lending to a potential borrower. The potential creditor will know in advance that, when making a risk assessment, it cannot rely on recovering a debt against a potential debtor's home.

This counterargument does not apply to involuntary creditors of judgment debtors – persons not in positions to avoid becoming creditors. A significant group of involuntary creditors have obtained judgments to recover monetary damages suffered as a result of the tortious conduct of a judgment debtor, such as when someone is injured because of someone else's negligence or intentional conduct. The court will award the injured party a judgment to compensate them for their injury, transforming them into a judgment creditor of the party at fault.[36] The *EMJA* recognizes this distinction between voluntary and involuntary creditors by providing that some classes of involuntary creditors can enforce against a debtor's active residence. There is no active residence exemption when a creditor is enforcing a judgment for damages resulting from physical injury intentionally inflicted on the judgment creditor by the judgment debtor.[37] Nor is there any exemption for the enforcement against the judgment debtor of a restitution order made pursuant to paragraph 738(1)(b) of the *Criminal Code*.[38] The home exemption does not apply in situations in which a debtor has engaged in serious misconduct.

Voluntary Disposition or Involuntary Loss of a Home

An active residence cannot be sold in judgment enforcement or bankruptcy proceedings in Saskatchewan. The exemption operates differently when a judgment debtor ceases to have a home as a result of destruction, expropriation, mortgage enforcement, or voluntary disposition of it. Although few exemption statutes expressly provide for the protection of a judgment debtor's equity up to the permissible statutory limit in the case of a mortgage enforcement sale or an expropriation up to the permissible statutory limit, generally courts have read this feature as implicit.[39] If the debtor voluntarily sells their home, then the *EMJA* provides that the debtor obtains the exempt value from the proceeds, and those proceeds remain exempt for up to six months from when they are received but only if they are kept separate and remain identifiable.[40] If the home is destroyed, then the *EMJA* provides that a debtor can retain proceeds from any insurance policy sufficient to restore the home.[41]

One possible explanation of these different outcomes is that, as a matter of public policy, it is necessary to distinguish between the loss of a home through seizure in judgment enforcement proceedings or bankruptcy and the loss of a home through other factors. As noted above, a noneconomic consideration in the design of home exemptions is to minimize as much as possible the social disruptions and psychological costs to the judgment debtor and their family resulting from the loss of possession of a home. It recognizes "the home" that they occupy as the important consideration and not the economic equivalent of the judgment debtor's interest in the home. This policy is implemented through full home exemption.

A different policy applies where the loss is a result of factors other than judgment enforcement or bankruptcy, such as mortgage enforcement, expropriation, destruction, or voluntary disposition of the home by the judgment debtor. In such cases, the policy focus is on providing the judgment debtor with a monetary exemption sufficient to permit them to obtain adequate alternative accommodation. The $50,000 (maximum) payment can be used by the debtor as a down payment on the purchase of a house or to pay rent on leased premises.

In 2012, when the *EMJA* came into force, the government concluded that $50,000 was adequate for this purpose.[42] Although this amount is the most generous in Canada,[43] inevitably it will cease to be sufficient unless it is increased as prices in the rental and real estate markets inflate. Although the amount is set through regulation, this does not guarantee that the necessary adjustments will be made. In most Canadian jurisdictions, exemption amounts have not taken into account the inflation of housing prices. For example, this aspect of Alberta judgment enforcement law was last updated in 1995.[44] There is no mechanism in any Canadian home exemption law through which the amount is automatically adjusted to reflect prevailing market conditions. However, there is nothing about exemption law that precludes the use of a formula under which this can be effected. For example, in California, the home exemption amounts are adjusted annually for inflation, based on a specified consumer price index.[45]

Full Home Exemption in Bankruptcy: A Trustee's Access to Excess Value

When a person starts formal bankruptcy proceedings, all of their property, including their exempt property, vests in their trustee.[46] The trustee then sells the nonexempt property or otherwise realizes value from it and distributes that value among the creditors. However, the trustee cannot treat exempt property as part of the distributable estate of the bankrupt person.[47] Provincial property exemptions apply when a debtor starts formal bankruptcy proceedings.[48] The result is that the trustee cannot treat the exempt property as part of the bankruptcy estate unless and until the property ceases to be exempt under the applicable provincial law.

The *EMJA* exempts from judgment enforcement an interest in one home "with a value that does not exceed $50,000," and an enforcement sale is barred as long as the debtor is using the home as an active residence.[49] When a debtor commences bankruptcy proceedings, any value of the bankrupt person's interest in the home in excess of $50,000 vests in the trustee as property of the bankruptcy estate, but the trustee cannot realize this excess through a sale as long as the bankrupt person occupies the home as an active residence.[50] The trustee can register a "caveat or caution"[51] affecting a bankrupt person's interest registered in the land titles registry.[52] The primary objective of such a registration is to ensure the trustee's priority over subsequent interests acquired in the bankrupt person's house. It also provides public notice of the trustee's claim to the value of a bankrupt person's or former bankrupt person's house that exceeds the $50,000 exemption.

These registrations raise difficult practical questions about what happens when a debtor's residence remains exempt at the end of a bankruptcy, when the debtor receives a "discharge" that releases most of their debts.[53] The trustee finishes administering the estate and then applies to a court for a discharge.[54] Before the trustee applies for it, they must return any property to the bankrupt person "that is found incapable of realization."[55] Must a trustee treat the excess value of the home vested in the estate as property "incapable of realization" if the debtor is discharged? Or can the trustee maintain their registration against the home to allow the trustee or a successor trustee to realize the excess value at some time in the future when the debtor stops using the home as an active residence or sells it, or the home is destroyed, expropriated, or sold in mortgage enforcement proceedings?

This practical question about registrations was addressed in *dicta* of the Saskatchewan Court of Appeal in *Deloitte, Haskins & Sells Ltd v Zemlak.*[56] It concluded that a trustee should file a claim of interest only when the trustee is prepared to carry on with administration of the estate after the discharge of the debtor.[57] While on the facts of the case before it, the court concluded that there was no excess value in the home, implying that, had the trustee established that there was, it could continue as the trustee and wait until the value of the surplus could be realized.

But can the trustee wait forever, or is there a point at which the excess value becomes "incapable of realization" and the trustee must discharge the "caveat or caution" filed against the title? If the home is being used as an active residence by the bankrupt person or one of their dependants on the date of discharge, then it might be impossible to predict when the home will be sold by the debtor or dependant or otherwise become capable of being realized by the trustee. In *Zemlak,* the court cited an earlier case for the following principles:

> Under s. 22(1) [now subsection 40(1)] of the Act, the trustee had an obligation, prior to applying for his discharge, to return to the appellant any property which he found incapable of realization. These claims, by their nature, would obviously have been difficult of realization and they were not exercised prior to his discharge. Although the trustee did not reassign them prior to his discharge, he did, in fact, reassign them to [the] appellant prior to the hearing of the exception. Had the trustee not done so, [the] appellant could have applied for a court order under s. 22(2) [now subsection 40(2)].[58]

In *Zemlak*, the trustee took the position that it remained "the trustee for the performance of such duties as may be incidental to the full administration of the estate."[59] Given the finding that there was no excess value in the home, the court did not address this argument directly. However, even if there had been excess value, then enforcing the trustee's right to sell the former home would amount to much more than an incidental duty. This duty could not have been performed at the date of discharge or in the foreseeable future.

The court in *Zemlak* stated that

> before parting from this case we observe that the appellant raised a subsidiary ground of appeal which questioned the Chambers judge's order reappointing the respondent as trustee under s. 23(11) [now subsection 41(11) *BIA*] of the *Act*. Since we have decided this case on the principal grounds of the appeal advanced, we do not find it necessary to deal with that point. We do not, however, want to be taken as approving the procedure. This point is left open for future consideration.[60]

Subsection 41(11) empowers a court, on being satisfied that there are assets of a bankruptcy estate that have not been realized or distributed, to appoint a trustee to complete the administration of the estate.[61] It is not clear what the court in *Zemlak* was signalling to trustees with this comment. However, it is clear that the court was not prepared to accept without further consideration the decision of the trial court that subsection 41(11) of the *BIA* is the appropriate method through which the value of the bankrupt person's interest in excess of $50,000 could be accessed for the benefit of former creditors after the bankrupt person's discharge.

One can only speculate why the Saskatchewan Court of Appeal in *Zemlak* was reluctant to accept without qualification that subsection 41(11) of the *BIA* can be the basis for capturing for a bankruptcy estate the value of a bankrupt person's interest in a home that exceeds the statutory dollar amount. There appears to be no technical legal reason for precluding its use in this context.[62] However, the basis of the court's concern might have been its unstated assumption that, in the great bulk of cases involving a trustee's attempt to access the value of a bankrupt person's interest in a home that exceeds the statutory dollar amount, the subsection would be inapplicable for logistical reasons.

There are, in fact, two logistical hurdles facing a trustee who wishes to sell a residence after the discharge of the debtor. First, the trustee might not be able to sell the home. As long as the discharged debtor remains in the home, the trustee cannot access any of its value. Subsection 41(11) is applicable only when the former bankrupt person sells the home or it is expropriated, totally destroyed, or sold in mortgage enforcement proceedings. The discharged debtor might well remain in the home for many years. Second, once the trustee sells the home, it is only entitled to the amount by which the value of the debtor's interest in the home *at the date of discharge* exceeds $50,000. In the time between the discharge and an eventual sale (or expropriation or destruction), the value of the home might increase substantially. The appreciation in value does not accrue to the trustee.[63] Thus, the trustee will also face a logistical difficulty in ascertaining the value of the home at the time of the discharge.

Undermining Exemptions with a Conditional Discharge Order in Bankruptcy

The public policies embodied in the *EMJA* that affected the outcome in *Zemlak* play a very important role in another aspect of bankruptcy proceedings. All noncorporate debtors who become bankrupt are discharged, conditionally or unconditionally, from most debts.[64] In most cases, the discharge is unconditional and automatic after a period of time specified in the *BIA*.[65] In cases that do not qualify for an automatic discharge, an application must be made to the court for an order of discharge.[66]

The court hearing an application for the discharge has wide discretion in terms of the order granted.[67] The court may, and under prescribed circumstances must,[68] grant a discharge order subject to conditions. Commonly, courts make a debtor's discharge conditional on the debtor paying a specified amount to the trustee. When deciding whether to make such an order, the court "must balance three things: the interest of the creditors in being paid, the interest of the rehabilitation of the bankrupt and the integrity of the bankruptcy process and the public's perception of it ... [T]he whole matter must be looked at in the light of reason, common sense and humanity, having regard to the fundamental policy of the Act."[69] Given the discretionary nature of a discharge order, it is not possible in most cases to isolate the significance given by a court to each of these factors. However, it is clear that the home exemption rights of the bankrupt person, including both the value of their interest and their right to retain possession of the home, affect the conditions that courts impose. In *Re Kreese*,[70] Registrar Herauf observed that

> in *Ramgotra (Trustee of) v. Northern American Life* (1996), 37 CBR (3d) 141 the Supreme Court of Canada, on the issue of exemptions stated at page 155: "One might well characterize exempt property collectively as the 'bare minimum' which a bankrupt is entitled to maintain in order to facilitate his or her rehabilitation following bankruptcy."
>
> I have no doubt that this is the philosophy behind exemption legislation. As stated previously, the difficulty arises when the size of the exemption is such that it would offend the majority of reasonable people and certainly diminish the integrity of the bankruptcy process. Notwithstanding this difficulty the courts must attempt to fashion orders that pay due deference to both these principles.[71]

When a bankrupt person applies for a discharge while retaining an exempt home, it raises three questions. First, to what extent should the value of the bankrupt person's interest in a home (which generally cannot be accessed by the trustee because the discharged bankrupt person continues to occupy it) play a role in conditional orders imposed on them? Second, can (or should) the courts use their power to impose conditional payments to deny directly or indirectly the bankrupt person exemption rights solely on the basis that to recognize those rights would offend the majority of reasonable people and diminish the integrity of the bankruptcy process? Third, should courts use their power to impose conditional payments to deny bankrupt people an exemption when they have engaged in misconduct? When seeking to answer these questions, it is important to distinguish, on the one hand, between taking the value of exempt assets into consideration when determining the financial capacity to fulfill conditional orders for the payment of money and, on the other, directly or indirectly negating exemption rights through the terms of the order.

The relevance of exempt assets in the decision to make a conditional order was addressed in *Re Biblow* by Registrar L. Schwann:

> To be clear, these cases do not stand for the bald proposition that no bankrupt should exit bankruptcy without a sizeable (or any) conditional order simply because the bankrupt has exempt assets. The dollar amount of the exempt assets coupled with the unique facts of each case informs the court on the appropriate disposition. In fact, there have been just as many cases where the facts did not justify a conditional order ... The most recent case where the issue came to the fore was an appeal from a decision of the

> Registrar who had granted an absolute discharge in the face of sizeable exempt assets. In dismissing the appeal, the court emphasized that the analysis was not reduced to a mere consideration of the ratio of exempt assets to proven claims; something more is required which is often an element of misconduct on the part of the bankrupt.[72]

Examples of the "misconduct" to which Registrar Schwann referred include pre-bankruptcy "reprehensible conduct";[73] failure to disclose assets to the trustee;[74] measures to escape a judgment for defamation;[75] using non-exempt assets to acquire a home[76] or other exempt assets;[77] the degree of fault of the debtor, such as excessive gambling, that led to the bankruptcy;[78] simple bad judgment;[79] the kind of bankruptcy claim, in particular tax claims;[80] and the value and kind of other exempt assets of the bankrupt person, such as RRSP and RRIF investments or a Deferred Profit Sharing Plan held by the bankrupt person in addition to a home.[81]

In *Re Brown,* Registrar Schwann stated that

> while the facts in both *Kreese* and *Biblow* evidence an element of misconduct on the part of the bankrupt, the ratio of those cases is not dependent on such a finding. The issue presented in this line of cases is simply whether the size of the bankrupt's exempt asset base would offend the majority of reasonable people and diminish the integrity of the bankruptcy process if the bankrupt were allowed to exit bankruptcy absent a conditional order. While evidence of misconduct animates the "integrity issue," the weight of case authority does not make it a constituent element.[82]

The policy conflict demonstrated in these statements between recognizing the exemption rights of a bankrupt person, on the one hand, and the integrity and public perception of the bankruptcy system, on the other, is put into stark relief in the decision of Registrar Thompson in *Re Hagerman.* At the date of his assignment, Mr. Hagerman had $294,233 in debt, of which $248,914 was unpaid income tax. Prior to his bankruptcy, he sold a business and used $313,000 to purchase a home. When addressing his application for a discharge, Registrar Thompson

> concluded that Mr. Hagerman's pre-bankruptcy conduct of transferring non-exempt funds into an exempt asset warrant[s] an order of payment. Mr. Hagerman purchased a newly built home in the year prior to his bankruptcy and, in doing so, moved non-exempt assets that would have been

> available to cover his debts out of the reach of his creditors[83] ... I have concluded that a reasonable person would be offended if I were to allow Mr. Hagerman to exit bankruptcy with a brand new home, without having paid his income tax debt. I have also concluded that an order for payment of $213,000.00, which represents the non-exempt equity in his home, is appropriate under the circumstances[84] ... For the foregoing reasons, an order will issue that Mr. Hagerman will be discharged from bankruptcy upon payment of $213,000.00 to the Trustee for the benefit of his creditors.[85]

In at least two cases when making a conditional order, the court suggested that the debtor could obtain a mortgage on the home and pay the mortgage money to the estate.[86] In both cases, the bankrupt person had sufficient earning capacity after discharge to make mortgage payments. However, in the absence of this capacity, a conditional order directly or indirectly requiring the bankrupt person to borrow money secured by a mortgage on the home and pay the proceeds to the trustee could be seen as an implicit rejection of the policy of Saskatchewan exemptions law (as recognized in the *BIA*) that has prevailed for many years. A mortgagor who does not have resources to discharge a mortgage on their home will inevitably face the loss of the home through mortgage enforcement proceedings. The result is an indirect denial of the provincial exemption given to debtors to retain an occupied home, as incorporated referentially into bankruptcy law.

This gives rise to the issue of whether *BIA* subsection 172(1) or (2) gives power to the courts to make orders that directly or indirectly deny a bankrupt person the exemption rights provided by subsection 67(1)(b), which unequivocally provides that the property divisible among the creditors of a bankrupt person "shall not comprise any property that against the bankrupt is exempt from execution or seizure under any laws applicable in the province within which the property is situated and with which the bankrupt resides."[87] When an order is made under subsection 172(1) or (2), the person subject to the order is a bankrupt person referred to subsection 67(1)(b). Subsection 172(1)(c) gives to the court the power to grant an order of discharge "subject to any terms or conditions with respect to any earnings or income that may afterwards become due to the bankrupt or with respect to after-acquired property," and subsection 172(2)(c) gives the court power to require the bankrupt person, "as a condition of his discharge, to perform such acts, pay such moneys, consent to such judgments or comply with such other terms as the court may direct." I believe that the more specific subsection 67(1)(b) prevails to the extent that a conflict arises in the application of the subsection and either subsection 172(1) or (2). With this approach, the court does not have the power under subsection 172(1) or (2) to order measures that place in jeopardy the bankrupt person's rights under provincial exemptions law to retain possession of the home. These rights are given by section 67 of the *BIA*. There is no power given to a court by section 172 to override section 67.

Conclusion

A long-standing policy of judgment enforcement law is that a judgment debtor should not be entitled to protect from judgment enforcement property of a kind and value greater than what is necessary for the maintenance of the debtor and family at a minimum level. The *EMJA*'s full home exemption extends this policy to take into account the importance of protecting, whenever possible, a judgment debtor and family from the trauma, dislocation, cost, and disruption that result from the dispossession of a home. This version of the policy, a feature of Saskatchewan law for many years, focuses on the home rather than an amount sufficient to obtain alternative accommodation necessitated by the seizure and sale of the home through judgment enforcement. The policy is vulnerable to attack when the value of the judgment debtor's interest in a home is substantially in excess of the value of a home that would be adequate for the debtor and family. The strength of the attack on the policy is somewhat diminished as a result of provisions of the *EMJA* for a monetary substitute for the home exemption when the judgment debtor sells the home or it is destroyed, expropriated, or sold in mortgage enforcement proceedings.

The home exemption has been a major concern to Saskatchewan courts in bankruptcy cases in which the value of a bankrupt person's interest in a home, whether more or less than $50,000, is greater than what is considered sufficient, when liquidated, for a "down payment" on a modest home. In several reported cases involving conditional discharges, the courts have taken into account the value of the bankrupt person's interest in a home as one of the factors justifying an order requiring that person to make payments to the trustee.[88] There are at least *dicta* suggesting that it is appropriate to make a conditional order solely on the basis that the home exemption seriously prejudices creditors or undermines the integrity of the bankruptcy system and to make it a condition of discharge that the bankrupt person pay to the trustee the difference between the bankrupt's interest in his or her home and the $50,000 exemption provided by the *EMJA*. My view is that a bankruptcy court does not have the power to force the bankrupt person to take measures that would place in jeopardy their possession of a home. The right to retain a home is guaranteed by the *EMJA*. As a result of subsection 67(1)(b) of the *BIA*, this right cannot be truncated in bankruptcy proceedings or made the sole basis for punitive measures under section 172(1), even in cases in which the homeowner has engaged in blameworthy conduct that induced the bankruptcy.

Notes

1 *General Comment No. 7: The Right to Adequate Housing (Art 11.1 of the Covenant): Forced Evictions*, UNCESCR, 16th Sess, UN Doc E/1998/22 (1997) at para 3.

2 This chapter does not address loss of homes as a result of enforcement of mortgages. For an example of protective measures applicable in this context, see *The Land Contracts (Actions) Act, 2018*, SS 2018, c L-3.001, which gives broad power to a Court of King's Bench judge to delay mortgage enforcement proceedings in order to give a defaulting mortgagor time to address default. The delay can be substantial; see Ronald Cuming, *Overview of Saskatchewan Real Property Law* (Regina: Office of the Queen's Printer, 2016) at 11-6–11-8.

3 The policy decision that homeowners be given this protection originated in the United States. Homestead legislation was first enacted in the Republic of Texas in 1838; see Laws of the Republic of Texas, 3rd Cong, 1st Sess, at 113 (1838–40). Current Texas homestead protection from creditors' liens is found in the Texas Constitution, art XVI, s 50, and *Texas Property Code*, ss 41.001–41.024 (2024). See, generally, Joseph W. McKnight, "Protection of Family Home from Seizure by Creditors: The Source and Evolution of a Legal Principle" (1983) 86:3 *Southwest Historical Quarterly* 369–99 at 369. For a compendium of references to pre-twentieth-century US exemption law, see Alison D. Morantz, "There Is No Place Like Home: Homestead Exemption and Judicial Construction of Family in Nineteenth Century America" (2006) 24:2 *Law and History Review* 245–95 at 248–49. I have avoided using the term "homestead exemption." The term "homestead" has been used traditionally in some Canadian jurisdictions in the context of two separate legal structures. One of them, the focus of this chapter, is exemption of an interest in a home from judgment enforcement and bankruptcy. The other is a reference to legislation such as *The Homesteads Act, 1989*, SS 1989–90, c H-5.1, which gives to an actual or deemed spouse a veto over disposition or encumbrance of the property owned by the other spouse that they occupy or have occupied as a family home. Many states of the United States deal with both policies in the same statutory provision. This is not the pattern employed in several Canadian jurisdictions.

4 Except in Saskatchewan, and possibly in Yukon, if in a particular case the judgment debtor has an interest in an urban home greater than the specified amount, then the home can be sold and the specified amount paid to the debtor.

5 *The Saskatchewan Farm Security Act*, SS 1988–89, c S-17.1, s 66(h) [*The Saskatchewan Farm Security Act*], exempts the house and buildings occupied by the farmer as a bona fide residence and the lot or lots on which they are situated to the extent of $32,000. However, in effect this is a full exemption; see note 12 and accompanying

text; *Civil Enforcement Act*, s 88(f), which exempts 160 acres of farmland on which the residence of an enforcement debtor is located if the primary occupation of the debtor is farming. There is no upper dollar value equivalent to that of a nonfarmer's residence.

6 *EMJA*, ss 93(1)(l), (2). See also *EMJA Reg*, s 23(10). A similar approach is implemented in a few states of the United States. See, for example, *Texas Constitution*, art XVI, and *Texas Property Code*, ss 41.001–41.024; *Code of the District of Columbia*, s 15-501(a)(14); *Florida Constitution*, art X, s 4; *Florida Statutes*, ss 222.01, 222.02; *Iowa Code*, s 561.16; *Kansas Statutes Annotated*, s 60-2301; *Oklahoma Statutes*, s 31-1; *South Dakota Codified Laws*, ss 43-31, 43–45-3. Many other states have enacted legislation exempting for judgment enforcement a limited portion of land and value of interest of the judgment debtor. The exemption offered by state law is affected by the *Bankruptcy Code*, 11 USC, s 522, which lists all property that a debtor may reclaim from the bankruptcy estate. However, a state may also elect to "opt out" of the federal exemption scheme. When a state does so, it removes the federal exemption scheme as an option, with the result that bankrupt debtors domiciled in that state can only invoke the state exemption laws.

7 *An Ordinance Exempting Certain Property from Seizure and Sale Under Execution*, RONWT, 1888, c 45 [1888 Ordinance].

8 The term "homestead" was not defined in the act. However, it was interpreted as referring to a "homestead" under *The Dominion Lands Act*, RSC 1906, c 55. See *McDougall v McDougall*, [1919] 2 WWR 637 at 640, 12 Sask LR 289.

9 1888 Ordinance, s 1(9).

10 Ibid, s 1(10).

11 *In re Demaurez* (1901), 5 Terr LR 84, en banc.

12 See *In re Hayes*, 1931 CanLII 211 (SK (KB)) at para 2; *Re Neuls* (1985), 17 DLR (4th) 554, 31 ACWS (2nd) 130 [*Neuls*].

13 When the home was sold by judicial sale and the mortgage debt discharged, the mortgagor was entitled to claim from any surplus proceeds the amount set out in *The Exemptions Act*; see *Charles v Hernandez Becerra*, 2016 SKCA 163; *Higgins Co Ltd v McNabb*, [1980] 2 WWR 385, 112 DLR (3rd) 407.

14 See, generally, Ronald Cuming and Donal Layh, *The Enforcement of* Money Judgments Act: *Commentary and Analysis* (Regina: Office of the Queen's Printer, 2012) at 293–94.

15 *EMJA*, s 93(1)(l); *EMJA Reg*, s 23(4).

16 *EMJA*, s 93(2). Under the *EMJA* at s 87, the dependant of a deceased judgment debtor is entitled to make an exemption claim on their property that could have been claimed as exempt by the judgment debtor were they not deceased. The term "dependant" is defined in the *EMJA* at s 84 as including a spouse of the judgment debtor, a child of the judgment debtor under the age of eighteen, and any other person who is or was at the time of death of the judgment debtor in whole or in part dependent on the judgment debtor's income.

17 Ibid at s 94(7)(c).

18 Ibid at ss 94(7)(c), (12)–(16).

19 Ibid at ss 94(8)–(11).

20 See note 50 and accompanying text.

21 George L. Haskins, "Homestead Exemptions" (1950) 63:8 *Harvard Law Review* 1289–1320 at 1290:

> The policy of the homestead laws is reflected in the three principal consequences which follow when particular property constitutes a homestead: (1) the property is exempt from execution for certain kinds of debts; (2) the owner's freedom of disposition is limited, since the consent of the spouse is required for a conveyance or encumbrance of the property; and (3) the use of the property, after the owner's death, is regulated for the benefit of his family.
>
> See also Richard E. Mendales, "Rethinking Exemptions in Bankruptcy" (1999) 40:4 *Boston College Law Review* 851–77 at 865: "The substantive purpose of personal exemptions in bankruptcy is to ensure that individual debtors will not emerge from bankruptcy completely destitute, but rather with certain basic properties needed both to live from day to day and for a quick reentry into normal economic life."

22 See the first section of Chapter 1 of this volume.

23 There is no home protection in mortgage foreclosure, builders' liens, or tax enforcement proceedings.

24 See note 4.

25 *Civil Enforcement Act* at s 89(2).

26 See, for example, *California Code of Civil Procedure* at s 704.730, California's Homestead Exemption Statute AB 1885, which provides a homestead exemption that is "the greater of the following: (1) The countywide median sale price for a single-family home in the calendar year prior to the calendar year in which the judgment debtor claims the exemption, not to exceed six hundred thousand dollars ($600,000); (2) Three hundred thousand dollars ($300,000).

27 See Superintendent of Bankruptcy, *Canadian Consumer Debt Profile – 2024* (Ottawa: Office of the Superintendent of Bankruptcy, 2025): "Only 14% of debtors owned a home, down from 21% in 2019. These homes had a median value or $322,000 and a median mortgage value of $248,000."

28 See, for example, *EMJA*, Part IV; *Civil Enforcement Act*, Part 8.

29 *Bankruptcy and Insolvency Act*, RSC 1985, c B-3 [*BIA*].

30 See also Anna J. Lund, "A Partial Fix: The 2019 Amendments to the Bankruptcy and Insolvency Act and Registered Disability Savings Plans" (2020) 2019 *Annual Review of Insolvency Law* 543–84.

31 See, generally, Royal Bank of Canada, "Housing Affordability" (n.d.), https://www.rbc.com/economics-articles/canadian-housing/house-affordability/ [perma.cc/7WJ8-U43V].

32 It also applies to money allocated to a retirement savings plan referred to in *The Registered Plan (Retirement Income) Exemption Act*, SS 2002, c R-13.01, and to registered retirement savings plans and registered retirement income funds referred to in the *BIA*, s 67(1)(b)(3). However, in the latter case, the contribution must have been made more than twelve months before the bankruptcy.

33 See, for example, *Re Hagerman*, 2014 SKQB 185 [*Hagerman*], discussed below.

34 In the United States, 11 US Code, s 522, prevents debtors from taking "unfair advantage" through state exemptions. S 522(o) prevents debtors from claiming an exemption in a residence otherwise exempt if the debtor acquired it anytime during the ten years preceding their petition by means of the conversion of nonexempt property "with the intent to hinder, delay or defraud creditors." S 522(p) prohibits debtors from exempting their interests in a residence in which such an interest was acquired by the debtor during the prescribed 1,215 days (three years) prior to the bankruptcy petition and in which it exceeds US $136,875 in value. When debtors have replaced their residences during the prescribed 1,215-day period, they are protected to the extent of the equity from their original residence being reinvested in a new home during the stated period.

35 See, for example, *Hagerman*.

36 In Saskatchewan, this group is not likely to include persons who suffered loss resulting from the operation of motor vehicles by judgment debtors. Under Saskatchewan law, all residents have the protection of mandatory no-fault insurance that covers loss resulting from an automobile accident.

37 *EMJA*, s 97; see also a comparable provision in the *Civil Enforcement Act*, s 93(e). Other involuntary creditors do not have alternative sources of recovery, such as a successful plaintiff in a defamation action against the debtor, but their numbers are not sufficient to reverse the policy of full home exemption.

38 *Criminal Code*, RSC 1985, c C-46.

39 See *Neuls*. In the context of mortgage enforcement, the issue arises only when there is a surplus from the sale of the home after the proceeds of the sale are applied to the mortgage obligation.

40 *EMJA*, s 94(12), provides that the "money" proceeds remain exempt for six months from the date that they are received by the judgment debtor but only if they are separately identifiable in specie or in a separate account with a deposit-taking institution. As a result of s 94(13), the proceeds are treated as exempt for a longer period if they remain identifiable and portions are used to obtain rental accommodation. Except as provided by the *EMJA*, s 94; the Alberta *Civil Enforcement Act*, s 98; and the *Judgment Enforcement Act*, s 135, a judgment debtor who sells their home loses the statutory exemption.

41 *EMJA*, s 94(6). In the case of "destruction" of the home, the judgment debtor is entitled to retain from the insurance proceeds an amount sufficient to replace the "item" "up to the prescribed $50,000 (s 94(6)(b))." Under ss 93(1)(l) and 93(2), the item is "a house, house trailer or equivalent facility, and the land on which it is permanently situated." A fire might destroy a house, but it will rarely destroy the land on which the house is located except where the land is rendered unusable for the purpose of rebuilding the house. Consequently, in most cases, the insurance proceeds of a fire that destroys the home will fall within the *EMJA*, s 94(6)(a) and not s 94(6)(b). If so, then the judgment debtor will be able to claim as exempt the total insurance proceeds (less any mortgage obligation) without regard to the $50,000 limit that otherwise would be imposed. It is possible, of course, for a home in the form of a house trailer or equivalent facility located on leased land to be totally destroyed.

42 Ibid, s 23(4)–(6).
43 The *Exemptions Act* provides the same amount.
44 See Anna J. Lund, "Uncertainty over the Scope of Borrower Protections in Mortgage Enforcement Proceedings in Alberta: The Problems and Potential Solutions" (2023) 60:4 *Alberta Law Review* 905–31 at 929.
45 *California Code of Civil Procedure*, s 704.730, California's Homestead Exemption Statute AB 1885.
46 *BIA*, s 71.
47 In *Royal Bank of Canada v North American Life Insurance Co*, [1996] 1 SCR 325 at para 49, [1996] SCJ No 17, Justice Gonthier stated that, "therefore, while an asset which is exempt under provincial law passes into the possession of the trustee at the time of bankruptcy, the exemption itself bars the trustee from dividing the asset among creditors where s 67(1)(*b*) is operative."
48 *BIA*, s 67(1)(b).
49 See notes 16 and 17 and accompanying text.
50 In this respect, there is an important difference between the approach contained in the *EMJA* and that contained in subsection 66(k) of *The Saskatchewan Farm Security Act*, which exempts a rural "homestead" regardless of the value of the property.
51 *BIA*, ss 74(3)–(4). This parallels the registration of a judgment against exempt property provided in *The Land Titles Act, 2000*, SS 2000, c L-5.1, s 173.3 [*The Land Titles Act, 2000*], under which an enforcement charge affecting land charges the judgment debtor's interest in land exempt from judgment enforcement pursuant to the *EMJA* may be registered against the land. However, the sheriff may not enforce the charge through seizure and sale of the interest.
52 *The Land Titles Act, 2000*, s 35(4), provides that a trustee in a bankruptcy must be registered as the owner of the title or the holder of an interest, as the case may be, in their capacity as trustee. See also *Land Titles Regulations, 2001*, RRS c L-5.1 Reg 1, ss 73–74, which address the transmission of title and interests by a trustee.
53 *BIA*, s 178(2).
54 Ibid, s 41(1).
55 Ibid, s 40(1).
56 *Deloitte, Haskins & Sells Ltd v Zemlak (Bankrupt)*, 1987 CanLII 4662 (SK CA) [*Zemlak*].
57 Ibid at para 24.
58 Ibid at para 22, citing *Thompson v Coulombe et al* (1985), 54 CBR (NS) 254 at 257. In *Shelson v Gowling Lafleur Henderson LLP*, 2004 CanLII 19412 (ON CA), the Ontario Court of Appeal refused to accept that it is a "bright-line rule" that, when a trustee applies for its discharge, it must elect, or be considered to have elected, to return to the bankrupt person its interest in nonrealizable property under the *BIA*, s 40(1), and, if it fails to do so, it holds that interest as the trustee for the bankrupt person and must return that interest to the person. The court cited as exceptions to the "rule" cases in which there has been misrepresentation or other misconduct by the bankrupt person (in not disclosing property) or otherwise discovery of a valuable asset within a reasonable time of the bankrupt person's application for discharge. See also *Deloitte & Touche LLP v Marino*, 2004 CanLII 4324 (ONCA).
59 This language refers to the then equivalent of the *BIA*, s 41(10).

60 *Zemlak* at para 27.
61 *BIA*, s 41(11).
62 In *Re Niekamp*, 2013 SKQB 288, at the date of discharge of the bankrupt person, his interest in his home was below the then exemption of $32,000. Four years later the house was sold by the mortgagee, with the result that there was a surplus of $162,288. The bankrupt person (who had not been discharged at the time of the sale) was given $32,000. The former trustee was reappointed, claiming the $130,288 as property of the estate. The court concluded that the date for determining the value of the home in a case in which the homeowner remains a bankrupt person is the date of disposition. Without specifically referring to the *BIA*, s 41(11), the court concluded that the surplus above the exemption was the property of the estate.
63 *Zemlak* at para 20.
64 *BIA*, ss 168.1–168.2, 172. However, not all debts are discharged; see ibid, s 178(1).
65 Ibid, s 168.1. The discharge is automatic unless it has been opposed by the superintendent, a creditor, or the trustee; see ibid, s 168.2(1). On the finding that about 90 percent of individual bankruptcies receive an automatic discharge, see Anna Lund, *Trustees at Work: Financial Pressure, Emotional Labour and Canadian Bankruptcy Law* (Vancouver: UBC Press, 2019) at 29.
66 *BIA*, s 172.1, requires a delay of the discharge application when a bankrupt person has $200,000 or more of personal income tax debt and whose personal income tax debt represents 75 percent or more of their unsecured claims. There is no automatic discharge for someone who has been bankrupt two or more times in the past; see ibid, s 168.1, 169.
67 The court has four options: first, refuse the discharge; second, grant an unconditional discharge; third, grant the order of discharge but suspend it for a specified period during which the applicant remains a bankrupt person, with the result that some income and nonexempt property acquired by that person during the period of suspension vest in the trustee, as provided by ibid, ss 67(1)(c) and 68; fourth, make a conditional order under which the debtor is discharged on the condition that the debtor pays money, consents to a judgment (enforced under provincial law), or performs some other act; ibid, s 172(3).
68 Ibid, ss 172(2), 173.
69 See *Re Nelson*, [1995] SJ No 384 at para 17, 133 Sask R 178 [*Nelson*].
70 *Re Kreese*, [1997] SJ No 129, 45 CBR (3rd) 36 [*Kreese*].
71 Ibid at paras 9–10.
72 *Re Biblow*, 2009 SKQB 76 at paras 33–34 [*Biblow*].
73 *Re Hubbard* (1999), 178 Sask R 307, 10 CBR (4th) 295 [*Hubbard*]; *Biblow*.
74 *Biblow*.
75 *Re Papazogou*, [1999] SJ No 240, 11 CBR (4th) 95 [*Papazogou*]; *Hubbard*.
76 *Hagerman*.
77 *Hubbard*; *Papazogou*.
78 *Biblow*.
79 *Todd (re)*, 2009 SKQB 120.
80 *Hagerman*; *Re Ferniuk*, [1998] SJ No 451, 169 Sask R 136.
81 For a description of cases in Saskatchewan prior to 2014 dealing with this issue, see *Hagerman* at paras 7–16.

82 *Re Brown*, 2010 SKQB 426 at para 30.
83 Ibid at para 23.
84 Ibid at para 25.
85 Ibid at para 26.
86 *Nelson; Hagerman.*
87 The reference in the provision to income exemptions must be read subject to the *BIA*, s 68, which provides a system for income exemption that displaces provincial law; see *Re Landry* (2000), 192 DLR (4th) 728, 50 OR (3rd) 1.
88 See, for example, *Nelson; Hubbard.*

Part 3

Legal Unhousing of Encampment Residents

8 Homeless by Design
When Institutionalized Indigenous Homelessness Meets Local Settler Government Intractability

YALE D. BELANGER

The measure of a society is how it treats its weakest members.

– attributed to both Mahatma Gandhi and former United States president Hubert Humphrey

Aboriginal peoples have a pre-occupation. It is of land. They occupied land in North America prior to others' arrival on its shores. Over the past 250 years Aboriginal people have been largely dispossessed of their lands and resources in Canada. This dispossession has led to another Aboriginal pre-occupation. It is with land. It is crucial to their survival as peoples. Its loss haunts their dreams. Its continuing occupation and/or reoccupation inspires their visions.

– John Borrows, Crown and Aboriginal Occupations of Land[1]

Introduction

Within weeks of the first tents being raised in a baseball stadium's overflow parking lot in Edmonton's Rossdale Flats in July 2020, hundreds of homeless individuals (the majority of them Indigenous) gathered at the Pekiwewin Prayer and Relief Camp (the "camp"). In the spirit of Pekiwewin, which in nêhiyawewin (the Cree language) loosely translates into the act of coming home, during the next 112 days, as many as 450 residents "returned home" to the camp in what was an era of unprecedented change for homeless individuals, elected officials, and public servants tasked with crafting housing and homelessness interventions.[2] Homeless encampments became familiar sites in a post-COVID-19 Canada marked by growing housing and employment precarity and housing affordability crises. Camp Pekiwewin was intentionally established on historically significant land that local government leaders and public officials acknowledged as municipally enclosed, traditional Indigenous territory. For most residents, Camp Pekiwewin was an attempt by those who lacked housing to create a "community – rekindling a lot of kinships that might have been sleeping for a while."[3]

This act of collective organizing did not begin in isolation: Indigenous homelessness in Edmonton dates to at least the 1970s and has been increasing steadily since 2006. Although the right to housing is enshrined in Canadian law,[4] Edmonton's (population of 1 million) homeless shelter capacity and programming notably remain ill equipped to address persistent urban Indigenous homelessness. Still, what drove this group of individuals in 2020 to take the extraordinary step of consolidating their community and asserting their presence in a city where Indigenous people experiencing homelessness remained historically invisible?[5] The camp leaders' publicly stated goal was to provide a space for housing, safety, and kinship to individuals who faced similar political and ideological pressures, in effect fashioning an environment of survivance[6] within their traditional land.[7] From the beginning, however, Mayor of Edmonton Don Iveson rejected these claims, choosing publicly instead to link the camp with social disorder, unable to guarantee its residents' dignity and safety. Chief of the Edmonton Police Service (EPS) Dale McFee similarly likened the camp to a group of law-breaking outsiders whose trespass on public land undermined public safety. In retrospect, despite the opportunity to develop more humane housing strategies in partnership with the leaders of a nascent community seeking similar prospects, both men opted to prioritize local control of municipal space to the exclusion of urban Indigenous people.

As I argue in this chapter, actions taken by Edmonton officials aligned with broader settler-colonial governance strategies that aim to displace Indigenous communities and evade long-term accountability. As Bruce Miller contends, "states uniformly have developed novel methods for sloughing off either entire Indigenous communities or Indigenous individuals from formal state-Indigenous relations, and any subsequent financial obligations or obligations under international conventions."[8] At the local government level, where Indigenous people's rights to and desires for land intersect with settler property regimes, municipal governance, and policing, city officials have identified urban Indigenous people as a federal (and, where applicable, provincial) policy responsibility. Such actions highlight a municipal approach that reorganizes Indigenous communities to reject "them as inauthentic and as lacking the qualities that the state imagines they ought to have."[9] In what I describe as the "Edmonton contact zone," a localized spatial logic compelled officials responsible for public health and safety to interpret the Canadian Constitution to justify their actions aimed at preserving the settler-colonial social and political order. Strategies such as forcibly removing unhoused Indigenous individuals from public spaces and relocating them in temporary accommodations were deemed necessary to uphold public order while proving to be useful in discounting covenants such as the *United Nations Declaration on the Rights of Indigenous Peoples*[10] as well as emergent legal, policy, and scholarly scaffolds elaborating urban Indigenous self-government's and self-determination's theoretical and applied milieus.

I have two objectives in this chapter. The first objective is to illustrate how Canadian law and policy, established and enacted at federal, provincial, and increasingly municipal government levels, have created and continue to develop pathways to homelessness that contribute to Indigenous people's displacement. It helps to answer the following question: How can Canadian law and policies "unhouse" people or, through various means, prevent them from becoming housed? The second objective is to show how historical and structural racism, in the form of settler colonialism, continues to influence law and policy and how settler-colonial ideas influenced local politicians and ancillary agents, such as the EPS, in their decision to dismantle Camp Pekiwewin. The chapter proceeds as follows. The first section details the evolution of contact zones and how settler-colonial hegemony subverted Indigenous claims to their traditional lands. The second section elaborates on the institutional drivers that predispose Indigenous people to become homeless. The third section charts Camp Pekiwewin's emergence, which represented a political statement of survivance defying the state's accepted land use protocols grounded in setter-colonial norms and its quick downfall facilitated by Edmonton City Council and the EPS.[11] To summarize, this chapter probes how Edmonton officials employed the method of exploiting jurisdiction to ignore responsibilities for Indigenous people to the city's benefit, which led to Camp Pekiwewin's closure and its residents' urban dispersal.

Contact Zones

On July 24, 2020, the Pekiwewin Prayer and Relief Camp was established near the site of the former Papaschase Indian Reserve, land that the City of Edmonton acknowledges as "the traditional territories of many First Nations such as the Nehiyaw (Cree), Denesuliné (Dene), Nakota Sioux (Stoney), Anishinaabe (Saulteaux) and Niitsitapi (Blackfoot)"[12] as well as "a gathering site for many Indigenous peoples" and the site of "traditional burial grounds."[13] The camp was located within Treaty 6 boundaries. Treaty 6 was signed in 1876, and a year later, a group led by Chief Papaschase adhered to it.[14] The Papaschase Indian Reserve was surveyed and allotted in 1880 on land in what is now southeast Edmonton that was once "owned" by the Hudson's Bay Company and then subdivided and sold in the 1870s for non-Indigenous settlement.[15] After the establishment of the reserve, federal officials promised Papaschase residents, who were confronting settler pressures to leave the region, that they could remain.[16] But Edmonton community residents had other ideas. As early as 1881, roughly one year after the reserve's assignment, municipal residents petitioned Prime Minister John A. Macdonald (also the superintendent general of Indian Affairs [1878–87, 1888] and minister of the interior [1878–83, 1888]), seeking its surrender and relocation of the Papaschase residents.[17] Pressure for a surrender increased as the regional economy came to rely on land-dependent agriculture and industry.[18] Nehiyaw promises to share the land were ignored as settlers promoted Indigenous exclusion. Succumbing to the pressure in 1886, Chief Papaschase and other members of his band surrendered their treaty rights and rights connected with the reserve. In 1888, the reserve was annulled, and in 1889, the remaining band members (three men and their families) entered into an agreement with the government to surrender their interest in the reserve for its sale or lease[19] and were removed to the current Enoch Cree Nation #440 site.[20] Edmonton was formally incorporated as a town in 1892.

The forced removal of Papaschase residents marked not just a political betrayal but also a transformation in the spatial logic of Indigenous-settler relations best understood through Mary Louise Pratt's concept of the "contact zone," defined as "an attempt to invoke the spatial and temporal copresence of subjects previously separated by geographic and historical disjunctures, whose trajectories now intersect."[21] Edmonton serves as a notable contact zone dating back to the precontact era, when diverse Indigenous Peoples engaged in trade, participated in ceremonies, and gathered for social and diplomatic purposes. Settlers arrived and disrupted the contact zone's previous relationships, introducing new elements that culminated in the signing of Treaty 6, a critical juncture in the history of regional Indigenous-settler relations.[22] Indigenous leaders perceived Treaty 6 as a co-created space where self-determining communities could establish co-governance institutions with settlers that could guide cross-cultural interactions on the land that the Nehiyaw had agreed to share.[23] In contrast, settlers presented the treaty signed under duress by Chief Papaschase and his fellow band members as proof that Indigenous leaders had ceded legal ownership of the land to Canadian control.[24] Afterward, lands not designated as First Nations communities remained under federal jurisdiction as territorial lands until 1905, when the Province of Alberta joined Confederation. The land that remained unoccupied was still subject to Indigenous usufructuary rights.[25] Reflecting the trends within the cognate literature, mutual claims to territory quickly devolved into ongoing jurisdictional feuds that were rarely resolved easily or quickly.[26]

Compartmentalizing the contact zone (Treaty 6 land) into "lands reserved for Indians" (First Nations) and distinct settler communities (towns and cities) embodied the nation-state's technique of structuring "political realities and subversive political imaginaries" that led to sovereignty being zoned suitably "to benefit some citizens systematically and, just as systematically, to disempower or otherwise harm other citizens."[27] As Renisa Mawani shows, colonial laws paved the way for separating treaty lands into First Nations space and urban space and for targeting Indigenous Peoples for sequestration in their lands.[28] Induced by the federal practice of opening the west to settlement, Edmonton's residents correspondingly endorsed European-Indigenous incompatibility to reject Indigenous territorial authority.[29] Imposing settler property regimes driven by a belief that settlers were "founders of political order"[30] expedited Indigenous territorial dispossession, disrupting Indigenous conceptions of land and home.[31] A dichotomy emerged, situating First Nations as natural, nonurban spaces in contrast to sanctified, constructed settler towns and later cities. More to the point, within settler-colonial legal and policy frameworks, space and the right of occupation were deemed culturally contingent.[32]

Edmonton's settler population particularly benefited from the federal *Indian Act*[33] enacted in 1876, which limited Indigenous Peoples to living in legally mandated reserves, rejected their self-determination claims, and significantly curtailed their self-government authority.[34] Unlocking the region's territorial wealth for settler society meant relocating and isolating

Indigenous communities onto discrete reserves.[35] Settler colonialism's logic interpreted Indigenous Peoples as a threat to nation building that was incorporated into municipal development and planning practices to regulate Indigenous urban permanency, also considered a risk to local political, economic, and social stability.[36] The legally and politically dubious justifications driving Indigenous dispossession in turn nurtured fears that Indigenous attempts to return to the city signalled a desire to reaffirm Indigenous sovereignty over settler-occupied lands.[37] In this setting, responding to residents' desires, municipal leaders employed bylaws to limit Indigenous access to the city.[38] Operating less as an event than a structure, settler colonialism evolved into an enduring process embedded in social relations, law, and policy that consistently remakes societies based on insider-outsider categorizations.[39] As a result, Indigenous Peoples were rendered outsiders within their traditional territories as they were simultaneously pressured through law and policy to abandon their First Nations communities for off-reserve residency.

This account of colonial dispossession in the late nineteenth century and early twentieth century reveals several assumptions that have continued to underlie law and policy since that time. The first is the innate connection of Indigenous Peoples to reserve communities along with the corollary assumption that they cannot establish a feeling of home in towns and cities. A third, related assumption is that by "choosing" to relocate from reserves to towns and cities, Indigenous individuals relinquish their Aboriginal and treaty rights accorded to Status Indians. Provincial and municipal officials push back against any assumption of "Indigenous rights," which federal leaders rarely reject, leading to the creation of a jurisdictional void that provincial and local government officials exploit to justify limiting the services that they provide to urban Indigenous people because "Indians" living on or off reserve are federal responsibility.[40] The first two points are baseless. In fact, in the Urban Aboriginal Peoples Study conducted in 2010 by the Environics Institute, a large majority (70 percent) of urban Indigenous people indicated that the city is home, and 60 percent believed that they could make a city their home better suited to their life demands while becoming a more visible part of the urban landscape.[41] Yet municipal officials continue to categorize (reorganize) urban Indigenous people as constitutional foreigners living in cities (and towns), a conclusion that I argue is generalizable to most municipalities in Canada, leaving Indigenous people institutionally liable to becoming and remaining homeless.

Institutional Foundation of Urban Indigenous Homelessness

Cities have evolved into networked spaces of relentless Indigenous displacement and dispossession, where a combination of consciously designed institutions remains informed by "individual thoughts, feelings, and behaviours" and structured by the "wider cultural process of meaning-making in historically rooted power dynamics."[42] Ideas are essential.[43] As Miller notes, these ideas shape and influence public policies that inspire novel methods used by settler-colonial governments to deny Indigenous communities or individuals formal state-Indigenous relations.[44] To reiterate, settler-colonial ideas target Indigenous Peoples for removal and are significantly impactful once institutionalized as laws, regulations, or formal policy frameworks. What tends to be overlooked or remain uncoupled from debates on modern-day state policies of Indigenous removal is how both the intended and the unintended negative consequences of past government policies on Indigenous Peoples have contributed to urban Indigenous homelessness.

Disproportionate Indigenous representation among Canada's unhoused population was already apparent by the 1960s.[45] Then, as now, First Nations people living off reserve and Métis and Inuit individuals were more likely to experience unsheltered homelessness compared with the non-Indigenous population.[46] Today, Indigenous people make up less than 5 percent of the national population but account for 29 percent of Canada's total homeless population.[47] On any night, 6.97 percent of the urban Indigenous population across Canada is considered homeless compared with 0.78 percent of the non-Indigenous population.[48] More than 1 of 15 urban Indigenous people are consequently homeless, compared with 1 of 128 non-Indigenous Canadians, which translates into urban Indigenous people being eight times more likely to be or become homeless than non-Indigenous urban individuals.[49] The overrepresentation of Indigenous people in Edmonton's unhoused population is especially acute. In Edmonton, between 2006 and 2021, the number of Indigenous people representing the city's homeless population grew from 38 percent to 54 percent.[50] From 2006 to 2023, the number of Indigenous individuals who identified as homeless nearly doubled to roughly 1,800.[51] On average,

- Indigenous individuals were homeless for 4.2 years, whereas non-Indigenous respondents experienced homelessness for 2.8 years.[52]
- Indigenous individuals were seven times more likely to be users of shelters compared with the city's total population.[53]

- Indigenous homeless individuals were more likely to be unsheltered, making up 62 percent of the unsheltered population.[54]

Understanding these disparities allows us to comprehend the impacts of urban Indigenous exclusion from housing and homelessness policies vis-à-vis Canada's legal and constitutional framework.

Despite clear evidence of need, urban Indigenous people remain trapped in what the Royal Commission on Aboriginal Peoples (1996) described as a policy vacuum (i.e., a space of jurisdictional ambiguity) marked by persistent government inaction.[55] This void is partly attributable to the federal and provincial governments' reliance on the constitutional division of powers, which enables these governments to avoid taking meaningful action to address urban Indigenous homelessness. In this contested space, federal, provincial, and municipal governments debate responsibility for urban Indigenous homelessness, only to respond reluctantly in times of unrest.[56] Allison Smith maintains that institutional legacies continue to shape municipal governance of homelessness.[57] Crucially, examining the policy vacuum's origins[58] serves as a proxy to understand the legal pathways to Indigenous homelessness, which includes two key dimensions: first, the jurisdictional responsibility for housing and homelessness policy, which often excludes or marginalizes Indigenous interests; second, the legal status of urban Indigenous people, which allows provinces and increasingly municipalities to deflect responsibility, thereby heightening urban Indigenous people's vulnerability to becoming and remaining homeless.

In the *Constitution Act, 1867,* sections 91 and 92 outline the respective responsibilities of the two orders of government: federal and provincial.[59] The federal government is granted jurisdiction over the collection of money through taxation. Provincial governments are assigned responsibility for "property and civil rights," "municipal institutions," and "all matters of a merely local or private nature." Territorial governments in Yukon, the Northwest Territories, and Nunavut have a constitutional right to self-governance under section 92 and are governed primarily by the federal government, with certain powers devolved to them through agreements. Notably, the Constitution does not explicitly specify which order of government is responsible for homelessness, nor does it provide explicit protection for housing rights.[60] Whereas the federal government has a greater capacity for revenue than the provinces, generating money through income and sales taxes, corporate taxes, and tariffs, the provinces rely on federal transfers as well as their own income and sales taxes. Municipalities are delegated bodies created by the provinces and therefore lack constitutional authority or significant revenue-generating capacity.[61] Yet both the national and subnational governments frequently exploit the ensuing jurisdictional ambiguity to forgo costly homelessness programs and poverty reduction initiatives in favour of other government priorities.[62]

Adding to the confusion when discussing urban Indigenous people is their tenuous constitutional status as "Indians." When the federal government accepted the exclusive legislative authority over "Indians, and Lands reserved for the Indians," Indigenous Peoples were then classified as wards of the state.[63] Their diversity was subsequently collapsed into a single administrative category known as "Indians." The Fathers of Confederation then drew from the British colonial civilization agenda, which encouraged Indigenous Peoples to move off reserves and assimilate into nearby non-Indigenous communities. One outcome was that Indigenous political participation was limited through law and policy.[64] Explicitly, Canada's *Indian Act* (1876) empowered the federal government to define who is considered an "Indian" and to exclude certain Indigenous Peoples from its responsibility.[65] This policy of distinction lingers, isolating "nonstatus" Indigenous Peoples, often nonreserve residents (i.e., town and city residents), for distinct treatment and limiting their access to resources and services.[66] Frequently, an Indigenous person lost status as the federal government reduced its corresponding financial commitments, which pressured residents of reserves to relocate to towns and cities, whose settler-colonial residents frequently opposed Indigenous residency. Impacted by complex legal and policy manoeuvring grounded by government desire to deflect responsibility for homelessness, housing, and Indigenous issues, urban Indigenous individuals have become disempowered, trapped in an unforgiving policy vacuum that aggravates homelessness.[67]

How, specifically, did settler-colonial beliefs embedded in law and policy find their expression in various government orders regarding urban Indigenous homelessness and how governments choose to respond? Briefly returning to the idea of group difference that anchors the agenda of civilization, we can see that they merged into a formidable barrier to Indigenous legal and policy inclusion, negatively influencing Indigenous housing and homelessness trends.

Governments resisted meaningful funding for on-reserve housing because officials feared that it would incentivize First Nations individuals to remain on reserves rather than leave them to become private homeowners or property holders.[68] Although new housing was needed in First Nations communities, providing it once again contradicted the goal of assimilation in the civilization agenda.[69] Regional programs were developed out of necessity, sometimes with provincial support. However, they were frequently undermined by limited funding and the involvement of multiple ministries and line departments, which added time and expense to what devolved into lengthy, convoluted, multi-governmental and multi-agency projects.[70] As a result, First Nations housing remains impoverished, even in 2025, prompting reserve residents to leave their communities in search of better housing.[71] The law created additional barriers for Indigenous people in their quest to access housing off reserve. Canada's first housing legislation, the *Dominion Housing Act* of 1935,[72] excluded Indigenous people from a program that assisted individuals in accessing government-funded mortgages, which initiated a long period of Indigenous prohibition from national and, where applicable, provincial housing programs. A growing body of literature confirms these trends and illustrates that the jurisdictional quagmire born in the civilization era continues to manufacture "intersecting sites of oppression" that increase the Indigenous "risk of ... homelessness."[73]

Indigenous people have not fared much better in national homelessness programs. For example, by the 1960s, the consequences of federal neglect had crystallized into the foundation of today's crisis. As remains the case today, overcrowding was common in most First Nations communities, and researchers warned government officials that ignoring existing conditions would have a significant adverse intergenerational effect.[74] Federal officials viewed Indigenous people as a rural policy concern, assuming that their housing needs would be adequately met once they were "assimilated" into urban spaces.[75] Indian Affairs officials also believed that assimilation would resolve all housing concerns.[76] Unfortunately, both perspectives failed to acknowledge the realities of First Nations individuals who migrated to cities in search of better housing, employment, and educational opportunities.[77] These migrants faced numerous obstacles, including ongoing settler-colonial racism, financial hardship, and lack of familiarity with urban housing systems. Federal interventions in the 1960s and beyond primarily targeted reserve housing needs while largely ignoring the needs of urban Indigenous people. By the 1990s, this gap became pronounced as urban Indigenous homelessness grew as federal officials deferred responsibility.[78] Reflecting contemporary times, federal officials looked to the provinces to intercede, only to be reminded of the federal section 91(24) responsibility for "Indians, and Lands reserved for the Indians."

Off-reserve Indigenous people remain primarily excluded from First Nations housing programs not transferable to non–First Nations settings, reflecting the ongoing government reliance on policies of group differentiation in nonreserve communities. In contrast, federal responses to Indigenous homelessness depend on large funding programs that delegate responsibility for planning and budgeting to various institutions, which lack effective coordination.[79] Reflecting on settler colonialism's lasting influence and how institutional legacies facilitate and sustain urban Indigenous homelessness, one can conclude that this persistent issue is a trade-off, and an acceptable one at that, for ensuring local government political stability and economic development. Despite the proven complicity of our legal and policy institutions in creating pathways to urban Indigenous homelessness, elected officials and bureaucrats across all government levels continue to deny their crucial role in maintaining this homelessness. Finally, urban Indigenous homelessness is not a policy failure in isolation. It is the direct outcome of a coordinated legal, political, and ideological framework rooted in the colonial project that continues to shape Canadian urban life. As I argue in the next section, this legacy of exclusion and neglect has had lasting effects, setting the stage for the urban Indigenous homelessness crisis that we face today.

Camp Pekiwewin: Case Study

Methodology

Encampments, such as Camp Pekiwewin, represent the most visible form of homelessness and have attracted significant public attention, epitomized by local press coverage. Providing us with critical timelines, the free press sporadically covered the rise of urban Indigenous homelessness, providing inconsistent reportage that occasionally offered flashes of insightful analysis.[80] The arrival of Camp Pekiwewin's first residents, months after the COVID-19 pandemic began, followed by the press, triggered a heated and lasting social debate about housing, homelessness, and encampments within Edmonton's contact zone. Journalists control how ideas originate and flow to the public, meaning that their views provide a valuable database of observations that help to explain how "social class practices and relations will embody certain characteristic values and meaning of the class so that its 'culture' is lived."[81] The unparalleled print and electronic media attention given to Camp Pekiwewin's rise and fall provides indispensable insights into how settler-colonial ideas influenced Mayor Don Iveson's (2013–21) and EPS Chief Dale McFee's (2019–25)[82] issue comprehension and subsequent application of law and policy, which, I contend, led to their implementation of policies that intensified a susceptible population's vulnerability to ongoing institutionalized homelessness.

To elaborate these dynamics, I begin with a discourse analysis of newspaper articles identified through searches in Canadian Newsstream, Canadian Newspaper Archive, and publicly accessible archives of various newspapers and television stations. Search terms included "Indigenous homelessness," "Edmonton," "Camp Pekiwewin," and "Edmonton Police Service." The media environment in Canada is characterized by a concentration of ownership that tends to privilege conservative values. Therefore, to reinforce data accuracy and reliability and counter potential bias and perspective, I also draw from academic, media, and grey literature, triangulating their conclusions with government reports and scholarly writing to examine critically the actions of politicians and police officials. Following a fundamental qualitative data analysis (thematic analysis), I analyzed all textual data using a critical discourse analysis approach, which enabled me to discern patterns (themes, taxonomies, exploratory-descriptive accounts) and unique occurrences in the data while examining how social and political domination is reproduced through text and talk.[83] Conducting a rigorous mixed-method study is the natural next step to help expand the findings in this chapter, revealing that urban Indigenous people's act of emerging from the shadows to demand social service support and to (re-)establish a community on reclaimed traditional land was fashioned into a threat that municipal residents demanded local officials neutralize.

Camp Pekiwewin

Camp Pekiwewin was established in the spring of 2020 by a coalition of individuals, including front-line outreach workers and Indigenous two-spirit women and femmes as well as Black, LGBTQ2S+, and settler allies. The camp provided unhoused people with a space in which to sleep, representing a united assertion of solidarity and a reclamation of the land. "It sets a tone that this isn't ... a protest," said one resident, but about "prayer ... [and] about creating community – rekindling a lot of kinships that might have been sleeping for a while."[84] One supportive journalist proposed that Camp Pekiwewin represented "collective liberation through occupation."[85] CTV News reported that "volunteers and social workers who spent time helping camp residents said the camps created a much-needed home base and sense of community for many who chose to stay in them."[86] One individual noted that "many of the residents of the camp were displaced and unhoused Indigenous people for whom the particular location of the camp had powerful spiritual and political resonance."[87] The first structure built was a teepee in the camp's centre, dubbed the heart of the community, where Elders led prayers and ceremonies. Although Mayor Iveson and other city officials recommended that residents relocate to city-funded shelters, many of them said that Camp Pekiwewin felt safer and more welcoming.[88] Others said that they avoided the shelters out of fear of contracting COVID-19.[89] At its peak, Camp Pekiwewin counted 170 tent homes hosting roughly 450 residents, representing nearly one-quarter of Edmonton's Indigenous homeless population.[90] What was the specific context of the encampment's emergence in 2020?

Indigenous homelessness had been on the rise in Edmonton since 2006. That year Indigenous people accounted for 38 percent of the city's homeless population, amounting to roughly 1,000 homeless Indigenous individuals.[91] This number increased to 54 percent in 2021 and 56 percent in 2023.[92] The lack of shelter capacity contributed to unsheltered homelessness in Edmonton, where Indigenous people were about seven times more likely to experience homelessness compared with the city's non-Indigenous population.[93] In August 2023, roughly two years after Camp Pekiwewin's closure, the number of Indigenous people alone who were homeless (roughly 1,800) exceeded the number of available shelter beds (843).[94] In an unparalleled turn of events, three forces collided in 2020, creating fertile ground for an unprecedented rise in urban Indigenous homelessness in Edmonton: an enduring opioid and drug poisoning crisis,[95] a pandemic, and an economic downturn exacerbating a local housing crisis. Several additional factors must be considered if we are to understand the spike in urban Indigenous homelessness, including major United Conservative Party budget cuts in 2019 and 2021 that affected provincial homelessness programs;[96] lower rates of Indigenous employment[97] and home ownership;[98] the onset of COVID-19, which limited shelter intake and drove people into the streets fearing for their health (heightened eviction rates followed);[99] and poor housing and overcrowding,[100] especially in First Nations communities, which resulted in higher rates of migration to cities for improved accommodations.[101]

As Federal Housing Advocate Marie-Josée Houle noted, encampments appeared across Canada in response to "a lack of affordable housing, limited support services, and nowhere safe to go."[102] They have often become "people's only housing option, or the only option that meets their needs for safety, security and dignity."[103] Although similar trends underscored the emergence of Camp Pekiwewin, Indigenous encampments must be acknowledged as unique spaces whose residents are particularly vulnerable to homelessness because of factors such as susceptibility to racism; lower health, education, and employment outcomes; precarious housing; and other structural determinants such as federal laws and policies that influence the social, economic, and political contexts of Indigenous people.[104] Reflecting these dynamics, the discourse analysis highlighted that, like the events leading to the dissolution of the Papaschase Indian Reserve in 1888, Camp Pekiwewin reflected the deep tensions and contradictions inherent in Indigenous struggles for freedom from settler-colonial power.[105] Triggering these responses was what I describe as Camp Pekiwewin's concentrated visibility – a troubling trend for non-Indigenous neighbours who were already fearful of urban Indigenous permanence. These neighbours, like those of the 1880s, demanded that local government officials remove a municipally bounded Indigenous community to safeguard Edmonton's settler-colonial interests.[106] Petitioners found the mayor and police chief receptive to their demands, much like Prime Minister Macdonald, and, in keeping with settler-colonial practice, branded Camp Pekiwewin an unbecoming symbol of social instability. Speaking to "the complex systemic onslaught of oppression that our community members face," the camp's leaders lobbied city and police officials to improve the safety of the residents.[107] Edmonton officials ignored these appeals, prompting objections from Indigenous leaders who understood the treaties as nation-to-nation agreements and that self-determination was being purposefully ignored.

Although the preceding discussion conveys some of the more overt settler-colonial dynamics that impeded the operations of Camp Pekiwewin, the following discussion elaborates the rationalities and shrewd tactics that underscored the actions of Mayor Iveson and Police Chief McFee. Notably, although the mayor and police chief seemed to act independently in representing their respective institutions, their responses were aligned, and they functioned as ideationally allied agents operating within the broader settler-colonial system structured to reject Indigenous encroachment into and assert authority in urban space.

From the outset, concentrated visibility threatened urban Indigenous permanence, compelling Edmonton officials and non-Indigenous residents to return to the settler-colonial playbook. In doing so, Camp Pekiwewin was portrayed as a threat to the city's interests, justifying state intervention. Urban Indigenous public visibility, according to Glen Coulthard, results from acts of self-recognition, which he defines as a practice of freedom critically evaluating, reconstructing, and redeploying "culture and tradition in ways that seek to prefigure ... a radical alternative to the structural facets of colonial domination."[108] Camp leaders elaborated two explicit outcomes. First, visibility was considered vital for improving public education, necessary to encourage elected officials to bolster social service provision. Second, and characteristic of visibility's role in asserting self-determination, camp leaders sought to shift the focus of their interactions with local officials from debating policy to promoting political partnerships based on a shared history and a mutual approach to understanding international rights.[109]

As Veracini predicted, amplified anxiety overwhelmed Edmonton residents being asked to help the urban Indigenous homeless in contravention of their settler-colonial heritage to eliminate urban Indigeneity. Camp Pekiwewin, then, symbolized the collision of settler colonialism and urban Indigenous self-determination, in which calculated and concentrated urban Indigenous visibility in pursuit of co-governance relations and self-government authority triggered a hitherto pacified public's outrage (the EPS confirmed a 113 percent rise in calls attributable to Camp Pekiwewin between August and mid-September 2020).[110] Driving residential resistance further were the apparent efforts of Iveson and McFee to align themselves with public opposition. Within less than three months of construction of the camp, for example, the mayor described its residents' living conditions as undignified and inhumane.[111] The police chief similarly insisted that such camps were crime incubators and endemic threats to their vulnerable residents.[112] Notably, the electronic and print media contributed to this narrative by habitually restating city and EPS press releases while prominently reporting on municipal government plans to demolish Camp Pekiwewin. These points, taken together, highlight the camp's unrealized public education strategy, as does the general lack of sympathy and empathy among city residents.

Camp leaders who advocated for negotiated co-governance agreements rooted in a shared history called on Edmonton's leaders to negotiate in good faith, respecting treaty principles of shared territory and joint political jurisdiction. The mayor's office and the EPS responded with two specific settler-colonial rationalities: first, reaffirm municipal jurisdiction to rebut Indigenous self-determination claims to civic lands; second, invoke local constitutional interpretations to redirect social service responsibilities to federal and provincial governments. Concerning the first rationality, Mayor Iveson and Police Chief McFee disregarded the spirit and intent of Treaty 6 as well as the attendant self-determination claims and community-building requests, which sought improved housing options and social service provision. The mayor specifically asserted local jurisdiction to deny urban Indigenous political legitimacy and, therefore, urban Indigenous requests to revive dormant government-to-government relationships.[113] Processes of daily jurisdiction endure and undermine urban Indigenous territoriality and self-determination.[114] For example, the actions of the mayor and police chief revealed that non-Indigenous demands took precedence over urban Indigenous self-determination and political rights to the city, particularly those involving municipal Indigenous land reclamation and self-determination. Iveson also deftly avoided discussing Indigenous self-government and self-determination.

Interestingly, the mayor's office and the EPS engaged in closed-door negotiations with camp leaders, leading to early concessions that included limiting police access to camp emergencies. The talks, however, were arguably a diversion calculated to ensure the camp's systematic dismantling, which both men appeared to be committed to from the start. This was despite the federal housing advocate's conclusion that people have a right to live in encampments and that tearing them down violates their human rights.[115] Iveson responded by reminding people that the EPS had dismantled a nearby encampment at 95th Street the previous November (2019), indicating that razing encampments had become normalized by the time of Camp Pekiwewin.[116] It remains to be seen whether Indigenous self-determination claims to traditional lands led Iveson to confront the growing social science and legal scholarship suggesting that urban Indigenous people, whether they are homeless or not, possess self-government rights and legal claims to traditional lands within municipal spaces. The discourse analysis nevertheless reveals that, at best, Indigenous self-determination and self-government were little more than abstract concepts. At worst, Mayor Iveson's and Police Chief McFee's words informed their actions, which in turn perpetuated and aggravated urban Indigenous homelessness.

Evident was that the mayor and police chief relied on negative portrayals of Camp Pekiwewin residents to justify external interventions in resolving publicly established problems rather than forging partnerships with camp leaders based on sharing power and pursuing structural reform.[117] As an example, the two men regularly portrayed the camp as a deficit community, making statements that had the dual effect of undermining Indigenous self-governance and reaffirming the city's capacity to regulate municipal space. Such actions exposed a historical settler-colonial manoeuvre. Consider the similar concerns expressed by future Canadian Minister of the Interior Frank Oliver in 1881. He noted that the Papaschase Reserve would cause "a lasting injury" to Edmonton "without any corresponding benefit occurring" to the Indigenous residents.[118] Settler-colonial leaders of each era similarly orchestrated an urban Indigenous community's closure based on various "concerns around safety ... for the neighbourhood, the surrounding community."[119]

Extending the deficit discourse beyond a public health trope, Camp Pekiwewin was also branded a collective of individual trespassers who faced "constant surveillance, criminalization, and hostility from the City of Edmonton, the police, and local homeowners."[120] Here jurisdiction forcefully emerged as a key pillar of Mayor Iveson's approach to interpreting the *Constitution Act, 1867* as assigning exclusive responsibility for "Indians, and Lands reserved for the Indians," to the federal government. Iveson subtly, albeit consistently, questioned whether municipal officials were accountable to urban Indigenous homeless individuals, whom he identified as federal charges. Regarding his municipal duty to ensure every resident's well-being, he argued that the province also shared liability, specifically because of the lacklustre funding for the requisite Indigenous services. The outcomes of the mayor's approach were telling. Edmonton, for example, allowed the material deprivation of urban Indigenous homeless individuals to occur by constantly engaging in jurisdictional bickering about local government responsibility for the homeless. Yet, when suitable, municipal officials directed resources to ensure police enforcement. In effect, Iveson wielded jurisdiction as a tool of municipal political empowerment to forsake Indigenous social service provision.

In what is a textbook example of perpetuating and exploiting the bemoaned policy vacuum, the discourse analysis exposed settler-colonial ideas that inspired the mayor's statements equating municipal space with non-Indigenous space. Iveson then reiterated his belief that urban Indigenous people fall under either federal or provincial jurisdiction and that the municipality's role is to deliver federal or provincial programs. Iveson, decisively, denied urban Indigenous self-determination and self-governance claims that likewise absolved Edmonton of any corresponding financial commitment. Homelessness advocates challenged the mayor's interpretations, urging caution while arguing that shutting down Camp Pekiwewin would violate the human right to housing and potentially Indigenous rights to self-government and self-determination.[121] Iveson conceded that the policy vacuum negatively influenced what he described as Edmonton's poor response, in turn aggravating urban Indigenous homelessness. Yet he invoked the policy vacuum that he had criticized by reminding people that the city's reliance on "action from all orders of government" for homelessness programs hindered Edmonton's ability to respond.[122] By shifting blame, Iveson engaged in what could be described best as strategic inaction, allowing him to avoid tackling the root causes of urban Indigenous homelessness (an outcome that Police Chief McFee perpetuated), all the while insisting that he would "push for a speedy response from provincial and federal governments to serve again the needs of vulnerable people in our city."[123]

As the mayor attempted to balance settler-colonial expectations with camp leaders' legitimate claims, the police chief seemed to be undaunted by Indigenous self-government or self-determination claims, relying on EPS jurisdiction to pursue Camp Pekiwewin's closure. Of note, he grudgingly accepted the camp residents' right to public protest, which EPS spokesperson Carolin Maran termed acceptable "within the context of the law and public health orders."[124] But by labelling Camp Pekiwewin as a demonstration (which camp leaders countered, arguing that it was not a protest but an exercise in community building), McFee deployed the standard policing device of reframing Indigenous political action as a precursor to disruption to justify state intervention.[125] During the summer of 2020, after Indigenous self-determination rights were invalidated as Camp Pekiwewin's threats to public health and safety were established, McFee turned to support neighbourhood residents out of fear that their concerns "aren't being heard," suggesting that they were unwitting victims of the encampment.[126] Unsurprisingly, his rhetoric of "both sides" ultimately prioritized settler homeowner complaints over Indigenous self-government and self-determination claims and requests for meetings.

Throughout this episode, both men consistently framed urban Indigenous presence as a threat while aggressively working to prevent the possibility of Indigenous permanence in the city. Efforts to reorganize the camp's residents into a community of Indigenous people in Edmonton who were neither a nation nor residents and lacked political legitimacy were also successful. What went unnoticed was that, dating to 2010, the mayor's office and the EPS routinely delivered territorial acknowledgments affirming Indigenous and municipal co-occupancy, even as Edmonton officials aggressively worked to raze Camp Pekiwewin and relocate its residents. This episode likewise prompts several critical questions. Did the coordinated effort to dismantle the camp signal a retreat from meaningful reconciliation with Edmonton's Indigenous people? Did it betray the city's public commitment to repairing this relationship?

Territorial acknowledgments are not merely symbolic gestures; they affirm precontact Indigenous sovereignty, counter settler-colonial erasure, and honour ongoing Indigenous relationships with the land.[127] Closely linked to the *UNDRIP*, which Parliament endorsed in May 2016 and enacted as the *UNDRIP Act* in 2021,[128] territorial acknowledgments identify Indigenous Peoples' historical and cultural ties to their lands, connections that the *UNDRIP* seeks to protect and fortify through its collective and individual rights frame. *UNDRIP* Articles 25–28, for instance, underscore Camp Pekiwewin's leaders' self-government and self-determination claims, illustrating that this was neither a protest nor a group of trespassers illegally occupying municipal land:

- Maintain spiritual relationships with their territories (Article 25).
- Own, use, develop, and control their lands and resources (Article 26).
- Uphold their laws, traditions, and customs relating to their lands (Article 27).
- Have redress for lands confiscated without their free, prior, and informed consent (Article 28).

Furthermore, interpreted through the dual lenses of the *UNDRIP* and international law, which stress the centrality of Indigenous self-determination, Camp Pekiwewin, an Indigenous-run camp operating on treaty land and led by democratically elected leaders who administered locally devised laws and policies, met international standards for self-government and self-determination.

From the start of Camp Pekiwewin to now, Edmonton officials have acknowledged that the city is situated on "the traditional territories of many First Nations"[129] and is "a gathering site for many Indigenous peoples" and the site of "traditional burial grounds" (a historical and ongoing contact zone).[130] These acknowledgments nevertheless stand in stark contrast to the actions of the city and EPS in displacing Indigenous people from the very land honoured. The discourse analysis, government documents reviewed, and public statements reviewed confirm that the *UNDRIP* did not guide the interactions of the city and EPS with urban Indigenous leaders, suggesting that reconciliation was viewed as situation specific and quickly halted when necessary. Even more troubling, it was typical for the mayor and police chief to perform territorial acknowledgments as they worked to close Camp Pekiwewin, challenging the state's understanding of land use.[131] In this context, the mayor prioritized local government jurisdiction over federal law, Supreme Court decisions, and international law to denounce an urban Indigenous community that he wanted removed. Significantly, Mayor Iveson's and Police Chief McFee's actions undermined their ability to honour a March 2019 agreement to collaborate with local organizations, businesses, academic institutions, governments, and citizens to "eliminate the systemic racism and discrimination that Indigenous Peoples face in Edmonton."[132]

In the wake of these events, sensing mounting residential resistance and the increasingly reticent stance of the EPS, and seeking to avoid a quasi-military conflict, the camp's leaders opted to negotiate a closure date. Iveson's promise to deliver dignified and safe shelter, the linchpin of his ten-week plan to end homelessness in August (which Iveson failed to deliver), prompted organizers to cap the camp's capacity and wind down operations.[133] Upon obtaining the approval of Edmonton City Council, on November 12, more than thirty EPS officers were dispatched to relocate the remaining fifteen residents of Camp Pekiwewin who had refused to retreat into Edmonton's shadows.[134] Thus ended a public episode (with more likely on the horizon) that disrupted the settler-colonial narrative, which, in turn, "created a lot of concerns around safety ... for the neighbourhood" that made "working toward the closure of Camp Pekiwewin ... an important goal for the city."[135] In the aftermath of the camp's closure, Mayor Iveson proudly noted that "Edmonton is one of the only cities where we've been able to disband those camps without arrests and without violence."[136] Not unlike the closure of the Papaschase Indian Reserve in 1888.

Conclusion

As the late Peter Russell noted, Western imperial ideologies form the backdrop of laws and policies that, I argue, create pathways to homelessness while imposing barriers that hinder our individual and collective abilities to respond to it.[137] In this chapter, I have clarified how social, economic, political, and legal conditions shape and produce people's experiences of housing and home by illustrating how Edmonton sustains "institutions that have eradicated value systems that existed for thousands of years, replacing them with doctrines that continue to disrupt life for Aboriginal peoples."[138] Correspondingly, I have exposed and explored the ideational foundation that elected leaders and policy makers use to underscore tactics designed to secure state hegemony and enhance local government authority through enduring processes of Indigenous elimination rather than political and social coexistence.

As this chapter's first epigraph admits, we routinely fail society's most vulnerable, including urban Indigenous people who experience homelessness. Camp Pekiwewin, for example, was neither understood as a result of homelessness nor recognized as a self-determining urban Indigenous community with self-government rights.[139] This urban collective quickly found itself (re)relegated to the margins, constrained by structures of settler colonialism that the local process of reconciliation sought to address.[140] Meaningful collaboration between Indigenous leaders and provincial and federal officials was not evident, showing that it is necessary to deepen their collective understanding of the city's obligations to Indigenous Peoples and their communities.[141] If local governments are to fulfill their role as democratic institutions within Canadian federalism, then they must abandon the polarizing colonial politics that shape the city's approach to urban Indigenous people and homelessness, starting with abandoning processes of dispossession and racialization that displaced the Papaschase Indian Reserve in 1888 and vindicated the dismantling of Camp Pekiwewin in 2020.[142] Territorial acknowledgments – already in practice as part of the processes of reconciliation – offer officials a much-needed relationship-building tool with which to devise co-governance agreements within shared spaces, thereby replacing the settler-colonial "project of replacement" invested in settler futurity.[143]

In summary, to address urban Indigenous homelessness effectively, all government actors must avoid jurisdictional gridlock, abandon immobilizing encampment politics, and pursue constitutional innovation and cooperative policy making. Absent these and other transformative shifts, the intersection of legal, policy, and social failures that underscores our current approach will persevere, intensifying the crisis of urban Indigenous displacement and threatening the well-being of an already vulnerable community experiencing homelessness.[144]

Acknowledgments

I would like to thank Sydney Rolfe for her research assistance, Jeff Coffman, Rylan Kafara, and Alli Moncrieff for reviewing and commenting on an earlier draft, and the editors of this volume for their helpful comments and patience.

Notes

1 John Borrows, *Crown and Aboriginal Occupations of Land: A History and Comparison* (Toronto: Ipperwash Inquiry, 2005) at 3.

2 Joshua Evans, Madeleine Stout, Damian Collins, and Kenna McDowell, "The Reticent State? Interpreting Emergency Responses to Homelessness in Alberta, Canada" (2023) 38:9 *Housing Studies* 1681–94.

3 Jordan Olmstead, "'This Is About Prayer': Inside Edmonton's Camp Pekiwewin," *CBC News* (August 12, 2020), https://www.cbc.ca/news/canada/edmonton/

this-is-about-prayer-inside-edmonton-s-camp-pekiwewin-1.5682391 [perma.cc/HM8B-7XFP].

4 *National Housing Strategy Act*, SC 2019, c 29, s 313.

5 Erin Dej, *A Complex Exile: Homelessness and Social Exclusion in Canada* (Vancouver: UBC Press, 2020). Dej notes that homeless individuals frequently avoid public spaces in their efforts to remain invisible, which she styles as a pre-emptive means of dodging social vilification and exclusion born of institutionalized behaviours and beliefs.

6 The term "survivance" is drawn from Gerald Vizenor, ed., *Survivance: Narratives of Native Presence* (Lincoln: University of Nebraska Press, 2008). Blending the words *survival* and *resistance*, survivance describes active Indigenous resistance to colonial oppression based on agency, storytelling, and cultural continuity grounded by asserting identity and reclaiming history, land being the philosophical and ideological anchor.

7 *Coalition for Justice and Human Rights Ltd v Edmonton (City)*, 2024 ABKB 26 (Affidavit, Dr. Yale Belanger) at paras 157–58 [*Coalition for Justice and Human Rights Ltd*, Belanger Affidavit].

8 Bruce Granville Miller, *Invisible Indigenes: The Politics of Nonrecognition* (Lincoln: University of Nebraska Press, 2003) at 211.

9 Ibid at 215.

10 United Nations General Assembly (UNGA), *United Nations Declaration on the Rights of Indigenous Peoples*, UNGA, 61st Sess, UN Doc A/RES/61/295 (2007) UNGAOR Res 61/295, Supp No 49, UN Doc A/RES/61/295 [*UNDRIP*].

11 Libby Porter and Janice Barry, "Bounded Recognition: Urban Planning and the Textual Mediation of Indigenous Rights in Canada and Australia" (2015) 9:1 *Critical Policy Studies* 22–40.

12 City of Edmonton, "Indigenous Land Acknowledgement: Home for Thousands of Years," https://web.archive.org/web/20240118123326/https://cityplan.edmonton.ca/indigenous-acknowledgement [City of Edmonton, "Land Acknowledgement"].

13 Mackenzie Brown, "Indigenous Landmarks and Spaces in Edmonton" (May 2, 2023), https://exploreedmonton.com/articles/indigenous-landmarks; Papaschase First Nation, "Highlights of Papaschase's History" (accessed February 6, 2026), https://papaschase.ca/brief-history.

14 Fred Fenwick, "Extinguishment of a Papaschase Indian Band (Death by Scrip)" (2004) 29 *Law Now* 88–91.

15 Dwayne Donald, "Edmonton Pentimento: Re-Reading History in the Case of the Papaschase Cree" (2004) 2:1 *Journal of the Canadian Association for Curriculum Studies* 21–54 at 36–37.

16 Irene Spry, "The Tragedy of the Loss of the Commons in Western Canada," in *As Long as the Sun Shines and Water Flows: A Reader in Canadian Native Studies*, ed. Ian Getty and Antoine S. Lussier (Vancouver: UBC Press, 1983), 203–28.

17 Papaschase First Nation, "A Brief History of the Papaschase Band: As Recorded in the Papaschase First Nation Statement of Claim" (n.d.), Wayback Machine, https://web.archive.org/web/20250427180716/papaschase.ca/text/papaschase_history.pdf.

18 Ibid.

19 *Canada (Attorney General) v Lameman,* [2008] 1 SCR 372, 2008 SCC 14.

20 Mill Woods Living Heritage. Ancestors claim that the government omitted certain members. Since 128 acres of land were assigned per treaty signatory, it was common for government officials to underestimate population sizes to save on land allocations. See Stephanie Dubois, "'I Can Feel My Ancestors Around Me': How the Papaschase Band Is Fighting to Be Recognized as an Official First Nation," *CBC News* (n.d.), https://newsinteractives.cbc.ca/longform/papaschase/ [perma.cc/G9LV-CUKA]; see also Papaschase First Nation, "Papaschase Brief History," https://papaschase.ca/history [perma.cc/C5V8-7V7G].

21 Mary Louise Pratt, *Imperial Eyes: Travel Writing and Transculturation,* 2nd ed. (New York: Routledge, 2008) at 8.

22 See, generally, John L. Taylor, *Treaty Research Report: Treaty 6 (1876)* (Ottawa: Treaties and Historical Research Centre, Indian and Northern Affairs Canada, 1985). For the Treaty 6 text and the Crown negotiator's reflections, see Alexander Morris, *The Treaties of Canada with the Indians of Manitoba and the North-West Territories* (1880; reprinted, Toronto: Coles Canadiana, 1971).

23 Richard T. Price, ed., *The Spirit of the Alberta Indian Treaties,* 3rd ed. (Edmonton: University of Alberta Press, 1999).

24 James Youngblood Henderson, "Implementing the Treaty Order," in *Continuing Poundmaker's and Riel's Quest: Presentations Made at a Conference on Aboriginal Peoples and Justice,* ed. Richard Gosse, James Youngblood Henderson, and Roger Carter (Saskatoon: Purich, 1994), 52–62 at 52. See also Arthur J. Ray, Jim Miller, and Frank J. Tough, *Bounty and Benevolence: A History of Saskatchewan Treaties* (Montreal and Kingston: McGill-Queen's University Press, 2000).

25 These rights allow Indigenous Peoples to use the land in traditional ways (e.g., hunting, fishing, gathering) without holding formal ownership of it. The Crown holds legal title. Indigenous Peoples, however, do retain a recognized right to access and benefit from these lands based on their historical use and occupation of them. These rights are inherent, long-standing, and often protected through treaties.

26 As it relates specifically to Indigenous housing and homelessness in Edmonton, see John D. Crookshanks, "Seeking Shelter Among Settlers: Housing, Governance, and the Urban/Aboriginal Dichotomy" (PhD diss., University of Alberta, 2013) [unpublished].

27 Thomas Biolsi, "Imagined Geographies: Sovereignty, Indigenous Space, and American Indian Struggle" (2005) 32:2 *American Ethnologist,* 231–47 at 240–41.

28 Renisa Mawani, *Colonial Proximities: Crossracial Encounters and Juridical Truths in British Columbia, 1871–1921* (Vancouver: UBC Press, 2009).

29 Kara Granzow, *Invested Indifference: How Violence Persists in Settler Colonial Society* (Vancouver: UBC Press, 2020).

30 Lorenzo Veracini, *Settler Colonialism: A Theoretical Overview* (London: Palgrave Macmillan, 2010) at 5.

31 Porter and Barry, "Bounded Recognition."

32 Glen Sean Coulthard, *Red Skin, White Masks: Rejecting the Colonial Politics of Recognition* (Minneapolis: University of Minnesota Press, 2014) at 173–74.

33 *Indian Act,* SC 1876, c 18.

34 Ibid. See also J.R. Miller, *Skyscrapers Hide the Heavens: A History of Native-Newcomer Relations in Canada,* 4th ed. (Toronto: University of Toronto Press, 2018); Yale D. Belanger and Maura Hanranhan, *Ways of Knowing: An Introduction to Indigenous Studies in Canada,* 4th ed. (Toronto: Nelson Education, 2021).
35 See Spry, "The Tragedy of the Loss of the Commons."
36 Eva Mackey, *Unsettled Expectations: Uncertainty, Land and Settler Decolonization* (Halifax: Fernwood, 2016).
37 Veracini, *Settler Colonialism.*
38 See, for example, Jordan Stanger-Ross, "Municipal Colonialism in Vancouver: City Planning and the Conflict over Indian Reserves, 1928–1950s" (2008) 89:4 *Canadian Historical Review* 541–80.
39 Patrick Wolfe, "Settler Colonialism and the Elimination of the Native" (2006) 8:4 *Journal of Genocide Research* 387–409.
40 Yale Belanger, "Breaching Reserve Boundaries: Canada v. Misquadis and the Legal Evolution of the Urban Aboriginal Community," in *Indigenous in the City: Contemporary Identities and Cultural Innovation,* ed. Evelyn Peters and Chris Andersen (Vancouver: UBC Press, 2013), 69–87 at 69.
41 Environics Institute, *Urban Aboriginal Peoples Study: Main Report* (Toronto: Environics Institute, 2010).
42 Jeffrey S. Denis, *Canada at a Crossroads: Boundaries, Bridges, and Laissez-Faire Racism in Indigenous-Settler Relations* (Toronto: University of Toronto Press, 2020) at 5.
43 See, for example, Daniel Béland, "Ideas and Social Policy: An Institutionalist Perspective" (2005) 39:1 *Social Policy and Administration* 1–18.
44 Miller, *Invisible Indigenes,* at 211.
45 See Yale D. Belanger, "The Policy of State as a Social Determinant of Health: Canada's Indigenous Homelessness Policy," in *International Handbook of Law, Policy and Homelessness,* ed. Chris Bevan (London: Routledge, 2024), 238–56 at 238; Yale D. Belanger, "A Critical Review of Canadian First Nations and Aboriginal Housing Policy, 1867–present," in *Exploring Effective Systems Responses to Homelessness,* ed. Naomi Nichols and Carey Doberstein (Toronto: Canadian Observatory on Homelessness, 2016), 442–59 at 442.
46 See Indian Affairs Branch, *A Survey of the Contemporary Indians of Canada: A Report on Economic, Political, Educational Needs and Policies,* vol. 1, by H.A.C. Cairns, S.M. Jamieson, & K. Lysyk, ed. H.B. Hawthorn, Catalogue No. R32-1267/1 (Ottawa: Information Canada, 1966); Indian Affairs Branch, *A Survey of the Contemporary Indians of Canada: A Report on Economic, Political, Educational Needs and Policies,* vol. 2, by M.A. Tremblay, F.G. Vallee, and J. Ryan, ed. H.B. Hawthorn, Catalogue No. R32-1267/2 (Ottawa: Information Canada, 1967).
47 Statistics Canada, *Census in Brief: Housing Conditions Among First Nations People, Métis and Inuit in Canada from the 2021 Census,* Catalogue No. 98-200-X (Ottawa: Statistics Canada, September 21, 2022).
48 Ibid.
49 Yale D. Belanger, Gabrielle Weasel Head, and Olu Awosoga, "Housing of Urban Aboriginal People in Urban Centres: A Quantitative Perspective" (2012) 2:1 *Aboriginal Policy Studies* 4–25.

50 See Canadian Observatory on Homelessness, "Community Profiles: Edmonton" (various dates), https://homelesshub.ca/community-profile/edmonton [perma.cc/ZQL4-LS8T].

51 Homeward Trust Edmonton, "Data, Analytics and Reporting" (n.d.), https://homewardtrust.ca/data-analytics-reporting/ [perma.cc/L2BK-7QW5] (this number will change as the database is updated).

52 Homeward Trust Edmonton, *2016 Edmonton Point in Time Homeless Count Final Report* (Edmonton: Homeward Trust Edmonton, 2016), http://homewardtrust.ca/wp-content/uploads/2016/11/2016-Edmonton-Homeless-Count-Final-Report.pdf. [perma.cc/KNE5-BJK3].

53 Employment and Social Development Canada, *Study of Indigenous Homelessness in Canada* (May 15, 2019), https://nickfalvo.ca/wp-content/uploads/2019/10/ESDC-HIFIS-analysis-Indigenous-ppls-15may2019.pdf [perma.cc/SP43-59PW], at 13.

54 Homeward Trust Edmonton, *2016 Final Report,* at 22.

55 Canada, Royal Commission on Aboriginal Peoples (RCAP), *Highlights of the Report of the Royal Commission on Aboriginal Peoples* (Ottawa: RCAP, 2010) at 542.

56 Chris Andersen and Jenna Strachan, "Urban Aboriginal Programming in a Coordination Vacuum: The Alberta (Dis)Advantage," in *Urban Aboriginal Policy Making in Canadian Municipalities,* ed. Evelyn Peters (Montreal and Kingston: McGill-Queen's University Press, 2011), 127–59.

57 Alison Smith, *Multiple Barriers: The Multilevel Governance of Homelessness in Canada* (Toronto: University of Toronto Press, 2022).

58 Standing Senate Committee on Aboriginal Peoples, *Urban Aboriginal Youth: An Action Plan for Change* (October 2003) at 18.

59 *Constitution Act, 1867* (UK), 30 & 31 Vict, c 3, reprinted in RSC 1985, App II, No 5.

60 Terry Skolnik, "Homelessness and Unconstitutional Discrimination" (2019) 15:1 *Journal of Law and Equality* 69–94; Shiri Pasternak, "Jurisdiction and Settler Colonialism: Where Do Laws Meet?" (2014) 29:1 *Canadian Journal of Law and Society* 145–61.

61 Price, *The Spirit of the Alberta Indian Treaties.*

62 John Graham, Yale D. Belanger, and Christine Walsh, "Homelessness in Canada," in *International Handbook of Law, Policy and Homelessness,* ed. Chris Bevan (London: Routledge, 2024), 225–37.

63 *Constitution Act, 1867* (1867), 30 & 31 Vict, c 3, s 91, ss 24.

64 Mawani, *Colonial Proximities;* Doug Owram, *Promise of Eden: The Canadian Expansionist Movement and the Idea of the West, 1856–1900* (Toronto: University of Toronto Press, 1992).

65 Sébastien Grammond, *Identity Captured by Law: Membership in Canada's Indigenous Peoples and Linguistic Minorities* (Montreal and Kingston: McGill-Queen's University Press, 2009).

66 John Borrows, "'Landed' Citizenship: Narratives of Aboriginal Political Participation," in *Citizenship in Diverse Societies,* ed. Will Kymlicka and Wayne Norman (Oxford: Oxford University Press, 2000), 326–42.

67 Sylvia Olsen, "Making Poverty: A History of On-Reserve Housing Programs, 1930–1996" (PhD diss., University of Victoria, 2016) [unpublished].

68 Belanger, "Policy of State."
69 Adele Perry, "From 'the Hot-Bed of Vice' to the 'Good and Well-Ordered Christian Home': First Nations Housing and Reform in Nineteenth-Century British Columbia" (2003) 50:4 *Ethnohistory* 587–610.
70 Olsen, "Making Poverty"; Belanger, "Policy of State."
71 Belanger, "Critical Review." This remains a historical trend. See Evelyn Peters and Vince Robillard, "Urban Hidden Homelessness and Reserve Housing" (2007) 4 *Aboriginal Policy Research Consortium International* 189–206.
72 *Dominion Housing Act*, SC 1935, c 58.
73 Belanger, "Critical Review"; Olsen, "Making Poverty"; Belanger, "Policy of State"; Amy M. Alberton, G. Brent Angell, Kevin M. Gorey, and Stéphane Grenier, "Homelessness Among Indigenous Peoples in Canada: The Impacts of Child Welfare Involvement and Educational Achievement" (2020) 111 *Children and Youth Services Review* 1–9.
74 H.B. Hawthorn, C.S. Belshaw, and S.M. Jamieson, *The Indians of British Columbia: A Study of Contemporary Social Adjustment* (Berkeley: University of California Press, 1958).
75 Federal and provincial elected officials still cling to the historical belief that homelessness is limited to industrial, urban environments and is not impactful in rural communities.
76 Perry, "From 'the Hot-Bed of Vice.'"
77 See, for example, Gabrielle Lindstrom, Steve Pomeroy, Nick Falvo, and Jodi Bruhn, *Understanding the Flow of Urban Indigenous Homelessness: Examining the Movement Between Treaty 7 First Nations and Calgary's Homeless-Serving System of Care* (Calgary: Calgary Homeless Foundation, 2020); Josh Brandon and Evelyn Peters, *Moving to the City: Housing and Aboriginal Migration to Winnipeg* (Winnipeg: Canadian Centre for Policy Alternatives, 2014).
78 Ryan Walker, "Social Housing and the Role of Aboriginal Organizations in Canadian Cities" (2008) 14:4 *Institute for Research and Public Policy: Choices* 1–18; Steve Pomeroy, "A New Beginning: A National Non-Reserve Aboriginal Housing Strategy," in *Aboriginal Policy Research Volume IV: Setting the Agenda for Change*, ed. Jerry P. White, Susan Wingert, Dan Beavon, and Paul Maxim (Toronto: Thompson Educational Publishing, 2007), 235–42.
79 Belanger, "Critical Review."
80 See, for example, Solina Richter, Katharina Kovacs Burns, Jean Chaw-Kant, et al., "Homelessness Coverage in Major Canadian Newspapers, 1987–2007" (2012) 36:4 *Canadian Journal of Communication* 619–35; Katharina Kovacs Burns, Solina Richter, and Jean Chaw Kant, "Portraits of People Who Are Homeless in the Canadian Media: Investigating the Journalists Behind the Stories" (2013) 1:2 *Studies in Media and Communication* 96–108.
81 Stuart Hall, "Culture, the Media, and the 'Ideological Effect,'" in *Mass Communication and Society*, ed. James Curran, Michael Gurevitch, and Janet Woollacott (London: Edward Arnold Harding, 1977), 315–48 at 322.
82 Upon retiring in February 2025, Dale McFee was appointed deputy minister of the Executive Council and head of the Alberta Public Service, where he helped the

United Conservative Party government to implement its "recovery-oriented" approach to addictions. See Janet French, "Edmonton Police Chief Dale McFee Hired as Alberta Premier's Top Bureaucrat," *CBC News* (December 12, 2024), https://www.cbc.ca/news/canada/edmonton/edmonton-police-chief-dale-mcfee-hired-as-alberta-premier-s-top-bureaucrat-1.7408991 [perma.cc/F7CS-PBBG].

83 See Teun A. van Dijk, *Discourse and Power* (New York: Palgrave Macmillan, 2008), and his "Critical Discourse Studies: A Sociocognitive Approach," in *Methods of Critical Discourse Studies, 3rd Edition,* ed. Ruth Wodak and Michael Meyer (Thousand Oaks, CA: SAGE Publications, 2016), 62–85 at 62.

84 Olmstead, "'This Is About Prayer.'"

85 "Collective Liberation Through Occupation: How Camp Pekiwewin Brings a Global Struggle to Edmonton" (n.d.), Progress Report,https://www.theprogressreport.ca/collective_liberation_through_occupation_camp_pekiwewin_is_the_world.

86 Jeremy Thompson, "The Pandemic, Politics, and Camp Pekiwewin: Don Iveson Reflects on 2020 in Edmonton," *CTV News* (December 30, 2020), https://www.ctvnews.ca/edmonton/article/the-pandemic-politics-and-camp-pekiwewin-don-iveson-reflects-on-2020-in-edmonton/ [perma.cc/4Z3P-CU35].

87 Robert Jackson, "Notes," *JumpCut: A Review of Contemporary Media* (n.d.), https://ejumpcut.org/archive//jc61.2022/RobertJackson/notes.html [perma.cc/UQT7-YNQG].

88 "Conditions at Edmonton Convention Centre Shelter Unsafe, Clients Say," *CBC News* (December 2, 2020), https://www.cbc.ca/news/canada/edmonton/conditions-at-edmonton-convention-centre-shelter-unsafe-clients-say-1.5824575 [perma.cc/46ER-VRUY].

89 Chris Stewart, "Camp Pekiwewin Closed and Residents Relocated as Edmonton City, Police Clear Site," *APTN News* (November 13, 2020), https://www.aptnnews.ca/national-news/homeless-shelter-edmonton-camp-pekiewin/ [perma.cc/66RM-RSJA].

90 Olmstead, "'This Is About Prayer.'"

91 Canadian Observatory on Homelessness, "Community Profiles."

92 Homeless Hub, "Edmonton" (various dates), https://homelesshub.ca/community-profile/edmonton [perma.cc/LK8Y-RBAK].

93 The United Conservative Party's draconian approach of pitting harm reduction against recovery likely exacerbated these trends. See Jeremy Appel, *Kenneyism: Jason Kenney's Pursuit of Power* (Toronto: Dundurn Press, 2024). According to the Alberta First Nations Information Governance Centre and Alberta Health, *Opioid Response Surveillance Report: First Nations People in Alberta* (Edmonton: Alberta Health, June 2021) at 3–4 [*Opioid Response Surveillance Report*], First Nations people experienced 22 percent of all opioid poisoning deaths during the first six months of 2020 (they make up roughly 6 percent of Alberta's population). The rate of apparently accidental opioid poisoning deaths was seven times higher among First Nations people compared with non–First Nations people. See also Homeward Trust Edmonton, *2016 Final Report,* at 29.

94 *Coalition for Justice and Human Rights Ltd*, Belanger Affidavit.

95 Appel, *Kenneyism.* See also Homeward Trust Edmonton, *2016 Final Report,* at 29.

96 See Nick Falvo, "Subsidized Rental Housing and Homelessness Under the UCP," in *Anger and Angst: Jason Kenney's Legacy and Alberta's Right,* ed. Trevor W. Harrison and Ricardo Acuña (Montreal: Black Rose Books, 2023), 349–72 at 349.

97 Twenty-six percent of Indigenous homeless individuals (versus 15 percent of non-Indigenous homeless individuals) cited job loss as a reason for their experience of homelessness. Eviction or family conflict was also listed as a contributing factor. See Homeward Trust Edmonton, *2016 Final Report,* at 29.

98 In Edmonton, 21 percent of Indigenous households were in core housing need (above the national average) compared with 11 percent of non-Indigenous households (below the national average). Canada Mortgage and Housing Corporation (CMHC), *The Housing Conditions of Off-Reserve Aboriginal Households* (Ottawa: CMHC, 2019) at 23.

99 Jakob Koziel, Maria Savidov, and Andrea Frick, *A Brief Scan of COVID-19 Impacts on People Experiencing Homelessness: System Impacts and Responses* (Edmonton: Bissell Centre, 2020).

100 Overcrowding was confirmed by the 2015 survey of First Nations housing by the Standing Senate Committee on Aboriginal Peoples. The same committee noted in 2022 that "overcrowding ... contributes to a host of social problems, such as family abuse, violence, suicide, alcoholism and addictions." Standing Senate Committee on Aboriginal Peoples, *Housing on First Nations Reserves: Challenges and Successes* (Ottawa: Canadian Senate, 2015) at 15–19.

101 The Assembly of First Nations pinpointed in 2011 a shortfall of 85,000 reserve housing units. A minimum of $17 billion would be required to alleviate reserve overcrowding. See Assembly of First Nations, *A Submission to the House of Commons Standing Committee on Finance* (Ottawa: House of Commons, August 12, 2011); Standing Senate Committee on Aboriginal Peoples, *Housing on First Nations Reserves.*

102 Office of the Federal Housing Advocate, *Upholding Dignity and Human Rights: The Federal Housing Advocate's Review of Homeless Encampments – Final Report* (Ottawa: Canadian Human Rights Commission, 2024) at 2.

103 Ibid.

104 See Jesse A. Thistle, *Definition of Indigenous Homelessness in Canada* (Toronto: Canadian Observatory on Homelessness Press, 2017), who argues for the need to reframe Indigenous homelessness through an Indigenous lens. Urban Indigenous homeless encampments likewise demand the same consideration.

105 James Tully, "The Struggles of Indigenous Peoples for and of Freedom," in *Political Theory and the Rights of Indigenous Peoples,* ed. Duncan Ivison, Paul Patton, and Will Sanders (Cambridge, UK: Cambridge University Press, 2000), 41–50 at 36.

106 Vizenor, *Survivance,* at 1.

107 Shima Robinson, "Encamping for Change: A Better World Is Possible," *Alberta Views: The Magazine for Engaged Citizens* (October 28, 2020), https://albertaviews.ca/encamping-for-change/ [perma.cc/6GVS-UNQQ].

108 Glen Coulthard, "Subjects of Empire: Indigenous Peoples and the 'Politics of Recognition' in Canada" (2007) 6:4 *Contemporary Political Theory* 437–60 at 456.

109 Paige Parsons, "Rossdale Green Space Occupied by Group Calling for Housing Rights, End to Police Violence," *CBC News* (July 26, 2020), https://www.cbc.ca/news/canada/edmonton/rossdale-green-space-occupied-by-group-calling-for-housing-rights-end-to-police-violence-1.5663902 [perma.cc/YVB8-J8MQ].

110 Lauren Boothby, "Police Calls Up 113 Per Cent in Rossdale Near Camp Pekiwewin over Last Year: Chief McFee," *Edmonton Journal* (October 7, 2020), https://edmontonjournal.com/news/local-news/police-calls-up-113-per-cent-in-rossdale-near-camp-pekiwewin-over-last-year-chief-mcfee [perma.cc/WE3B-CBZ9].

111 City of Edmonton, "24/7 Temporary Accommodation in Works as City Announces Plan to Help Homeless Edmontonians" (October 5, 2020), https://transforming.edmonton.ca/24-7-temporary-accommodation-in-works-as-city-announces-plan-to-help-homeless-edmontonians/ [perma.cc/5XMM-MU8M].

112 Boothby, "Police Calls Up 113 Per Cent."

113 Shari Pasternak, *Grounded Authority: The Algonquins of Barrier Lake Against the State* (Minneapolis: University of Minnesota Press, 2017) at 3.

114 Shaunnagh Dorsett and Shaun McVeigh, *Jurisdiction* (London: Routledge-Cavendish, 2012); Pasternak, "Jurisdiction and Settler Colonialism."

115 Office of the Federal Housing Advocate, *Upholding Dignity and Human Rights.*

116 Vinesh Pratap, "Edmonton Homeless Encampments Being Removed," *Global News* (November 1, 2019), https://globalnews.ca/news/6114164/edmonton-homeless-encampments-removed/ [perma.cc/439R-KLNT].

117 J. Rick Ponting and Cora Voyageur, "Challenging the Deficit Paradigm: Grounds for Optimism Among First Nations in Canada" (2001) 21:2 *Canadian Journal of Native Studies* 275–307.

118 Dwayne Trevor Donald, "Edmonton Pentimento Re-Reading History in the Case of the Papaschase Cree" (2004) 2:1 *Journal of the Canadian Association for Curriculum Studies* 21–54 at 38.

119 Emily Mertz, "Camp Pekiwewin in Rossdale Closed, Police and City Crews on Site," *Global News* (November 12, 2020), https://globalnews.ca/news/7458802/camp-pekiwewin-in-rossdale-closed-police-and-city-crews-on-site/ [perma.cc/C2J9-BZZM]. See also Rob Shields, Kieran Moran, and Dianne Gillespie, "Edmonton, Amiskwaciy Waskahikan, and a Papaschase Suburb for Settlers" (2020) 64:1 *Canadian Geographer* 105–19.

120 Robert Jackson, "Grounded Abstractions: An Interview with Conor McNally," *Jump-Cut: A Review of Contemporary Media* (n.d.), https://ejumpcut.org/archive//jc61.2022/RobertJackson/index.html [perma.cc/L6U7-DNCF].

121 See Sandeep Agrawal, "COVID Is a Wakeup Call that Rights and Freedoms Can Be Tested in a Crisis," *Edmonton Journal* (December 8, 2020), https://edmontonjournal.com/opinion/columnists/opinion-covid-is-a-wakeup-call-that-rights-and-freedoms-can-be-tested-in-a-crisis [perma.cc/3GMS-VUHC]; Jordan Olmstead, "Organizers to Leave Pekiwewin Encampment as Temporary Shelter Opens," *CBC News* (October 30, 2020), https://www.cbc.ca/news/canada/edmonton/organizers-to-leave-pekiwewin-encampment-as-temporary-shelter-opens-1.5782997 [perma.cc/BKQ8-2TP2].

122 "City of Edmonton Working to Move Camp Pekiwewin Residents," *Global News* (August 27, 2020), https://globalnews.ca/video/7302570/city-of-edmonton-working-to-move-camp-pekiwewin-residents, at 00h:1m:27s.

123 Ibid at 00h:00m:40s.

124 Parsons, "Rossdale Green Space Occupied by Group."

125 Yale D. Belanger and P. Whitney Lackenbauer, eds., *Blockades or Breakthroughs? Aboriginal Peoples Confront the Canadian State* (Montreal and Kingston: McGill-Queen's University Press, 2014).

126 Boothby, "Police Calls Up 113 Per Cent."

127 See Chelsea Vowel, "Revisiting 'Beyond Territorial Acknowledgments'" (November 21, 2024), https://apihtawikosisan.com/2024/11/revisiting-beyond-territorial-acknowledgments/ [perma.cc/E3B6-WXGB].

128 See Yale D. Belanger, "The United Nations Declaration on the Rights of Indigenous Peoples and Urban Aboriginal Self-Determination in Canada: A Preliminary Assessment" (2011) 1:1 *Aboriginal Policy Studies* 132–61; *UNDRIP*.

129 City of Edmonton, "Land Acknowledgement."

130 Brown, "Indigenous Landmarks and Spaces in Edmonton."

131 Porter and Barry, "Bounded Recognition."

132 City of Edmonton, "Community Engagement: Indigenous Framework" (n.d.), https://www.edmonton.ca/city_government/initiatives_innovation/community-engagement-indigenous-framework [perma.cc/3JMF-YPNP].

133 "'Whatever It Takes': Edmonton Mayor Pledges to End Homelessness This Fall," *CBC News* (October 2, 2020), https://www.cbc.ca/news/canada/edmonton/homelessness-edmonton-encampment-covid-1.5747337 [perma.cc/2G4V-B4B7].

134 Mertz, "Camp Pekiwewin in Rossdale Closed."

135 Ibid.

136 Thompson, "The Pandemic, Politics, and Camp Pekiwewin."

137 Peter H. Russell, *Recognizing Aboriginal Title: The* Mabo *Case and Indigenous Resistance to English-Settler Colonialism* (Toronto: University of Toronto Press, 2005).

138 Peter Menzies, "Homeless Aboriginal Men: Effects of Intergenerational Trauma," in *Finding Home: Policy Options for Addressing Homelessness in Canada,* ed. J. David Hulchanski, Philippa Campsie, Shirley B.Y. Chau, Stephen W. Hwang, and Emily Paradis (Toronto: Cities Centre Press, 2009), 457–81.

139 See, for example, Allison K. Moncrieff, "Settler Colonialism, Race and Space: Articulating the Criteria and Disparities of Municipal In(ex)clusion in Lethbridge, Alberta" (MA thesis, University of Lethbridge, 2023) [unpublished].

140 Julia Christensen, "'Our Home, Our Way of Life': Spiritual Homelessness and the Sociocultural Dimensions of Indigenous Homelessness in the Northwest Territories (NWT), Canada" (2013) 14:7 *Social and Cultural Geography* 804–28.

141 Alexandra Flynn, "With Great(er) Power Comes Great(er) Responsibility: Indigenous Rights and Municipal Autonomy" (2021) 34 *Journal of Law and Social Policy* 111–27.

142 Shields, Moran, and Gillespie, "Edmonton, Amiskwaciy Waskahikan."

143 Eve Tuck and Rubèn Gaztambide-Fernández, "Curriculum, Replacement, and Settler Futurity" (2013) 29:1 *Journal of Curriculum Theorizing* 72–89.

144 The phrase "immobilizing politics around encampments" is found in an opinion piece by Keith Gerein, "As Edmonton Freezes, so Goes the Immobilizing Politics Around Encampments," *Edmonton Journal* (January 15, 2024), https://edmontonjournal.com/opinion/columnists/keith-gerein-as-edmonton-freezes-so-goes-the-immobilizing-politics-around-encampments [perma.cc/BW5W-YXZ8]. The phrase "constitutional creativity and cooperative flexibility" is found in *Fedération des producteurs de volailles du Québec v Pelland*, 2005 SCC 20 at para 15.

9

The Rights of Unhoused Indigenous People

Linking the Right to Housing and Indigenous Rights in Canadian Responses to Encampments

ALEXANDRA FLYNN AND ESTAIR VAN WAGNER

Introduction

Canadian cities were experiencing extreme shortages of public, private rental, and "affordable" housing, as well as rising homelessness, even before the pandemic began in March 2020.[1] As the associated economic downturn unfolded in the following months and years, the impact of COVID-19 pushed these already failing housing systems to the brink of collapse.[2] Already overcrowded shelters experienced outbreaks, and people experiencing homelessness were increasingly forced to seek refuge outside to avoid congested settings.[3] This led to the growth of encampments because people were better able to distance themselves physically.[4] At the start of the pandemic, some Canadian cities imposed moratoriums on encampment evictions; however, they later resumed this long-standing practice, contrary to public health advice. Although advocates urgently argued in favour of an approach to encampments that upheld the right to housing, including the rights of Indigenous Peoples, cities went to court asserting their rights to evict encampment residents through trespass orders and injunctions.[5] In this chapter, we focus on the rights of Indigenous encampment residents in the context of ongoing encampment clearances and other human rights violations in encampments across Canada.

Within the general reality of housing precarity and inequality in Canada, the disproportionate number of Indigenous people who are unhoused reveals a specific example of the long-standing systemic failure to address housing needs in Indigenous communities. On-reserve housing is chronically underfunded by the federal government, compounded by a lack of secure infrastructure and safe drinking water.[6] Indigenous people are consistently overrepresented in the unsheltered population.[7] They are also more likely to stay outside or with others than non-Indigenous people who are unhoused.

We set out the legal obligations of governments with respect to the constitutionally protected rights of Indigenous Peoples and the requirements of the *United Nations Declaration on the Rights of Indigenous Peoples.*[8] We argue that these obligations must inform all decisions about encampments and engagements with encampment residents, including the adoption of robust consultation approaches that enable meaningful participation.[9] We set out how the constitutional status of Indigenous Peoples, the evolution of the duty to consult and accommodate, the adoption of the *UNDRIP,* the presence of encampments on Indigenous lands, and the disproportionate number of Indigenous people within encampment populations must all inform encampment engagement, eviction, and service provision.

In making this argument, we first outline the magnitude of Canada's housing crisis and the degree to which Indigenous people are disproportionately represented in homeless populations. Next we summarize the jurisprudence in which courts have recognized the rights of encampment residents in limited circumstances under the *Canadian Charter of Rights and Freedoms,*[10] and we reference decisions in which courts have engaged with the connections between Indigeneity and homelessness. We then introduce the meaning and context of the right to housing in Canada, specifically the application of the right to housing in regard to encampments. Finally, we argue that the right to housing must be informed by constitutionally protected Indigenous rights, the *UNDRIP,* and encampment case law, offering possible steps forward in recognizing these connections.

This chapter engages primarily with Canadian case law, legislation, and policy to ground our understanding of Canadian government obligations. As settler law professors trained in colonial law, our aim is to set out Canadian government obligations in the context of nation-to-nation relations with Indigenous governments and authorities that are the experts in and practitioners of their own diverse laws and systems of governance. In crafting these arguments, we acknowledge that housing policy and responses to encampments must be done alongside Indigenous communities and informed by Indigenous laws. Indeed, in our view, Indigenous laws are vital sources of understanding relationships and obligations as we work toward more just and equitable approaches to housing for all, and we acknowledge the important work that has taken place and continues to take place.

The Staggering Reality of Homelessness in Canada

Homeless encampments in Canada exist at the nexus of multiple and overlapping crises, all of which were compounded by COVID-19.[11] Encampments are a symptom of the lack of adequate affordable housing and the shortcomings of housing and other policies at all levels of government across Canada. The lack of affordable housing, the opioid crisis, racial injustice, police misconduct, and ongoing colonization all converge at these sites. As Kaitlin Schwan and Leilani Farha, the former United Nations special rapporteur on the right to adequate housing, have stated, encampments are simultaneously a prima facie violation of the right to housing and a form of rights claim in the face of exclusionary formal systems.[12] Where systems have so egregiously failed unhoused individuals, "refusing to be made invisible" and claiming space are expressions of the right to housing.[13]

The Context of Unhousing in Canada

Homelessness and living unsheltered affect a substantial number of Canadians: a 2016 study estimated that at least 235,000 people in Canada experience homelessness each year.[14] More recent data demonstrate a significant increase, particularly since the pandemic. Nearly 60,000 people were living on streets and in shelters across seventy-four communities in the 2024 single night count. This represents a 79 percent increase from the 2020–22 count, with unsheltered homelessness growing the fastest at 107 percent since 2020–22 and 303 percent since 2018.[15] In Vancouver, 5,232 people were living in shelters, in cars, or on streets in 2025, an increase of 30 percent since 2023, with a 30 percent increase in unsheltered homelessness.[16] Many municipalities conduct point-in-time counts annually, but these studies are widely considered to underestimate the actual number of unhoused people.[17] And unhoused Indigenous people are particularly likely to be undercounted.[18] The rise in the rate of homelessness in Canada since the 1980s is generally attributed to three broad trends: a nationwide disinvestment in affordable housing, shifts in employment away from permanent positions and toward precarious labour, and the broad defunding of social welfare programs.[19] Up to the late 2000s, municipalities (by then the primary social housing providers) largely focused on crisis responses such as shelters and drop-in programs and policing unhoused populations through anti-panhandling laws and municipal bylaws.[20] Federal and provincial plans to reduce homelessness began proliferating, often focusing on "chronic homelessness" and housing first strategies, culminating in calls for a new national housing strategy.[21]

In the context of declining state investment in housing and social supports and rising rates of homelessness, encampments have become a regular facet of urban life in Canada. During COVID-19, they became increasingly visible and as a result attracted increasing attention from the media and governments.[22] Unhoused people have long been subject to increased police surveillance and punishment by virtue of lacking private property rights in land and depending on public spaces to meet basic needs, pressuring many into shelters to escape this persecution and harassment.[23] However, the long-standing limitations of a shelter-based response were compounded by COVID-19.[24] Safety concerns about congested settings and the lack of available shelter spaces were factors in the growth of encampments early in the pandemic, although encampment residents have long cited personal safety and privacy; a lack of protection of their belongings; health issues; a lack of availability of shelter and housing; conditions within shelters or shelter rules; proximity to partners, family members, community members, and service providers; and relative independence as important factors in the establishment and growth of encampments.[25] Indigenous people have raised particular concerns about the lack of appropriate and safe shelter services.[26]

With few exceptions, municipal governments across Canada have adopted punitive responses to encampments established by unhoused people. The legal bases for these responses include statutory sources from criminal offences to bylaws, with enforcement ranging from forced eviction, police violence, and criminal charges to fines and trespass notices. This punitive approach persisted during the pandemic despite the disproportionately negative effects of COVID-19 on unhoused people.[27] Municipal and public transportation bylaw offences were already unevenly applied to people experiencing homelessness, and COVID-19 fines and distancing requirements that followed had the same disproportionate effects.[28] Given the high incidence of encampments in public spaces, their regulation tends to involve municipal bylaws. Prohibitions or restrictions on erecting shelters in parks and/or camping in parks are some of the most commonly used legal tools.[29] In other instances, encampments on private properties can engage other specific legislation regulating access and use.[30] In either case, violations of underlying regulations are often enforced through trespass laws that facilitate police involvement.[31]

Indigenous Peoples and Unhousing in Canada

Thirty years ago, in 1996, the report of the Royal Commission on Aboriginal Peoples recognized that "Aboriginal housing and community services are in a bad state, by all measures falling below the standards that prevail elsewhere in Canada and threatening the health and well-being of Aboriginal people."[32] As Métis-Cree scholar Jesse Thistle states, "the observable manifestations of intergenerational trauma in Indigenous Peoples, such as intemperance, addiction and street-engaged poverty, are incorrectly assumed to be causes of homelessness in popular and worldwide blame-the-victim discourses. Obscured behind these discourses are the historical processes and narrative prejudices practiced by the Canadian state and settler society that have produced Indigenous homelessness."[33] Homelessness and housing insecurity disproportionately affect Indigenous people in Canada.[34] Indigenous households in Canada are 1.5 times more likely to be in core housing need than non-Indigenous households, with the difference growing to 1.7 and 1.8 in Manitoba and Saskatchewan.[35] They are more likely to live in crowded conditions and in housing in need of repair than non-Indigenous households.[36] Just over half of Inuit people living in Inuit Nunangat live in crowded housing.[37] Although 5 percent of the population identifies as Indigenous, 33 percent of the respondents to the last point-in-time homelessness count identified as Indigenous. The number increased among those in unsheltered locations, such as encampments.[38] In Toronto, Hamilton, and Ottawa, three of Ontario's largest cities, from 15 percent to 30 percent of Indigenous people were unhoused in 2020.[39] In Toronto, 9 percent of people experiencing homelessness were Indigenous, but 31 percent of those living outside in 2024 were Indigenous.[40] A street census in Winnipeg found that 79.9 percent of unsheltered respondents were Indigenous.[41] In Vancouver, Indigenous people make up 2 percent of the urban population but 34 percent of the homeless population.[42] In 2024, 54 percent of people unsheltered in Metro Vancouver were Indigenous.[43]

Nationally, Indigenous people access emergency shelter services ten times more than those who are non-Indigenous.[44] Even so, shelter-based and point-in-time statistics underestimate the number of unhoused people identifying as Indigenous.[45] In 2024, Indigenous people made up 34 percent of those staying in unsheltered locations and 43 percent of those staying with others nationally, so the point-in-time counts are likely an underestimate.[46] Research shows that Indigenous people are less likely to use shelters than other unhoused people since they can "replicat[e] patterns of colonial oppression" and thus be inaccessible to Indigenous people.[47] Hidden homelessness, such as staying with friends or family members, is also prevalent for Indigenous people.[48]

Indigenous overrepresentation in the homeless population is even more striking when broken down by gender.[49] For example, in Winnipeg, 82 percent of women experiencing homelessness were Indigenous.[50] Indigenous women are fifteen times more likely to use a shelter than non-Indigenous women.[51] They remain overrepresented in domestic violence shelters, and they are six times more likely to be the victims of sexual assault than Indigenous men and more likely to experience post-traumatic stress disorder.[52] *The Final Report of the National Inquiry into Missing and Murdered Indigenous Women and Girls* heard detailed testimony about the link between inadequate and unsafe housing in Indigenous communities, homelessness, and violence.[53] Indigenous women remain the group most likely to experience hidden or concealed homelessness.[54] They might avoid shelters for fear of violence and because of the lack of culturally appropriate services, or they simply might not have accessible options in rural or remote areas.[55] Without culturally sensitive shelters, Indigenous women continue to face discrimination when attempting to access emergency housing.[56] Community-based researchers with the Downtown Eastside Women's Centre Carol Muree Martin and Harsha Walia assert that current shelter systems are inherently paternalistic since they position Indigenous women as "clients" of shelters and undermine their right to safety and shelter.[57] Indigenous women are often expected to be polite and civil and express gratitude to receive basic services.[58] Furthermore, although they do experience higher rates of violence, narratives portraying them as victims contribute to marginalization while ignoring their resilience and resistance to colonialism.[59] These issues are amplified for gender-diverse Indigenous people who often experience discrimination when accessing a gender-segregated shelter system.[60]

The data are scant on the experience of homelessness among 2SLGBTQ+ women and gender-diverse people. However, a 2019 study affirmed that Indigenous 2SLGBTQ+ youth experience homelessness earlier than their Indigenous peers and have higher rates of mental health and addiction challenges.[61] Culturally sensitive services are generally important for Indigenous youth, disproportionately dislocated or displaced from their families by colonial child welfare systems.[62] When the youth return to their communities as adults, they can be cultural outsiders, leading to housing precarity with either no home to stay in or feeling unable to stay in their family homes.[63]

This profound violation of Indigenous Peoples' human rights is a result of historical and ongoing processes of colonization and racism that have resulted in separation from land, community, and culture. As Mikaela Gabriel notes, "to say that the Indigenous housing crisis is a modern problem is incorrect; Indigenous Peoples have had a housing crisis for 530 years."[64] Existing reports on Indigenous homelessness, including those authored by Indigenous scholars and advocates, illustrate how its roots in disconnection from lands and community have resulted in a distinctively Indigenous experience of homelessness that cannot be easily reconciled with a simple socio-economic narrative.[65] Thistle describes the resulting "spiritual homelessness" as "being without All My Relations."[66] Thus, understanding Indigenous homelessness requires engagement with the ongoing dispossession of land and displacement from territory, broken treaty promises, residential schools and removal of children into foster care, intergenerational disconnection from language and culture, chronic underfunding of housing and social services, and systemic discrimination in employment and housing.[67] The profound discrimination in securing and maintaining housing that Indigenous people face is well documented.[68] Indeed, the experience of housing discrimination against Indigenous people reflects broader systemic failings in housing in Indigenous communities.[69] Gabriel adopts the term "houselessness" to reflect this structural element and place the onus on colonial structures: "Indigenous Peoples are home on Turtle Island. However, since it is land sovereignty and safe access to housing that has been interfered with by colonial governments, this land relationship is a result of various intersecting housing crises."[70] Thus, for Indigenous people, addressing homelessness "requires a holistic approach that reconstructs the links between the individual, family, community and Nation."[71]

Thistle notes that the colonial definition of homelessness[72] ignores Indigenous worldviews and argues for a conceptualization of Indigenous homelessness that includes a disconnection from one's Indigeneity, be it cultural, spiritual, emotional, and/or physical.[73] He identifies twelve dimensions of Indigenous homelessness: historical displacement, contemporary geographic separation, spiritual disconnection, mental disruption and imbalance, cultural disintegration and loss, overcrowding, relocation and mobility, going home, having nowhere to go, escaping or evading harm, emergency crisis, and climate refugee.[74] These twelve dimensions were born from his consultation with Indigenous scholars, front-line workers, community members, those with lived experiences of homelessness, and those who work in the area of Indigenous homelessness.[75] Thistle found that the greater the number of dimensions affecting an individual or a community, the greater the severity of the experience of homelessness.[76] In other words, these dimensions can be layered over one another, and in identifying these layers we can also identify the factors that led to the individual's experience of homelessness.

Research on Indigenous homelessness has consistently identified self-determination as core to any approach to homelessness and housing precarity.[77] This is consistent with the *UNDRIP,* which specifically notes the right to "be actively involved in developing and determining health, housing and other economic and social programmes affecting them and, as far as possible, to administer such programmes through their own institutions."[78] The top-down Western model prevalent in housing policy and programs is practically and ideologically unsuited to addressing the context of colonization, racism, and discrimination at the heart of Indigenous homelessness. Community organizations desire Indigenous-led social housing in consultation and partnership with Indigenous organizations.[79] Some of the language used regarding future steps is "policy co-production" between governments (municipal, provincial, and federal) and Indigenous Peoples. Rather than simple consultation on and consideration of issues, co-production of policy involves working with Indigenous Peoples on an equal footing. At the basis is a recognition of their rights to self-government and self-determination.

Cathryn Rodrigues and co-authors point to the need for "culturally safe and appropriate services."[80] Such services would require understanding the distinctiveness of urban Indigenous populations compared with other equity-deserving groups. This would include recognizing that unhoused Indigenous people are not a monolithic group. For example, some unhoused Indigenous people have strong relationships with nearby reserves or might be connected to home communities in other areas, whereas others do not.[81] The complex context of urban Indigenous homelessness has been a barrier to the adoption of holistic approaches specific to Indigenous people and families, including difficulties in identifying appropriate representatives for urban Indigenous people. Also, the lack of comprehensive urban Indigenous policy and the reliance on a patchwork of policies and programs mean that models are rarely informed by or responsive to the specific needs of unhoused Indigenous individuals or families. As Rodrigues and co-authors note, a human rights approach means that policy should be shaped by lived experience rather than by models developed for chronic homelessness in the non-Indigenous population.[82]

A human rights approach to encampments has particular implications for unhoused Indigenous people. For example, forced evictions of encampments are a gross violation of human rights and inconsistent with Canada's obligations under international law, including the *UNDRIP*.[83] The right to participate meaningfully in policy development and decision making is a core element of the right to housing and critical to self-determination for Indigenous Peoples. Furthermore, encampments are located on Indigenous territories, and residents are disproportionately Indigenous. Thus, governments must recognize the role of Indigenous communities in responding to encampments and respect the unique needs and rights of Indigenous people as encampment residents and as decision makers in realizing the right to housing in Canada.[84]

Realizing this right is inextricably linked to recognizing Indigenous rights and implementing the *UNDRIP* at all levels of government. In our view, these areas of human rights advocacy must be advanced together.

Rights Established Under Encampments Litigation

Early in the COVID-19 pandemic, Leilani Farha, the UN special rapporteur on the right to adequate housing, and Kaitlin Schwan published *A National Protocol for Homeless Encampments in Canada* (the *Protocol*), advocating for cities to adopt a human rights–based approach and respect the dignity of encampment residents when working with them to secure adequate affordable housing.[85] Based on international human rights instruments to which Canada is a signatory, the *Protocol* sets out principles for governments to respond to encampments. Indigenous rights and self-determination are central components of the *Protocol*, guided by the *UNDRIP* and recognition of the distinct constitutional framework for Indigenous Peoples in Canada. Principle 8 points to four broad requirements for compliance with international human rights law: first, a recognition of the distinct relationship between Indigenous Peoples and their lands and territories; second, a guarantee of self-determination as well as free, prior, and informed consent and meaningful consultation; third, a prohibition on forced eviction, displacement, and relocation; and fourth, protection from and guarantees against all forms of violence and discrimination for Indigenous women, girls, and gender-diverse people.[86]

Our research indicates that, though some governments have attempted to implement individual components of the *Protocol*, at present no Canadian government is taking a human rights–compliant approach.[87] As we have argued elsewhere, bylaw enforcement grounded in a property rights framework has generally taken primacy over meaningful outreach to and provision of appropriate support for encampment residents.[88] Although some cities claim to have adopted human rights–compliant approaches, encampment residents and advocacy groups have disputed the efficacy of many outreach efforts and the effectiveness of supports, particularly for Indigenous residents.[89]

The Role of the Courts in Setting Out the Legal Rights of Encampment Residents

Amid the lack of adequate services, disputes have arisen between encampment residents and officials over the conditions of emergency shelter spaces, the availability of shelter spaces or housing opportunities, and the rights of encampment residents to continue residing where they are.[90] Courts have thus played a key role in setting out the basic rights of encampment residents. The landmark decision in *Victoria (City) v Adams* was a Charter challenge brought by encampment residents in response to the city's injunction application against them loitering and "taking up temporary abode overnight" in the park.[91] The British Columbia Court of Appeal affirmed the Supreme Court's decision that the municipal *Parks Regulation Bylaw*[92] and the *Streets and Traffic Bylaw*[93] had breached the defendants' section 7 rights to life, liberty, and security of the person and were not saved under section 1 of the Charter. It declared the infringing sections of the bylaws "of no force and effect insofar and only insofar as they apply to prevent homeless people from erecting temporary shelter."[94] The Court of Appeal's 2009 decision declared the bylaws "inoperative insofar and only insofar as they apply to prevent homeless people from erecting temporary overnight shelter in parks when the number of homeless people exceeds the number of available shelter beds in the City of Victoria."[95] The decision did not establish a daytime right to shelter even where there were insufficient shelter beds.

With a few exceptions noted below, the courts have narrowly construed government obligations post-*Adams*. In *Abbotsford (City) v Shantz*,[96] the court clarified that the Charter did not create positive obligations with respect to housing and rejected homelessness as a protected ground under the Charter's section 15 equality rights protection, relying on the *Tanudjaja v Canada (Attorney General)*[97] decision of the Ontario Court of Appeal.[98] Rather than acknowledging housing as a human right, the courts have considered cases one by one, examining the number of housing and shelter spaces created by governments, encampment conditions, and the balance between the costs incurred by the province/city and the benefits gained by the encampment residents.[99]

Since 2020, as encampments proliferated during the pandemic, courts across Canada have cautiously expanded the *Adams* framework in a handful of claims decided in favour of encampment residents and unhoused persons. This expansion includes a more robust inquiry into shelter conditions rather than simply looking at the number of available beds. In *Sanctuary et al v Toronto (City) et al,* the Ontario Superior Court sanctioned the City of Toronto for not adhering to rules surrounding the distancing of beds.[100] This decision was a victory in terms of accountability and revealed the shortcomings of the city's shelters in responding to the pandemic. In Quebec, outbreaks at shelters were considered a valid reason for people to avoid them on top of the issues raised about shelters denying admittance.[101] Likewise, in 2021, the lack of sufficient and appropriate indoor options was an important factor in *Prince George (City) v Stewart.* The court held that the existing shelter beds were not "low barrier" enough to provide for accessibility.[102] For example, the shelters imposed eligibility criteria that often excluded those with substance abuse issues or mental health issues from accessing them.[103] Other barriers that the court mentioned included a lack of identification or bank accounts or records.[104] Notably, the judge also commented on the cold climate and the lack of both suitable housing and daytime facilities. That might imply that Charter protections regarding shelter at nighttime could be extended to daytime situations in which cold weather is a significant threat. In a subsequent injunction application by the city in *Prince George (City) v Johnny,*[105] the court still found a lack of low-barrier shelter spaces accessible to some encampment residents as well as issues with the limited daytime facilities.

The 2021 *Bamberger* decision involved a judicial review of two orders made by the Vancouver Parks Board, an elected local body that governs city parks, to clear an encampment located at CRAB Park. Encampment residents raised procedural issues about the lack of consultation with them and questions about the reasonableness of the Parks Board's decision.[106] Although the residents did not raise a section 7 claim, the court was attentive to the constitutional issues, which informed the conclusion that residents had a right to notice and an opportunity to be heard before being ordered to leave.[107] The court also decided that the Parks Board was unreasonable because there was no reasonable factual basis for concluding that there were sufficient and appropriate indoor shelter options for those who sought shelter at CRAB Park.[108] On these bases, the court set aside the order prohibiting overnight shelter in the park and remitted the decision for reconsideration.[109] *Bamberger* highlights the role of administrative law in ensuring substantive and procedural fairness for encampment residents. Nonetheless, the decision does not go as far as the human rights obligations enshrined in international law for notice, meaningful participation in decision making, and the prohibition on forced evictions.[110] This is notable because the lands are federally owned and governed by the Parks Board, and thus the decision could have been directly informed by the concept of meaningful engagement.[111]

In the 2023 *Waterloo* decision, the court was asked to provide direction to the regional government on how to enforce its legal rights to evict unhoused persons living in an encampment on municipally owned land.[112] Although the region brought the application with respect to a specific encampment, it proposed to use the court's decision as a precedent for the treatment of other encampments. In *Waterloo,* the court criticized the risk assessment tool developed by the municipality as lacking a basis in research, failing to analyze adequately the types of "incidents" included, and perhaps most significantly not consulting any of the encampment's residents or including any comparative consideration of the potential risks of eviction for encampment residents in the analysis.[113] The judge concluded that the risk assessment "has no way to measure the relative risk of choosing between eviction, allowing Encampment residents to stay, or pursuing other options."[114]

Going forward, the above decisions clarify that it is incumbent on Canadian municipalities to engage meaningfully with encampment residents and to undertake a balanced assessment of risks regarding the impact of encampments and the impact of evictions on encampment residents.

Judicial Engagement with the Disproportionate Number of Indigenous Residents in Encampments

Courts in some encampment cases have acknowledged the high number of Indigenous people who are unhoused. In an early case in 2003, the court accepted evidence that one-third of the occupants of the named encampment were Indigenous.[115] In a 2015 decision, the court acknowledged that 21 percent of the City of Abbotsford's homeless individuals identified as Indigenous.[116] In 2020, in *Vancouver Fraser Port Authority v Brett,* the court noted the 2019 Vancouver Homeless Count, which identified 2,223 individuals who were experiencing homelessness, 495 (22.3 percent) of whom identified as Indigenous. In *Black v Toronto,* Justice Schabas found that the applicants had raised a serious issue to be tried related to a potential breach of section 15 of the Charter and the Ontario *Human Rights Code*,[117] specifically noting the disproportionate number of Indigenous and gender-diverse people among encampment populations.[118] This reference to the high number of residents who are Indigenous did not factor into the court's decision making.

In the following two cases from British Columbia, the court went further in its consideration of Indigeneity and homelessness. First, in *BC/Yukon Association of Drug War Survivors v Abbotsford (City)*, the British Columbia Human Rights Tribunal dealt with various allegations of discrimination by the City of Abbotsford and the Abbotsford Police Department brought by five unhoused Indigenous men.[119] The five applicants alleged that the use of pepper spray on one applicant's tent and property, the spreading of chicken manure on an area where the applicants were living, and the destruction or disposal of their personal property constituted discrimination based on race, ancestry, disability, and place of origin.[120] The tribunal described the incident as "a degrading and deplorable experience" for those subjected to it and rejected the city's claim that new protocols prohibiting the destruction of property in encampments had remedied the discrimination.[121] The tribunal also pointed to evidence that the officer knew, or ought to have known, of the applicants' protected characteristics.[122] The city argued that the claim of discrimination based on place of origin should be dismissed because "being homeless is not connected to a person's place of origin."[123] However, the tribunal allowed the applicants to proceed based on their novel argument that place of origin here meant "placelessness" – those experiencing homelessness are treated as though they do not belong and so are "placeless" within their own country, province, and city.[124]

Second, in the 2021 *Stewart* case, the City of Prince George sought various declarations and orders to remove two encampments on city property. The court found that the city had failed to consider various barriers (e.g., lack of identification, substance use disorders, lack of bank accounts) to access to the emergency shelter beds. Ultimately, the court granted the city an injunction against only one of the encampments and allowed the other to stay. Crucially, the court took judicial notice of the ongoing impacts of colonization such as residential schools and noted the disproportionate number of Indigenous individuals in the encampment. Regional Chief Terry Teegee, a member of Takla Nation, deposed in an affidavit that a 2018 count found that 79 percent of the homeless population in Prince George were Indigenous, though Indigenous people accounted for only 10–15 percent of the city's overall population. He also stated that the Lower Patricia encampment "is just down the hill from the original site of a Lehidli T'enneh village and cemetery."[125] The court's connection of colonialism and homelessness links the lived realities of unhoused populations with the dispossession of Indigenous Peoples from their lands and cultures and the ongoing lack of adequate services and resources both on and off reserve.

The Right to Housing, Encampments, and the Rights of Indigenous Peoples

Advocates and people with lived experiences of homelessness have long argued for a human rights approach to housing, including to encampments.[126] A human rights approach is rooted in the self-determination of encampment residents and focused on the provision of adequate housing and other necessary and culturally appropriate resources.[127] Where the human rights of encampment residents are fully recognized, they can serve both as a shield against punitive government action and as leverage to force positive government action.

A true human rights approach to housing goes beyond the existing Charter case law, in which the courts have resisted to date any legal implications of a positive right to housing.[128] As this section outlines, a right to housing prohibits the evictions of encampment residents until accessible and adequate housing is available, guarantees the provision of necessities and protection from the elements, and ensures that residents are active participants in the development and implementation of the policies that directly affect their lives, communities, and belongings.[129] We argue that, in addition to these features, the right to housing must ensure that the unique rights and interests of Indigenous Peoples are recognized and fulfilled.

An Emerging Right to Housing in Canada

In 2017, the federal government published a preliminary National Housing Strategy document, which outlined a commitment to a rights-based approach.[130] In the 2019 *National Housing Strategy Act,* the federal government enshrined the right to adequate housing in federal law, informed by strong feedback from civil society organizations on the need to articulate clearly the recognition of housing as a human right and to provide for effective monitoring and remedies.[131] The act recognizes that the right to adequate housing is a fundamental human right affirmed in international law and commits to the progressive realization of the right to adequate housing as recognized in the *International Covenant on Economic, Social and Cultural Rights.*[132] Under the *NHSA,* the federal government is obligated to maintain and implement a National Housing Strategy that accounts for human rights obligations.[133] However, the content of a right to adequate housing is not yet defined in Canadian law. The federal government's description of the right to adequate housing focuses on "implement[ing] housing rights progressively (ie, over time and to the maximum of its available resources)."[134] Although the government acknowledges that future cases could clarify the "minimum core obligations" owed by governments, it has not proactively defined what they could be.[135] Efforts to establish a positive right to adequate housing through the courts have been unsuccessful.[136] Neither courts nor governments have explained what a right to housing means for those in encampments.

The *NHSA* does not specifically create a justiciable right to housing. However, this does not mean that it will not have an impact on future judicial decisions. As Bruce Porter argues, it should have a "positive influence" on courts in future cases to ensure that Charter interpretation is consistent with Canada's international human rights obligations.[137] As we have argued elsewhere, this is an underdeveloped area of the case law on encampments, particularly post-*NHSA*.[138] The federal housing advocate established under the *NHSA* could request a review of litigation strategy in housing-related cases, including encampment cases, and could intervene as a friend of the court where appropriate.[139] This is particularly important for cases involving areas of federal jurisdiction, such as Indigenous Peoples and lands, but also federally owned lands or federal funding and programs. Furthermore, given the failure of Canadian courts to contribute to the realization of the right to housing in Canada to date, Porter notes that the *NHSA*'s provision of effective remedies outside the courts might serve as a "unique form of access to justice ... for systemic issues."[140] This systemic focus and emphasis on alternatives to the courts might offer unique opportunities to engage with Indigenous legal systems and develop culturally appropriate approaches in partnership with Indigenous Nations and organizations connected to the territory.

Other governments have been reluctant to adopt similar rights-based approaches to homeless encampments. This is significant because core elements of housing policy fall under provincial jurisdiction and then are often delegated to municipal governments. Thus, this lack of corresponding legal and policy frameworks to implement the right to housing has profound effects on those living in encampments. In practice, all levels of government have failed to secure access to permanent, adequate housing for encampment residents. Even while officials acknowledge the lack of available housing, enforcement measures such as tickets, arrests, forced evictions, and destruction of tents and personal property are widespread responses to encampments in Canada.[141] The complexity of the problem of homelessness, the polarization of views among stakeholders, the cross-departmental and interjurisdictional issues raised by encampments, and the absence of intergovernmental coordination on this issue have fortified a largely punitive response to encampments across the country. At the time of writing, no provincial framework has yet expressly adopted the right to housing. Some municipalities have done so; however, these commitments have not yet led to a human rights–compliant response to encampments.[142]

Although vastly understudied and reported, First Nations have acknowledged a right to housing for their citizens on reserve lands.[143] However, on-reserve housing rights are complicated by the application of the *Indian Act*[144] and the role of the federal government. Notably, in 2025, the federal court held that Canada owes both a *sui generis* fiduciary duty and a common law duty of care regarding on-reserve housing in a class action brought by a number of First Nations.[145]

The Right to Housing Informed by the Rights of Indigenous Peoples

All governments in Canada have distinct obligations and responsibilities to Indigenous Peoples under section 91(24) of the *Constitution Act, 1867,*[146] section 35 of the *Constitution Act, 1982,*[147] and pursuant to treaties. These obligations are complex, extending from the provision of on-reserve housing, to the funding of safe and culturally appropriate housing programs and emergency shelters, to the treatment of Indigenous encampment residents in off-reserve locations. These obligations are unfulfilled, with governments either denying their responsibilities outright or underplaying their respective obligations to Indigenous Peoples by arguing that they are not primarily responsible.[148]

It is indisputable that the federal government has clear and distinct responsibilities for reserve lands and specific obligations to Indigenous Peoples, pursuant to section 91(24) of the *Constitution Act, 1867* and the *Indian Act.* Section 35 of the *Constitution Act, 1982* requires all governments in Canada to recognize and affirm the "existing [A]boriginal and treaty rights of the [A]boriginal [P]eoples of Canada." Canadian courts have interpreted this to include rights and title as well as a prospective duty by all levels of government to consult and accommodate Indigenous Peoples about decisions that can affect them and their lands.[149] These obligations are also informed by international law, so the right to housing must also be understood as "interdependent with and indivisible from the rights and legal principles set out in the *UNDRIP*."[150] Thus, self-determination and Indigenous legal orders and systems of governance are central to defining the right to housing for Indigenous Peoples. In our view, Canada's statutory right to housing must be informed by the rights of Indigenous Peoples further to the following obligations.

Section 91(24) of the Constitution Act, 1867: Federal Obligations and the Unhousing of Indigenous People

The federal government's role in housing in Indigenous communities on reserves, and the profound failures to provide safe and adequate housing, ground its responsibility for addressing Indigenous housing precarity more broadly. The failure to provide safe, healthy, and accessible housing in Indigenous communities has been well documented for decades.[151] The groundbreaking Royal Commission on Aboriginal Peoples report of 1996 found it to be "possible and desirable to achieve adequate housing for Aboriginal people in ten years."[152] Yet the Senate Committee on Aboriginal Peoples' *Report on On-Reserve Housing and Infrastructure* in 2015 found "severe housing shortages and overcrowding; poorly constructed housing that is in serious disrepair"; and barriers to First Nations meeting their housing needs.[153] The Senate report linked these risks directly to federal government decisions, particularly inadequate funding and the lack of a federal framework for enforceable fire or building codes, and ill-suited federal guidelines for planning and designing on-reserve houses.[154]

Despite its distinct responsibilities for reserve lands and specific obligations to Indigenous Peoples, the federal government has consistently taken the position that the provision of housing on reserves is a matter of social policy and not an enforceable right pursuant to treaties or section 35 of the *Constitution Act, 1867*.[155] In our view, and as the federal court in *St. Theresa Point First Nation v Canada* held, this position contradicts the Crown's historical and ongoing role in on-reserve housing and the funding of programs related to Indigenous housing and homelessness off reserve.

ON-RESERVE HOUSING

The Crown holds legal title to reserve land for the "use and benefit" of a First Nation.[156] The *Indian Act* provides for band councils to be empowered and authorized to "borrow money for band projects of housing purposes" and "making of loans out of moneys so borrowed to members of the band for housing purposes" and to take action related to overcrowding and sanitary conditions of housing.[157] Nonetheless, the Crown has substantial power in relation to reserve land, including with respect to most land transactions, and tenurial relationships on reserves are complex because of the *Indian Act*.[158] Historically, the federal government was directly involved in the provision of housing on reserves. However, such housing was provided as a "temporary" measure and neither properly funded nor built to meet minimum standards.[159] Furthermore, as some scholars have argued, the imposition of standard "suburban-style" housing entirely divorced from the local climate, culture, and geography was yet another manifestation of the colonial desire to assimilate Indigenous Peoples into a settler-colonial way of life through confinement on reserves and separation from territories, Indigenous economies, and ways of life.[160] Thus, housing policy for reserves has long been defined by a "paternalistic approach of dictating housing design and underfunding housing – creating conditions of enforced poverty."[161] Studies have documented a range of issues with on-reserve housing: a higher risk of respiratory tract infections and asthma[162] because of overcrowding and mould,[163] a correlation between overcrowding and poor mental health outcomes,[164] and an increased risk of fires.[165] In 2007, the Canada Mortgage and Housing Corporation (CMHC) found that the rate of death from fire for First Nations members living on reserves was 10.4 times higher than for the non–First Nations population.[166] Research has also shown a chronic shortage of housing units.[167]

Although policy shifts since the mid-1990s have theoretically emphasized self-determination with respect to on-reserve housing, in practice federal policy has failed to incorporate Indigenous perspectives and crucially has not effectively shifted control and funding to First Nations. Thus, though the federal government contends that "the provision and management of housing on reserve lands is under the jurisdiction of First Nations, with support provided by the Government of Canada,"[168] it has maintained effective control over decision making and therefore retains responsibility and liability in relation to the provision of adequate housing for Indigenous Peoples, both on and off reserve.[169] Indeed, a core issue identified by the 2021 House of Commons Committee report on Indigenous housing was the lack of "adequate, long-term, and sustainable funding" for Indigenous organizations to realize control over housing.[170] Furthermore, recent efforts to improve access to the private sector and market-based support for housing development ignore, and might even conflict with, distinctive Indigenous approaches to housing as part of a holistic conception of home as "emplacement" within a "web of relationships and responsibilities" rather than a built environment that can be commodified.[171]

OFF-RESERVE HOUSING

The lack of adequate housing on reserves directly contributes to the over-representation of Indigenous people in the unhoused population in Canada.[172] The 2021 House of Commons report on off-reserve housing noted the roots of Indigenous homelessness in the failures of federal housing policy for northern communities and the withdrawal of federal support for social housing.[173] Multiple witnesses cited housing shortages and poor housing conditions on reserves as reasons that people relocate to urban centres from their home communities as well as reasons that they are unable to return to those communities.[174] Indeed, most Indigenous people live off reserve and face significant systemic discrimination in the housing market.[175] Indigenous households off reserve are more likely to be in core housing need and to live below the standards of adequacy and suitability, putting them at increased risk of being unhoused.[176]

Some argue that housing off reserve is an area of provincial jurisdiction under section 92 of the *Constitution Act, 1867,* through which provinces regulate landlord-tenant relationships as part of their "property and civil rights" jurisdiction.[177] However, until the 1990s, the federal government played a strong and active role in housing affordability.[178] At present, its connection to off-reserve housing and homelessness is primarily as a funder for other levels of government or agencies delivering housing, shelters, and outreach programs, although the federal government also oversees the Canada Mortgage and Housing Corporation and conducts research and collects data on housing.[179]

Issues with the inadequacy of funding for Indigenous-led and -controlled off-reserve housing solutions have been identified by Indigenous leaders and housing providers, including within the Indigenous National Housing Strategy.[180] Regardless of how the federal government defines its role with respect to housing broadly, its funding for housing constitutes a "service" under human rights law since there is "a benefit or assistance offered to the public" in the context of a "public relationship."[181] The federal government must recognize its human rights obligations – including the rights of Indigenous Peoples – in its funding relationships.

Enhanced Consultation and Procedural Fairness

Federal and provincial governments have a duty to consult and accommodate Indigenous Peoples, as the Supreme Court set out in *Haida Nation.* While the application of the duty to municipal decision makers is less clear, with some appellate court decisions finding municipalities do not have an independent constitutional duty to consult, provincial planning frameworks delegate significant power, and procedural responsibility, to local governments and thus the associated constitutional obligations.[182] To date, this duty has not been applied in the context of homelessness and encampments, perhaps in part because of this ambiguity about municipal obligations, but also because the doctrine has been developed largely in the context of land-based claims and natural resource extraction projects rather than urban Indigenous social and economic cases. As Jula Hughes and Roy Stewart have noted, courts have "taken a predominantly property-based approach that is in tension with the sovereign and self-governance dimensions of Aboriginal rights."[183] The application of the duty to consult and accommodate in encampment cases is also challenged by the communal nature of section 35 rights, which largely prohibits individuals from bringing a claim.[184]

In our view, the duty should nonetheless inform the context of encampments at two levels: first, respect for the self-determination of urban Indigenous communities and the systems of governance that they develop; second, obligations to the holders of section 35 rights to the relevant territory as decision makers, including the increasing involvement of Indigenous Nations in the development, provision, and governance of housing and programs for unhoused individuals.[185] Restricting the duty to consult to a property-based framework in the context of encampments would compound the exclusionary property rights approaches that municipalities have taken thus far. Furthermore, though representational issues are genuinely complex, as Hughes and Stewart point out, there is a significant risk that urban Indigenous people are being left out of processes and decisions that directly affect their rights and therefore that processes are failing to meet constitutional requirements.[186] This is particularly important in the context of encampments, where residents experience marginalization on multiple intersecting bases.

Even if applied in the context of homelessness and encampments, the existing understanding of the duty to consult does not account for the extent of obligations to Indigenous Peoples. The *UNDRIP* requires governments to obtain the free, prior, and informed consent of Indigenous Peoples in all decisions that affect their socio-economic development.[187] Canadian courts have also recognized that the right to self-determination applies to urban Indigenous people and communities with respect to social programs and decisions that affect them.[188] Therefore, though there is limited case law in this context, in our view relevant government actors have legal duties to consult and engage with Indigenous governments as partners, as well as with regional and urban Indigenous organizations that provide programs and services, about policies and priorities related to housing and homelessness policy. Programs and services aimed at Indigenous people that exclude input and participation from urban Indigenous communities can affect their human dignity and violate section 15 equality rights under the Charter.[189] Furthermore, forced evictions of Indigenous people from encampments *prima facie* do not comply with requirements for meaningful good faith consultation about and involvement in social programs, nor are they consistent with the recognition of Indigenous self-determination. Given that almost half of all Indigenous people live off reserve, constitutionally compliant policy making requires robust frameworks for urban Indigenous consultation across the spectrum of housing precarity. As Hughes and Stewart note, a lack of consultation about changes to funding or policy in areas such as housing, cultural services, and employment supports can have "devastating impacts when programs and services are altered or eliminated."[190]

Indigenous Rights and the *NHSA:* Pathways Toward the Right to Housing

Federal obligations regarding unhoused Indigenous people have been strengthened by the enactment of the *NHSA* and the *UNDRIP Implementation Act,* which imposes obligations to bring federal law into compliance with international human rights law as per the *UNDRIP.* That declaration sets minimum standards to support the survival, dignity, and well-being of Indigenous people. Many of the principles and obligations that the *UNDRIP* enshrines are grounded in binding international law and are thus already relevant sources to inform the interpretation of domestic law and the review of government decision making.[191] Indeed, in *Reference re An Act respecting First Nations, Inuit and Métis children, youth and families,* the Supreme Court held the *UNDRIP* "has been incorporated into the country's positive law."[192] Beyond the federal *UNDRIP* statute, several Canadian governments at the federal, provincial, and municipal levels have endorsed or adopted the declaration.[193] In 2025, the British Columbia Court of Appeal held the *UNDRIP* "engages the common law interpretive presumption of conformity arising out of Canada's obligations and solemn commitment as a member of the international community to apply and implement *UNDRIP* in domestic law."[194] International human rights obligations extend to all levels and branches of government, including municipalities, and inform the interpretation of domestic law, including section 35.[195]

A number of the *UNDRIP* articles are directly relevant to government responses to encampments, though we note, per the *Gitxaala* decision, that the application of the *UNDRIP* to Canadian law requires "due regard for the extent to which a relevant article expresses a binding international rule or general principle, minimum standard, or aspiration."[196] Article 1 guarantees Indigenous Peoples' right to full enjoyment of all human rights and fundamental freedoms recognized in international law. Article 3 recognizes the right to self-determination and the freedom to determine political status and pursue economic, social, and cultural development, which the British Columbia Court of Appeal notes is a "peremptory norm of international law and which is enshrined in binding conventions."[197] Article 10 establishes that Indigenous Peoples "shall not be forcibly removed from their lands or territories." Article 21 states that Indigenous Peoples have the right to the improvement of their economic and social conditions, including housing and sanitation. Article 23 recognizes that self-determination requires that Indigenous Peoples have the ability to develop and administer health, housing, and other economic and social programs affecting them through their own institutions and in accordance with their needs. Furthermore, the declaration does not differentiate between urban and rural and remote Indigenous populations in recognizing the right to self-determination.

Despite repeated calls for a federal Indigenous Housing Strategy, including most recently from the 2021 House of Commons Committee report,[198] Canada has not formally recognized the right to housing for Indigenous Peoples in the context of section 35 and treaty relationships. Rather than adopting a rights-based approach, Canada has continued to download responsibility without the necessary support for and recognition of Indigenous self-determination. In the federal government's words, "housing is the responsibility of First Nations with some support from" the ministry.[199] In our view, federal Indigenous housing policy should be grounded in a renewed nation-to-nation relationship consistent with a rights-based approach and informed by the interrelated commitments to self-determination and the right to housing in the *NHSA* and the *UNDRIP Implementation Act.* This federal leadership would be a strong indication to other levels of government that encampment responses must also be rights based and start from a nation-to-nation relationship.

The *NHSA* provides some hopeful pathways to this transformation. Structures for accountability are organized around the newly established Office of the Federal Housing Advocate. They include authority for the advocate to initiate studies of areas of federal jurisdiction and report findings and offer advice and recommendations to Parliament. Section 91(24) establishes that the federal government has clear and distinct obligations in relation to Indigenous Peoples and on-reserve housing.[200] These obligations include the established link between the deplorable conditions of on-reserve housing and the lack thereof and Indigenous housing precarity and homelessness off reserve. The advocate is also empowered to initiate studies of systemic issues based on submissions or their own initiative.[201] The advocate can consult widely, including with Indigenous Nations, people, and organizations, on systemic housing issues.[202] The advocate's mandate specifically includes monitoring "the implementation of the housing policy and assess[ing] its impact on people who are members of vulnerable groups."[203] Thus, there are several avenues through which the advocate can initiate research, engage with Indigenous communities and organizations, and make recommendations to Parliament relevant to Indigenous homelessness.

Although the *NHSA* does not directly bind provincial and municipal governments, which are directly involved in housing and homelessness services on the ground, the advocate's mandate to provide advice is not limited to federal jurisdiction, which could help to ensure that the systemic aspects of Indigenous homelessness are addressed and not limited by narrow jurisdictional concerns.[204] Therefore, despite the fact that municipal bylaws, often invoked in encampment responses, are not under federal jurisdiction, the advocate is able to consider the implications of the *NHSA* and the right to housing for bylaw powers in examining the broader context of encampments. Crucially, the advocate's advice can define areas in which the federal government might not have jurisdiction but can and should take a leadership role through funding conditions, policy coordination, and other inter-jurisdictional initiatives. Thus, though provincial, territorial, and municipal governments are not directly affected by the *NHSA* in the same way as the federal government, there are important implications of the act and its relationship with section 35 obligations and the *UNDRIP* for how other levels of government respond to encampments.

In her first annual report, the federal housing advocate urgently and immediately identified encampments as a core violation of human rights.[205] The report identifies how decision makers have failed to engage meaningfully with encampment residents on many matters. In particular, the report is critical of how residents are left out of the decision-making process and the few routes by which they can challenge decisions, propose alternative solutions, and inform decision makers of their priorities and needs. In response to this failure, the report advocates a rights-based approach to encampments, including through direct engagement with and genuine participation of residents.[206] Following the report, the advocate's office announced that the first formal review would be about encampments as "one of the most visible and most serious failures of governments to protect the human right to adequate housing."[207]

The advocate's interim report, released in October 2023, provided an overview of her findings regarding the human and Indigenous rights violations concerning encampment residents.[208] In her review, the advocate met with Indigenous encampment residents as well as national and local organizations representing Indigenous Peoples to learn about the distinct harms experienced by unhoused Indigenous people, including the distance from their home communities and the lack of local supports.[209] Of specific concern was the jurisdictional confusion regarding service provision and, in particular, the federal government's failure to provide services to urban Indigenous populations.[210] The advocate specified that Indigenous understandings of encampments must be respected, incorporating Thistle's definition of homelessness.[211] The interim report provided nuance on the rights involved, clarifying that both human rights and Indigenous rights are engaged in the treatment of encampments and their residents.[212] The report noted that Indigenous rights are engaged because encampments occur on Indigenous lands and since Indigenous people are overrepresented in encampments.[213] The advocate's final report in 2024 provided recommendations both to address the dignity, security, and protection of the human rights of all unhoused people and to uphold the rights of Indigenous Peoples.[214]

In addition, encampment litigation is ongoing, bolstered by successes in the *Waterloo, Stewart,* and *Bamberger* decisions. There are specific arguments that engage Indigenous rights in connection with these decisions. First, the court in *Bamberger* recognized that, under decisions such as *Adams,* the constitutionally protected rights of encampment residents include procedural dimensions.[215] Depending on the populations involved in future encampment decisions, the court might also reference existing procedural and other protections under the Constitution and through statutory instruments such as British Columbia's *Declaration on the Rights of Indigenous Peoples Act.* Second, courts might build upon established procedural requirements in *Waterloo* and *Bamberger,* including the right to notice and an opportunity to be heard before being ordered to leave, by acknowledging the unique rights of Indigenous Peoples as established under the duty to consult and accommodate them and the human rights obligations enshrined in the *UNDRIP* and international law.[216] Third, where an encampment exists on federally owned land, the court might look to the obligations under the *NHSA*, including requirements under international law, and recognize the enhanced rights that underscore the progressive realization of the right to housing.[217]

Finally, creative solutions might also lie in legislative commitments made in federal legislation. For example, the *NHSA* creates statutory duties to realize the right to adequate housing for Indigenous Peoples in the federal government's role as a funder, requiring Canada to place conditions on any funding agreements with other governments or agencies.[218] The *NHSA* commits the government to support improved housing outcomes, furthering the progressive realization of the right to adequate housing and developing a National Housing Strategy that must focus on "improving housing outcomes for people in the greatest need."[219] These commitments provide a strong basis for funding conditions on transfers to other levels of government to ensure that funding specifically addresses Indigenous housing needs and homelessness, which can lead to better accountability for funding priorities under the National Housing Strategy. In the context of language rights, the Federal Court of Appeal found a funding agreement that did not comply with the federal obligations under the *Official Languages Act*[220] had to be terminated or renegotiated to comply with the statutory obligations to "enhance the vitality of the linguistic minority and not to hinder it."[221] Just as protections in the *Official Languages Act* are rooted in constitutional protection of language rights,[222] Canada's constitutional obligations to Indigenous Peoples and emerging *UNDRIP* obligations give these statutory commitments to the right to housing additional meaning in the context of homelessness.

Conclusion

The COVID-19 pandemic exposed the long-standing failures of Canada's housing systems, particularly in urban contexts where affordable housing has been in acute shortage. The rise of encampments during this period – driven by overcrowded shelters and public health mandates – brought renewed visibility to the crisis of homelessness and especially to the disproportionate number of Indigenous people who experience unsheltered homelessness. As we have argued in this chapter, these failures are both unjust and contrary to Canada's constitutional obligations.

Indigenous people are disproportionately affected by the housing crisis and by increased housing precarity and homelessness across the country.

Recognition of the right to housing at the federal scale has not yet resulted in concrete changes to decision making about homelessness and encampments at any level of government. Courts have become a last resort for seeking the basic recognition of human rights where governments lack a consistent policy framework to guide the treatment of encampment residents. Recent court decisions have brought some additional protections for encampment residents, recognizing the lack of adequate shelter spaces and the need for consultation. Justices have also acknowledged the high number of Indigenous residents in encampments. However, recourse to the courts in addressing encampments is deeply inadequate. Access to the courts is challenging for precariously housed and unhoused populations. Moreover, even after successful litigation, municipalities can introduce measures that undermine the safety and security of unhoused people and those living in encampments. The assertion of municipal authority through encampment evictions, often in direct contradiction to public health advice and human rights standards, underscores the deep disjuncture between state practices and rights-based approaches to housing. It also illustrates the failures of governments to recognize and respect Indigenous Peoples' authority and constitutional rights.

We have situated homelessness and encampment responses within a broader legal and constitutional framework. In our view, governments' obligations to Indigenous Peoples must fundamentally inform all decisions related to homelessness and encampments. These obligations include constitutionally protected Aboriginal and treaty rights, the evolving duty to consult and accommodate Indigenous Peoples, and commitments to self-determination arising from the *UNDRIP*. The disproportionate presence of Indigenous people in encampments, the historical and ongoing failures of housing provision in Indigenous communities, and the presence of encampments in Indigenous territories all demand a legal and policy response grounded in recognizing Indigenous authority.

Our analysis highlights the limitations of current judicial engagement with encampments and homelessness. We call for a reconceptualization of the right to housing in Canada – one informed by Indigenous legal orders, meaningful consultation, and recognition of the structural conditions that produce and sustain the particular experiences of Indigenous homelessness. A rights-based, nation-to-nation approach is essential not only to addressing the immediate realities of encampments but also to advancing substantive justice in housing policy more broadly. As we argue here and elsewhere, the right to housing, legislated at the federal level, together with constitutional and legislative protections for Indigenous Peoples, must inform how encampments are regulated and how governments engage with unhoused people and their belongings.

Understanding the right to housing as a binding framework for all governments is a step in the right direction. However, the right to housing, and its application in the context of encampments, must be informed by Indigenous perspectives and legal responses to caring for members of their nations and other vulnerable people living within their territories. The housing crisis is intertwined with colonialism and the erosion of home on Indigenous lands, with specific and devastating effects on First Nations and people. We have explored a broad understanding of Indigenous rights under domestic and international instruments, including the *UNDRIP*. These commitments bind governments and inform the specific meaning of the right to housing as it relates to Indigenous people and communities. As we noted at the outset, our exploration of state law is one limited step in holding governments accountable; however, it must be understood and inextricably linked to supporting Indigenous-led approaches grounded in Indigenous legal orders and modes of governance. Indigenous rights, and respect for Indigenous authority, can transform government responses to encampments and should be the foundation of finding meaningful solutions to the crisis of homelessness and its disproportionate impacts on Indigenous people.

Acknowledgments

We are grateful for the outstanding research assistance of Emma Smyth, Jennifer Nguyen, and Kiera Schuller, and for the comments of anonymous peer reviewers. We thank the many advocates and people with lived experience who have consistently reminded us and others of the treaty and constitutional obligations owed to Indigenous Peoples. Many thanks to Anna Lund, Sarah Buhler, and the contributors to the Legal Unhousing project for their thoughtful feedback. All errors and omissions are our own.

Notes

1 Alexandra Flynn, Joe Hermer, Caroline Leblanc, Sue-Ann MacDonald, Kaitlin Schwan, and Estair Van Wagner, *Overview of Encampments Across Canada: A Right to Housing Approach* (Ottawa: Office of the Federal Housing Advocate, 2022).

2 See, for example, Leilani Farha, and Kaitlin Schwan, “The Front Line Defence: Housing and Human Rights in the Time of COVID-19,” in *Vulnerable: The Law, Policy, and Ethics of COVID-19*, ed. Colleen M Flood, Vanessa MacDonnell, Jane Philpott, Sophie Thériault, and Sridhar Venkatapuram (Ottawa: University of Ottawa Press, 2020); Terry Skolnik, “The Punitive Impact of Physical Distancing Laws on Homeless People,” in Flood et al., *Vulnerable*, 287–97 at 288–89, 293–95.

3 See, for example, Isaac Olson, "Forced Out of Montreal Encampment, Disbanded Homeless Community Spreads Out into City," *CBC News* (December 9, 2020), https://www.cbc.ca/news/canada/montreal/homeless-montreal-shelters-encampment-1.5834917 [perma.cc/9LGP-NZSJ].

4 By "encampments," we mean temporary outdoor campsites on all property – whether categorized under colonial laws as "public" or "private." These informal settlements result from a lack of accessible affordable housing. This distinguishes them from efforts to assert a claim to the property as a whole (as in squatting or adverse possession) or to the occupation of public space as a form of expression (as in protest occupations), which are likely to engage different rights and obligations. For example, courts have distinguished between homeless encampments where s 7 Charter rights to life, liberty, and security of the person are engaged and protest encampments where s 2 rights related to freedom of expression are most relevant. See, generally, Tracy Heffernan, Fay Faraday, and Peter Rosenthal, "Fighting for the Right to Housing in Canada" (2015) 24:2 *Journal of Law and Social Policy* 10–45.

5 See, for example, *Vancouver Fraser Port Authority v Brett*, 2020 BCSC 876 [*Brett*]; *Prince George (City) v Stewart*, 2021 BCSC 2089 [*Stewart*].

6 Office of the Auditor General of Canada, *Report 3 – Access to Safe Drinking Water in First Nations Communities – Indigenous Services Canada* (Ottawa: Office of the Auditor General of Canada, 2021), https://www.oag-bvg.gc.ca/internet/English/parl_oag_202102_03_e_43749.html.

7 In the 2020 point-in-time count, 35 percent of respondents were Indigenous, whereas only 5 percent of the population in Canada identify as Indigenous. See Infrastructure Canada, *Everyone Counts 2020–2022: Preliminary Highlights Report* (Ottawa: Infrastructure Canada, 2024), https://housing-infrastructure.canada.ca/homelessness-sans-abri/reports-rapports/pit-counts-dp-2020-2022-highlights-eng.html [perma.cc/9T5P-2SEP]. This is consistent with past counts, which ranged between 29 percent and 37 percent; see Employment and Social Development Canada (ESDC), *Everyone Counts 2018: Highlights – Preliminary Results from the Second Nationally Coordinated Point-in-Time Count of Homelessness in Canadian Communities* (Ottawa: ESDC, 2019), https://housing-infrastructure.canada.ca/homelessness-sans-abri/reports-rapports/pit-counts-dp-2018-highlights-eng.html [perma.cc/TF7R-BRFK]; ESDC, *Everyone Counts – Guide to Point-in-Time Counts in Canada – 2nd Edition* (Ottawa: ESDC, 2017), https://publications.gc.ca/collections/collection_2017/edsc-esdc/Em12-9-2017-eng.pdf [perma.cc/T9KQ-6RVQ]. See also Yale D. Belanger, Olu Awosoga, and Gabrielle Weasel Head, "Homelessness, Urban Aboriginal People, and the Need for a National Enumeration" (2013) 2:2 *Aboriginal Policy Studies* 4–33.

8 United Nations General Assembly (UNGA), *United Nations Declaration on the Rights of Indigenous Peoples*, UN GAOR, 61st Sess, UN Doc A/RES/61/295 (2007), arts 3, 23 [*UNDRIP*].

9 In understanding the meaning of "Indigenous," we acknowledge that questions about Indigenous identity and nationhood are complex. We recognize the importance of centring Indigenous Nations and communities in deciding who is Indigenous. We use "First Nations" to refer to governments that represent Indigenous

Peoples, whether recognized as band councils under the *Indian Act* or by Indigenous Peoples under Indigenous legal and governance traditions. The Canadian Constitution recognizes Indigenous Peoples as those who meet the definition of First Nations in the *Indian Act* as well as Métis and Inuit. We speak broadly of Indigenous Peoples in all of these contexts.

10 *Canadian Charter of Rights and Freedoms,* Part I of the *Constitution Act, 1982,* being Schedule B to the *Canada Act 1982* (UK), 1982, c 11, s 7 [Charter].

11 Governments, the law, scholarship, and front-line groups tend to focus attention and resources on urban homelessness. However, we acknowledge that rural homelessness and rural homeless encampments are a significant issue in Canada. For a useful primer on the difficulties of responding to rural homelessness, see Sue-Ann MacDonald and Dominique Gaulin, "The Invisibility of Rural Homelessness in a Canadian Context" (2020) 29:2 *Journal of Social Distress and Homelessness* 169–83.

12 Leilani Farha and Kaitlin Schwan, *A National Protocol for Homeless Encampments in Canada* (United Nations Special Rapporteur on the Right to Housing, 2020) at 4, 23, https://make-the-shift.org/wp-content/uploads/2020/04/A-National-Protocol-for-Homeless-Encampments-in-Canada.pdf [perma.cc/8MKK-S3WL].

13 Ibid at 15.

14 Stephen Gaetz, Tanya Gulliver, and Tim Richter, *The State of Homelessness in Canada: 2014* (Toronto: Homeless Hub Press, 2014) at 42.

15 Housing, Infrastructure and Communities Canada, *Everyone Counts 2024: Highlights Report Part 1 – Enumeration of Homelessness* (Ottawa: Infrastructure Canada, 2025); Marc-Antoine Dionne, Christine Laporte, Jonathan Loeppky, and Alexander Miller, *A Review of Canadian Homelessness Data* (Ottawa: Statistics Canada, 2023), https://www150.statcan.gc.ca/n1/en/pub/75f0002m/75f0002m2023004-eng.pdf?st=TmBjn7V1 [perma.cc/Z5XW-XFYV].

16 Homelessness Services Association of BC, James Caspersen, and Stephen D'Souza, in consultation with The Indigenous Homelessness Steering Committee, *2025 Point-in-Time Homeless Count in Greater Vancouver: Preliminary Data Report* (Vancouver: Lu'ma Native Housing Society, July 2025); CBC News, "Vancouver-Area Homeless Numbers Show Sharpest Spike Between Counts Since Survey Began" (October 5, 2023), https://www.cbc.ca/news/canada/british-columbia/greater-vancouver-homeless-count-2023-1.6987718 [perma.cc/CM94-8END].

17 Homeless counts have been criticized for not capturing adequately the actual number of people experiencing homelessness or its different forms of expression (e.g., hidden homelessness). See, for example, Sue-Ann MacDonald, Philippe-Benoit Côté, Annie Fontaine, Élisabeth Greissler, and Stéphanie Houde, *Démarche qualitative du Deuxième portrait de l'itinérance au Québec: Regards croisés et approfondissement des connaissances* (Montréal: CREMIS, 2022), https://api.cremis.ca/wp-content/uploads/2021/12/Rapport-final_2020-05-26_Version-finale_murale.pdf [perma.cc/YC68-ULBA], at 7.

18 See the literature review on this in Evelyn J. Peters and Selena Kern, "The Importance of Hidden Homelessness in the Housing Strategies of Urban Indigenous People," in *Indigenous Homelessness: Perspectives from Canada, Australia, and New Zealand,* ed. Evelyn J. Peters and Julia Christensen (Winnipeg: University of Manitoba Press, 2016), 49–66.

19 See Stephen Gaetz, Erin Dej, Tim Richter, and Melanie Redman, *The State of Homelessness in Canada: 2016* (Toronto: Homeless Hub, 2016) at 12. See Heffernan, Faraday, and Rosenthal, "Fighting for the Right to Housing in Canada."

20 See Gaetz et al., *The State of Homelessness in Canada 2016,* at 13. See also *Safe Streets Act,* 1999, SO 1999, c 8.

21 Gaetz et al., *The State of Homelessness in Canada 2016,* at 13–14.

22 See Flynn et al., *Overview of Encampments,* at 11.

23 See Skolnik, "The Punitive Impact," at 295–96.

24 See Justine Levesque, Jordan Babando, Nathaniel Loranger, Shantel Johnson, and David Pugh, "COVID-19 Prevalence and Infection Control Measures at Homeless Shelters and Hostels in High-Income Countries: A Scoping Review" (2022) 11:223 *Systematic Reviews* 1–20; Stefan Baral, Andrew Bond, Andrew Boozary, et al., "Seeking Shelter: Homelessness and COVID-19" (2021) 6 *FACETS* 925–58.

25 See Nicholas Olson and Bernie Pauly, "Forced to Become a Community: Encampment Residents' Perspectives on Systemic Failures, Precarity, and Constrained Choice" (2022) 3:2 *International Journal on Homelessness* 124–38.

26 See, for example, Katie McCallum and David Isaac, *Feeling Home: Culturally Responsive Approaches to Aboriginal Homelessness* (Burnaby: Centre for Native Policy and Research, 2011).

27 See Skolnik, "The Punitive Impact."

28 See ibid at 291. Skolnik only references anecdotal cases of fines being issued to people experiencing homelessness and notes that many courts closed or reduced capacity during the pandemic, so the extent of the impact might take years to be fully revealed.

29 See, for example, Joe Hermer and Elliot Fonarev, "The Mapping of Vagrancy Type Offences in Municipal By-Laws" (2020), https://homelesshub.ca/blog/mapping-vagrancy-type-offences-municipal-laws [perma.cc/U2BY-7CZK]. For examples in which park bylaws are engaged, see *Victoria (City) v Adams,* 2008 BCSC 1363 [*Adams 1*]; *Victoria (City) v Adams,* 2009 BCCA 563 [*Adams 2*]; *Bamberger v Vancouver (Board of Parks and Recreation),* 2022 BCSC 49 [*Bamberger*]; *Poff v Hamilton,* 2021 ONSC 7224.

30 See, for example, *Fraser Health Authority v Evans,* 2016 BCSC 1708.

31 See, generally, Sarah E. Hamill, "Property Says No: Relational (In)Equality, Encampments, and Property Rights" (2023) 36:7 *Journal of Law and Social Policy* 119–38.

32 Royal Commission on Aboriginal Peoples (RCAP), *Report of the Royal Commission on Aboriginal Peoples: Volume 3: Gathering Strength,* Catalogue No. Z1-1991/1-3E/PDF (Ottawa: Supply and Services Canada, 1996) at 341.

33 Jesse A. Thistle, *Definition of Indigenous Homelessness in Canada* (Toronto: Canadian Observatory on Homelessness Press, 2017) at 7, https://homelesshub.ca/sites/default/files/attachments/COHIndigenousHomelessnessDefinition.pdf [perma.cc/F95M-AKG3].

34 Statistics Canada, *Housing Conditions Among First Nations People, Métis and Inuit in Canada from the 2021 Census* (Ottawa: Statistics Canada, 2022); Caryl Patrick, *Aboriginal Homelessness in Canada: A Literature Review* (Toronto: Canadian Homelessness Research Network Press, 2014) at 15.

35 Parliamentary Budget Officer (PBO), *Urban, Rural, and Northern Indigenous Housing* (Ottawa: PBO, February 11, 2021), https://distribution-a617274656661637473.pbo-dpb.ca/5b2407108abe40544f4c66d4a7fe08c47aecce914911c2f7e3bbcad23a2070fc [perma.cc/L2LP-P88T].

36 Statistics Canada, *Housing Conditions.*

37 Ibid.

38 Housing, Infrastructure and Communities Canada, *Everyone Counts 2024: Highlights Report Part 2 – Survey of People Experiencing Homelessness* (Ottawa: Infrastructure Canada, 2025) at 19.

39 Homeless Hub, "Indigenous Peoples" (2021), https://homelesshub.ca/collection/population-groups/indigenous-peoples/ [perma.cc/RYA4-ZWVN].

40 City of Toronto, *Street Needs Assessment 2024* (Toronto: City of Toronto, 2025).

41 End Homelessness Winnipeg, *2024 Winnipeg Street Census or Point-In-Time Count Report* (Winnipeg: End Homelessness Winnipeg, 2014), https://endhomelessnesswinnipeg.ca/wp-content/uploads/2024-Winnipeg-Street-Census-Report_Aug2025.pdf.

42 Homelessness Services Association of BC, *2025 Point-in-Time Homeless Count*; City of Vancouver, *City of Vancouver's* UNDRIP *Strategy: Report of the* UNDRIP *Task Force to the City of Vancouver Mayor and Council* (Vancouver: City of Vancouver, October 25, 2022) at 17, https://council.vancouver.ca/20221025/documents/p1.pdf [perma.cc/J5ET-66BT].

43 Homelessness Services Association of BC, *2025 Point-in-Time Homeless Count* at 14; BC Non-Profit Housing Association, *2020 Indigenous Homeless Count: Results in Metro Vancouver* (Vancouver: BC Non-Profit Housing Association, 2020), https://infocusconsulting.ca/wp-content/uploads/Homeless-Count-Infographic-2020-FINAL.pdf [perma.cc/58FU-2PFZ].

44 ESDC, *The National Shelter Study 2005–2014* (Gatineau: ESDC, 2019), https://publications.gc.ca/collections/collection_2017/edsc-esdc/Em12-17-2017-eng.pdf [perma.cc/MQ5F-CJPW]. See also Housing, Infrastructure and Communities Canada, *Homelessness Data Snapshot: The National Shelter Study 2024 Update* (Ottawa: Housing, Infrastructure and Communities, 2025), https://housing-infrastructure.canada.ca/alt-format/pdf/homelessness-sans-abri/reports-rapports/data-shelter-2024-donnees-refuge-en.pdf.

45 See Infrastructure Canada, *Everyone Counts 2020–2022.*

46 Infrastructure Canada, *Everyone Counts 2024: Highlights Report Part 2.*

47 Leilani Farha, *Report of the Special Rapporteur on Adequate Housing as a Component of the Right to an Adequate Standard of Living, and on the Right to Non-Discrimination in This Context,* UNGA, 74th Sess, UN Doc A/74/183 (2019), at 10 [*SR Report 2019*].

48 See, for example, Jino Distasio, Gina Sylvestre, and Susan Mulligan, "Hidden Homelessness Among Aboriginal Peoples in Prairie Cities," in *Finding Home: Policy Options for Addressing Homelessness in Canada,* ed. J. David Hulchanski, Philippa Campsie, Shirley B.Y. Chau, Stephen W. Hwang, and Emily Paradis (Toronto: Cities Centre, University of Toronto, 2010), chap 6.3; Evelyn J. Peters and Vince Robillard, "Urban Hidden Homelessness and Reserve Housing" (2007) 104 *Aboriginal Policy Research Consortium International* 189–205.

49 Carol Muree Martin and Harsha Walia, *Red Women Rising: Indigenous Women Survivors in Vancouver's Downtown Eastside* (Vancouver: Downtown Eastside Women's Centre, 2019), https://yellowheadinstitute.org/wp-content/uploads/2019/04/mmiw-report-final-march-10-web.pdf [perma.cc/PYZ4-A97D].

50 End Homelessness Winnipeg, *2024 Winnipeg Street Census or Point-In-Time Count Report*; Connecting the Circle, *Connecting the Circle: A Gender-Based Strategy to End Homelessness in Winnipeg* (Winnipeg: Connecting the Circle, 2019), https://wcwrc.ca/wp-content/uploads/2019/09/Connecting-the-Circle-Full-Web.pdf [perma.cc/RFP6-638V], at 11.

51 Nick Falvo, "The Use of Homeless Shelters by Indigenous Peoples in Canada" (2019), https://homelesshub.ca/blog/use-homeless-shelters-indigenous-peoples-canada [perma.cc/7DCK-NUJB].

52 Ibid; ESDC, *Highlights of the National Shelter Study 2005 to 2016* (Ottawa: ESDC, 2019); Brittany Bingham, Akm Moniruzzaman, Michelle Patterson et al., "Gender Differences Among Indigenous Canadians Experiencing Homelessness and Mental Illness" (2019) 7 *BMC Psychology* 57, https://bmcpsychology.biomedcentral.com/articles/10.1186/s40359-019-0331-y.

53 National Inquiry into Missing and Murdered Indigenous Women and Girls (MMIWG), *Reclaiming Power and Place: The Final Report of the National Inquiry into Missing and Murdered Indigenous Women and Girls, Volume 1a* (Ottawa: MMIWG, 2019) at 537–45 [*MMIWG Report*].

54 Julia Christensen, "'Our Home, Our Way of Life': Spiritual Homelessness and the Socio-Cultural Dimensions of Indigenous Homelessness in the Northwest Territories (NWT), Canada" (2013) 14:7 *Social and Cultural Geography* 804–28.

55 See Farha and Schwan, *A National Protocol for Homeless Encampments in Canada*; *MMIWG Report*.

56 Native Women's Association of Canada (NWAC), *Native Housing for First Nations, Inuit, and Métis Women* (Ottawa: NWAC, 2018), https://nwac.ca/resource/fact-sheet-housing-2018/?wpdmdl=1976&refresh=61fcd9fb588291643960827 [perma.cc/PH3C-G7R3].

57 See Martin and Walia, *Red Women Rising*.

58 See NWAC, *Native Housing for First Nations, Inuit, and Métis Women*.

59 Ibid.

60 Christensen, "Our Home."

61 Sean A. Kidd, Jesse Thistle, Travis Beaulieu, Bill O'Grady, and Stephen Gaetz, "A National Study of Indigenous Youth Homelessness in Canada" (2019) 176 *Public Health* 163–71.

62 Patrick, *Aboriginal Homelessness in Canada;* Mikaela D. Gabriel, "Our Home Is Native Land: Teachings, Perspectives, and Experiences of Indigenous Houselessness" (2013) 14:S1 *Canadian Journal of Nonprofit and Social Economy Research* 89–105 at 90.

63 Jeffrey Paul Ansloos, Amanda Claudia Wagner, and Nicole Santos Dunn, "Preventing Indigenous Youth Homelessness in Canada: A Qualitative Study on Structural Challenges and Upstream Prevention in Education" (2021) 50:4 *Journal of Community Psychology* 1918–34.

64 Gabriel, "Our Home Is Native Land," at 92.
65 Peters and Kern, "The Importance of Hidden Homelessness."
66 Thistle, *Definition of Indigenous Homelessness in Canada,* at 16.
67 Ibid at 8.
68 See, for example, *Desjarlais v Kanganilage and Another*, 2012 BCHRT 243; *Smith v Mohan,* 2018 BCHRT 207; *Copenace v West,* 1979 CanLII 3893 (ON HRT); *Bishop v Markowski,* 1993 CanLII 9117 (SK HRT).
69 Shelagh McCartney, Jeffrey Herskovits, and Lara Hintelmann, "Failure by Design: The On-Reserve First Nations' Housing Crisis and Its Roots in Canadian Evaluation Frameworks" (2018) 38:2 *Canadian Journal of Native Studies* 101–24 at 113; Shelagh McCartney, Jeffrey Herskovits, and Lara Hintelmann, "Developing Occupant-Based Understandings of Crowding: A Study of Residential Self-Assessment in Eabametoong First Nation" (2021) 36:2 *Journal of Housing and the Built Environment* 645–62.
70 Gabriel, "Our Home Is Native Land," at 92.
71 Peter Menzies, "Developing an Aboriginal Healing Model for Intergenerational Trauma" (2008) 46:2 *International Journal of Health Promotion and Education* 41–48 at 47.
72 See, for example, Urban Matters CCC and BC Non-Profit Housing Association, *Vancouver Homeless Count 2018* (Vancouver: Urban Matters CCC and BC Non-Profit Housing Association, 2018), https://vancouver.ca/files/cov/vancouver-homeless-count-2018-final-report.pdf [perma.cc/QNF8-2KZY]. The counts of 2018 and 2019 included those who did not "have a place of their own where they pay rent and can expect to stay for 30 days" as homeless. This number included people who were unsheltered: staying on streets or beaches; staying in alleys, doorways, parkades, or vehicles; staying in parks and other public spaces; using homelessness services or staying in hospitals or jails and having no fixed address; and staying at someone else's place where they did not pay rent (i.e., couch surfing). This definition also included sheltered people staying in temporary emergency shelters, detox centres, and transition houses.
73 Thistle, *Definition of Indigenous Homelessness in Canada.*
74 Ibid.
75 Ibid.
76 Ibid.
77 Canadian Observatory on Homelessness, *Closing the Circle: Discussing Indigenous Homelessness in Canada* (Toronto: Homeless Hub, 2019), https://homelesshub.ca/resource/closing-circle-discussing-indigenous-homelessness-canada [perma.cc/4ZZM-VPUQ].
78 *UNDRIP*, art 23. See also *United Nations Declaration on the Rights of Indigenous Peoples Act*, SC 2021, c 14, s 5 [*UNDRIP Act*], which states that "the Government of Canada must, in consultation and cooperation with Indigenous peoples, take all measures necessary to ensure that the laws of Canada are consistent with the Declaration."
79 Lou Seltz and Dimitrios Roussopoulos, *Montréal Homelessness and Indigenous Housing* (Montreal: Milton-Parc Citizens' Committee, 2020), https://ccmp-mpcc.com/wp-content/uploads/2020/11/Montreal_Homelessness_2020_EN-2.pdf [perma.cc/QE3N-5UYL].

80 Cathryn Rodrigues, Rita Henderson, Katelyn Lucas, Sean Bristowe, Kaylee Ramage, and Katrina Milaney, *Understanding Homelessness for Urban Indigenous Families: How Can We Envision Gendered and Culturally Safe Responses* (Toronto: Homeless Hub, 2020), https://homelesshub.ca/sites/default/files/attachments/SafeInterventionReport_Aug_7%205.31.46%20PM%20%281%29.pdf [perma.cc/Y23T-GQAP].

81 Evelyn J. Peters, ed., *Urban Aboriginal Policy Making in Canadian Municipalities* (Montreal and Kingston: McGill-Queen's University Press, 2011).

82 Rodrigues et al., *Understanding Homelessness for Urban Indigenous Families.*

83 Ibid.

84 Right to Housing in Toronto (R2HTO), *Encampments Rights Review: Report on Encampments in Toronto During COVID-19* (Toronto: R2HTO, 2020), https://right2housingto.ca/wp-content/uploads/2020/09/R2HTO-Encampents-Rights-Review-final.pdf [perma.cc/97BZ-EVVP].

85 Farha and Schwan, *A National Protocol for Homeless Encampments in Canada.*

86 Ibid at 29–31.

87 Flynn et al., *Overview of Encampments Across Canada.*

88 Estair Van Wagner and Alexandra Flynn, "Human Rights Cities: Realizing the Right to Housing at the Municipal Scale" (2024) 57:1 *University of British Columbia Law Review* 235–94.

89 Office of the Federal Housing Advocate, *Upholding Dignity and Human Rights: The Federal Advocate's Review of Homeless Encampments – Interim Report* (Ottawa: Canadian Human Rights Commission, 2023) [Office of the Federal Housing Advocate, *Interim Report*]. See also Bobby Hristova, "Indigenous Community Leaders in Hamilton Say City Lacking Consultation About Encampments," *CBC News* (November 24, 2021), https://www.cbc.ca/news/canada/hamilton/encampment-indigenous-consultation-1.6261117 [perma.cc/N4NV-X3P7]. See also Union of BC Indian Chiefs (UBCIC), "UBCIC Alarmed by Vancouver's Violent Plan to Clear DTES" (2023), https://www.ubcic.bc.ca/ubcic_alarmed_by_vancouver_s_violent_plan_to_clear_dtes. Indigenous organizations have specifically noted the lack of consultation about encampments despite the disproportionate number of Indigenous residents.

90 See, for example, Flynn et al., *Overview of Encampments Across Canada.*

91 *Adams 1* at paras 7–10. Canadian case law dealing with encampments began in 2003 in British Columbia; see *Vancouver Parks Board v Mickelson*, 2003 BCSC 1271 [*Mickelson*]; *Vancouver Board of Parks and Recreation v Sterritt*, 2003 BCSC 1421 [*Sterritt*]. There are earlier Canadian cases dealing with protest occupations that reference homelessness and a 1939 case involving federal relief camps established during the Great Depression intended in part to address homelessness. There is also *Vancouver (City) v Maurice*, 2002 BCSC 1421, though this was described at the time as a squat/protest rather than an encampment, and the reasoning is thinner and less influential than the cases of the following year. Therefore, we see the examined cases as the start of the current line of jurisprudence.

92 City of Victoria, Bylaw No 07-059, *Parks Regulation Bylaw.*

93 City of Victoria, Bylaw No 92-84, *Streets and Traffic Bylaw*, as repealed by City of Victoria, Bylaw No 09-079, *Streets and Traffic Bylaw.*

94 *Adams 1* at para 239.

95 *Adams 2* at para 166.

96 *Abbotsford (City) v Shantz*, 2015 BCSC 1909 [*Shantz*].
97 *Tanudjaja v Canada (Attorney General)*, 2014 ONCA 852 [*Tanudjaja*], and see the discussion of *Tanudjaja* in Chapter 1 of this collection.
98 *Shantz* at paras 148, 177, 231–34.
99 See *British Columbia v Adamson*, 2016 BCSC 1245.
100 See *Sanctuary et al v Toronto (City)*, 2020 ONSC 4708 at paras 6–7.
101 See *Clinique juridique itinérante c Procureur général du Québec*, 2023 QCCS 1949; *Clinique juridique itinérante c Procureur général du Québec – Ministère des transports et de la mobilité durable du Québec*, 2023 QCCA 855.
102 Ibid at para 81.
103 Ibid at para 73.
104 Ibid at paras 67–68, 73.
105 *Prince George (City) v Johnny*, 2022 BCSC 282.
106 Ibid at para 40.
107 Ibid at paras 65–73.
108 Ibid at para 150.
109 Ibid at paras 63–64.
110 Ibid.
111 See *Government of the Republic of South Africa and Others v Grootboom and Others*, [2000] ZACC 14 (SamLII) [*Grootboom and Others*]; Michèle Biss, Bruce Porter, Sahar Raza, and David Desbaillets, *Progressive Realization of the Right to Adequate Housing: A Literature Review* (National Right to Housing Network, 2022), https://housingrights.ca/wp-content/uploads/NHC-Progressive-Realization-Paper_EN.pdf [perma.cc/6QWB-KGQ7], at 7.
112 *The Regional Municipality of Waterloo v Persons Unknown and to Be Ascertained*, 2023 ONSC 670 [*Waterloo*].
113 Ibid at paras 37–46.
114 Ibid at para 46.
115 *Sterritt* at para 6.
116 *Abbotsford (City) v Shantz*, 2015 BCSC 1909 [*Shantz 3*].
117 *Human Rights Code*, RSO 1990, c H.19.
118 *Black v City of Toronto*, 2020 ONSC 6398 at paras 60–61.
119 *BC/Yukon Association of Drug War Survivors v City of Abbotsford*, 2020 BCHRT 86 [*BC/Yukon*].
120 Ibid at paras 1–4.
121 Ibid at para 76.
122 Ibid at para 98.
123 Ibid at para 100.
124 Ibid.
125 *Stewart* at para 14.
126 See, for example, Nicholas Olson and Bernadette Pauly, "Homeless Encampments: Connecting Public Health and Human Rights" (2021) 112:6 *Canadian Journal of Public Health* 988–91; Emily Paradis, *If You Build It, They Will Claim: Rights-Based Participation and Accountability in Canada's National Housing Strategy* (June 1,

2018), https://maytree.com/wp-content/uploads/Paradis-submission-Rights-based-participation-and-accountability-1-June-2018.pdf [perma.cc/KQ5K-PSUR].

127 See Olson and Pauly, "Homeless Encampments," at 993. See also Bruce Porter, "International Human Rights in Anti-Poverty and Housing Strategies: Making the Connection" (September 25, 2014), https://ssrn.com/abstract=2500384 [perma.cc/LKY8-UPJ2]. See also Bruce Porter, "International Human Rights, Health and Strategies to Address Homelessness and Poverty in Ontario: Making the Connection" (2014) Institute of Population Health, Exchange Working Paper Series 3:3, https://papers.ssrn.com/sol3/papers.cfm?abstract_id=2469947 [perma.cc/NJL2-ATYK].

128 Charter, s 7. See, especially, *Tanudjaja.*

129 See *Tanudjaja.*

130 See ESDC, *Canada's National Housing Strategy – A Place to Call Home* (Gatineau: ESDC, 2018), https://eppdscrmssa01.blob.core.windows.net/cmhcprodcontainer/sf/project/placetocallhome/pdfs/canada-national-housing-strategy.pdf [perma.cc/TAG5-KPA2].

131 *National Housing Strategy Act*, SC 2019, c 29, s 313 [*NHSA*]; see Bill C-97, *An Act to Implement Certain Provisions of the Budget Tabled in Parliament on March 19, 2019 and Other Measures*, 42nd Parl, 1st Sess, 2019 (first reading April 8, 2019). See also the discussion of the process in Bruce Porter, *Implementing the Right to Adequate Housing Under the* National Housing Strategy Act*: The International Human Rights Framework* (Ottawa: Office of the Federal Housing Advocate, 2021), https://www.socialrights.ca/2021/Porter%20-%20NHSA%20&%20IHRL.pdf, at 12–13.

132 *NHSA*, Preamble; *International Covenant on Economic, Social and Cultural Rights*, 993 UNTS 3 (December 16, 1966, entered into force January 3, 1976) [*ICESCR*].

133 *NHSA*, s 5(1).

134 Ryan van den Berg, *A Primer on Housing Rights in Canada*, Publication No. 2019-16-E (Ottawa: Library of Parliament, 2019) at 11.

135 Ibid at 11–12.

136 See *Tanudjaja* at paras 30–32. Leave to appeal to the SCC denied: *Jennifer Tanudjaja et al v Attorney General of Canada, et al*, 2015 CanLII 36780 (SCC). Notably, a 2022 decision allowed a hearing about a positive right to health care to go ahead on human rights grounds after the UNHRC found that Canada had violated its international commitments. See *Toussaint v Canada (Attorney General)*, 2022 ONSC 4747. See also *Views Adopted by the Committee Under Article 5 (4) of the Optional Protocol Concerning Communication No 2348/2014*, UNHRC, 123rd Sess, UN Doc CCPR/C/123/D/2348/2014 (2018).

137 Porter, *Implementing the Right to Adequate Housing*, at 23.

138 Van Wagner and Flynn, "Human Rights Cities," at 235.

139 Porter, *Implementing the Right to Adequate Housing*, at 23; *NHSA*, s 13.

140 Porter, *Implementing the Right to Adequate Housing*, at 24.

141 Ibid.

142 See, for example, City of Toronto, "Toronto Housing Charter – Opportunity for All" (2020), https://www.toronto.ca/wp-content/uploads/2022/02/948f-Toronto-Housing-Charter-2020.pdf [perma.cc/R4X3-LMLJ].

143 See, for example, *Kwandibens v Whitesand First Nation*, 2018 ONSC 2318 [*Kwandibens*].

144 *Indian Act*, RSC 1985, c I-5.

145 *St. Theresa Point First Nation v. Canada*, 2025 FC 1926 [*St. Theresa Point First Nation*].

146 *Constitution Act, 1867*, 30 & 31 Vict, c 3 [*Constitution Act, 1867*].

147 *Constitution Act, 1982*, being Schedule B to the *Canada Act 1982* (UK), 1982, c 11 [*Constitution Act, 1982*].

148 See, for example, John Borrows, "Canada's Colonial Constitution," in *The Right Relationship: Reimagining the Implementation of Historical Treaties*, ed. John Borrows and Michael Coyle (Toronto: University of Toronto Press, 2017), 17–38 at 17; *St. Theresa Point First Nation*.

149 See, for example, *Tsilhqot'in Nation v British Columbia*, 2014 SCC 44; *Haida Nation v British Columbia (Minister of Forests)*, 2004 SCC 73 [*Haida Nation*].

150 *UNDRIP Act*.

151 RCAP, *Report of the Royal Commission on Aboriginal Peoples*, at 341; Canada, Minister of Indian and Northern Affairs, *Government Response to the Seventh Report of the Standing Committee on Aboriginal Affairs and Northern Development: Aboriginal Housing* (Ottawa: Parliament of Canada, 2007); Truth and Reconciliation Commission (TRC) of Canada, *Canada's Residential Schools: The Legacy (Volume 5)* (Montreal and Kingston: McGill-Queen's University Press, 2015) at 163; Leilani Farha, *Report of the Special Rapporteur on Adequate Housing as a Component of the Right to Adequate Standard of Living, and on the Right to Non-Discrimination in This Context*, UNGAOR, 28th Sess, UN Doc A/HRC/28/62 (2014) at para 9 [*SR Report 2014*]; *MMIWG Report*; House of Commons Standing Committee on Human Resources and Social Development and the Status of Persons with Disabilities (HUMA), *Indigenous Housing: The Direction Home*, 43-2 (May 2021) at 60.

152 RCAP, *Report of the Royal Commission on Aboriginal Peoples*, at 352.

153 Ibid; Senate Standing Committee on Aboriginal Peoples, *On-Reserve Housing and Infrastructure: Recommendations for Change*, 41-2 (June 2015) at 1.

154 Senate Standing Committee on Aboriginal Peoples, *On-Reserve Housing*, at 13–14, 16–18, 23–25.

155 This was noted in the RCAP report and was articulated by senior civil servant Daniel Leclair, director general, Community Infrastructure Branch, Aboriginal Affairs and Northern Development Canada, before the Standing Senate Committee on Aboriginal Peoples; see Standing Senate Committee on Aboriginal Peoples, *Issue 9 – Evidence*, 41-2 (November 5, 2014) at 19:50 (Daniel Leclair), https://sencanada.ca/en/Content/Sen/committee/412/appa/09ev-51716-e [perma.cc/3GUS-TPN5].

156 *Indian Act*, s 18.

157 Ibid, s 73(1)(i)–(m).

158 Note that some First Nations have more substantial control over lands, including with respect to housing, pursuant to the *First Nations Land Management Act*, modern treaties, or self-government agreements, though it does not change the underlying ownership of land.

159 McCartney, Herskovits, and Hintelmann, "Failure by Design," at 113.

160 McCartney, Herskovits, and Hintelmann, "Failure by Design," at 115.

161 Ibid.

162 Gisèle M. Carrière, Rochelle Garner, and Claudia Sanmartin, "Housing Conditions and Respiratory Hospitalizations among First Nations People in Canada" (2017) 28:4 *Health Reports* 9–15; Michael Optis, Karena Shaw, Peter Stephenson, and Peter Wild, "Mold Growth in On-Reserve Homes in Canada: The Need for Research, Education, Policy, and Funding" (2012) 74:6 *Journal of Environmental Health* 14–21.

163 Paul C. Webster, "Housing Triggers Health Problems for Canada's First Nations" (2015) 385:9967 *Lancet* 495–96.

164 Ibid.

165 Lori Chambers, "Fanning the Flames: Racism in Government Recommendations for the Prevention of Deaths by Fire on First Nations Reserves" (2018) 38:2 *Canadian Journal of Native Studies* 25–42 at 28.

166 CMHC, *Fire Prevention in Aboriginal Communities* (Ottawa: CHMC, 2007), https://publications.gc.ca/collections/collection_2008/cmhc-schl/nh18-23/NH18-23-107-009E.pdf [perma.cc/9NYM-LSP5]. See also provincial coroners' reports: BC Coroners Service, *Residential Structure Fire Deaths in BC, 2007–2011* (Burnaby: Office of the Chief Coroner, 2012), https://www2.gov.bc.ca/assets/gov/birth-adoption-death-marriage-and-divorce/deaths/coroners-service/statistical/fire.pdf; Ontario Chief Coroner, *Ontario Chief Coroner's Table on Understanding Fire Deaths in First Nations* (Government of Ontario, 2021), https://www.ontario.ca/document/ontario-chief-coroners-table-understanding-fire-deaths-first-nations/introduction [perma.cc/X5TS-V7J8].

167 Christopher Alcantara, "Certificates of Possession and First Nations Housing: A Case Study of the Six Nations Housing Program" (2005) 20:2 *Canadian Journal of Law and Society* 183–205; TRC, *Canada's Residential Schools*, at 165; Indigenous Housing Caucus Working Group, *Addressing the Housing Needs of Indigenous Families and Individuals in the Urban, Rural and Northern Parts of Canada* (Ottawa: Canadian Housing Renewal Association, 2018), https://chra-achru.ca/wp-content/uploads/2015/09/2018-06-05_for-indigenous-by-indigenous-national-housing-strategy.pdf [perma.cc/B6Y5-XSH5], at 14.

168 Leclair, Standing Senate Committee on Aboriginal Peoples.

169 Ibid; *St. Theresa Point First Nation*; McCartney, Herskovits, and Hintelmann, "Failure by Design."

170 HUMA, *Indigenous Housing*, at 60.

171 Thistle, *Definition of Indigenous Homelessness*, at 14–15. See also *SR Report 2019* at 10; HUMA, *Indigenous Housing*.

172 Evelyn J. Peters and Vince Robillard, "'Everything You Want Is There': The Place of the Reserve in First Nations' Homeless Mobility" (2009) 30:6 *Urban Geography* 652–80; Thistle, *Definition of Indigenous Homelessness; MMIWG Report* at 445.

173 HUMA, *Indigenous Housing*.

174 Ibid at 41, 43.

175 Patrick, *Aboriginal Homelessness in Canada*, at 12.

176 Statistics Canada, *Canadian Housing Survey, 2018* (Ottawa: Statistics Canada, 2020), https://www150.statcan.gc.ca/n1/pub/11-627-m/11-627-m2020024-eng.htm [perma.cc/X24J-P4Q3].

177 *Constitution Act, 1867*, s 92(13).

178 Heffernan, Faraday, and Rosenthal, "Fighting for the Right to Housing in Canada," at 18.
179 The funding streams and structures are laid out in detail in HUMA, *Indigenous Housing;* Senate Standing Committee on Aboriginal Peoples, *On-Reserve Housing;* PBO, *Urban, Rural, and Northern Indigenous Housing.*
180 Indigenous Housing Caucus Working Group, *Addressing the Housing Needs of Indigenous Families.*
181 *First Nations Child and Family Caring Society of Canada et al v Attorney General of Canada (for the Minister of Indian and Northern Affairs Canada),* 2016 CHRT 2 at paras 40–45.
182 *Neskonlith Indian Band v Salmon Arm (City of),* 2012 BCCA 379. See also Shin Imai and Ashley Stacey, "Municipalities and the Duty to Consult Aboriginal Peoples: A Case Commentary on Neskonlith Indian Band v Salmon Arm (City)" (2014) 47 *University of British Columbia Law Review* 293–312; Alexandra Flynn, "Indigenous-Municipal Legal Relationships: Moving Beyond the Duty to Consult and Accommodate" (2020–21) 25 *Review of Consitutional Studies/Revue d'études constitutionnelles* 181–204; Felix Hoehn and Michael Stevens, "Local Government and the Crown's Duty to Consult" (2018) *Alberta Law Review* 971–1008.
183 Jula Hughes and Roy Stewart, "Urban Aboriginal People and the Honour of the Crown – A Discussion Paper" (2015) 66 *University of New Brunswick Law Journal* 263–99 at 265.
184 Ibid at 290.
185 Ibid at 296. See, for instance, Mississaugas of the New Credit First Nation, *Trailblazers: The Mississaugas of the New Credit First Nation Strategic Plan* (Hagersville, ON: Mississaugas of the New Credit First Nation, 2017) at 39, 48; BC Indigenous Homelessness Strategy Steering Committee, *BC Indigenous Homelessness Strategy* (Vancouver, BC: Aboriginal Housing Management Association, 2022).
186 Hughes and Stewart, "Urban Aboriginal People and the Honour of the Crown," at 294. See also Yale D Belanger, "Breaching Reserve Boundaries: *Canada v. Misquadis* and the Legal Creation of the Urban Indigenous Community," in *Indigenous in the City: Contemporary Identities and Cultural Innovation,* ed. Evelyn Peters and Chris Anderson (Vancouver: UBC Press, 2013), 69–87.
187 *UNDRIP,* arts 10, 11(2), 19, 28(1), 29(2), 32(2).
188 *Canada (AG) v Misquadis,* 2003 FCA 370; *Ardoch Algonquin First Nation v Canada (AG),* 2003 FCA 473 at para 36 [*Ardoch Algonquin*].
189 *Ardoch Algonquin* at para 141.
190 Hughes and Stewart, "Urban Aboriginal People and the Honour of the Crown," at 296.
191 *Baker v Canada (Minister of Citizenship and Immigration),* [1999] 2 SCR 817 at 861, 243 NR 22; *Reference re Public Service Employee Relations Act (Alta),* [1987] 1 SCR 313 at 394, 74 NR 99; *Quebec (Attorney General) v 9147-0732 Québec Inc,* 2020 SCC 32 at para 32. See Government of Canada, "Implementing the United Nations Declaration on the Rights of Indigenous Peoples Act" (last modified June 20, 2024), https://justice.gc.ca/eng/declaration/index.html [perma.cc/6XE7-653Z].

192 *Reference re An Act respecting First Nations, Inuit and Métis children, youth and families* 2024 SCC 5.
193 See, for example, *Declaration on the Rights of Indigenous Peoples Act*, SBC 2019, c 44 [*DRIPA*]; *UNDRIP Act.*
194 *Gitxaala v British Columbia (Chief Gold Commissioner)*, 2025 BCCA 420, at 125 [*Gitxaala*].
195 *SR Report 2014.*
196 *Gitxaala* at 129.
197 Ibid at 66.
198 HUMA, *Indigenous Housing.*
199 See the description of the on-reserve housing policy in Indigenous and Northern Affairs Canada, *Evaluation of On-Reserve Housing* (Ottawa: Government of Canada, January 2017) at 16.
200 *National Housing Strategy Act*, ss 13(d), (g), (h).
201 Ibid, ss 13(d), (h), 13.2(1).
202 Ibid, ss 13(e), (f).
203 Ibid, s 13.
204 Ibid, ss 13(d), (h).
205 Marie-Josée Houle, *Housing Is a Human Right: The Office of the Federal Housing Advocate's 2021–2022 Annual Report to the Minister* (Ottawa: Canadian Human Rights Commission, 2022), https://2021.housing.chrcreport.ca/pdfs/office_of_the_federal_housing_advocate-annual_report_2021.pdf.
206 Ibid.
207 Canadian Human Rights Commission, "Encampments" (last modified June 6, 2025), https://www.chrc-ccdp.gc.ca/individuals/right-housing/encampments [perma.cc/3Y9E-K6KS].
208 Ibid; Office of the Federal Housing Advocate, *Interim Report*, at 2. The final report was released after this chapter was completed and can be found at Office of the Federal Housing Advocate, *Upholding Dignity and Human Rights: The Federal Housing Advocate's Review of Homeless Encampments* (Ottawa: Canadian Human Rights Commission, 2024), https://www.chrc-ccdp.gc.ca/publications/upholding-dignity-and-human-rights-federal-housing-advocates-review-homeless [perma.cc/FG8A-CH8Z] [Office of the Federal Housing Advocate, *Upholding Dignity and Human Rights*, final report].
209 Office of the Federal Housing Advocate, *Interim Report*, at 3, 13.
210 Ibid at 14.
211 Ibid at 2, 7.
212 Ibid at 3.
213 Ibid.
214 Office of the Federal Housing Advocate, *Upholding Dignity and Human Rights*, final report.
215 *Bamberger* at para 150.
216 See *Waterloo; Bamberger; Haida Nation;* Hughes and Stewart, "Urban Aboriginal People and the Honour of the Crown."
217 See *Grootboom and Others;* Biss et al., *Progressive Realization*, at 7.

218 *Canada (Commissioner of Official Languages) v Canada (Employment and Social Development)*, 2022 FCA 14 [*Commissioner v ESD*]. On conditional grants and the division of powers, see *Finlay v Canada (Minister of Finance)*, 1993 CanLII 129 (SCC); *Reference re Canada Assistance Plan (BC)*, 1991 CanLII 74 (SCC).

219 *NHSA*, ss 4–5.

220 Official Languages Act, RSC 1985, c 31 (4th Supp).

221 *Commissioner v ESD* at para 88.

222 Ibid at para 110.

Part 4

Legal Unhousing in Institutions

10

Legal Unhousing and the Right of Persons with Disabilities to Live Independently and in the Community

Contemplating Accessibility Standards

LAVERNE JACOBS

Introduction

The legal unhousing of persons with disabilities occurs in a number of ways. Disabled people in Canada face barriers to housing that include a lack of appropriately designed spaces, insufficient supports in the community, and financialization. Consequently, they often end up living in institutions. Although the human rights model of disability forms the foundation of international disability rights law and should guide the development of law and policy related to adequate housing, current approaches to rectifying housing issues for persons with disabilities often do not build on the human rights model of disability. As a result, the inclusion and recognition of persons with disabilities in mainstream communities have been hindered. Government, through the creation of public policy, has an important role to play in safeguarding the right to adequate housing for disabled people. In this chapter, I propose that appropriately designed accessibility standards can help to realize this right using the human rights model of disability.

In the second section, I introduce the right to housing for disabled persons as it exists in Canada, situating it within the broader rights to adequate housing and to equality and nondiscrimination of persons with disabilities that are safeguarded in international law. I also define the human rights model of disability and examine its impact on the right to adequate housing. In the third section, I discuss the decision in *Disability Rights Coalition v Nova Scotia (Attorney General)*[1] to illustrate how institutionalization and wait times for community housing constitute systemic disability discrimination. That case also points toward additional systemic obstacles that regularly hinder disabled individuals who wish to live prosperously in their community. In the fourth section, I consider two contexts in which legislative and policy reforms that rely on the human rights model of disability can help to reduce the risk of unhousing once a person with disabilities is living in the community. The first context concerns inadequate personal supports for persons with disabilities living in the community. The second context relates to remedies for housing-related issues experienced by persons with disabilities living in the community. I explain the theoretical and practical underpinnings of accessibility legislation and how the product of such legislation – housing accessibility standards – can bring us closer to removing these obstacles to living in the community, even if imperfectly. I complete the discussion by suggesting that, where remedial pathways are legislated through the administrative state, the existence of standards for housing that are informed by the human rights model of disability can equally assist in resolving disputes over remedies.

Persons with Disabilities and the Right to Housing

The Right to Adequate Housing in International Law

The right to housing for persons with disabilities is enshrined in international and domestic law. The right exists most explicitly at the international level. The *Convention on the Rights of Persons with Disabilities* (*CRPD*),[2] adopted in 2006 by the United Nations General Assembly and ratified by Canada in 2010, indicates that persons with disabilities have a right to adequate housing as part of the broader right to an adequate standard of living and social protection. Article 28(1) of the *CRPD* states that

> States Parties recognize the right of persons with disabilities to an adequate standard of living for themselves and their families, including adequate food, clothing and housing, and to the continuous improvement of living conditions, and shall take appropriate steps to safeguard and promote the realization of this right without discrimination on the basis of disability.

One can observe from reading this article that the right to housing, although explicit, is part of a bundle of rights required for an adequate standard of living. In this way, the right to housing is both explicit and tempered, in the sense that it is not provided as directly as many other rights in the *CRPD,* such as the right to education or work.[3] Furthermore, the fact that the right to adequate housing is connected to other elements of an adequate standard of living is a reminder of the indivisibility of human rights and, more specifically, that adequate housing can be a stepping stone to achieving and retaining other essentials of socio-economic well-being, such as good health.[4]

In terms of its design, the right to adequate housing is strengthened by obliging states parties to ensure the continuous improvement of living conditions and to take steps to safeguard and promote the realization of this right.[5] These obligations must be fulfilled without discrimination on the basis of disability.[6]

The right to adequate housing under the *CRPD* presents a more robust version of the right set out in the earlier *International Covenant on Economic, Social and Cultural Rights* (*ICESCR*) of 1966.[7] The *ICESCR* recognizes the right of everyone to an adequate standard of living, including adequate housing, and to the continuous improvement of living conditions.[8] By contrast, the right to adequate housing under the *CRPD* focuses explicitly on persons with disabilities. Moreover, interpretations of the right to adequate housing can build upon the *CRPD*'s preamble, which recognizes the diversity of disability[9] and that multiple or aggravated forms of discrimination can be experienced by persons with disabilities.[10] In this way, the *CRPD* opens the door to deeper understandings and interpretations of the meaning of adequate housing that reflect a more authentic recognition of the lived experiences of persons with disabilities, including their intersectional marginalization.

"Adequate housing" is not defined in the *CRPD*. However, ideas about what this concept means can be drawn from the *ICESCR*. In 1991, the United Nations Committee on Economic, Social and Cultural Rights, the treaty body responsible for monitoring the implementation of the *ICESCR*, published *General Comment No. 4* on adequate housing.[11] It identifies seven factors that need to be present in order for housing to be considered adequate in any particular context.[12] These factors are: (1) the legal security of tenure; (2) the availability of services, materials, facilities, and infrastructure; (3) affordability; (4) habitability; (5) accessibility; (6) location; and (7) cultural adequacy.[13] In the context of ensuring housing for persons with disabilities, all these factors are relevant, although the degree to which some are more relevant than others will vary depending on the circumstances. In other words, though factors such as habitability (i.e., housing that provides adequate space and safety) and location (i.e., housing located in a place that gives access to employment options, health-care services, etc.) might appear to be particularly important for persons with disabilities, other factors, such as cultural adequacy, might be equally important, especially in light of the diversity of the disability community. The contributions of Indigenous Elders to individuals and families in Indigenous communities, for example, have been noted to promote individual and community wellness.[14] Indigenous persons with disabilities might therefore consider the ability to maintain connections with Indigenous Elders within traditional communities (or cultural adequacy) to be a fundamental part of adequate housing.

Another international legal provision that addresses the right to housing for persons with disabilities is Article 9(1) of the *CRPD*. This article guarantees the right of access for persons with disabilities and touches on the accessibility of housing. It asserts that states parties must ensure access on an equal basis with others to services and facilities that include housing, and it requires the identification and elimination of barriers and obstacles to access in these domains.

Finally, Article 19 of the *CRPD* is important for ensuring that those with disabilities live and thrive in the community. Article 19 guarantees the right of persons with disabilities to live independently and be included in the community. It requires states parties to recognize the equal right of all persons with disabilities to live in the community. It also obliges states parties to take appropriate and effective measures to facilitate the full enjoyment of this right and to facilitate the full inclusion of persons with disabilities and their participation in the community. The choice of where to live and with whom, and the right of access to adequate personal assistance to support living and inclusion in the community, have been emphasized in international law. The Committee on the Rights of Persons with Disabilities has indicated that persons with disabilities should have funding and be at the centre of decisions made about their personal assistance.[15] In summary, the right to adequate and accessible housing for persons with disabilities and the right to live independently and be included in the community are strongly anchored in international law.

The Human Rights Model of Disability and Its Impact on the Right to Adequate Housing

A state party that has ratified the *CRPD* is obligated to implement the right to housing for persons with disabilities as it is found in the convention. Moreover, the implementation of any aspect of the *CRPD* should be done in conformity with the principles related to equality and nondiscrimination established by the CRPD Committee.

In its *General Comment No. 6*, the CRPD Committee defines the human rights model of disability as part of its extensive and detailed guidance on the right to equality and nondiscrimination for persons with disabilities. The human rights model of disability recognizes disability as a social construct. It therefore works to avoid reducing persons with disabilities to their medical impairments (as is done in the medical model) and instead emphasizes that disability arises from the interaction between persons with impairments and barriers in society. In this way, the human rights model of disability builds upon the social model of disablement. The human rights model guards against the use of a person's impairment to exclude that person from being considered a rights holder. It protects the human rights of persons with disabilities, seeks to safeguard their dignity, and does not grant benefits or protections based on charity or pity. Furthermore, it recognizes the diversity of persons with disabilities and that disability is only one layer of a person's identity.[16]

Overall, the human rights model of disability emphasizes the human dignity of persons with disabilities. The model encompasses values that can further social change, such as respect for the autonomy, independence, and full inclusion in society of persons with disabilities.[17] The human rights model also embraces human variation and sees impairment as a part of it. The complexity and politics of identity, including intersectional identity, are recognized through the human rights model. Finally, that model provides a road map for change; it goes beyond describing disability as the social model of disability has done.[18]

The right to equality and nondiscrimination also reflects the inclusive equality approach that underpins the *CRPD*. That approach is grounded in substantive equality, which means that it recognizes and aims to rectify systemic and structural inequalities as well as power imbalances. The inclusive equality approach has four main dimensions: a distributive dimension concerned with fair distribution of resources; a recognition dimension that aims to combat stigma, stereotyping, and violence and to recognize intersectionality; a participative dimension that aims for inclusion in society; and an accommodation dimension "to make space for difference as a matter of dignity."[19] It is important to consider the dimensions of inclusive equality when engaging with the human rights model of disability, as the two concepts are inextricably intertwined in the international protection of disability rights.

When it comes to adequate housing for persons with disabilities, the CRPD Committee has specifically stated that ensuring equality and nondiscrimination requires that states parties take appropriate measures to see that "persons with disabilities are not denied the possibility to rent or disadvantaged in the housing market."[20] Although *General Comment No. 6* does not provide additional explanation, it seems to be clear that analyzing how persons with disabilities can be excluded from rental accommodations and disadvantaged (individually, systemically, and structurally) in seeking, obtaining, and retaining housing is a necessary first step to provide an equality-based right to adequate housing for persons with disabilities. Moreover, policies for preventing exclusion and disadvantage in domestic rental accommodation and housing markets should attempt to dismantle barriers to housing for disabled members of the community. Finally, there needs to be a way for information about barriers affecting persons with disabilities to be addressed not only in policy creation but also in remedial responses when disabled persons have experienced loss or injury, including to their dignity, as a result of these barriers.

The Right to Housing in Domestic Law

In Canada, the international law instruments discussed above reinforce housing rights that are more immediately justiciable. On a domestic level, the right to housing for persons with disabilities is protected through a patchwork of different laws. The clearest protection arises from statutory human rights law (anti-discrimination law). Canadian anti-discrimination statutes generally provide explicit protection from discrimination on the ground of disability, including in rental accommodations.[21] The law is centred on the concept of reasonable accommodation, which requires persons with disabilities to be accommodated by a landlord to the point of undue hardship. The protection against discrimination under human rights law is sometimes twinned with an explicit protection from harassment by landlords, their agents, or other occupants.[22] Renovations to make a rental space more physically accessible are commonly discussed within the context of reasonable accommodations in housing for persons with disabilities. Yet, there are less often referenced circumstances that also fit within the realm of reasonable accommodations requested by persons with disabilities, such as reorganizing where and how garbage is collected to accommodate an individual's physical disabilities or finding ways to ensure that a person with noise sensitivity is not affected by the noise of neighbours.[23] Finally, outside rental accommodations, Canadian human rights law protections in the conclusion of contracts inescapably guard against disability discrimination in the purchase of property as well.

Although disability rights protection occurs most frequently through anti-discrimination law, other legal frameworks can also come into play. These frameworks include landlord and tenant law, the *Canadian Charter of Rights and Freedoms,*[24] and the federal *National Housing Strategy Act.*[25] Nevertheless, there is currently no domestic legal framework that explicitly and directly focuses on housing rights issues for persons with disabilities. When one surveys the Canadian jurisprudence on disabled people and housing, one notes that it similarly contains few decisions that markedly advance the right to live independently and in the community. A notable exception is the case of *Disability Rights Coalition.* It is one of the most important judicial decisions for exposing and addressing unnecessary institutionalization and extensive wait times for housing in the community. Institutionalization has deep historical significance in the disability rights movement.[26] That is because the risk of being institutionalized is disproportionately higher for persons with disabilities, and disabled people have at times been institutionalized for reasons that neither firmly connect them to medical impairment nor respect their will and preferences. With respect to the concept of legal unhousing, the *Disability Rights Coalition* decision, which I examine next, makes valuable contributions to both law and policy development in the area of community living for persons with disabilities.

Deinstitutionalization: *Disability Rights Coalition v Nova Scotia (Attorney General)*

Disability Rights Coalition is a landmark decision regarding the deinstitutionalization of persons with disabilities in Canada. Three disabled appellants sought damages after having spent several years in institutions because of the province's inordinate delay in providing appropriate community housing.[27] The appellants were persons with mental disabilities in need of social assistance in the form of supportive housing. They were placed in institutions because of a lack of available housing.[28] They alleged discrimination on the grounds of mental disability and source of income. In the *Disability Rights Coalition* decision, the appellants and their lawyers successfully demonstrated the existence of both individual and systemic discrimination in the province's actions. The case illustrates how persons with disabilities can be deprived of the right to adequate housing and specifically the rights to be included in the community, to live independently, and to reside in places of their choosing.

In *Disability Rights Coalition,* the Nova Scotia Court of Appeal held that the appellants had experienced discrimination not only when they were placed in Nova Scotia's mental health institution but also when they were housed in residential or rehabilitation centres or in communities other than their own.[29] The court held that they had been placed in these institutions in order to access their basic needs even though the province had an obligation to provide those needs. Moreover, they did not need to be institutionalized.

In its comprehensive reasons for the decision, the Court of Appeal observed that the province's course of action ran contrary to its long-standing knowledge of the impacts of institutionalization on persons with disabilities. Between 1984 and 1998, the responsible government department had appointed committees to consider and modernize the care provided to seniors and disabled persons (particularly those with mental disabilities).[30] Through four major reports published during this time period, the province recognized the importance of integrating persons with intellectual disabilities into the mainstream community and started to move along the path to deinstitutionalization. As the Court of Appeal noted, the province had known that institutionalization was not required for persons with intellectual or psychosocial disabilities and that it could have detrimental personal impacts, including the loss of opportunities to engage with others and to thrive as members of the mainstream community.[31] Nevertheless, persons with disabilities continued to be placed or kept in institutions. For example, Beth MacLean resided in the Nova Scotia mental health facility for over a decade. The Court of Appeal observed that

> it is apparent on the evidence accepted by the Board that the Province's conduct towards Ms. MacLean had a significant and lasting impact on her. She was eligible to be discharged from the Nova Scotia Hospital in 2002 but languished there for the next 13 or 14 years. She was capable of living a productive life in the community but was denied that opportunity. Her mental and physical well-being deteriorated while she was institutionalized.[32]

In addition to the risk of institutionalization and its impacts, the court accepted that extensive wait times for community placement constituted a further adverse consequence facing persons with disabilities who seek social assistance in housing.

These two adverse consequences – institutionalization and inordinate wait times – are often intertwined. As noted above, MacLean spent thirteen or fourteen years institutionalized in the Nova Scotia Hospital because the province was unable to provide her with a home in the community with the supports that she needed. Another appellant, Sheila Livingstone, was put on a wait list to obtain a community placement in a small options home (a home that typically houses three disabled individuals and is staffed by a third-party agency that provides support to the residents twenty-four hours a day).[33] She remained on the wait list for nine years and lived in the mental health facility even though she no longer required mental health services. Livingstone ultimately accepted a placement in an adult residential centre in Yarmouth, Nova Scotia, several kilometres away from her family. Although it was not a small options community home, this placement was the "only offer of alternative shelter made by the Province for Ms. Livingstone in the nine years she was eligible for assistance."[34] She also accepted the placement because of concerns about her safety as she had been physically assaulted more than once by other patients in the mental health facility.[35] However, the relocation to a different community brought further adverse consequences. The distance from her family members made visiting and maintaining connections with them extremely difficult. Livingstone passed away in the adult residential centre in Yarmouth two years later.[36]

Inordinate wait times had been identified as a problem with the system much earlier in an independent review in 2001. At that time, the reviewer, Dr. Michael Kendrick, signalled two significant issues within the functioning of the provincial government system that underpinned the decisions preventing disabled persons from moving (back) into their communities. The first issue was that government departments were reluctant to fund vacant community spots for individuals during their temporary hospital admissions, with the result that their community spots often were lost. Alluding to the homelessness that the interplay between government services engenders for people with disabilities, the Board of Inquiry highlighted this aspect of the independent review:

> Dr. Kendrick ... recommended: "The Department of Community Services And The Department of Health Need To Restructure The Fiscal Incentives Regarding Community Placement" (Emphasis in original). He wrote:
>
> > *when a person who is currently living in a CBO [community-based option] goes into a psychiatric in-patient unit with the Health Department, the Department of Community Services still has to fund the now vacant space of the person while they are in hospital. If they are unable to do this for a lengthy period while the individual is in hospital, then the person will lose their home.* The reason for this is that the Department of Community Services cannot afford to fund empty spaces indefinitely, and therefore has to set some point where the person is no longer a

> resident ... *This effect thereby renders people unnecessarily homeless, and denies them the continuity of abode that most reasonable people would see as sensible.*[37]

The second issue was that if an individual placed in a psychiatric hospital subsequently wanted to move into the community, then they would not necessarily be given priority for a placement or even considered for funding of a community spot. Their wait time could therefore be exceptionally lengthy and, ironically, more costly to taxpayers than the community placement itself.[38]

The Nova Scotia Court of Appeal determined that the risks of institutionalization and prolonged wait times constituted two systemic adverse impacts experienced by persons with disabilities who sought social assistance from the province. Prolonged wait times existed uniquely in relation to persons with disabilities and arose because they required supports and services to live in the community.[39] The Court of Appeal accepted the argument put forward by the Disability Rights Coalition comparing the province's provision of services to disabled persons seeking social assistance under the applicable statute with the its provision of services to nondisabled persons seeking social assistance.[40] In the case of nondisabled social assistance recipients, there were no lengthy delays, no requirement of relocation, no risk of institutionalization, and an absence of the arbitrary and discretionary classification/assessment practices that plagued the administration of the social assistance regime when it came to persons with disabilities.[41]

As a result, one of the major conclusions of the *Disability Rights Coalition* decision was that the province's treatment of persons with disabilities in the delivery of social assistance could constitute systemic discrimination. Addressing a lingering question relating to the nature of the evidence required to demonstrate systemic discrimination, the Nova Scotia Court of Appeal clarified that when a complaint of systemic discrimination is made, it is not necessary to prove that everyone with the protected characteristic has experienced the adverse impacts.[42] Such a requirement would be impractical and unnecessary, and would prevent the advancement of numerous systemic discrimination claims which generally seek to improve policies and practices rather than to provide individualized remedies such as compensation.[43] The Board of Inquiry therefore erred in its analysis of the systemic discrimination claim submitted by the Disability Rights Coalition. The Court of Appeal held that the Disability Rights Coalition had established a *prima facie* case of systemic discrimination and ordered that the issue of systemic discrimination be returned to a new Board of Inquiry for a fresh and full examination.[44] The Court of Appeal also clarified the nature of the systemic discrimination in this case as affecting persons with disabilities in the receipt of social assistance *generally*.[45] The court held that it was inappropriate for individuals in the situation of the appellants to be compared only with other persons with disabilities who received social assistance.[46] In contrast, systemic discrimination occurs because of the disproportionate negative impacts on persons with disabilities caused by the province's administration of the social assistance program.[47] Persons with disabilities are the only individuals subject to be institutionalized as they wait to receive social assistance, to face the risk of having to relocate from their communities, and to wait for extended periods of time for a home in the community, possibly to no avail.[48]

In addition to arguing successfully for the court's conclusions on systemic discrimination, the Disability Rights Coalition of Nova Scotia executed an agreement with the province that aims to reduce wait times for placements in the community and to expedite deinstitutionalization.[49] This five-year path-breaking agreement is overseen by an expert independent monitor selected by the parties who reports yearly on the progress.[50] The Nova Scotia Human Rights Board of Inquiry will retain jurisdiction until the systemic discrimination addressed in this agreement has ended.[51]

The *Disability Rights Coalition* case serves as an illustration of how legal remedies can be pursued to address the unhousing of persons with disabilities arising from government administration of social assistance. The case has had a significant impact on the use of human rights law (anti-discrimination law) as a tool to identify and redress individual and systemic disability discrimination in the context of adequate housing for persons with disabilities. Furthermore, although concern has been expressed about the pace of change pursuant to the agreement,[52] the agreement with the province promises to have a positive effect in the long run for disabled people who wish to move out of institutions and find adequate housing in the community. At the time of the hearing on remedies, the board accepted the parties' request to develop collaboratively a remedy that would be feasible to implement and effective in addressing the multiple issues in the systemic discrimination.[53] The remedy pursued is based on an expert report commissioned jointly by the Disability Rights Coalition and the government of Nova Scotia's Department of Community Services.[54]

Nevertheless, beyond what the *Disability Rights Coalition* decision establishes in terms of disability discrimination and wait times for housing, it also hints at several fault lines in the path to community living. More specifically, although avoiding unnecessary institutionalization is an important and common aspect of the right to live independently and be included in the community, other obstacles regularly hinder disabled individuals who wish to live prosperously in the community. These obstacles serve to unhouse the rights of persons with disabilities to live independently and in the community. These everyday situations of unhousing include inadequate personal supports, evictions for financial gain by landlords (or renovictions), a lack of remedial avenues, and insufficiently responsive remedial actions. These obstacles could be addressed through the development of laws and policies that better reflect the human rights model of disability, including the concepts of recognition and redistribution.

In the final part of this chapter, I consider how legislative and policy reform that furthers the human rights model of disability could be impactful. I discuss the instrument of accessibility legislation and how standards created to ensure adequate housing for persons with disabilities could offer promise in a range of areas and serve to address these obstacles.

Creating Accessibility Standards to Address Housing Barriers for Persons with Disabilities

Accessibility legislation is a proactive form of equality law. It aims to identify potential disabling barriers and to eradicate them before they are established in society. Accessibility legislation establishes a process by which committees of individuals representing disabled persons, industry, and government work together to create standards. The standards become legally binding regulations after public consultation and ministerial review.[55] Accessibility legislation has developed extensively in Canada. Seven provinces, as well as the federal government, have adopted accessibility legislation and are developing accessibility standards.[56]

Standards have been developed in many social areas, including customer service, transportation, employment, information and communication, and the built environment. Standards in these areas focus on narrow technical requirements as well as broader normative goals. The technical requirements are typically in place to ensure that persons with disabilities have sufficient space for mobility aids, can use websites and other communication devices, and (along with manufacturers and vendors of assistive devices) are aware of the specifications within which they need to work. Ontario's accessibility standards for transportation, for example, require that conventional transportation service providers ensure that vehicles have a certain amount of internal physical space specified in square millimetres.[57] These standards apply to transit buses, streetcars, subways, and other vehicles identified in the regulation. In summary, accessibility standards indicate what must be included in goods, facilities, and services though with varying degrees of technical detail.

Some accessibility standards incorporate broader philosophical goals in addition to technical requirements. Such standards are helpful in delineating the foundations of the standards, in turn showing how the standards work to further disability equality.[58] For example, the foundational principles of Ontario's recommended postsecondary education standards emphasize that disability is part of diversity and intersectionality and the importance of recognizing the compounded impacts of intersecting identities.[59] This orientation is helpful in interpreting the standards since it might prompt administrators in the postsecondary education context to ask about additional simultaneous experiences of marginalization that could erect or contribute to barriers experienced by a student with an impairment. This approach connects clearly with the human rights model of disability.

Indeed, that model is a useful guide when it comes to creating accessibility standards for persons with disabilities in the area of adequate housing. The key elements of the human rights model of disability are the (re)distribution of resources to avoid socio-economic disadvantage, the appropriate recognition of persons with disabilities (without stigmatizing, stereotyping, etc.) that respects their dignity, the participation of persons with disabilities in society, and a dimension for individualized accommodation.[60] In addition to these elements, which stem from the inclusive equality grounding of the human rights model of disability, the model emphasizes human variation, the diversity of disability, the intersectional identities of persons with disabilities, and the removal of barriers in society.[61] The human rights model of disability therefore fits well with accessibility legislation and complements its goals.[62]

Accessibility standards could be helpful in the area of housing. Similar to the recommended postsecondary education standards, they could both regulate the technical design of spaces to ensure that they are physically accessible and legislate an approach to housing consonant with the human rights model of disability. Moreover, legislating an intersectional approach, as was done within the postsecondary education context, would assist in ensuring that persons with disabilities and the barriers to housing that they face are fully recognized. This approach would work to safeguard the dignity of persons with disabilities.

Legislated standards could be used to counteract some of the precise situations experienced in the *Disability Rights Coalition* case. For example, it is clear that the allocation of funding was one of the reasons why disabled people could not find supported housing in the community. Housing accessibility standards could be directed to the government on issues such as resource allocation, which would assist with an equitable redistribution of resources to ensure funding for housing development and renovation as well as community supports for persons with disabilities. In addition to standards that are binding on the government, standards could be created that require developers to build a certain number of accessible or accessible-ready homes.[63]

Accessibility standards for adequate housing could include a requirement that governments pay attention to ensuring that there are sufficient and appropriate quality services in the community. Once in the community, personal supports can be essential for living independently and participating as a member of the community. The Committee on the Rights of Persons with Disabilities has defined "personal assistance" as "person-directed/'user'-led human support available to a person with disability," noting also that it is a tool for independent living.[64] Locally, in Canada, the term "personal supports" is more commonly used. The Erie St. Clair Healthline, for example, defines such supports as "services that assist people at home with their daily care, [ensure] mobility of routine activities of daily living, and provide respite care" – referring to essentially the same services.[65] The problem is that such services are often difficult to find. Often the supports available are insufficient for the level of demand or not designed to match what is actually needed by consumers of the services.[66] They might also simply be of poor quality.[67] Accessibility standards could address these shortcomings by requiring that a pool of funding, indexed to inflation, be set aside by the government, ensuring that certain types of services are always available (e.g., meal preparation, homemaking, and outings at the request of the person with the disability). In addition to basic elements of personal care (e.g., bathing and dressing), these services are essential if one is to thrive in the community.

At the same time, it is important not to overlook the practical challenges associated with the creation and implementation of accessibility standards. Housing accessibility standards have rarely been created through the processes of accessibility legislation in Canada, and those that have been created have generally not been mandatory,[68] so one of the first challenges that can arise is the need to convince the government that housing is a priority area in which accessibility standards should be developed through the consultative co-production processes of accessibility legislation.[69] This work often falls on the shoulders of disability advocacy groups. Using as an example Ontario, the first Canadian jurisdiction in which standards were created under the legal framework of accessibility legislation, we can observe that the social areas in which standards were developed have typically been designated by the responsible minister without public consultation. This makes it harder for organizations dedicated to disability issues to express their views on the need for specific standards.

Once the social areas are selected for standard development, the process of designing standards through standard development committees engages issues of what I have termed elsewhere a "deliberative democracy battlefield."[70] Since consensus may be required for standards to be created, compromises often occur, sometimes leaving standards weaker than desired by the disability community. The human rights model of disability as it relates to adequate housing might not always emerge in its fullest form. Finally, issues concerning a lack of compliance with and enforcement of standards have arisen because of a lack of political will, inadequate budgetary resources, or other reasons.[71] These phenomena can result in standards that exist on paper but not in practice. Despite these challenges, however, the establishment of accessibility standards in housing, even if imperfect, has the benefits of opening the door to strengthening the housing standards over time and bringing about social change on the issue.

Housing standards can also assist with remedies. When one considers issues related to adequate housing for disabled persons, issues concerning effective remedies are often overlooked. An essential element of enjoying the right to live independently and in the community is the ability to pursue remedies when that right has not been adequately fulfilled. To be effective, remedies need to be easily accessible and reflective of the human rights model of disability as opposed to furthering charitable or medical models. Yet independent remedial pathways do not always exist. For example, people with disabilities who receive inadequate personal assistance often have few meaningful (as well as timely and inexpensive) remedial options. In Ontario, disputes about the quality of community services provided to individuals requiring personal supports or about an alleged violation of a person's rights by the agency approved to deliver those services do not give rise to a right of appeal to an independent tribunal. Instead, the agency involved is required to review the complaint and respond to the person who made it.[72] It is therefore essential that these agencies recognize the right to live independently and be included in the community and the human rights model of disability that underlies it. Housing standards could require the government to ensure the existence of independent dispute resolution mechanisms, as well as training for personal support agencies to ensure that their work is grounded in the human rights model of disability and respectful of the right of persons with disabilities to live independently and in the community.

Even where independent remedial avenues do exist, it is necessary to support administrative tribunals so that they can adopt perspectives in their interpretations and adjudications in line with obligations under the *CRPD.* Renovictions offer a useful example. They form part of financialization – a process through which rental housing properties are transformed into products for financial investors.[73] Systemic inequality has been noted to exist in financialization.[74] The landscape of those disproportionately affected by renovictions includes persons with disabilities from intersectional backgrounds, such as women and those of lower income. The Disabled Women's Network of Canada has highlighted that when it comes to the negative impacts of financialization, including renovictions, women with disabilities figure prominently.[75] The impacts include institutionalization, loss of supports in the community, and loss of accessible homes.[76]

Renoviction decisions in Ontario engage the use of discretion by independent administrative tribunal decision makers (usually Landlord and Tenant Board adjudicators) in the context of contested evictions. This use of discretion raises the question of which factors influence the exercise of discretion toward approval or denial of renovictions. In the exercise of their discretion, administrative adjudicators are required to apply the human rights law of the province.[77] It is therefore important that the right to be free from discrimination in accommodations (found in the human rights statutes of the provinces and territories[78]) be understood liberally and purposively as intended.[79] Accessibility standards in housing can assist in this context as well. They can serve to remind adjudicators of the obligations that exist for Canada as a state party under the human rights model of disability and the CRPD, more broadly. They can serve to prompt the jurisdiction's Human Rights Commission to issue policy guidelines for the interpretation of the *Human Rights Code,* and/or they might be considered directly by adjudicators in their exercise of discretion. For example, the Ontario Human Rights Commission issued its *Policy on Ableism and Discrimination Based on Disability,* which serves as an interpretive guideline available to the Human Rights Tribunal of Ontario and the general public and refers to the role of Ontario's accessibility legislation (the *Accessibility for Ontarians with Disabilities Act*).[80]

In summary, there are several reasons for the adoption of accessibility standards to ensure adequate housing for disabled people. Accessibility standards can help to ensure that there are sufficient and appropriate places for occupancy, recognize and respond meaningfully to the diversity of disability and the need for personal supports, and assist with creating remedial pathways with adjudicated outcomes that respect the right to adequate housing for persons with disabilities and engage with the human rights model of disability.

Conclusion

The Committee on the Rights of Persons with Disabilities has noted that domestic laws and policies often poorly reflect the human rights model of disability. In its words, "laws and regulatory frameworks often remain imperfect and incomplete or ineffective, or reflect an inadequate understanding of the human rights model of disability. Many national laws and policies perpetuate the exclusion and isolation of and discrimination and violence against persons with disabilities. They often ... lack effective mechanisms of legal redress and reparation."[81]

Closer to home, the Ontario Human Rights Commission has called upon the federal government to address systemic inequality in housing on the basis of disability and other grounds.[82] In this chapter, I have discussed the need for law and policy reform to protect and further the right to adequate housing for persons with disabilities. Accessibility standards in housing are an equality law instrument that would be helpful in achieving this goal, particularly if they are informed by the human rights model of disability.

I have outlined the right to adequate housing as it exists under the United Nations *CRPD* and more broadly in international law under the *ICESCR*. I have further situated the right within the tenets of the human rights model of disability, the model that underlies the right to equality and nondiscrimination under the *CRPD*. Turning to the domestic context, I have explored, primarily through an examination of the *Disability Rights Coalition* case from Nova Scotia, the use of domestic law to protect the right to housing of disabled people in Canada. That case made groundbreaking advances in recognizing the elements of individual and systemic discrimination that can exist within the public service delivery of social assistance where housing in the community with disability supports is part of the assistance sought. The decision focused primarily on the risk of institutionalization and the experience of lengthy wait times. In addition to its pursuit of a resolution through the provincial human rights system, the Disability Rights Coalition concluded a multi-year agreement to operationalize a robust process of deinstitutionalization and ensure that persons with disabilities can be placed in the community more rapidly.

The *Disability Rights Coalition* decision also pointed to several obstacles that disabled people face while living in the community, though it did not address them directly. These everyday obstacles constitute forms of legal unhousing. They include a lack of appropriately designed spaces, inadequate personal supports, a lack of remedial avenues, and the possibility of insufficiently responsive remedial outcomes. I have reviewed these obstacles and, using various examples, argued that the use of accessibility standards in housing has positive implications for both policy and remedial reform. Without steps to render the right to adequate housing more concrete, persons with disabilities in Canada and elsewhere will be left in situations in which the right exists but without effective means of realization. Ensuring legal and policy reforms that reflect the human rights model of disability and bolster the distribution of housing resources, the availability of personal supports, remedial options, and responsive remedies through the administrative justice system are achievable goals. Moreover, these goals can be significantly enriched by the use of accessibility standards for housing.

Acknowledgments

The opinions expressed in this article are those of the author and do not aim to represent any organization. Thanks to Anna Lund and Sarah Buhler for the invitation to take part in this edited collection. Thanks also to Victoria Cino and Dawn Hadwen for their excellent research assistance. Portions of this chapter appear in Laverne Jacobs, Odelia Bay, Ruby Dhand, David Ireland, Richard Jochelson, and Freya Kodar, *Law and Disability in Canada: Cases and Materials* (Toronto: LexisNexis, 2026).

Notes

1 *Disability Rights Coalition v Nova Scotia (Attorney General)*, 2021 NSCA 70 [*Disability Rights Coalition*], and see the discussion of this case in Chapter 1 of this collection.

2 *Convention on the Rights of Persons with Disabilities*, December 13, 2006, 2515 UNTS 3 (entered into force May 3, 2008) [*CRPD*].

3 Ibid, arts 24, 27.

4 On the connections between socio-economic rights and the social determinants of health equity, see Carolyn B. Swope and Diana Hernández, "Housing as a Determinant of Health Equity: A Conceptual Model" (2019) 243:112571 *Social Science and Medicine* 1–13.

5 *CRPD*, art 28(1).
6 Ibid.
7 *International Covenant on Economic, Social and Cultural Rights*, December 16, 1966, 993 UNTS 3 (entered into force January 3, 1976) [*ICESCR*].
8 Ibid, art 11.
9 See *CRPD*, Preamble "i."
10 Ibid, Preamble "p," states "concerned about the difficult conditions faced by persons with disabilities who are subject to multiple or aggravated forms of discrimination on the basis of race, colour, sex, language, religion, political or other opinion, national, ethnic, indigenous or social origin, property, birth, age or other status."
11 Committee on Economic, Social and Cultural Rights (CESCR), *General Comment No. 4: The Right to Adequate Housing (Art. 11 (1) of the Covenant)*, OHCHR, 6th Sess, UN Doc E/1992/23 (1991), https://www.refworld.org/legal/general/cescr/1991/en/53157 [perma.cc/JP7G-EWP6].
12 Ibid at para 8.
13 Ibid.
14 See Chantal Viscogliosi, Hugo Asselin, Suzy Basile et al., "Importance of Indigenous Elders' Contributions to Individual and Community Wellness: Results from a Scoping Review on Social Participation and Intergenerational Solidarity" (2020) 111 *Canadian Journal of Public Health* 667–81 at 669; see also the discussion of the role that Indigenous traditional knowledge plays in early childhood learning in John Ward, "Reconceptualizing Learning Disabilities in Light of Indigenous Ways of Learning," in *Law and Disability in Canada: Cases and Materials*, ed. Laverne Jacobs, Odelia Bay, Ruby Dhand, David Ireland, Richard Jochelson, and Freya Kodar (Toronto: LexisNexis, 2026).
15 Committee on the Rights of Persons with Disabilities [CRPD Committee], *General Comment No. 5 on Living Independently and Being Included in the Community*, UN CRPD/C/GC/5 (2017) at para 16(d).
16 See CRPD Committee, *General Comment No.* 6, 19th Sess, UN CRPD/C/GC/6 (2018) at paras 1–11.
17 See the set of eight underlying principles in *CRPD*, art 3.
18 See Theresia DeGener, "A Human Rights Model of Disability" (2014) [unpublished, archived at ResearchGate], https://www.researchgate.net/publication/283713863_A_human_rights_model_of_disability [perma.cc/426H-X3K9].
19 See CRPD, *General Comment No. 6 (2018) on Equality and Non-Discrimination*, OHCHR, 19th Sess, UN Doc CRPD/C/GC/6 at para 11.
20 Ibid at para 60.
21 See, for instance, *Human Rights Code*, RSO 1990, c H.19, s 2(1).
22 See ibid, s 2(2).
23 See, for example, *Portman v Midwest Property Management*, 2022 CanLII 69462 (NT HRAP); *Stewart v Jordan*, 2023 AHRC 4.
24 *Canadian Charter of Rights and Freedoms*, Part I of the *Constitution Act, 1982*, being Schedule B to the *Canada Act 1982* (UK), 1982, c 11 [Charter].
25 *National Housing Strategy Act*, SC 2019, c 29, s 313 [*NHSA*].
26 For an international assessment of the impact and extent of institutionalization of persons with disabilities, see CRPD, *Guidelines on De-Institutionalization, Including*

in Emergencies, UN Doc CRPD/C/5 (2022), https://www.ohchr.org/en/documents/legal-standards-and-guidelines/crpdc5-guidelines-deinstitutionalization-including. For a discussion of the history of the institutionalization of persons with intellectual disabilities in Canada, see Madeline C. Burghardt, *Broken: Institutions, Families, and the Construction of Intellectual Disability* (Montreal and Kingston: McGill-Queen's University Press, 2018). For a discussion of the history of institutionalization of psychiatric consumers and survivors, see Geoffrey Reaume, *Remembrance of Patients Past: Patient Life at the Toronto Hospital for the Insane, 1870–1940* (Toronto: University of Toronto Press, 2000).

27 The three appellants were Joseph Delaney, Sheila Livingstone, and Beth MacLean. Sheila Livingstone passed away in 2016 before the first hearing of the *Disability Rights Coalition* case, and her complaint was consequently brought by her estate. Beth MacLean passed away in 2021, a few days before the Nova Scotia Court of Appeal rendered its decision. The Nova Scotia Court of Appeal held that two appellants, Joseph Delaney and Beth MacLean, were entitled to damages. However, because Sheila Livingstone's death occurred before the adjudication of her complaint, her claim for damages was barred by the *Survival of Actions Act,* RSNS 1989 c 453, which does not allow estates to obtain damages for pain and suffering. See *Disability Rights Coalition* at paras 286–96. The discretionary compensation awarded by the Board of Inquiry to Sheila Livingstone's sister and niece was also revoked as they had not requested it. See *Disability Rights Coalition* at paras 297–303.

28 The Nova Scotia Court of Appeal provides a description of the appellants' medical impairments and life experience in *Disability Rights Coalition* at paras 16–19.

29 *Disability Rights Coalition* at paras 179–80. The "mental health institution" and the "mental health facility" refer to the Nova Scotia Hospital, described by the NSCA as a psychiatric facility with a rehabilitation unit (Maritime Hall) and a locked acute-care psychiatric ward (Emerald Hall) (see ibid at paras 16, 18). I use the expression "residential or rehabilitation centres" in this chapter to refer to Nova Scotia's Adult Residential Centres (ARCs), Regional Rehabilitation Centres (RRCs), and Residential Care Facilities (RCFs) (see ibid at paras 25, 26).

30 Ibid at para 23.

31 Ibid at para 179.

32 Ibid at para 273.

33 See ibid at para 18, note 6.

34 Ibid.

35 Ibid at para 19. Olga Cain, Livingstone's sister and representative, accepted the position on her behalf.

36 Ibid.

37 As reproduced in ibid at para 25.

38 Ibid.

39 Ibid at para 67.

40 This argument and the corresponding evidence are discussed in ibid at paras 67, 196–200.

41 Ibid at para 67.

42 Ibid at para 209.
43 Ibid at para 210.
44 Ibid at para 223.
45 Ibid at para 149.
46 Ibid at para 129.
47 Ibid at para 222.
48 The court summarized these arguments made by the Disability Rights Coalition in ibid at paras 62–67.
49 Disability Rights Coalition of Nova Scotia, "Interim Agreement Reached on a Systemic Human Rights Remedy for Persons with Disabilities," press release (April 26, 2023), https://www.disabilityrightscoalitionns.ca/wp-content/uploads/2023/04/Rev-DRC-Media-Release-April-26-2023-130pmwith-links.pdf [perma.cc/E88U-72MU].
50 At the time of writing, the first two annual monitoring reports had been issued: Michael J. Prince, *Monitoring Report 2023–24: Getting on Track* (Nova Scotia Human Rights Commission, 2024); and Michael J. Prince, *Monitoring Report 2024–25: Gaining Traction* (Nova Scotia Human Rights Commission, 2025).
51 *Disability Rights Coalition v Province of Nova Scotia* (June 28, 2023), Nova Scotia Human Rights Commission File No 51000-30-H14-0148 (Decision Reporting Interim Settlement and on Retention of Jurisdiction Pending Final Anticipated Settlement) at para 25.
52 Blair Rhodes, "Disability Rights Group 'Severely Disappointed' After Province Misses Deadline," *CBC News* (May 8, 2024), https://www.cbc.ca/news/canada/nova-scotia/disability-rights-coalition-disappointed-missed-deadline-1.7198153 [perma.cc/JH8J-4FEC]; Disability Rights Coalition of Nova Scotia, "The Disability Rights Coalition Is Disappointed in the Province's Failure to Meet Human Rights Remedy Timelines," press release (January 20, 2025), https://www.disabilityrightscoalitionns.ca/2025/01/20/disability-rights-coalition-disappointed-in-the-provinces-failure/ [perma.cc/E75V-DFV7].
53 On the history of the development of the collaborative remedy, see Nova Scotia Human Rights Commission, "February 11, 2022: Newly Constituted Board of Inquiry Announced," https://humanrights.novascotia.ca/remedy#June2025 [perma.cc/E75V-DFV7]; Nova Scotia Human Rights Commission, "April 26, 2023: Human Rights Review and Remedy for the Finding of Systemic Discrimination Against Nova Scotians with Disabilities Released," https://humanrights.novascotia.ca/remedy#June2025 [perma.cc/E75V-DFV7].
54 See Eddie Bartnik and Tim Stainton, "Human Rights Review and Remedy for the Findings of Systemic Discrimination Against Nova Scotians with Disabilities: Technical Report of the Independent Experts to the Disability Rights Coalition and the Province of Nova Scotia" (February 6, 2023), https://novascotia.ca/coms/disabilities/human-rights-remedy-dsp-final-report.pdf [https://perma.cc/PZR8-HEL9].
55 For a more extensive discussion and critique of accessibility legislation in Canada, see Laverne Jacobs, Odelia Bay, Ruby Dhand, David Ireland, Richard Jochelson, and Freya Kodar, *Law and Disability in Canada: Cases and Materials* (Toronto: LexisNexis, 2021) at 33–38; Laverne Jacobs, Britney De Costa, and Victoria Cino, "The

Accessibility for Manitobans Act: Ambitions and Achievements in Antidiscrimination and Citizen Participation" (2016) 5:4 *Canadian Journal of Disability Studies* 1–24.

56 In the order that they were enacted, the accessibility legislation of the provinces include *Accessibility for Ontarians with Disabilities Act, 2005,* SO 2005, c 11 [*AODA*]; *Accessibility for Manitobans Act,* CCSM, c A1.7; *Accessibility Act,* SNS 2017, c 2; *Accessible British Columbia Act,* SBC 2021, c 19; *Accessibility Act,* SNL 2021, c A-1.001; *An Act Respecting Accessibility in Saskatchewan,* SS 2023, c 19; *Accessibility Act,* SNB 2024, c 27. At the federal level, see *Accessible Canada Act,* SC 2019, c 10.

57 *Integrated Accessibility Standards,* O Reg 191/11, s 55.

58 See Jacobs, De Costa, and Cino, "The *Accessibility for Manitobans Act.*"

59 Ontario, Postsecondary Education Standards Development Committee, *Development of Proposed Postsecondary Education Standards: Final Recommendations Report 2022* (Toronto: Government of Ontario, 2022) at 6–7 (subsection entitled "Guiding Principles"). The report contains various recommendations that incorporate intersectionality, including the requirement for training of all employees of postsecondary institutions using an intersectional and anti-oppressive lens, including Recommendation 24. At the time of writing, the recommended standards had not yet received final approval by the responsible minister, although they had met all other requirements.

60 See the discussion above in "The Human Rights Model of Disability and Its Impact on the Right to Adequate Housing."

61 Ibid.

62 A description of their complementarity can be found in Accessible Standards Canada's explanation of its approach to the development of standards under the *Accessible Canada Act.* See Accessibility Standards Canada, *Accessible-Ready Housing,* CAN/ASC-2.8:2025 (Ottawa: Government of Canada, 2025), https://accessible.canada.ca/creating-accessibility-standards/can-asc-282025-accessible-ready-housing?mode=full-html, at s 1 [*Accessible-Ready Housing 2025*]; Accessibility Standards Canada, "Accessible Standards Canada: About Us," https://accessible.canada.ca/about-us [perma.cc/N859-KHQK].

63 The term "accessible-ready housing" has been used by the government of Canada to mean "housing that is designed in such a way that it can be readily adapted into an accessible house ... with minimal effort and cost (ie without requiring major or significant changes to the structural systems, electrical systems, or mechanical systems of the house)." See *Accessible-Ready Housing 2025,* s 9.1.

64 CRPD, *General Comment No. 5,* at para 16(d).

65 Erie St. Clair Healthline, "In-Home Personal Support – Erie St. Clair," https://eriestclairhealthline.ca/listservices.aspx?id=10363 [https://perma.cc/ED3K-934G].

66 Spinal Cord Injury Ontario, "Case for Support-Transforming PSW Services as a Sustainable Career in Community Settings," https://www.sciontario.org/advocacy-scio/strengthening-retention-and-recruitment-of-psws-in-ontario/ [https://perma.cc/GB8W-USB6].

67 See Dalson Chen, "This Amherstburg Man Says the In-Home Care He Receives Is Inadequate – Despite His Complaints," *CBC News* (December 19, 2024), https://www.cbc.ca/news/canada/windsor/disability-care-assisted-living-paraplegic-wheelchair-1.7411441 [https://perma.cc/VT7V-LVPM].

68 The government of Canada has created voluntary housing accessibility standards using consultation processes typical of accessibility legislation. See *Accessible-Ready Housing 2025* and the related standard, Accessibility Standards Canada, *Accessible Dwellings*, CAN/ASC-B652:23 (Ottawa: Government of Canada, 2023), https://www.csagroup.org/wp-content/uploads/2430606.pdf [*Accessible Dwellings 2023*].

69 Through the *Accessible Canada Act*, the federal government created standards related to accessible housing, published in January 2023 and May 2025. These standards are voluntary, not binding; see *Accessible Dwellings 2023* and *Accessible-Ready Housing 2025*, s 3.3.

70 Laverne Jacobs, "The Universality of the Human Condition: Theorizing Transportation Inequality Claims by Persons with Disabilities in Canada, 1976–2016" (2018) 7:1 *Canadian Journal of Human Rights* 35–66.

71 See, for example, Laurie Monsebraaten, "Ontario Vows to Enforce Accessibility Law: Businesses Flout Requirements to Report on How They Are Meeting Needs of Customers with Disabilities, While Enforcement Strategy Lags," *Toronto Star* (February 20, 2014), https://www.thestar.com/news/gta/ontario-vows-to-enforce-accessibility-law/article_fc5bb7d2-e046-5576-b24a-99cf03391ed1.html. The situation in Ontario has improved since that time.

72 See *Home Care and Community Services Act, 1994*, SO 1994, c 26, s 39.

73 Office of the Federal Housing Advocate, *The Financialization of Multi-Family Rental Housing in Canada: A Report for the Office of the Federal Housing Advocate*, by Martine August, Catalogue No. HR34-4/2022E-PDF (Ottawa: Canadian Human Rights Commission, 2022), https://homelesshub.ca/wp-content/uploads/2024/04/august-financialization-rental-housing-ofha-en.pdf [perma.cc/JV7G-X33K], at iii. For a discussion of financialization in Canada, see Chapter 4 of this collection.

74 Disabled Women's Network, *Financialization of Purpose-Built Rental Housing: Written Submission to the National Housing Council* (Montreal: Disabled Women's Network, 2023), https://dawncanada.net/media/uploads/page_data/page-64/NHR_Financialization_of_Housing-DAWN-August31_2023_EN_BH.pdf [perma.cc/DMU9-2FBY].

75 Ibid at 1, 8–9.

76 Ibid.

77 *Tranchemontagne v Ontario (Director, Disability Support Program)*, 2006 SCC 14; *Northern Regional Health Authority v Horrocks*, 2021 SCC 42. On the divergent ways in which landlord-tenant tribunals engage with human rights legislation, see Chapter 3 in this collection.

78 See, for example, *Human Rights Code*, s 2.

79 *Quebec (Commission des droits de la personne et des droits de la jeunesse) v Montréal (City); Quebec (Commission des droits de la personne et des droits de la jeunesse) v Boisbriand (City)*, 2000 SCC 27.

80 Ontario Human Rights Commission, *Policy on Ableism and Discrimination Based on Disability* (2018), https://www3.ohrc.on.ca/en/policy-ableism-and-discrimination-based-disability [https://perma.cc/3EMS-U7JC]. On the purpose of the policy and of commission policies generally, see *Human Rights Code*, ss 30, 45.5. See also *AODA*.

81 CRPD, *General Comment No. 6*, at para 3.

82 See the letter from Renu Mandhane to Jean-Yves Duclos and Evan Siddall (May 18, 2018), in Ontario Human Rights Commission, "Recommendations to Strengthen the National Housing Strategy," ohrc.on.ca/en/recommendations-strengthen-national-housing-strategy [perma.cc/4HHJ-SJTE].

11

From Failure to Fulfillment
Analyzing Incarcerated Women's Human Rights to Adequate Housing in Canada

CAYDENCE MARLEY

The Human Right to Adequate Housing: Not as Easy as "A B C, 1 2 3"

(A) Incarcerated women are humans. (B) Humans have human rights. (C) The right to adequate housing is a human right. Therefore, incarcerated women have the human right to adequate housing. This "A B C" framework might appear to be obvious or even elementary, but the realization of this chain of reasoning – and, more importantly, this reality – continue to confound the Canadian legal system, correctional system,[1] and government.

In an ideal state, an "A B C" formula would guide the implementation of incarcerated women's right to adequate housing. However, the realities of complex legislation and the unique experiences of incarcerated women in Canada mandate that the recognition and fulfillment of the human right to adequate housing not be reduced or minimized to a simple formula. Paying homage to these complexities, in this chapter I aim to expose how the Canadian correctional system fails to foster environments that fulfill incarcerated women's, and in particular incarcerated Indigenous women's, right to adequate housing. In doing so, I seek not to dwell on the current failures of the correctional system. Rather, I intend to recast adequate housing not merely as a human right of incarcerated women but also as a responsibility of the government. Canada must fulfill its duty to reflect on the intersectional needs of incarcerated women and actively seek to meet those needs.

My objective in this chapter is to forward Call to Action 55 of the Truth and Reconciliation Commission of Canada's 94 Calls to Action:

> 55. We call upon all levels of government to provide annual reports or any current data requested by the National Council for Reconciliation so that it can report on the progress towards reconciliation. The reports or data would include, but not be limited to ...
>
> vii. Progress on reducing the overrepresentation of Aboriginal people in the justice and correctional systems.[2]

As this chapter demonstrates, it is not just that Canada owes a duty to provide adequate housing for as long as women continue to be incarcerated but also that women, particularly Indigenous women, will continue to be overincarcerated as long as Canada fails to fulfill its duty. Prison living conditions are inadequate, and the right to and standards of adequate housing can be used as benchmarks for remedying these inadequacies. Hence, Canada must challenge itself not only to "develop a legal framework for protecting the right to housing"[3] but also to use that right in and of itself as a framework for prison reform.

In fulfilling the objectives of this chapter and Call to Action 55, in the second section I briefly outline the scope of the human right to adequate housing. In the third section, I assess whether the current conditions in Canadian correctional facilities are fulfilling incarcerated women's right to adequate housing, giving special consideration to the intersectional experiences of Indigenous women and their overrepresentation in corrections. More precisely, I examine six criteria of adequate housing and conclude that they are not being fulfilled for incarcerated women. In the fourth section, I adopt a prospective lens to assess how legislative and institutional amendments could remedy the current systemic failures in realizing incarcerated women's right to adequate housing. I present a brief conclusion in the fifth section.

The Scope of Adequate Housing: "More than Four Walls and a Roof"

The right to adequate housing is multi-faceted and currently informed by numerous policies, various legislative schemes, and a host of jurisprudence. Michèle Biss's chapter in this volume unearths the human right to adequate housing as it is currently understood in both international and Canadian legislative and judicial contexts. As her chapter demonstrates, the right to adequate housing expands beyond simply having four walls and a roof over one's head.[4] Rather than merely providing an adequate physical shelter, adequate housing encompasses "sustainable and non-discriminatory access to facilities essential for health, security, comfort and nutrition."[5]

According to the United Nations, there are seven specific criteria that "must be met before particular forms of shelter can be considered to constitute 'adequate housing'":[6] (1) security of tenure; (2) availability of services, materials, facilities, and infrastructure; (3) affordability; (4) habitability; (5) accessibility; (6) location; and (7) cultural adequacy.[7] In the third section, I examine six of these criteria in detail within the carceral context, focusing on how adequate housing is experienced by incarcerated Indigenous women. I do not examine affordability since the United Nations conceptualizes it in terms of whether the cost of housing "threatens or compromises the occupants' enjoyment of other human rights."[8] Since inmates do not pay for their time in corrections in a manner akin to paying rent or a mortgage, this factor is beyond the scope of this analysis.

The discussion of adequate housing throughout this chapter ties into a broader discussion of the *lack* of adequate housing. Jesse Thistle, a Métis scholar, has constructed a framework to understand Indigenous homelessness, which draws from his lived experiences with homelessness,[9] and which ties into the themes explored in his book *From the Ashes: My Story of Being Métis, Homeless, and Finding My Way.*[10] Thistle identifies twelve dimensions of Indigenous homelessness, the most pertinent to this discussion being "Spiritual Disconnection Homelessness."[11] This concept differs from what he describes as "Nowhere to Go Homelessness," which encapsulates the stereotype of the individual who has no physical shelter or home. Rather, Thistle describes "Spiritual Disconnection Homelessness" as an "Indigenous individual's ... separation from Indigenous worldviews or connection to the Creator or equivalent deity."[12] As this chapter details, his more nuanced conceptions of homelessness are experienced by a disproportionate number of Indigenous women incarcerated in Canada.

Thistle's framework of homelessness is salient to this chapter because it sheds light on the complexity of Indigenous people's experiences of lacking a home or adequate housing, including Indigenous women's experiences in prison. As Thistle notes, "because a lack of home, much as a sense of place or homeplace, is a culturally understood experience, we must develop and recognize an Indigenous definition of homelessness that must inform policy-making to solve the tragedy of Indigenous homelessness."[13]

My choice to focus on Indigenous women and to supplement the United Nations definition of adequate housing with Thistle's definition of homelessness is twofold. First, "Indigenous peoples suffer discrimination in almost all aspects of housing."[14] Considering that one of the pillars of this discussion is "equal and non-discriminatory access to adequate housing,"[15] it is crucial to examine how Indigenous incarcerated women are discriminated against in the carceral context. Second, Indigenous women are vastly overrepresented in both provincial and federal correctional facilities in Canada.[16] They are incarcerated at a rate over twelve times higher than non-Indigenous women[17] and "make up 4% of the Canadian population, yet [they] account for roughly 40% of the federal women's prison population."[18] A recent report even indicates that "on April 28, 2022, the number of incarcerated Indigenous women reached 50% for the first time (298 Indigenous and 298 non-Indigenous women in federal custody)."[19] These statistics not only justify but demand a focus on incarcerated Indigenous women's experiences.

The Right to Adequate Housing in Canadian Correctional Facilities

The right to adequate housing has not yet been assessed in the context of Canadian correctional facilities. This is evident not only from a lack of legal or socio-political research on the topic but also from the absence of express intersections between correctional legislation and housing and homelessness legislation.

For instance, the United Nations *Fact Sheet* on *The Right to Adequate Housing* assesses how this right applies to women, children, "slum dwellers," homeless persons, persons with disabilities, displaced persons and migrants, and Indigenous people.[20] The document does not expand on incarcerated individuals' right to adequate housing; there is promise in its consideration of Indigenous people's and women's right to adequate housing, but the fact sheet falls short of assessing the intersectional experiences of Indigenous women in a carceral context. In fact, and disappointingly, a search in the document for terms including "jail," "prison," "custody," "penitentiary," "correctional center/centre," "correctional facility," "correctional institution," "inmate," "incarceration," and "incarcerated" comes up bare. Similar searches in the *National Housing Strategy Act*[21] and the *National Housing Act*[22] produce the same lack of results. Interestingly, there is also no mention of "housing" or "adequate housing" in the *Corrections and Conditional Release Act*,[23] Canada's chief piece of legislation governing inmates' living conditions. Hence, as incarcerated women seek legislative recourse to enforce their human right to adequate housing, they find themselves in a double bind: they can rely either on correctional legislation with no mention of housing or on housing legislation with no mention of corrections.

Despite the absence of explicit recognition of incarcerated women's right to adequate housing, that right is implicitly contemplated by legislation. The *Corrections and Conditional Release Act* states that "offenders retain the rights of all members of society except those that are, as a consequence of the sentence, lawfully and necessarily removed or restricted."[24] This affirms that offenders retain the right to adequate housing, providing the basis for a novel analysis. More notably, the *NHSA* seeks to "support improved housing outcomes for the people of Canada"[25] and to "monitor the implementation of the housing policy and assess its impact on persons who are members of vulnerable groups, persons with lived experience of housing need and persons with lived experience of homelessness."[26] A broad interpretation of the language of "members of vulnerable groups" invites and warrants a nuanced consideration of the impacts of housing for incarcerated individuals. Indeed, "the United Nations Committee on Economic, Social and Cultural Rights has underscored that the right to adequate housing should not be interpreted narrowly,"[27] and case law and Parliament have recognized that incarcerated individuals, particularly incarcerated Indigenous women, are vulnerable populations.[28] Similarly, the reference in the *NHSA* to "persons with lived experience of housing need and persons with lived experience of homelessness"[29] would include incarcerated persons with said lived experiences. Astounding amounts of research highlight the correlation between incarcerated people and housing insecurity or homelessness either before or after their incarceration.[30] Such research further justifies a novel, carceral analysis of the right to adequate housing.

Capitalizing on this opportunity to conduct a novel analysis, I turn to assessing whether Canadian correctional facilities are meeting the minimum criteria for adequate housing. Before proceeding, I offer two caveats. Although the discussion assesses the criteria as they relate to Indigenous incarcerated women as a group, these criteria could also be assessed against the unique circumstances of an individual incarcerated woman.[31] Second, the criteria are set apart for organizational purposes in this discussion but should not be conceptualized in silos; each informs the other, particularly when considered in the light of incarcerated Indigenous women's experiences.

Security of Tenure

The first criterion of adequate housing is security of tenure: "Housing is not adequate if its occupants do not have a degree of tenure security which guarantees legal protection against forced evictions, harassment and other threats."[32] As this definition suggests, security of tenure is typically conceptualized and assessed in terms of residential evictions. However, the phrase "and other threats" opens this factor up for consideration in the carceral context. The United Nations has also stated that "the concept of legitimate tenure rights extends beyond mainstream notions of private ownership and includes multiple tenure forms deriving from a variety of tenure systems,"[33] justifying an examination of such systems in correctional facilities.

Security of tenure has become a key issue for incarcerated Indigenous women. Take, for example, the fact that Indigenous women are more likely than non-Indigenous women to be subject to arbitrary security designations and unit changes, such as being placed in maximum security and solitary confinement.[34] Changes in level of security and movement from communal quarters to solitary confinement can be conceptualized as insecurity of tenure because women subject to these discriminatory and often arbitrary changes do not experience the predictable or stable living conditions like those who remain consistently assessed. Furthermore, women who are moved from minimum- to medium- or maximum-security units or placed in segregation or confinement are effectively "evicted" from their living quarters; they are uprooted, forced to move to different units, and placed in spaces with more constraints on their physical, mental, and spiritual autonomy,[35] which exacerbates existing vulnerabilities for Indigenous women.[36]

The rates at which and the reasons for which Indigenous women are moved to higher security units in Canadian custodial institutions are further examples of the lack of security of tenure. Current security classification regimes in federal penitentiaries are inherently prejudicial to Indigenous women and result in their movement from minimum to medium or maximum security and placement in solitary confinement at higher rates than those for non-Indigenous women.[37] Regarding the former, around 65 percent of the women classified as maximum-security risks in federal correctional facilities are Indigenous.[38] Some of this overrepresentation can be attributed to the fact that mental health issues and self-harm are disproportionately experienced by Indigenous women: "Aboriginal women account for 78.2% of all self-harm incidents in prison and this is the main reason why they are moved to a higher security level."[39] Compared with non-Indigenous women, Indigenous women experience high rates of non-trauma-informed measures of force and control in prisons, which "aggravates pre-existing trauma and engenders additional trauma," leading women to externalize their internal trauma in the form of self-harm or suicidal behaviour.[40] Hence, the high rates of self-harm among incarcerated Indigenous women can be understood as manifestations of "the ongoing impacts of colonialism – for example, their construction as having non-human bodies deemed worthy of abuse and death."[41]

Turning to the issue of solitary confinement, the auditor general of Canada found that "around half of the female offenders placed in segregation are Indigenous women."[42] They are segregated more frequently and for longer spells than non-Indigenous women offenders.[43] Exposing this gruelling reality, "in 2003, the Canadian Human Rights Commission reported that one Aboriginal woman had been held in segregation for 567 days. In 2006, another Aboriginal woman is reported to have spent the majority of her sentence in isolation, [and] for over 1500 days she was classified as being in segregation."[44]

According to the correctional investigator of Canada, "this overrepresentation is largely the result of systemic bias and racism, including discriminatory risk assessment tools, ineffective case management, and bureaucratic delay and inertia."[45] A specific instance of systemic bias and racism in the security assessment regime is evident from the fact that, as a result of traumas related to colonization and attempted assimilation, Indigenous women are likely to have more extensive criminal histories involving violence and to suffer from higher rates of mental illness compared with non-Indigenous women.[46] Violence, crime, and mental health make up the crux of the security assessment criteria,[47] necessarily disadvantaging Indigenous women. Systemic bias is also perpetuated throughout the criminal justice system in the form of stereotypes, such as the "Indian savage," "drunken Indian," or "sq*aw," which frame Indigenous women as more dangerous, violent, and impure than their non-Indigenous counterparts.[48] Such stigmas can be manipulated into erroneous justifications for placing Indigenous women in higher security classifications or in solitary confinement.

Overall, the insecurity of tenure experienced by incarcerated women is littered with discrimination against Indigenous women's cultures and experiences with colonization, thus violating the right to adequate housing.

Availability of Services

The next criterion of adequate housing is the availability of services, materials, facilities, and infrastructure, collectively referred to as availability of services: "Housing is not adequate if its occupants do not have safe drinking water, adequate sanitation, energy for cooking, heating, lighting, food storage or refuse disposal."[49]

Incarcerated women's lack of access to clean drinking water, sanitation and hygiene products, heating, ventilation, and refuse disposal has featured prominently in Canadian media. Faith Eagle made headlines when she undertook a hunger strike to protest the poor living conditions and lack of access to essential services at the Pine Grove Correctional Centre for women in Prince Albert, Saskatchewan.[50] Her protest was intended "to raise awareness about her living conditions, which she still calls too cold, too isolated and too unsanitary."[51] Eagle noted that "the cells are cold; [it] blows cold air from the window, from the vent. The vents are filthy. They have never been cleaned. There's a lot of sick people in here."[52]

The abysmal living conditions of incarcerated women are not unique to Pine Grove. Research has shown that incarcerated women across Canada lack access to proper menstrual and reproductive hygiene products, a concept known as "period poverty."[53] Such realities expose the unmet right to access sanitation products and refuse disposal as mandated by the right to adequate housing.

Related is the fact that, until 2021, incarcerated women reasonably suspected of hiding contraband in their vaginal canals could be subjected to "dry-celling" per section 51(b) of the *Corrections and Conditional Release Act,* as it existed in the version of the act in force until June 22, 2022:

> **Use of X-ray, "dry cell"**
> **51** Where the institutional head is satisfied that there are reasonable grounds to believe that an inmate has ingested contraband or is carrying contraband in a *body cavity,* the institutional head may authorize in writing one or both of the following:
>
> ...
>
> **(b)** the *detention of the inmate in a cell without plumbing fixtures,* with notice to the penitentiary's medical staff, on the expectation that the contraband will be expelled.[54]

For clarity, "body cavity" is defined as "rectum or vagina" under the *Corrections and Conditional Release Act.*[55]

The court in *Adams v Nova Institution*[56] considered this provision and interpreted its constitutionality in depth. Lisa Adams was placed in a dry cell at the Nova Institution for Women in Nova Scotia on May 6, 2020, on the basis of the warden's suspicion that she was concealing contraband in her vagina.[57] Despite adamantly and consistently denying the allegation, Adams remained in the dry cell until May 22.[58] She was released "after a pelvic examination demonstrated that, in fact, she was not carrying any contraband in her vagina."[59] After considering her extended confinement in the dry cell and the wording of the *Corrections and Conditional Release Act*, the court in *Adams* held that section 51(b) of that act, as it then was, discriminated against women with female anatomy[60] because "the predominantly involuntary menstrual process by which bodily fluids or waste (including contraband) might be expelled through the vagina is not as frequent as through the digestive tract. As such, women may become subjected to longer periods of dry cell detention."[61]

In response to the declaration in *Adams* that section 51(b) violated the right to equality under section 15 of the Charter,[62] Parliament amended the wording of section 51 to include "rectum" only.[63] Hence, the *Corrections and Conditional Release Act* still allows for the dry-celling of women if they are suspected of concealing contraband in their rectums.

Under any circumstances, dry-celling deprives women of their right to adequate housing by denying them access to water, sanitation, and refuse disposal. To understand this argument, one must understand the barren conditions of a dry cell. *Adams* notes that "it is called a 'dry cell' because there are no plumbing fixtures, and the water is turned off."[64] There are no toilets or sinks,[65] and "the purpose of such a placement is to prevent the prisoner from flushing anything down the toilet should the prisoner excrete anything while in custody."[66]

Considering these facts, dry-celling necessarily and undeniably deprives women of access to adequate sanitation and proper refuse disposal not only for their urine or fecal excrement but also for any menstrual waste. Although I could find no research on the following points, I would make reasonable inferences that women in dry cells would need to pass along their used menstrual products to a security guard for proper disposal; they would not be able to wash themselves properly with soap and water prior to applying, inserting, or removing menstrual products; and, *if* they are provided with and permitted to use menstrual products, then they would have to apply, insert, or remove them under the direct and unrelenting supervision of staff. Without a toilet, sink, or shower, women cannot insert, remove, or dispose of menstrual products in any sanitary, comfortable, or dignified way. In this sense, any dry-celling of women – even if not for the purpose of extracting contraband from a vagina – violates the right to adequate housing.

From conditions like those at Pine Grove, to exacerbating period poverty, to dry-celling, correctional facilities are failing to facilitate women's right to adequate housing by restricting and denying access to services such as adequate heating, ventilation, sanitation, and refuse disposal.

Habitability

The third criterion of adequate housing is habitability: "Housing is not adequate if it does not guarantee physical safety or provide adequate space, as well as protection against the cold, damp, heat, rain, wind, [or] other threats to health and structural hazards."[67] Given that this is one of the most closely studied and scrutinized aspects of Canadian correctional facilities, the assessment of habitability is organized into three subsections: lack of adequate space, threats to physical safety and health by structural health hazards and violence, and threats to mental health, as contemplated by "other threats to health."[68]

Lack of Adequate Space in Correctional Facilities

The lack of adequate space within Canadian correctional facilities has been well documented as the rates of overcrowding in jails and prisons soar. For instance, Pine Grove was over capacity on every day tracked during an observation period from September 2022 to January 5, 2023.[69] Sydney Wouters, the executive director of the Elizabeth Fry Society of Saskatchewan, indicated that "inmates [at Pine Grove] reported delays or temporary cancellation of programs due to lack of space, which can be a problem for women who need to take programs to be considered for reintegration leaves or transfer to the reintegration unit."[70] Because of the "chronic overcapacity," the gym facilities at Pine Grove have been converted into dorm units, women have experienced increased wait times to access medical care, and the overall culture of the institution has plummeted.[71] In fact, Pine Grove is so overcrowded that Saskatchewan Hospital in North Battleford, a psychiatric hospital, has designated two of its own units for "overflow" from Pine Grove.[72]

The Elizabeth Fry Society has also documented overcrowding at the Edmonton Institution for women.[73] In its case, it is significant to note that overcrowding can still occur when a prison, even if under capacity, does not provide adequate living space. For example, Correctional Services Canada states that "Edmonton prison is at capacity, but is not breaching policy on overcrowding ... Ten double bunks are approved in the secure unit, which was operating at less than 75 per cent capacity during the August investigation."[74] Even though the facility is technically under capacity by 25 percent, the women nevertheless lack adequate space and are literally living on top of one another. Edmonton's prison perfectly explicates why an assessment of adequate space in prison should concentrate not on overcapacity but on overcrowding. In other words, Canada must be critical not only of facilities that are over capacity (i.e., over the technical limit for the individuals whom it was built to house) but also of facilities not built to adequately accommodate the housing needs of women even when under capacity.

Researchers have noted that some of the chief issues stemming from a lack of adequate space in correctional facilities include higher rates of violence, security problems, and increased health risks because of higher rates of contraction of infectious diseases.[75] These points delineate how a lack of adequate space and habitability are intimately intertwined with other aspects of adequate housing, such as access to services.

The current dilemma of overcrowding in Canadian corrections draws a close parallel to Thistle's concept of "Overcrowding Homelessness."[76] Such homelessness occurs when "the number of people per dwelling in urban and rural Indigenous households ... exceeds the national Canadian household average, thus contributing to and creating unsafe, unhealthy and overcrowded living spaces, in turn causing homelessness."[77] Since the overrepresentation of Indigenous people in Canadian correctional facilities far surpasses their representation in the public population, and since Indigenous women commonly live in overcrowded quarters such as in Pine Grove, their living situations can be like those who experience "Overcrowding Homelessness." The fact that the living conditions of incarcerated Indigenous women so closely resemble Indigenous definitions of homelessness provides a blunt answer to the question of whether habitability and the right to adequate housing are being fulfilled in a carceral context: they are not.

Threats to Physical Safety in Correctional Facilities

In addition to living in overcrowded residences, incarcerated women are deprived of their right to habitable, adequate housing by two main threats posed to their physical safety in and by correctional facilities. The first is infection and illness resulting from structural hazards such as overcrowding and poor living conditions. The second is violence and abuse at the hands of oneself, other inmates, and correctional officers and other staff.

STRUCTURAL HAZARDS TO PHYSICAL HEALTH

Structural hazards and deficiencies in correctional facilities such as overcrowding, poor design and layout, and poor living conditions are increasing health-care risks among incarcerated women. These concerns took on a new dimension during the onset of the COVID-19 pandemic:

> Due to overcrowding, poor ventilation, and decreased hygiene standards and healthcare services compared with in the community setting, the prison environment is highly conducive to the transmission of infections, including COVID-19. Physical distancing and other prevention measures are difficult to implement adequately in the prison environment as people in prison live in close quarters, share toilet and hygiene facilities, and may not be able to access personal protective equipment.[78]

The transmission of infections and illnesses in correctional facilities poses a particular detriment to Indigenous women "given the increased prevalence of chronic conditions, including respiratory illnesses, among Indigenous women," all of which make them susceptible to worse health outcomes when infected.[79] As researchers Chaneesa Ryan, Hollie Sabourin, and Abrar Ali rightly note, "the global pandemic is not creating health or social inequities, it is shining a light on and exacerbating inequities that have long existed and been perpetuated by systems of oppression."[80]

Another reality that is conducive to and aggravates the spread of illnesses in correctional facilities is that women are less inclined to disclose symptoms of potential infections because of the fear of being segregated while ill.[81] As the above discussion notes, Indigenous women are at an increased risk of being placed in segregation or solitary confinement, and thus they might be reluctant to expose themselves as potential health hazards within institutions by disclosing their symptoms. The fear of being stigmatized as a health threat[82] and being subsequently marginalized might trump the fear of coping with an untreated respiratory disease, thus contributing to higher counts of uncontrolled and uncontained illnesses.

PHYSICAL VIOLENCE

In addition to the health risks perpetuated by the layout and organization (or lack thereof) of correctional institutions, incarcerated women's physical safety is threatened by violence from themselves, other inmates, and correctional staff. Prison violence is a continuum that includes personal, emotional, and psychological harm; physical and sexual assault; verbal abuse; and self-harm and suicide, which can be consequences of being institutionalized.[83]

It is well documented that "the prison setting generates a landscape of violence through the languages of gender and security, along with routine practices that come together to facilitate and heighten the conditions for violence to occur in seemingly normal, benign, and necessary ways."[84] This is one aspect of what researchers Ben Crewe, Susie Hulley, and Serena Wright have conceptualized, albeit in the British context, as the "gendered pains of imprisonment."[85]

There are numerous disturbing examples of these devastating abuses in Canada. Consider the life of Ashley Smith. She was a teenage girl who spent nearly all of her time in prison in administrative segregation and on suicide watch, far exceeding the legal limit for time spent in segregation.[86] While in segregation, Ashley "was subject to repeated body cavity and strip searches," "was frequently tasered and pepper-sprayed," and was sometimes given medication or drugs "by force via involuntary injections."[87] On October 19, 2007, she self-asphyxiated at the age of nineteen.[88] Numerous guards watched complacently as Ashley took her own life: "Ashley Smith [died] in a hospital gown on the concrete floor of her segregation cell in Grand Valley Institution in Kitchener, Ontario, while several prison guards watched and videotaped her last moments from a few feet away in the hall outside her cell, not intervening or performing CPR for forty-five minutes as she lay dying before their eyes."[89] After her passing, "the news media accounts, Ombuds reports, and the Coroner's inquest focused on Ashley's disruptive behaviour throughout her two years in prison and largely framed the event as a mental health issue without much consideration of how her ongoing experiences were a reflection of institutional violence."[90] Her story is a heart-breaking example of how violence against women in prisons is "not only ... removed from public view, but ... is also harder to identify – hidden by security discourses and routine practices that trivialize, legitimate, and erase what would often be considered violence in any other context."[91]

Ashley's story depicts the power of euphemism, showing how vilifying language such as "manipulative, abused, needy, aggressive, disadvantaged, unfortunate, conniving, complex, intimidated, vulnerable, anti-social, unadjusted, unstable, and cunning"[92] is used to sanitize and normalize abuse of and violence against women in prison.[93] The use of such language creates a "security logic"[94] that simultaneously casts violence by correctional staff as "necessary for security purposes" while depicting women as "deserving of such treatment."[95]

For Indigenous women, the minimization of violence in a carceral context is not novel. The use of euphemism goes back to residential schools, which have been "described ... as 'prison camps that we euphemistically and ... wrongly call residential schools. They weren't residences, they weren't schools.'"[96] Today violence against incarcerated Indigenous women continues to be minimized by its underreporting by correctional staff and other inmates,[97] by the perpetuation of racist stigmas such as the sq*aw that frame Indigenous women as asking for or deserving of violence,[98] and by the use of euphemistic language. For example, as noted earlier, "'Indigenous women continue to experience lengthy periods of solitary confinement, defined instead as modified movement, clinical seclusion, and structured or enhanced supervision. *This shift in vocabulary does not necessarily mean a change to the conditions of confinement.*'"[99]

Let me clarify: to euphemize these realities is not to erase them. Incarcerated women, particularly Indigenous women, experience heightened rates of carceral violence and self-harm; this is a product of historical and continued racism and colonization. An Indigenous woman incarcerated at the former Kingston Prison for Women noted that "the critical difference is racism. We are born to it and spend our lives facing it. Racism lies at the root of our life experiences. The effect is violence, violence against us, and in turn our own violence."[100] Across Canada, Indigenous women are three and a half times more likely than non-Indigenous women to be victims of violence, and Indigenous women between the ages of twenty-five and forty-four are five times more likely to die because of violence.[101] Given these high rates of abuse, Indigenous women are also at risk to internalize racism and violence: "We carry the burden of our memories: of pain inflicted on us, of violence done before our eyes to those we loved, of rape, of sexual assaults, of beatings, of death. For us, violence begets violence."[102] This internalization results in high rates of self-harm and suicide among incarcerated Indigenous women.[103]

Incarcerated Indigenous women also experience higher levels of sexual violence from correctional staff[104] in the form of unwelcome sexualized looks and comments, sexual harassment and assault, and violating strip searches.[105] According to the final report of the National Inquiry into Missing and Murdered Indigenous Women and Girls, "almost all incarcerated Indigenous women have a history of sexual abuse, yet they are continually subjected to strip-searches," which "involve the removal or rearrangement of clothing to permit visual inspection of a prisoner's genitals, breasts, or buttocks."[106] Up to 30 percent of strip searches violate policy and the constitutional rights of inmates.[107] For example, "a woman is meant to have her top or bottom on at all times during a strip-search, but the National Inquiry heard that, in most instances, incarcerated Indigenous women are completely naked during the strip-search."[108] Considering the violation of their rights and the history of sexual violence against Indigenous women, strip-searching is incredibly traumatizing for them. Some have even gone as far as to note that strip searches are experienced, particularly by women and minorities, "as a form of state-sanctioned sexual assault"[109] or "'visual rape'"[110] that can contribute to self-injurious behaviour as a response to the trauma.[111]

Considered alone, the above stories and statistics of violence against incarcerated women might appear to be "random, isolated, or episodic."[112] However, considered as a whole, they highlight how "violence is endemic to the regulation of women in Canadian prisons."[113] The disproportionate instances of self-harm, physical abuse, and sexual violence experienced by Indigenous inmates are indicative of how correctional facilities fail to protect and guarantee the physical safety of women and therefore their right to habitable, adequate housing.

Threats to Mental Health in Correctional Facilities

Correctional facilities also fail to provide habitable housing to incarcerated women by exacerbating mental health issues and failing to provide essential mental health services.

In Canadian correctional facilities, the provision of mental health care is governed by the *Corrections and Conditional Release Act:*

> **Obligations of Service**
>
> **86 (1)** The Service shall provide every inmate with
>
> **(a)** essential health care; and
>
> **(b)** reasonable access to non-essential health care.[114]

Section 86 is the only legislation governing inmates' right to health since the *Canada Health Act*[115] does not apply to incarcerated Canadians. Critics have rightfully pointed out how the ambiguous language of "essential" and "non-essential" health care in section 86 of the *Corrections and Conditional Release Act* "implies that health issues are to be addressed only out of necessity";[116] this interpretation is in stark contrast to the preamble of the *Canada Health Act* that confirms Parliament's progressive commitment to "health promotion."[117] Furthermore, the *Corrections and Conditional Release Act* refers to its beneficiaries as "inmates," whereas the *Canada Health Act* refers to its subjects as "Canadians," which "create[s] dichotomies between the 'citizen' and the 'offender,' and the type of care to which each is entitled."[118]

These ambiguities contribute to inconsistencies in the quantity and quality of mental health care across correctional facilities.[119]

For starters, "the burden of mental illness in Canada's prisons is estimated to be 3 times that of the general population,"[120] and nearly 80 percent of incarcerated women suffer from mental health disorders.[121] Deepening this issue is the disproportionate placement of Indigenous women in segregation, which "can lead to deteriorating mental well-being, aggravate existing mental illnesses, and increase the risk of self-injury and suicide."[122] Despite these inequities, mental health services are less accessible to incarcerated women than to the general Canadian public.[123] Furthermore, mental health services are often deemed nonessential and therefore offered less frequently than physical health-care services in correctional facilities.[124] I agree that "to separate mental health from physical health is an alarming oversight given the histories of people in prison, but an oversight made possible given the particular (and limited) representation of 'health,' which is produced in [the *Corrections and Conditional Release Act*]."[125]

The vast majority of mental health programming available in correctional facilities is only offered to the general prison population, excluding the 50 percent of Indigenous women in maximum security.[126] For mental health services available to maximum-security individuals, access is inconsistent and unpredictable.[127] Likewise, mental health services are limited for women serving life sentences. This limitation flows from the fact that one of the expressed purposes of the *Corrections and Conditional Release Act* is "assisting the rehabilitation of offenders and their *reintegration into the community* as law-abiding citizens through the provision of programs in penitentiaries."[128] This purpose, when considered in tandem with section 86, "suggests that any 'nonessential' care is [only] provided to persons who will be re[-]entering the broader community and does not specify that such care should be extended to persons who are not being released to the community. One effect of this law is that it delegitimizes the health of people serving life sentences."[129] The Correctional Service of Canada has revealed that nearly 20 percent of all federally incarcerated women serve in-custody life sentences[130] and that Indigenous offenders are less likely to be granted full parole than non-Indigenous offenders.[131] Under the *Corrections and Conditional Release Act,* these individuals would be exempt from "nonessential" mental health programs.

A funnel of access to mental health services emerges: first, women in the general Canadian population; second, incarcerated women; third, incarcerated women in maximum-security units or serving life sentences without parole, who are disproportionately Indigenous women. Such restricted and intersectionally discriminatory access to mental health services exacerbates and threatens incarcerated women's mental health, thus violating the right to habitable, adequate housing.

Location

Location is another aspect of adequate housing: "Housing is not adequate if it is cut off from employment opportunities, health-care services, schools, childcare centres and other social facilities, or if located in polluted or dangerous areas."[132] The most pertinent aspect of this definition for an analysis centred on incarceration is that housing must not be cut off from child-care centres and other social facilities.

In Canada, there are only five institutions for federally incarcerated women, located in Abbotsford, British Columbia; Edmonton, Alberta; Kitchener, Ontario; Joliette, Quebec; and Truro, Nova Scotia.[133] There are few women-only secure correctional centres in each province and territory for provincially or territorially sentenced women; in Saskatchewan, that centre is Pine Grove.[134] The limited numbers and dispersed locations of these facilities mean that inmates, particularly federally incarcerated inmates and women from the northern territories, must move far from their homelands and communities when serving their sentences. This is particularly detrimental for incarcerated mothers. In Canada, "sixty-four per cent of incarcerated Indigenous mothers are single mothers, meaning they are the primary caregivers for their children."[135] Although mother-child programs exist to allow some incarcerated mothers to keep their children with them while incarcerated, subject to specific eligibility criteria, participation in them is low.[136] It demonstrates that, across Canada, incarcerated women are almost completely disconnected from their families, children, and child-care programs foundational to the right to adequate housing. Incarcerated women's loss of contact with family is another element of the gendered pains of imprisonment articulated by Crewe, Hulley, and Wright.[137]

The scattered locations of women's institutions also interfere with Indigenous women's ability to access social facilities. The United Nations does not explicitly define them, but in Indigenous cultures "social facilities" or "social institutions"[138] expand beyond physical structures that offer social services and include family and community connections, spiritual centres, ceremonial places, and natural ecosystems (i.e., lands, waters, and all living creatures).[139] More notably, "Indigenous women, girls, and 2SLGBTQQIA people have long had critical rights and responsibilities in creating safe communities by ... creating social security nets."[140] Hence, by relocating Indigenous women to correctional facilities away from their communities, they are divorced from the facilities in and on which their social interactions manifest and deprived of adequate housing.

The separation of Indigenous women from child-care and social institutions is summarized in Thistle's definition of "Relocation and Mobility Homelessness," which occurs when Indigenous people must travel "over geographic distances between urban and rural spaces for access to work, health, education, recreation, legal and childcare services, to attend spiritual events and ceremonies, have access to affordable housing, and to see family, friends and community members."[141] Since the circumstances of incarcerated Indigenous women so closely parallel Thistle's definition of homelessness, it is apparent that correctional facilities are failing to providing adequate housing to this demographic.

Accessibility and Cultural Adequacy

For housing to be adequate, it must be accessible and culturally adequate. Accessibility means that "housing is not adequate if the specific needs of disadvantaged and marginalized groups are not taken into account," and cultural adequacy means that "housing is not adequate if it does not respect and take into account the expression of cultural identity."[142] As the definitions reveal, these factors operate hand in hand and therefore are assessed in tandem.

In Canadian correctional facilities, rehabilitative programming attempts to address the unique physical, mental, spiritual, and cultural identities and needs of Indigenous peoples as disadvantaged and marginalized groups. Such programming can include "programming regarding life skills; parenting skills; education; employment; alcohol and substance abuse; anger management; and spiritual programming."[143] Mental health programs are also becoming more prevalent,[144] corresponding to "the parallel prevalence of disability and involvement in the criminal justice system amongst Indigenous peoples in Canada."[145] The array of potential programming seems to be promising, but existing programs are not accessible to all inmates, nor are they culturally adequate because most are pan-Indigenous.

Cultural programming is not readily accessible in all women's facilities. Fortunately, some form is offered at Pine Grove in Saskatchewan.[146] At Pine Grove, cultural lodges offer inmates access to services such as pipe ceremonies, one-on-one Elder counselling, smudging, traditional parenting teachings, singing, drumming, beading, and medicine gathering (among others).[147] Yet enrolment and participation in cultural programs across Canadian institutions are not immediate. One report notes that, from the date of admission into corrections, Métis women wait an average of 265 days to enter programming, and First Nations women wait 238 days.[148] Another report indicates that Indigenous offenders had to wait up to five months before starting necessary programming.[149] Such programming is also limited for those ineligible to access nonessential health care and for women in maximum-security units.[150] These severe delays and restrictions to accessing programming mean that incarcerated women's right to accessible and culturally adequate housing is unmet altogether or for significant time periods.

Even if such programming were immediately available to all incarcerated women, it would be accessible and culturally adequate only if it catered to the various cultures co-existing in each institution. Thus, creating "one size fits all" pan-Indigenous programs is insufficient.[151] To combat this shortcoming, the Correctional Services of Canada "should [and must] design programs that recognize the differences between First Nations, Métis, and Inuit women, as well as the distinct identities within these groups."[152] This is incredibly important because, for example, "'what might be protocol, a teaching, or culture in Treaty No. 6 territory ... would quite simply not be relevant to Inuit, Anishinaabeg, or Maliseet attendees.'"[153] A clear failure in this regard is that there exists no programming in any women's institution specifically tailored to Inuit women.[154]

Finally, culturally adequate programming must ensure that the circumstances surrounding participation are appropriate and cater to the unique circumstances of Indigenous women as marginalized people. Much of the cultural programming in Canadian correctional facilities cannot be accessed without Indigenous women undergoing some form of trauma, a counterintuitive deterrent. For instance, "a serious disincentive to accessing programming is that female inmates are regularly strip searched when they return to prison after participating in programs."[155] Given the earlier discussion of Indigenous women's disproportionate histories of sexual violence, administering programming to fulfill their cultural rights cannot simultaneously undermine their right to habitable, safe housing. Thus, the development of cultural programming in prisons must not only be meaningful but also mindful of how programs can inadvertently engage carceral practices that impede access to those very programs.

The current overarching failure to offer accessible and culturally adequate programming resonates with Thistle's definition of "Spiritual

Disconnection Homelessness," which encompasses an "Indigenous individual's ... separation from Indigenous worldviews or connection to the Creator or equivalent deity."[156] Indigenous women can become disconnected from their worldviews because of systemic injustices such as delay, ineligibility, pan-Indigeneity, and retraumatization that often coincide with access to programming in correctional facilities. The prevalence of spiritual disconnection homelessness inside corrections exposes how incarcerated women's right to adequate housing is unmet.

The Future of the Human Right to Adequate Housing for Incarcerated Women

The prior discussion might have left readers feeling disheartened, distraught, or even disturbed. It should have. This is not because I have sought to burden readers, particularly Indigenous readers, with reinvigorated trauma (indeed, we have endured enough) but because I refuse to replicate the euphemisms that Canada has employed for decades to mask its failure to provide incarcerated women with adequate housing. Yet I also do not intend merely to point out a problem without offering some solution. Moving forward, the human right to adequate housing for incarcerated women is not as far-fetched as it might seem. It is feasible. Ensuring incarcerated women's human right to adequate housing is twofold. It must take place on paper and in the flesh.

First, legislatively, incarcerated individuals must be declared to be "people of Canada" who are "members of vulnerable groups" within the meaning of sections 4(c) and 13(a) of the *NHSA*, respectively; this declaration will hold the government of Canada and federal housing advocate accountable for "the progressive realization of the right to adequate housing,"[157] not just in a residential or commercial context but also in a carceral context.

Second, "essential" health care in the *Corrections and Conditional Release Act* must be clearly explicated to include mental health services and cultural programming for all women, irrespective of potential reintegration into the community.

Third, existing correctional and housing legislation must contemplate definitions of homelessness unique to Indigenous communities. Current legislation focuses primarily on the adequacy of physical structures but, as Thistle has articulated, homelessness and inadequate housing for Indigenous people is more than just not having four walls and a roof over one's head. If Canada's relationship with Indigenous peoples has taught us anything, it is that if Indigenous experiences are not documented, then our government denies their existence and any reason for action. To propel our government into action, Thistle's definitions of Indigenous homelessness ought to be incorporated into housing legislation.

Nevertheless, Canada has a history of breaking its paper promises to Indigenous communities. Hence, legislation is only part of the answer. The bulk of the work needs to be done on the ground with the support of Indigenous communities, for Indigenous peoples of Canada "have the right to ... be actively involved in developing and determining health, housing and other economic and social programmes affecting them."[158] There is a strong argument that efforts should focus on reducing and eliminating incarceration; if women were not incarcerated at such high rates – or, thinking optimistically, at all – then there would be fewer issues with the human right to adequate housing in a carceral context.

Prison abolition is a favourable housing solution for two key reasons. First, it would help to curb the cycle of inadequate housing. Many Indigenous women lose physical and, in some cases, legal possession of their homes once they are incarcerated because of foreclosure, eviction (be it by family members, friends, or landlords), or abandonment: "Offenders serving lengthy sentences are especially likely to become isolated from family and community, and lose social connections that may be beneficial in terms of securing employment or housing."[159] When these women are released from prison, either they must find other people to live with, or they are forced to live on the streets or in shelters, where they are more vulnerable to violence or exploitation.[160] Such women might participate in criminal activities to obtain income, which results in further convictions,[161] or have more incentive to commit petty crimes with the intention of securing the shelter (albeit inadequate shelter) of a prison cell.[162] In this sense, prison triggers a cycle of inadequate housing. Abolishing prisons, for women in circumstances similar to those described above, would reduce the likelihood of losing their homes and entering a cycle of inadequate housing.

I would be remiss not to note that many Indigenous women lack housing entirely prior to being incarcerated, which Thistle describes as "Nowhere to Go Homelessness."[163] For these women, prison abolition might seem to be counterintuitive insofar as it purports to take away the only housing that the women might have. However, recall that women living on the streets might have more incentive to commit crimes to secure prison shelter, increasing their criminal records and in turn making it more difficult for them to obtain employment and resources necessary to secure adequate housing once released from prison.[164] Over the past decade, Canada has seen a 60 percent increase among federally sentenced Indigenous women[165] and high rates of recidivism, often among low-income or homeless individuals.[166] These rates have no realistic prospect of diminishing under the current inadequate carceral conditions: "Under inhumane conditions ... the prisoner has to focus on the basic interest of survival and 'would lack even the capacity to understand [themself] as a subject of interests worth fulfilling.'"[167] For those stuck in survival mode, incarcerated women cannot concentrate on restoration, cultural reconnection, and rehabilitation, which would set them up with the tools necessary to access adequate housing. Abolishing prison could benefit these women by curbing the cycle of recidivism by removing the "benefit" of obtaining shelter in exchange for committing criminal offences. Although prison abolition might not seem to be ideal for these women, the bottom line is that prison is not adequate housing. Inadequate housing in the form of "Nowhere to Go Homelessness" cannot be resolved by offering alternative inadequate housing. Returning to Indigenous methods of justice that do not involve incarceration is one way to relieve women of the inadequacies of housing in prison and allow them to focus more closely on preparing themselves to reintegrate into society and access adequate housing.

Perhaps a less drastic alternative to prison abolition is to focus on decarceration, or finding alternatives to incarceration, an idea which Angela Davis explores in Chapter 6 of her book, *Are Prisons Obsolete?*[168] Such an approach could reduce significantly the number of incarcerated Indigenous women, which would allow more funds to be allocated to addressing adequate housing concerns. Prison abolitionists might argue that funding correctional facilities has the reverse effect of inflating rates of incarceration, quoting the age-old maxim "if you build it, they will fill it."[169] To play the devil's advocate, I would argue that, if prisons are to continue existing, more funding could be used in a progressive way to create Indigenous-specific women's institutions: that is, to Indigenize the correctional system. These institutions should exist in every province and territory and be designed and operated by Indigenous individuals because Indigenous peoples have the right to administer "housing and other economic and social programmes affecting them ... through their own institutions."[170] Indigenous institutions should exist not only in urban centres but also near rural Indigenous communities. Healing for many Indigenous peoples is closely tied to land and kinship relations and reclaiming and reconnecting with one's culture, territory, language, and ways of knowing.[171] As such, closer connections to one's geographic and social communities would be more likely to aid in rehabilitation, not create recidivism.[172] Ultimately, creating Indigenous women's correctional centres could remedy the failures of current facilities to provide adequate housing, particularly in terms of location, accessibility, and cultural adequacy.

However, given Canada's reluctance to entrust Indigenous communities with governance over their own affairs, creating new Indigenous-focused women's institutions appears to be radical and unlikely. Even with decades of litigation supporting Indigenous peoples' inherent jurisdiction over their traditional ways of living,[173] the Supreme Court of Canada only recently recognized that jurisdiction over family and child services.[174] At this rate, and being optimistic, it could be decades or perhaps centuries before Indigenous jurisdiction over Indigenous systems of justice and corrections will be recognized. Funding therefore needs to be allocated to Indigenize and nurture existing institutions (back) to a state of adequate housing.[175] Among a plethora of other examples, funding could be entrusted to Indigenous communities to redesign security-screening regimes that acknowledge and do not chastise women for their state-imposed experiences of trauma, violence, and mental health struggles. Funding could be used to ensure that women have access to proper hygiene and menstrual products, clean running water, and proper heating and ventilation. It could also be used to design programming to accommodate various Indigenous worldviews and to shorten the wait time for access to cultural programming.

Funding cannot be the only material solution to inadequate housing in a carceral context. It is a promising starting point, but it cannot become "a patchwork of individual and minimalist 'band-aid solutions'" to deep-seated, systemic injustice. Canada must also engage in socio-political reform with a focus on women of colour feminism, anticolonialism, and Indigenous self-governance.[176] In doing so, Canada must abide by its legislative obligations to respect, protect, and fulfill the right to adequate housing in correctional facilities.

Conclusion: From Failure to Fulfillment

This chapter has canvassed how current conditions in Canadian correctional facilities are failing to measure up to the standards of adequate housing contemplated by housing legislation and policy. Most incarcerated women experience insecurity of tenure, lack access to essential services, live in uninhabitable conditions, are located far from family members and social facilities, and lack access to culturally adequate living conditions. These inadequacies are pronounced for incarcerated Indigenous women.

The irony here is palpable. Correctional staff are being paid healthy salaries[177] while observing masses of incarcerated Indigenous women living in inadequate conditions. As André Bear, advocate of inherent and treaty rights, notes, "the Canadian legal system seems eager to fill its prisons mostly with Indigenous peoples," and at some point society must "recognize how the ongoing injustice seems to be paying off mortgages for many non-Indigenous professionals."[178] Incarcerated Indigenous women's inadequate housing is funding the adequate housing of legal professionals, correctional staff, government workers, legislators, and policy makers.

As Canada ventures forward, it must actively seek to reconcile these realities of inadequate housing in correctional facilities with its legislative and reconciliatory responsibilities. To reiterate the beginning of this chapter, women will continue to be incarcerated at alarming rates as long as Canada fails to fulfill its duty to provide adequate housing. The starting point for fulfilling this responsibility and embarking on true reconciliation per the Truth and Reconciliation Commission's Call to Action 55 involves a thorough review of Indigenous definitions of homelessness and a genuine effort to implement adequate housing in a carceral context through socio-political reform and funding. This funding, unlike reconciliation, does not go both ways; those with adequate housing must fund those without adequate housing – not the other way around.

Acknowledgments

I express my gratitude to Professor Sarah Buhler and Professor Anna Lund for their trust and guidance throughout the publication process. I also acknowledge each and every incarcerated woman whose experiences have informed the development of this chapter. As an Indigenous woman myself, I see these women not as statistics but as my sisters.

Notes

1 The terms "correctional systems," "facilities," and "institutions" in this chapter encompass federal and provincial prisons and jails in Canada. For the purpose of brevity, I do not assess the fulfillment of adequate housing by transitional housing and healing lodges.

2 Truth and Reconciliation Commission (TRC) of Canada, *Truth and Reconciliation Commission of Canada: Calls to Action* (Winnipeg: TRC, 2015), https://www2.gov.bc.ca/assets/gov/british-columbians-our-governments/indigenous-people/aboriginal-peoples-documents/calls_to_action_english2.pdf, at 6.

3 Office of the United Nations High Commissioner for Human Rights and UN-Habitat, *The Right to Adequate Housing: Fact Sheet No 21/Rev 1* (May 2014), https://unhabitat.org/sites/default/files/documents/2019-05/fact_sheet_21_adequate_housing_final_2010.pdf [perma.cc/V6GW-RMMG], at 27 [UN *Fact Sheet*].

4 Ibid at 3.
5 Ibid at 8.
6 Ibid at 3.
7 Ibid at 4.
8 Ibid.
9 Jesse A. Thistle, *Definition of Indigenous Homelessness in Canada* (Toronto: Canadian Observatory on Homelessness, 2017), https://homelesshub.ca/sites/default/files/attachments/COHIndigenousHomelessnessDefinition.pdf [perma.cc/3L3X-VVM9].
10 Jesse Thistle, *From the Ashes: My Story of Being Métis, Homeless, and Finding My Way* (Toronto: Simon and Schuster, 2019).
11 Thistle, *Definition of Indigenous Homelessness*, at 9–12.
12 Ibid at 10.
13 Ibid at 8.
14 UN *Fact Sheet* at 28.
15 Ibid at 3.
16 National Inquiry into Missing and Murdered Indigenous Women and Girls (MMIWG), *Reclaiming Power and Place: The Final Report of the National Inquiry into Missing and Murdered Indigenous Women and Girls, Volume 1a* (Ottawa: MMIWG, 2019) at 635–36, https://mmiwg-ffada.ca/wp-content/uploads/2019/06/Final_Report_Vol_1a-1.pdf [perma.cc/V2CP-MBQG] [MMIWG *Final Report*].
17 Government of Canada, "Overrepresentation of Indigenous People in the Canadian Criminal Justice System: Causes and Responses" (last modified January 20, 2023), https://justice.gc.ca/eng/rp-pr/jr/oip-cjs/p4.html [perma.cc/BMG4-SF6M].
18 MMIWG *Final Report* at 635.
19 Ivan Zinger, *Office of the Correctional Investigator Annual Report 2021–2022* (Ottawa: Office of the Correctional Investigator, June 30, 2022), https://oci-bec.gc.ca/sites/default/files/2023-06/annrpt20212022-eng.pdf [perma.cc/U8BZ-TWNZ], at 20.
20 UN *Fact Sheet* at iii.
21 *National Housing Strategy Act*, SC 2019, c 29, ss 313, 4(a) [*NHSA*].
22 *National Housing Act*, RSC 1985, c N-11.
23 *Corrections and Conditional Release Act*, SC 1992, c 20.
24 Ibid, s 4(d).
25 *NHSA*, s 4(c).
26 Ibid, s 13(a).
27 UN *Fact Sheet* at 3.
28 *Bacon v Surrey Pretrial Services Centre (Warden)*, 2010 BCSC 805 at para 342; *R v Feeney*, 2008 ONCA 756 at paras 6–7; Senate of Canada, Standing Senate Committee on Human Rights, *Interim Report – Study on the Human Rights of Federally-Sentenced Persons: The Most Basic Human Right Is to Be Treated as a Human Being* (February 2019) at 6.
29 *NHSA*, s 13(a).
30 See, generally, Julie Moschion and Guy Johnson, "Homelessness and Incarceration: A Reciprocal Relationship?" (2019) 35:4 *Journal of Quantitative Criminology* 855–87; Penelope Abbott, Parker Magin, Joyce Davison, and Wendy Hu, "Medical Homelessness and Candidacy: Women Transiting Between Prison and Community Health

Care" (2017) 16:130 *International Journal for Equity in Health* 1–10; JoAnn S. Lee, Gilbert Gimm, Maya Mohindroo, and Louise Lever, "Assessing Homelessness and Incarceration Among Youth Aging Out of Foster Care, by Type of Disability" (2022) *Child and Adolescent Social Work Journal* 743–59; Brianna Remster, "Homelessness Among Formerly Incarcerated Men: Patterns and Predictors" (2021) 693:1 *Annals of the American Academy of Political and Social Science* 141–57; Janani Umamaheswar, "'On the Street, the Only Person You Gotta Bow Down to Is Yourself': Masculinity, Homelessness, and Incarceration" (2022) 39:2 *Justice Quarterly* 379–401; Amanda Geller and Marah A. Curtis, "A Sort of Homecoming: Incarceration and the Housing Security of Urban Men" (2011) 40:4 *Social Science Research* 1196–213.

31 See, for example, *Tanudjaja v Attorney General (Canada)*, 2013 ONSC 5410 at para 129.

32 UN *Fact Sheet* at 4.

33 Raquel Rolnik, *Report of the Special Rapporteur on Adequate Housing as a Component of the Right to an Adequate Standard of Living, and on the Right to Non-Discrimination in This Context*, UNHRC, 25th Sess, Supp No 3, UN Doc A/25/54 (2013) at 4.

34 See David Milward, *Reconciliation and Indigenous Justice: A Search for Ways Forward* (Winnipeg: Fernwood, 2022) at 187–88.

35 Canadian Association of Elizabeth Fry Societies, Prisoners' Legal Services, and John Howard Society of Canada, *By Any Other Name: A 15 Day Spotlight on Solitary Confinement in Canada: Summary Report – November 2021* (Ottawa: Canadian Association of Elizabeth Fry Societies, 2021), https://caefs.ca/wp-content/uploads/2021/12/2021-11-30-SC-RPT-BY-ANY-OTHER-NAME-A-15-Day-Spotlight-on-Solitary-Confinement-in-Canada.pdf [perma.cc/MGR2-PZGR], at 5, 6, 24 [Elizabeth Fry Societies, *Solitary Confinement*].

36 Ibid at 12; House of Commons, *A Call to Action: Reconciliation with Indigenous Women in the Federal Justice and Correctional Systems: Report of the Standing Committee on the Status of Women* (June 2018) at 33–34, 126; Milward, *Reconciliation and Indigenous Justice*, at 187. I expand on the mental health impacts of segregation and maximum security in the "Habitability" section of this chapter.

37 Milward, *Reconciliation and Indigenous Justice*, at 187–88.

38 Zinger, *Office of the Correctional Investigator Annual Report*. See also the MMIWG *Final Report* at 635.

39 Ontario Women's Justice Network, "Over-Represented and Over-Classified: Crisis of Aboriginal Women in Prison" (June 1, 2014), perma.cc/7JFU-N9ZV.

40 Michaela M. McGuire and Danielle J. Murdoch, "(In)-Justice: An Exploration of the Dehumanization, Victimization, Criminalization, and Over-Incarceration of Indigenous Women in Canada" (2022) 24:4 *Punishment and Society* 529–50 at 536.

41 Ibid at 535. See also Neha A. Pandeya, Philip J. Schluter, Geoffrey K. Spurling, Claudette Tyson, Noel E. Hayman, and Deborah A. Askew, "Factors Associated with Thoughts of Self-Harm or Suicide Among Aboriginal and Torres Strait Islander People Presenting to Urban Primary Care: An Analysis of De-Identified Clinical Data" (2022) 19:1 *International Journal of Environmental Research and Public Health* 153–67 at 153.

42 House of Commons, *A Call to Action,* at 89.

43 Mandy Wesley, *Marginalized: The Aboriginal Women's Experience in Federal Corrections* (Ottawa: Public Safety Canada and Wesley Group, 2012), https://www.publicsafety.gc.ca/cnt/rsrcs/pblctns/mrgnlzd/mrgnlzd-eng.pdf, at 33; see also Elizabeth Fry Societies, *Solitary Confinement.*

44 Wesley, *Marginalized,* at 33.

45 Zinger, *Office of the Correctional Investigator Annual Report.*

46 Milward, *Reconciliation and Indigenous Justice,* at 189–90; MMIWG *Final Report* at 384, 525, 636–37; House of Commons, *A Call to Action,* at 84.

47 Milward, *Reconciliation and Indigenous Justice,* at 189.

48 In *R v Williams,* the Supreme Court of Canada noted how these racist stereotypes influence how the public views Indigenous people's "credibility, worthiness, and criminal propensity"; *R v Williams,* 1998 CanLII 782 (SCC) at para 58. See also Angela Nagy, Carla Cesaroni, and Aziz Douai, "Media Depictions of Crimes Committed by Aboriginal Peoples: Sensationalizing and Reaffirming Stereotypes" (2022) 22:2 *Journal of Criminal Justice and Popular Culture* 77–93 at 89; see, generally, Debra Merskin, "The S-Word: Discourse, Stereotypes, and the American Indian Woman" (2010) 21:4 *Howard Journal of Communications* 345–66; Elizabeth Fry Societies, "Solitary Confinement," at 37.

49 UN *Fact Sheet* at 4.

50 Andrew Benson, "Sask Prisoner Now 3 Months into Hunger Strike over Indigenous Inmate Conditions," *Global News* (December 4, 2022), https://globalnews.ca/news/9324886/indigenous-prisoner-hunger-strike-conditions/ [perma.cc/C55G-JKHB].

51 Ibid.

52 Connor O'Donovan, "3 of 4 Saskatchewan Correctional Centres Overcapacity," *Global News* (December 8, 2022), https://globalnews.ca/news/9334712/saskatchewan-correctional-centres-capacity-issues/ [perma.cc/XDN2-5XDA].

53 Allison R. Casola, Kierstin Luber, Amy Henderson Riley, and Lynette Medley, "Menstrual Health: Taking Action Against Period Poverty" (2022) 112:3 *American Journal of Public Health* 374–77; see, generally, Martha J. Paynter, *Reproductive (In)-Justice in Canadian Federal Prisons for Women: Final Report for the 2019–2020 Reproductive Justice Workshop Project* (Ottawa: Canadian Association of Elizabeth Fry Societies, 2021), https://ac935091-bf76-4969-8249-ae3a107fca23.filesusr.com/ugd/d2d30e_13d22f66c3eb41449c2e52c519913b35.pdf [perma.cc/VX4D-JEMZ].

54 *Corrections and Conditional Release Act,* s 51(b) [emphasis added].

55 Ibid, s 46.

56 *Adams v Nova Institution,* 2021 NSSC 313 [*Adams*].

57 Ibid at para 1.

58 Ibid at paras 4–5.

59 Ibid at para 5.

60 I use the phrase "women with female anatomy" because I recognize that not all women have female anatomy.

61 *Adams* at para 142.

62 Ibid at paras 14, 169; Charter, s 15.

63 *Corrections and Conditional Release Act*, s 51.
64 *Adams* at para 2.
65 *R v Johnson*, 2016 ONSC 3947 at para 37.
66 *R v Multani*, 2017 BCPC 210 at para 31.
67 UN *Fact Sheet* at 4.
68 Ibid.
69 Thia James, "Pine Grove, Other Sask Jails Consistently Overcapacity, Provincial Data Shows," *StarPhoenix* [Saskatoon] (January 14, 2023), https://thestarphoenix.com/news/saskatchewan/pine-grove-womens-jail-consistently-overcapacity-provincial-data-shows [perma.cc/JB7Q-XCBM].
70 Ibid.
71 Ibid.
72 I visited both Saskatchewan Hospital and Pine Grove Correctional Centre and confirmed this fact with staff from both facilities.
73 Zoe Todd, "Tensions Mounting at Overcrowded Edmonton Women's Prison, National Advocacy Group Warns," *CBC News* (October 9, 2017), https://www.cbc.ca/news/canada/edmonton/edmonton-institution-women-prison-corrections-criminal-1.4342583 [perma.cc/Y4YA-T8CC].
74 Ibid.
75 Henny Nuraeny and Tanti Kirana Utami, "The Impact of Overcapacity on Fulfilling the Basic Rights of the Assisted Citizen in Prison in the Perspective of Human Right" (2019) 317:1 *Advances in Social Science, Education and Humanities Research* 149–52 at 151.
76 Thistle, *Definition of Indigenous Homelessness*, at 11.
77 Ibid.
78 Chaneesa Ryan, Hollie Sabourin, and Abrar Ali, "Applying an Indigenous and Gender-Based Lens to the Exploration of Public Health and Human Rights Implications of COVID-19 in Canadian Correctional Facilities" (2020) 111 *Canadian Journal of Public Health* 971–74 at 972. See also Adelina Iftene, "COVID-19 in Canadian Prisons: Policies, Practices and Concerns," in *Vulnerable: The Law, Policy and Ethics of COVID-19*, ed. Colleen Flood, Vanessa MacDonnell, Jane Philpott, Sophie Thériault, and Sridhar Venkatapuram (Ottawa: University of Ottawa Press, 2020), 367–80; Adelina Iftene, "COVID-19, Human Rights and Public Health in Prisons: A Case Study of Nova Scotia's Experience During the First Wave of the Pandemic" (2021) 44:2 *Dalhousie Law Journal* 477–510.
79 Ryan, Sabourin, and Ali, "Applying an Indigenous and Gender-Based Lens," 972.
80 Ibid at 973.
81 Ibid at 972.
82 See, generally, World Health Organization, "A Guide to Preventing and Addressing Social Stigma Associated with COVID-19" (February 24, 2020), https://cdn.who.int/media/docs/default-source/epi-win/stigma/covid19-stigma-guide.pdf?sfvrsn=48f6ac1_2&download=true.
83 Vicki Chartrand, "Landscapes of Violence: Women and Canadian Prisons" (2015) 12:1 *Champ pénal* 1–20 at 5.
84 Ibid at 1.

85 Ben Crewe, Susie Hulley, and Serena Wright, "The Gendered Pains of Long-Term Imprisonment" (2017) 57:6 *British Journal of Criminology* 1359–78.

86 Rebecca Bromwich and Jennifer M. Kilty, "Introduction: Law, Vulnerability, and Segregation: What Have We Learned from Ashley Smith's Carceral Death?" (2017) 32:2 *Canadian Journal of Law and Society* 157–64 at 158–59.

87 Ibid at 159.

88 Ibid at 157.

89 Ibid at 159.

90 Chartrand, "Landscapes of Violence," at 2.

91 Ibid at 10.

92 Ibid at 9.

93 Ibid at 10.

94 Ibid.

95 Ibid at 2.

96 MMIWG *Final Report* at 516.

97 Canadian Association of Elizabeth Fry Societies, *Sexual Coercion and Violence in Prisons Designated for Women* (Ottawa: Canadian Association of Elizabeth Fry Societies, 2021), https://caefs.ca/wp-content/uploads/2021/10/2021-04-14-SVC-Submission-Sexual-Coercion-and-Violence-in-Prisons-Designated-for-Women.pdf [perma.cc/R6PC-438N], at 4.

98 Merskin, "The S-Word," at 347, 359; see also Chartrand, "Landscapes of Violence," at 2.

99 House of Commons, *A Call to Action,* at 91–92 [emphasis added].

100 Wesley, *Marginalized,* at 5.

101 Ibid.

102 Ibid at 23 [emphasis added], citing Aboriginal Justice Inquiry, *Survey of Federally Sentenced Aboriginal Women in the Community* (Ottawa: Native Women's Association of Canada, 1990) at 8.

103 Chartrand, "Landscapes of Violence," at 3.

104 Elizabeth Fry Societies, *Sexual Coercion and Violence,* at 3, 5–6.

105 Ibid at 6.

106 MMIWG *Final Report* at 637.

107 Ibid.

108 Ibid.

109 Ibid at 637–38.

110 *R v Golden,* 2001 SCC 83 at para 90.

111 Elizabeth Fry Societies, *Sexual Coercion and Violence,* at 5, 11.

112 Chartrand, "Landscapes of Violence," at 2.

113 Ibid at 4.

114 *Corrections and Conditional Release Act,* s 86(1).

115 *Criminal Code,* RSC 1985, c C-6; *Canada Health Act,* RSC 1985, c C-6.

116 Eilish Scallan, Kari Lancaster, and Fiona Kouyoumdjian, "The 'Problem' of Health: An Analysis of Health Care Provision in Canada's Federal Prisons" (2021) 25:1 *Health* 3–20 at 9.

117 Ibid.

118 Ibid at 15.
119 Ibid at 9, 15.
120 Ibid at 10.
121 House of Commons, *A Call to Action,* at 40.
122 Ibid at 90.
123 Scallan, Lancaster, and Kouyoumdjian, "The 'Problem' of Health," at 10.
124 Ibid.
125 Ibid.
126 MMIWG *Final Report* at 638.
127 Ibid.
128 *Corrections and Conditional Release Act,* s 3(b) [emphasis added].
129 Scallan, Lancaster, and Kouyoumdjian, "The 'Problem' of Health," at 8.
130 Correctional Service Canada, "Federal Offenders Serving Life Sentences: 2015–16 to 2019–20" (May 2021), https://www.canada.ca/content/dam/csc-scc/migration/005/008/092/005008-rib-21-08-en.pdf.
131 Public Safety Canada, *Corrections and Conditional Release Statistical Overview: 2021 Annual Report* (2022), https://www.publicsafety.gc.ca/cnt/rsrcs/pblctns/ccrso-2021/ccrso-2021-en.pdf [perma.cc/2JGT-EGSY], at 128.
132 UN *Fact Sheet* at 4.
133 Correctional Service Canada, "Women's Facilities" (last modified May 16, 2019), https://www.canada.ca/en/correctional-service/programs/offenders/women/womens-facilities.html [perma.cc/PTE9-3MQG].
134 Government of Saskatchewan, "Correctional Facilities and Community Corrections Offices" (n.d.), https://www.saskatchewan.ca/residents/justice-crime-and-the-law/correctional-facilities-and-probation/correctional-facilities-and-community-corrections-offices [perma.cc/285U-BSVT].
135 MMIWG *Final Report* at 637.
136 Wesley, *Marginalized,* at 21; see also Correctional Service Canada, "Commissioner's Directive 768: Institutional Mother-Child Program" (January 24, 2020), https://www.canada.ca/en/correctional-service/corporate/acts-regulations-policy/commissioners-directives/768.html [perma.cc/29W3-AYL7].
137 Crewe, Hulley, and Wright, "The Gendered Pains of Long-Term Imprisonment," at 1367–69.
138 MMIWG *Final Report* at 51.
139 Ibid at 56, 137, 157.
140 Ibid at 157.
141 Thistle, *Definition of Indigenous Homelessness,* at 11.
142 UN *Fact Sheet* at 4.
143 Wesley, *Marginalized,* at 7.
144 Ibid.
145 David Ireland, Richard Jochelson, and Brayden McDonald, "Arrest, Detention and Disability in Canada," in *Law and Disability in Canada: Cases and Materials,* ed. Laverne Jacobs, Ruby Dhand, David Ireland, Richard Jochelson, Freya Kodar, and Odelia Bay (Toronto: LexisNexis Canada, 2021), 145–66 at 146.
146 Tyler Barrow, "Sask Adding Cultural Services to Four Correctional Centres to Reduce Reoffending," *CTV News* (January 19, 2021), https://www.saskatoon.

ctvnews.ca/sask-adding-cultural-services-to-four-correctional-centres-to-reduce-reoffending-1.5273263 [perma.cc/6G2G-3XMN].

147 Ibid.

148 Wesley, *Marginalized,* at 8.

149 House of Commons, *A Call to Action,* at 94.

150 Ibid at 87, 98; MMIWG *Final Report* at 638.

151 MMIWG *Final Report* at 639.

152 House of Commons, *A Call to Action,* at 102.

153 Ibid.

154 Wesley, *Marginalized,* at 17; MMIWG *Final Report* at 639.

155 House of Commons, *A Call to Action,* at 95.

156 Thistle, *Definition of Indigenous Homelessness,* at 10.

157 *NHSA,* s 4(d).

158 *United Nations Declaration on the Rights of Indigenous Peoples Act,* SC 2021, c 14, art 23 [*UNDRIP Act*].

159 Ben Roebuck, *Homelessness, Victimization, and Crime: Knowledge and Actionable Recommendations* (Ottawa: Institute for the Prevention of Crime, University of Ottawa, n.d.), https://www.publicsafety.gc.ca/lbrr/archives/cnmcs-plcng/cn35305-eng.pdf, at 19.

160 Women's National Housing and Homelessness Network, "Women and Girls' Homelessness in Canada" (n.d.), https://womenshomelessness.ca/women-girls-homelessness-in-canada/ [perma.cc/CQW3-N474].

161 See, for example, Christine A. Walsh, Paula MacDonald, Gayle E. Rutherford, Kerrie Moore, and Brigette Krieg, "Homelessness and Incarceration Among Aboriginal Women: An Integrative Literature Review" (2011) 9:2 *Pimatisiwin: Journal of Aboriginal and Indigenous Community Health* 363–86 at 368.

162 See, for example, Sarah Smellie, "Amid Housing Crisis, Jail Seen as Preferable to Living on the Street," *Toronto City News* (December 2, 2023), https://toronto.citynews.ca/2023/12/02/housing-crisis-jail-preferable-to-living-on-the-street/ [perma.cc/X7LM-2VFM].

163 Thistle, *Definition of Indigenous Homelessness,* at 12.

164 Walsh et al., "Homelessness and Incarceration Among Aboriginal Women," at 368.

165 Government of Canada, "Overrepresentation."

166 Correctional Service Canada, "A Comprehensive Study of Recidivism Rates Among Canadian Federal Offenders" (April 2019), https://www.canada.ca/content/dam/csc-scc/migration/005/008/092/err-19-02-en.pdf.

167 Lisa Kerr, "How the Prison Is a Black Box in Punishment Theory" (2019) 69:1 *University of Toronto Law Journal* 85–116 at 110–11.

168 Angela Y. Davis, "Abolitionist Alternatives," in *Are Prisons Obsolete?* (New York: Seven Stories Press, 2003), 105–15.

169 Joshua Guetzkow and Eric Schoon, "If You Build It, They Will Fill It: The Consequences of Prison Overcrowding Litigation" (2015) 49:2 *Law and Society Review* 401–32.

170 *UNDRIP Act,* art 23.

171 MMIWG *Final Report* at 78, 409.

172 Ibid at 457, 484, 490.

173 See *R v Sparrow*, 1990 CanLII 104 (SCC); *R v Van der Peet*, 1996 CanLII 216 (SCC); *R v Powley*, 2003 SCC 43.

174 *Reference re An Act Respecting First Nations, Inuit and Métis Children, Youth and Families*, 2024 SCC 5.

175 I place the term "back" in parentheses because some correctional facilities in Canada have *never* constituted adequate housing. As such, they are not being "brought back" to adequacy; they are being made adequate for the first time.

176 See, for instance, Bronwyn Dobchuk-Land, "Resisting 'Progressive' Carceral Expansion: Lessons for Abolitionists from Anti-Colonial Resistance" (2017) 20:4 *Contemporary Justice Review* 404–18; see also Heather Dorries and Laura Harjo, "Beyond Safety: Refusing Colonial Violence Through Indigenous Feminist Planning" (2020) 40:2 *Journal of Planning Education and Research* 210–19.

177 See, for example, Government of Canada, "Wages: Correctional Service Officer in Canada" (last modified February 9, 2023), https://www.jobbank.gc.ca/marketreport/wages-occupation/6670/ca [perma.cc/E9L7-ZJQU]; Government of Canada, "Wages: Prison Warden in Canada" (last modified December 3, 2024), https://www.jobbank.gc.ca/marketreport/summary-occupation/1799/ca [perma.cc/YK9A-AMYH].

178 André Bear, "Maintaining the Canadian Legal System Is Obstructing Justice for Indigenous Peoples," *CBC News* (March 21, 2023), https://www.cbc.ca/news/canada/saskatchewan/opinion-andre-bear-maintaining-legal-system-obstructing-justice-indigenous-1.6781527 [perma.cc/8TCQ-MJWJ].

Contributors

Yale Belanger is a professor and chair of political science at the University of Lethbridge.

Michèle Biss is a practising lawyer and the Executive Director of the National Right to Housing Network.

Sarah Buhler is a professor at the University of Saskatchewan College of Law.

Distinguished Professor **Ronald CC Cuming** (emeritus) has fifty-four years of experience as a professor of commercial law at the University of Saskatchewan and University of British Columbia and more than thirty years of experience as an international and domestic commercial consultant.

Alexandra Flynn is an associate professor at the Allard School of Law, University of British Columbia.

Laverne Jacobs is a professor in the Faculty of Law at the University of Windsor, where she holds the Research Chair in Disability Equality and Administrative Justice. She is also a member of the United Nations Committee on the Rights of Persons with Disabilities.

Jason Leslie is a solicitor for Housing and Municipal Affairs in the Justice, Health and Revenue group at the Ministry of Attorney General for British Columbia.

Anna Lund is the F.R. (Dick) Matthews Q.C. Professor of Business Law in the Faculty of Law at the University of Alberta.

Caydence Marley is a proud Métis woman and lawyer from Treaty 4 Territory near Lebret, Saskatchewan. She works and resides on both Treaty 4 and Treaty 6 Territories.

Estair Van Wagner is an associate professor at the University of Victoria Faculty of Law.

Jonnette Watson Hamilton is a professor emerita in the Faculty of Law, University of Calgary.

David Wiseman is an associate professor in the Faculty of Law, Common Law Section, English Program, University of Ottawa.

Index

Note: "(t)" after a page number indicates a table. CMHC stands for Canada Mortgage and Housing Corporation; HTC, for Herongate Tenant Coalition (Ottawa); and *NHSA*, for *National Housing Strategy Act*. Courts and tribunals are abbreviated as follows: CA (for provincial Courts of Appeal); Sask QB (Saskatchewan Court of Queen's Bench [now Court of King's Bench]); SC (for British Columbia and Nova Scotia Supreme Courts; Ontario Superior Court); SCC (Supreme Court of Canada); SKORT (Saskatchewan Office of Residential Tenancies); ZA CC (South Africa Constitutional Court); and ZA HC (South Africa High Court). Abbreviations for various UN treaties and committees appear in parentheses in main entries.

About the Cover Artwork

A Safe Neighborhood for Your Neighbors (2025), sculptural painting by Daniel Lee Whyte, featuring works by J.D Hunter, Nicholas Martain, Sam Paolini, and Theo Donovan. Oil on stitched canvas, paper and fabric mache, wood, iron pipe, 84 × 84 × 30 inches.

A Safe Neighborhood for Your Neighbors is a collaborative, three-dimensional painting featuring decolonial works by local artists and activists. Embedded in the surface are 421 stitches, each representing a life lost due to houselessness in Edmonton in 2023. The piece was informed by conversations with unhoused community members and community service workers.

Artist Statement – Daniel Whyte

My work draws from my wider social environment and lived experience. I focus on vulnerability, centring conversations around abuse in its various forms. I work closely with my unhoused neighbours, distributing essential supplies and responding to hostile policies enacted by our municipal government. I prioritize depicting the resilience and warmth found in the margins, highlighting humanity and strong community ties. I believe a compassionate and attentive community is essential to overcoming systemic barriers.

Set in Warnock Pro and Futura by Apex CoVantage, LLC
Copyeditor: Dallas Harrison
Proofreader: Kristy Lynn Hankewitz
Indexer: Cheryl Lemmens
Cover designer: JVDW Designs
Cover image: *A Safe Neighborhood for Your Neighbors* (2025), sculptural painting by Daniel Lee Whyte, featuring works by J.D. Hunter, Nicholas Martin, Sam Paolini, and Theo Donovan
Authorized Representative: Easy Access System Europe – Mustamäe tee 50, 10621 Tallinn, Estonia, gpsr.requests@easproject.com

Kolibri 360 GmbH
Ferdinand-Jühlke-Straße 7
99095 Erfurt, Deutschland
produktsicherheit@kolibri360.de